DICTIONARY OF RACE AND ETHNIC RELATIONS

Fourth Edition

ROUTLEDGE BOOKS BY ELLIS CASHMORE

The Black Culture Industry

. . . and there was television

Making Sense of Sports

Out of Order? Policing black people
(with Eugene McLaughlin)

Black Sportsmen

HIS OTHER BOOKS

The Logic of Racism

United Kingdom? Class, race and gender since the war

Having To – The world of oneparent families

No Future: Youth and society

Rastaman: The rastafarian movement in England

Introduction to Race Relations
(with Barry Troyna)

Black Youth in Crisis
(with Barry Troyna)

Approaching Social Theory
(with Bob Mullan)

DICTIONARY OF RACE AND ETHNIC RELATIONS

FOURTH EDITION

ELLIS CASHMORE

with

MICHAEL BANTON • JAMES JENNINGS,
BARRY TROYNA • PIERRE L. VAN DEN BERGHE

and specialist contributions from
Heribert Adam • Molefi Kete Asanti • Stephanie Athey
Carl Bagley • Kingsley Bolton • Roy L. Brooks
Richard Broome • Bonnie G. Campodonico
Robin Cohen • James W. Covington • Guy Cumberbatch
John A. Garcia • Ian Hancock • Michael Hechter
Gita Jairaj • Robert Kerstein • Zeus Leonardo
Timothy J. Lukes • Peter McLaren • Eugene McLaughlin
Robert Miles • Kogila Moodley • Marshall Murphree
George Paton • Jan Nederveen Pieterse • Peter Ratcliffe
Amy I. Shepper • Betty Lee Sung • John Solomos
Stuart D. Stein • Roy Todd • Robin Ward
Steven Vertovec • Loretta Zimmerman

London and New York

First published 1984
Second edition published in 1988
Third edition published in 1994; reprinted 1995
Fourth edition published in 1996 by
Routledge
11 New Fetter Lane
London EC4P 4EE
29 West 35th Street
New York, NY 10001

© Routledge & Kegan Paul 1984, 1988
This edition © Routledge 1996
Set in 10/12pt Times, Linotronic 300 by
Intype London Ltd
Printed and bound in Great Britain by
Clays Ltd, Bungay, Suffolk
Printed on acid free paper

British Library Cataloguing in Publication Data
A catalogue record for this book is available from the British Library

Library of Congress Cataloging in Publication Data
A catalogue record for this book is available from the Library of Congress

ISBN 0–415–15167–8 (hb)
     0–415–13822–1 (pb)

CONTENTS

In memory of
BARRY TROYNA
1952–1996
A pioneering scholar and a beloved friend

CONTRIBUTORS

ELLIS CASHMORE
Professor of Sociology
Staffordshire University

PRIMARY CONTRIBUTORS

MICHAEL BANTON
Professor Emeritus of Sociology
University of Bristol

JAMES JENNINGS
Professor of Political Science
University of Massachusetts

BARRY TROYNA
Professor of Education
University of Warwick

PIERRE VAN DEN BERGHE
Professor of Anthropology & Sociology
University of Washington

SPECIALIST CONTRIBUTORS

HERIBERT ADAM
Simon Fraser University

MOLEFI KETE ASANTI
Temple University, Philadelphia

STEPHANIE ATHEY
Stetson University

CARL BAGLEY
Staffordshire University

KINGSLEY BOLTON
University of Hong Kong

ROY L BROOKS
San Diego Law School

RICHARD BROOME
La Trobe University, Melbourne

BONNIE G. CAMPODONICO
Santa Clara University

ROBIN COHEN
University of Warwick

JAMES W COVINGTON
University of Tampa

GUY CUMBERBATCH
Aston University

JOHN A GARCIA
University of Arizona

IAN HANCOCK
University of Texas

MICHAEL HECHTER
University of Arizona/Oxford University

GITA JAIRAJ
Freelance Writer
London

ROBERT KERSTEIN
University of Tampa

ZEUS LEONARDO
University of California

TIMOTHY J LUKES
Santa Clara University

PETER McLAREN
University of California

EUGENE McLAUGHLIN
Open University

ROBERT MILES
University of Glasgow

KOGILA MOODLEY
University of British Columbia

MARSHALL MURPHREE
University of Zimbabwe

GEORGE PATON
Aston University

PETER RATCLIFFE
University of Warwick

AMY I SHEPPER
University of South Florida

JOHN SOLOMOS
University of Southampton

STUART D STEIN
University of the West of England

BETTY LEE SUNG
City College of New York

ROY TODD
University of Leeds

STEVEN VERTOVEC
University of Warwick

ROBIN WARD
Formerly of Nottingham Trent University

LORETTA ZIMMERMAN
University of Portland

INTRODUCTION

What makes race so intractable, so resilient to every known policy, program or provision? More than thirty years after the first legislation designed to reduce the effects of discrimination, we find ample proof of the presence of race in public and private life.

Since the publication of the third edition of this book, four key episodes have reawakened us to the fact that race remains a relentless, enervating issue of our times. There can be few, if any, issues that command so much attention and effort with so little yield. Each time, we relax our concentration, a new disclosure reveals the complexity, virulence and sheer obduracy of what has become arguably *the* problem of the late twentieth century.

As the trial of O. J. Simpson progressed through 1994–5, research indicated a curious difference in interpretation of the evidence and testimony presented. Only five percent of whites polled believed Simpson was innocent, while twenty percent were convinced he was guilty before the trial had even started. Twenty-eight percent of blacks said they were certain Simpson was innocent of the brutal stabbings which took place on the night of June 12, 1994, on the steps of Nicole Simpson's Brentwood apartment. (See *Causes célèbres* for more on the Simpson case.)

Near the conclusion of the trial, a perverse symmetry began to emerge. Sixty four percent of whites interviewed found the evidence against Simpson convincing and would have returned a guilty verdict had they served on the jury; fifty nine percent of African Americans, when presented with the same evidence, opted for an acquittal.

Four years before, a *Wall Street Journal*/NBC News Poll in 1991 revealed a "chasm in attitudes" between whites and African Americans. Whites saw a country where relations between blacks and themselves had improved over the previous decade; blacks saw exactly the opposite. One of the most emotive issues dividing the two groups was federal government assistance. Many blacks welcomed the government's efforts, especially affirmative action. But, whites were skeptical of such efforts and encouraged blacks to fend for themselves.

Study after study had depicted the United States as what the writer Andrew Hacker called "two nations," divided by race. The segregation that had endured long after the end of slavery left an indelible imprint in the form of institutions, customs, beliefs, languages, cuisine, and so on. That was to be expected. Not so understandable was the difference in consciousness, of outlook, of mentality. It was as if blacks and whites were looking at the world through entirely different prisms.

Those wishing to explain this difference by reference to natural, as opposed to social, phenomena would have found sustenance in the research of Richard Herrnstein and Charles Murray, published in 1994, under the title of *The Bell Curve*. The sensation caused by its publication is the second of the four pivotal events. (See **Intelligence and race**.)

Reheating overcooked dishes rarely produces a satisfactory meal. Doing likewise with scientific debates sometimes has different results. The debate joined by Herrnstein and Murray was started in the 1960s by Arthur Jensen, who soared to international infamy after publishing the results of his research in a respectable scientific journal, the *Harvard Educational Review*. The title of the article was "How can we boost IQ and scholastic achievement?" Jensen's project had been to unravel the riddle of nature versus nurture. Are we born with intelligence, or do we acquire it as we grow up? he asked, though in rather more erudite terms. Specifically, he wanted to test the intelligence of three groups of children: white, black, and Latino. Jensen found that blacks consistently scored 15 points below whites. Nothing shocking in this: indeed, it would have been a major surprise had African American children fared any better, given the history of slavery and the denial of civil rights they and their forbears would have endured; the impact of this and other factors on intellectual development is plain enough.

Jensen, though, did not accept that social, cultural or environmental forces, the nurture side of the equation, were the cardinal causes of the persistently low scores of black children. He concluded that genes bore 80 percent of the responsibility for intelligence. Nature, in his experiments, won hands down. Even if, as Jensen stressed, the motives behind the research were all about the spirit of scientific inquiry, the conclusions could not have been designed better for the truth-seeking racist (if that is not an oxymoron). Caucasians are more intelligent than other groups that have been called races *and* the reason they are lies in the realm of biology. We can do nothing about it: blacks are naturally inferior.

Nobel prize-winner William Shockley threw his scalpel into the arena when he proposed that blacks be sterilized to prevent them from passing on their inferior genes. Unlike Jensen, Shockley did not insist that his motives were pure. Few would have believed him anyway.

The notorious article bearing Jensen's findings drew fire from all quarters and, only years later, after several other studies had produced contrasting results, did the debate die down. Few noticed the embers glowing. Years later, *The Bell Curve*, entitled thus to convey the parabola formed when plotting the distribution of intellience in a population, strengthened Jensen's suggested link between IQ and race.

Many studies, said the authors, demonstrated about a 15 point difference in the mean scores of black and white Americans. There is also more equivocal evidence that Asians score significantly higher than whites. Herrnstein died while the book was in production, though Murray survived the trauma and robustly defended its argument. Nature may be unfair in its distribution of talent genes, but it does not determine our destinies. *Differences in IQ don't much matter*, emphasized Murray. "We put it in italics; if we could we would put it in neon lights."

The riposte was as sharp and resonant as that which followed Jensen. No one was seriously entertaining Murray's meek apology about IQ differences not mattering, nor his insistence that the results told us only about group differences, not individual ones. In the sample studied, there were many blacks who outscored whites. Glib as it sounded, Murray asserted his commitment to individualism: being born to a group that is collectively inferior does not mean the individual should accept his or her own inferiority. They should travel as far as their natural talent would take them along the road to success; this was the gist of Murray's message.

When Jensen's article was published, the United States was in the throes of a series of changes that were to transfigure America's social and political landscape. The civil rights movement led by Martin Luther King had literally marched its way into public prominence figuratively holding a mirror to white America. The dear, untutored land that created tragedy by either its own ignorance or its own malevolence had turned a nation sundered by slavery into one serrated by class and ethnic divisions. Tormented by the lack of progress that followed the 1954 *Brown vs. Board of Education of Topeka* decision to dissolve the legal boundaries that segregated whites and blacks in educational institutions, the United States had to negotiate the commission of full civil rights to an African

American population openly dissatisfied and prepared, in some instances, to take violently to the streets.

Predictably, the white backlash to desegregation brought an unwelcome reminder that, for many, the traditional institution of slavery was still the favored social arrangement and the segregated society that succeeded it was a move in the wrong direction. But, the context in which *The Bell Curve* was published was altogether different. The decision by the Supreme Court limiting affirmative action rules designed to favor minorities highlighted a marked shift to the right by the highest court in the land. (See **Affirmative action**.)

This brings us to the third episode and one which has its origins in a 1989 legal action brought by Randy Pech, a white construction contractor, whose bid for a contract to build guard rails on a Colorado freeway was rejected. Instead, the contract was awarded to the more expensive but Latino-owned Gonzalez Construction Company. Congress required that at least ten percent of all federal money spent on road building should go to businesses run by "disadvantaged" groups. Pech sued and, in 1995, gained a significant victory: affirmative action programs were to be subject to scrutiny and should survive only if they served "a compelling government interest" (*Adarand Constructors, Inc. v. Peña*).

That judgment represented a crucial doctrinal shift. The court stopped short of outlawing affirmative action, but set a far more exacting standard by which any preferential programs were deemed acceptable. The ruling issued a victory for the "angry white male," that endangered species which believed it had been fair game for too long. But, it also pleased an increasing number of disillusioned liberals, who believed that, far from being a panacea to eradicate racism, affirmative action had actually exacerbated it by perpetuating the very racial divisions they sought to remove.

The decision coupled with a ruling that invalidated an educational program to attract white students to predominantly black schools in Kansas City, stunned minority group leaders. Interestingly, Clarence Thomas, the conservative African American judge appointed amid controversy under the Bush administration, voted for a review of affirmative action, his argument being that, lurking behind such programs, is "a theory of injury that was predicated on black inferiority." Ironically, Thomas himself had benefited from such a program. (See **Thomas, Clarence**.)

African-American organizations pointed out, that black children are still three times more likely to live in poverty than white children. (Herrnstein and Murray would have an obvious expla-

.nation for that, of course.) They might also have added that African Americans account for almost 40 percent of the prison population, have a shorter life expectancy than whites and almost double the rate of infant mortality. (See **African Americans**.) Drug use and dealing is also disproportionately high among blacks. (See **Drugs and racism**.)

Affirmative action was the main prong of the U.S. attack on racism and racial discrimination from the mid-1960s onwards. Britain, having never experienced *de jure* segregation and the multiple inequities it bred, saw no need for such radical preferential schemes. It opted for a more conservative egalitarian policy of equal opportunity as a way of reducing the racial inequalities that were laid bare after innercity riots in the early 1980s. (See **Equal opportunity** and **Riots: Britain**.)

Unlike affirmative action, the British approach entailed equalizing the conditions of entry into the job market and promotion races. When major corporations began to set the trend and adopt equal opportunities policies, a solution to Britain's racial problems seemed to be at hand. By the early 1990s, virtually every employer had reorganized its employment policies so as to include some provision for equality of opportunity. Typically, job advertisements would be appended with a message along the lines of: "is an equal opportunities employer and appoints and promotes strictly on merit. The company especially welcomes applications from . . ." and a delineation of minority groups would follow.

The premise of equal opportunity is that the root of racial ills lies in disparate employment prospects. Historically, the major uprisings and disturbances in Britain have been precipitated by job-related issues. In the 1950s, attacks on blacks were triggered by the perception of whites that migrants from South Asia and the Caribbean were unwanted competitors in a shrinking job market. The 1980s riots took place against a background of unbearably high unemployment; black youths were the most affected group. If the stratified world of work could be evened out, then, it was thought, racism and associated problems could be confronted. It seemed a reasonable assumption and one which worked well for a decade. Britain's troubled streets seemed to be a thing of the past.

So, it was disarming to discover that, according to an official report published in 1996, racial abuse had increased. Police figures showed that violent incidents in which race was a motivating factor had risen by 25 percent in 1993–4, most of the increases occurring in innercity areas. This constitutes the fourth episode: reported incidents included racial attacks, threats, verbal abuse, intimidation, harassment, graffiti, and the distribution of offensive literature. In the three years leading to January 1996, there were thought to have been twelve racist murders, the most famous being that of eighteen-year-old Stephen Lawrence, who was stabbed to death by white youths while waiting at a bus stop in London in 1993.

More typically, a black single mother with three children was forced to move from her home in Dagenham, London, after years of racial harassment. Several middle-aged white neighbors constantly shouted abuse at her, threatened her children and said they would burn down her house. (See **Harassment: racial and racist**.)

There are two ways of looking at this. One is more sanguine than the other. It is: that the actual amount of racial harassment is not increasing and may indeed be on the decrease. What *is* increasing is the number of incidents reported to the police. The 1996 figures, in this perspective, reflect both a greater willingness of the police to take offenses related to racism seriously and the confidence of ethnic minorities in the criminal justice system. In other words, victims once mistrusted the police so much that they saw little point in reporting their misfortunes. In the mid-1990s, their faith had been secured. (See **Police and racism**.)

The other way of looking at the report is more straightforward: ethnic minorities were getting beaten up more regularly. Maybe the streets of London, Birmingham and Manchester were not incendiary hotspots any more. But, there was little cause for self-satisfaction: racism and racial attacks, once thought to be a remnant of the 1970s, served to remind the British that its problems had not disappeared, almost thirty years after its first legislation to outlaw discrimination. (See **Law: race relations [Britain]**.)

The four episodes capture some of the tensions that beset today's debates about race and ethnic relations. Some insist that the general situation has improved in both the U.S.A. and Britain since the war; while others argue that racism operates in more surreptitious ways that are less open to inspection. Many stay loyal to official policies designed to alleviate the consequences of racism and wish to pursue them further; others believe they were ill-conceived and argue that no social policy in existence can cure what is, at source, an individual phenomenon. They will have derived sustenance from the theories of Herrnstein and Murray.

Disagreements over the solutions to the problems posed by racism have counterparts in disagreements over the source of those problems. We may even be nearing a time when there will be disagreement over whether a solution is possible at all. Certainly, a variety of scholars from all points on the political spectrum have at least entertained this grim prospect. Arthur Schlesinger, for example, in his *The Disuniting of America*, (Norton, 1992) launches a pithy and vituperative attack on attempts to create a genuinely multicultural society where the riven U.S.A. presently stands. Schlesinger blasts what he calls the "cult of ethnicity," which has "reversed the movement of American history, producing a nation of minorities – or at least of minority spokesmen – less interested in joining with the majority in common endeavor than in declaring their alienation from an oppressive, white, patriarchal, racist, sexist, classist, society."

The argument is one of several to question the viability of, or indeed, desirability of a multicultural society. The United States has been sliced apart by what Schlesinger calls "congeries of distinct and inviolable cultures." Yet the intention of the United States was to be a "transforming nation, developing a unique national character based on common political ideals and shared experiences. The whole point of the union was not to preserve old cultures but to forge a new American culture." We might add that the "whole point" was defined by whites.

Schlesinger tosses a few new arguments into the so-called pot. But, the main constituent remains assimilation. (See **Assimilation**.) This seemingly obsolete concept has returned at a time when ethnic diversity is increasing. Ethnic homogeneity is seen by many as indispensable to a peaceful existence. Schlesinger acknowledges that assimilation, as an ideal, once had a "coercive edge" in that it attempted to impose Eurocentric, or, more specifically, Anglocentric images and values on everybody. But he also believes it is imperative that diversity be translated into unity. Amalgamation of this sort does not please all, but one cannot deny its urgency in current debates. (See **Amalgamation**.)

Ironically, many champions of diversity have similar premises, if different propositions. Writers such as Molefe Kete Asanti and Leonard Jeffries have raised doubts about the validity of ethnic pluralism or cultural heterogeneity. (See **Afrocentricity**.) Black empowerment through cultural revitalization is the ambition here: the contestations and negotiations are strategies designed to secure cultural space. Subversion of the dominant order comes through a realignment of history and experience. In this perception culture is an active site chock full of possibilities. In other words, a sense of black collectivity must be found if African Americans are to empower themselves and the implication of this perspective is that we cannot find it through gradual integration or any of the other processes that are thought to lead to a multicultural society. Multiculturalism is seen as a chimera: a fanciful conception of hybrid character. (See **Multiculturalism**.)

Even the concept that underlies most conceptions of multiculturalism has come under attack of late. "Speaking of ethnicity allows a more or less explicitly racial definition of the group concerned to be re-introduced by the back door" writes Michel Wierviorka, in *The Arena of Racism* (Sage, 1995), "or, alternatively, that the term provides a cover for social problems to which it is unwilling to refer directly."

In a rather different way, Robert Young, in his *Colonial Desire* (Routledge, 1995), argues that advancing a fluid conception of culture in contrast to fixed, essentialist notions of race is tantamount to repeating an historical error. "Today it is common to claims that in such matters we have moved from biologism and scientism to the safety of culturalism," writes Young. But: "Culture and race developed together, imbricated within each other." Multiculturalism and the plurality of ethnic identity it encourages is steering us towards a new form of essentialism in which we reify individual and group identities, on this account. (See **Hybridity**.)

Perhaps, there is mileage in the approach favored by Ella Shohat and Robert Stam: "For us, the word 'multiculturalism' has no essence; it points to a debate," they write in their *Unthinking Eurocentrism* (Routledge, 1994). "While aware of its ambiguities, we would hope to prod it in the direction of a radical critique of power relations, turning it into a rallying cry for a more substantive and reciprocal intercommunalism." This is a challenging conception of multiculturalism and one which calls for a "profound restructuring and reconceptualization of the power relations between cultural communities." In other words, it sees multiculturalism as avoiding the Balkanization implied by many interpretations, in which groups divide and subdivide on the basis of actual or perceived cultural differences and identities. Instead, it envisages a coalescing and regrouping of minorities to form more formidable "communities" readied for empowerment.

Shohat and Stam call this "polycentric multiculturalism" which "thinks and imagines from the margins," as they put it. "Minoritarian communities" are not special interest groups to be pasted on to a preexisting nucleus, "but rather as active, generative participants at the very core of a shared, conflictual history." Plurality, diversity, difference: defenders of multiculturalism rhapsodize over these; but sometimes without pausing to think out the implications of encouraging the coexistence of diverse cultural practices. How about practices that openly deprecate women, such as footbinding and clitoridectomy, both of which are still practised today? "Active, generative" participants to multiculturalism they may be; but hardly likely to elicit the approval of those who rail against the subjugation of women. If multiculturalism is more than a grandiloquent gesture, we have to see history, culture and, most importantly, suffering as more than different centers in a great assorted box of chocolates. (See **Patriarchy and ethnicity**.)

Peter McLaren has ventured toward a resolution to this in his article "White terror and oppositional agency" in which he endorses a "critical multiculturalism" (in *Multiculturalism: A Critical Reader* edited by David T. Goldberg, Blackwell, 1994). "Diversity must be affirmed within a politics of cultural criticism and a commitment to social justice," writes McLaren, adding that: "We need to refocus on 'structural' oppression in the forms of patriarchy, capitalism, and white supremacy." This means that, for all the relativism implied by multiculturalism, a residual absolutism should not be surrendered – like an invariant opposition to the persecution of women brought about by patriarchy, or the class divisions engineered by capitalism.

Ethnicity and multiculturalism have, since the 1970s, shouldered the burden of being the principal alternative to a racist society. Perhaps they are in danger of collapsing beneath the enormous weight. If this is so, then is time for the whole area to reevaluate itself, its analytical importance, its political goals and its moral responsibilities. All of the contributors in this volume are in some way engaged in this project. Each has studied, pursued research and published scholarly work that has enhanced our knowledge of race and ethnic relations. In preparing this edition, I have asked them all to stay mindful of developments in the field in recent years.

A book such as this needs to change as quickly as society. It is constantly vitiated by both events and intellectual trends. Developments threaten the explanatory adequacy of theories and a healthy discipline needs to replenish itself. Given the colossal size of the problems faced, it is at least an encouraging sign. This edition reflects the replenishment.

Many terms have either entered the lexicon or have been fused with new significance in recent years. So, the reader will find newly-commissioned entries on **Others**, a term revivified by **Postcolonial** studies. **Hybridity** has also entered the discourse, as has **Subaltern**. The term **Colonial discourse** itself, of course, has emerged as central to race and ethnic relations. This turn in the study of race and ethnic relations has effected another understanding of the concept of race, or more appropriately "race." In addition to the two perspectives of previous editions, there is now a third, **"Race" as signifier**.

A warrantable intellectual school and social movement called **Black feminism** has gained coherence over the past several years and this too features. And, as if to perpetuate the interrogative spirit that guides many new entries, I have included **Whiteness** to demonstrate that much of what we take for granted needs to be rendered problematic.

The debates over Affirmative Action have given us cause to reflect on the philosophical premises of such programs; the need to interrogate the concept of **Merit** arises. Racism might properly be pluralized to capture its various, mutatating manifestations. One such manifestation is **Environmental racism**, which demands our attention. **Multiracial/biracial** are terms that have crept into our vocabulary, though they are not welcome by many – as the entry indicates. *Causes célèbres*, while not a term popularly associated with race and ethnic relations, is a new addition that conceptually accommodates the multiplying number of high-profile legal cases that attract worldwide attention and focus on racial themes.

The relevance of the work of Brazilian scholar **Paulo Freire** to race and ethnic relations has been reconsidered in recent years and an essay on his theoretical approach is included. A new entry on **Roma**, popularly though misleadingly known as "gypsies," has been commissioned for this edition. And there is a new entry on *Aztlán*, which is of great significance to the Latino experience.

Many of the other terms, as diverse as **Darwinism**, **Diaspora**, **Genocide**, **Segregation**, **Rap**, and **Xenophobia** have been completely rewritten to take account of the significance they have gained over the past few years. The opposite reason justifies the omission of other items. My decisions in these and many other matters have been influenced by the advice of other contributors, in particular Michael Banton, James Jennings, Pierre van den Berghe, and my dear friend Barry Troyna, who died so tragically young shortly before this book was completed.

I have been supported by an able and constructive team led by Seth Denbo at Routledge. Amy Shepper, of University of South Florida, has made a valuable contribution in many areas.

I include the same caveat as in other editions: my failed attempt at omniscience will inevitably render me guilty of errors, many that derive from my attempt to deal with matters of which I have no first-hand knowledge. Over the past several years, I have received many letters informing me of my shortcomings and I am grateful for them. I have used the information to improve this edition. I acknowledge my correspondents and thank in advance those who will take the trouble to write to me in future.

A

Aboriginal Australians

The original Aboriginal Australians have been called "intellectual aristocrats" of early peoples by Claude Lévi-Strauss because of the rich cultural heritage these hunter-gatherers evolved in Australia since at least 50,000 B.C.E. These people were among the first mariners, artists, and religious thinkers.

1770–1930: Assimilation

In 1770, the sovereignty of the 250 distinct Aboriginal cultural-linguistic groups was contested by Lt. James Cook, when he claimed the eastern half of the Australian continent for the British. Cook took possession without negotiation or treaty since he judged the indigenous people to be few and not to have blended their labor with the land in an agricultural manner. Colonialism in Australia was born with his unilateral and incorrect declaration that the land was *terra nullius* or waste – a perception still in dispute today.

The 300,000 Aborigines (Noel Butlin suggests a precontact figure of 800,000 in his book on smallpox, *Our Original Aggression: Aboriginal Populations of Southeastern Australia, 1788–1850*, Allen & Unwin, 1983) were pressured by a pastoral and mining frontier that spread in spurts from southeast and coastal areas across Australia in the century after 1788. A sporadic frontier guerrilla war was waged over the land in most areas causing about 2,000 settler and possibly 20,000 Aboriginal deaths. There was no policy of genocide, but at times government forces supported the settlers in local killing actions. However, the clash between a hunter-gatherer economy and the pastoral arm of British industrial capitalism created unintended relations of genocide. Within a generation many Aboriginal groups had been reduced by over 80 percent while others totally disappeared through the action of introduced diseases, economic disruption, white and *inter se* killings, and a reduced birth rate through infertility and some cultural fatalism.

Many Aborigines took a vital attitude to contact and were not passive victims of colonial expansion despite this death toll. They defended their land and resources, tried to control settlers through reciprocity and kinship, and sought out Europeans by way of curiosity or to extend their cultural opportunities and traditional power. Some material items such as glass and steel were valued but only as adjuncts to their own cultural imperatives. Many Aborigines, particularly in the north, worked in the pastoral industry which supplanted their own traditional economy. They provided cheap, servile, and essential labour, but their nearness to traditional lands and the indifference of their employees to their culture, enabled the maintenance of the old ways.

The gaining of responsible government by the Australian colonies after the 1850s put the settlers, not the British Colonial Office, in charge of Aboriginal policy. This led to a century of restrictive and racist controls supported by social developmentalist and Social Darwinist rationalizations. In southeastern Australia where two or three generations of contact and miscegenation had left an Aboriginal population of mixed decent, policy after 1886 sought to end the "Aboriginal problem" through assimilation and absorption. People of mixed descent were forced from reserves formed earlier, and children were removed from their families for so-called neglect, into orphanages, training homes, apprenticeships, and white foster care. The real reason for the removals that took an estimated 8,000 children from this region alone in sixty years and affected most Aboriginal extended families, was the children's Aboriginality. Such removals lasted into the 1970s and only now are welfare placements made after consultation with the Aboriginal community.

In the north and southwest, where people remained mainly of full decent, the policy was to confine them on reserves under petty and strict controls and in practice half were moved to reserves. Thereafter they could be consigned to white employers as domestics or as pastoral laborers. The Aboriginal Acts removed many civil rights including freedom of movement, rights over property, freedom of marriage especially across racial lines, power over one's family, and the right to practice cultural activities. A dozen Christian missions carried out a similar but more benignly paternal role.

From the 1930s: Self-sufficiency

Aboriginal activism from the 1930s, belated white Australian receptiveness by the 1950s to Aboriginal demands, and federal government leadership, led to a dismantling of state discriminatory legislation in the 1960s. A landmark referendum in 1967 voted overwhelmingly to include Aborigines in the census with other Australians and to allow the federal government to legislate on Aboriginal affairs. Policy moved from assimilation to integration. The reformist federal Labor government in 1972 introduced a policy of self-determination, transformed to self-management by the succeeding Liberal-Nationalist government. Aboriginal community organizations mushroomed with federal finance, empowering people. The Northern Territory Lands Rights Act (1976) and South Australian legislation led to a handback of a quarter of those states' lands – mostly arid – to Aboriginal people. These people had then to face difficult negotiations with an aggressive mining industry. At this time a plethora of welfare officers and social scientists "found" the Aborigines, adding to the outside pressures.

The great optimism of the 1970s in Aboriginal affairs was tempered by growing political and economic difficulties in the 1980s which pushed Aboriginal concerns off the major political agenda. An Australian-wide land rights push was stymied by a white backlash in the 1980s. Also the self-managed reserves often fell to a new welfare colonialism – as white and black federal bureaucrats set overall funding and community development priorities, leaving local Aboriginal communities to decide about trivia within imposed frameworks.

Aboriginal people, less than 2 percent of the Australian population, continue to suffer marginalization and disadvantage despite antidiscrimination laws. Some of this social closure is due to the desire for cultural solidarity by Aboriginal people but white prejudice plays a large part. Their life expectancy, health, income and educational levels, and political power are still dramatically below that of other Australians despite considerable funding programs. Their drug abuse and imprisonment rates are ten times as high. Recent opinion polls show two-thirds of Australians agree that Aborigines lack social and economic equality. Almost 100 Aboriginal deaths in custody over seven years led to a Royal Commission (1987–91). While it found little official criminality in the deaths, it condemned indifferent and racist treatment of Aborigines by prison officers, police, and the community. This has led to new regimes of prison treatment and $4 billion spending on Aboriginal drug rehabilitation, education and job programs. This Commission, which received enormous daily publicity, also alerted the public to the extent of the removal of Aboriginal children since 1900.

This Royal Commission and the Bicentennial celebrations of white settlement in 1988 revived earlier calls for a compact between white and Aboriginal Australians. A government commission representing both sides is to create a strategy for reconciliation by 2001, which many hope could include the treaty or compact never made in 1788.

A High Court ruling in the Mabo Case (1992) over land claims at Murray Island in the Torres Strait finally overturned the notion of *terra nullius*. After a year of fierce controversy, the Keating Labor government passed the landmark Native Title Act in late 1993; this gave Aboriginal people with traditional links to vacant crown land an opportunity to seek communal native title. However, legal wrangles and High Court decisions deadlocked claims for over two years, creating anxiety among Aborigines, mining companies and white pastoral leaseholders alike.

However, the 1995 Federal Court decision on the Wik people's native title claim (Cape York Peninsula), upholding that pastoral leases extinguished native title, led to a novel reconciliation agreement in early 1996 between local pastoralists and Aborigines to avoid any further High Court action. The parties mutually recognized leasehold and native title and agreed to forge voluntary access agreements. The federal government has agreed to fund environmental management by both parties and to sponsor World Heritage listing for half of Cape York Peninsula – an immense 17 million hectares of rain forest and wetlands.

Traditional Aboriginal culture which was forced underground in the century of paternalist control is now flourishing in rural areas and many urban Aborigines are reclaiming their Aboriginal heritage. An Aboriginal artistic renaissance, touching remote communities and youths in custody alike, won much international interest and fostered pride.

Reading
Aboriginal Australians 2nd edition by Richard Broome (Allen & Unwin, 1994) is an overview of two centuries of cultural contact.
Australians for 1788 edited by J. Mulvaney & P. White (Fairfax, Syme & Weldon, 1987) is an account of the diversity of traditional hunter-gatherer in Australia and may be read in conjunction with *Economics and Dreamtime* by Noel Butlin (Cambridge University Press, 1993).
Koori. A Will to Win by J. Miller (Angus & Robertson, 1985) is the first Aboriginal writer's view of black–white history since 1788.
Annual Bibliography (1975/76), Australian Institute of Aboriginal and Torres Strait Islander Studies, is a guide to sources.

See also: GENOCIDE; NATIVE AMERICANS; NATIVE PEOPLES
Richard Broome

Affirmative action
This policy is directed toward reversing historical trends that have consigned minority groups and women to positions of disadvantage, particularly in education and employment. It involves going beyond

trying to ensure equality of individual opportunity by making discrimination illegal, by targeting for preferential benefits members
of groups that have faced discrimination.

Employment
In the United States, the Civil Rights Act of 1964 was the initial
important legislative effort that has served as a basis for later
affirmative action efforts regarding employment. Title VII of this
Act forbade employment discrimination on the basis of race, sex,
religion, and national origin. This legislation also established the
Equal Employment Opportunity Commission (EEOC) to investigate
complaints of employment discrimination. Although initially the
EEOC had to refer cases to the Civil Rights Division of Department
of Justice for litigation, in 1972 Congress amended Title VII by
passing the Equal Employment Opportunity Act. This legislation
authorized the EEOC to file lawsuits in federal district courts against
private employers if attempts at voluntary conciliation failed. It
also authorized the Justice Department to bring local and state
governments to court to challenge their hiring practices. Although
many saw Title VII as merely a protection against discrimination,
it has been interpreted in several court decisions as justifying
affirmative action programs.

A significant early decision in the area of employment was *United
Steelworkers of America v. Weber*, 1979. This was the first Title VII
case to come before the Supreme ·Court in which the plaintiff
charged "reverse discrimination." The Court ruled that an affirmative action plan that was agreed upon by both the company and
the union, and which included preferential promotions for blacks
working for the company, was an acceptable policy designed to
enhance the job opportunities for minorities, and did not constitute
"reverse discrimination." The Court accepted this plan even though
the company had not been found guilty of past discrimination. The
Supreme Court ruled that, at least in this voluntary plan, Title VII
does not forbid race-conscious affirmation action plans.

In *Johnson v. Transportation Agency, Santa Clara County*, 1987,
the Supreme Court again approved a voluntary affirmative action
plan as legitimate under Title VII. The Court noted that the plan
can be acceptable even when the racial or sexual hiring imbalance
is due to societal forces beyond the employer's control, rather than
to discrimination by the employer.

The Supreme Court also has upheld court-ordered affirmative
action challenges under Title VII (e.g., *Sheet Metal Workers Local*

28 v. EEOC, 1986, *United States v. Paradise*, 1987), although it has made clear that it will accept court-ordered plans under more limited circumstances than voluntary plans. For example, in *Sheet Metal Workers*, the Court ruled that affirmative action must be a remedy for past discrimination, although the majority agreed that affirmative relief was not confined to actual victims of discrimination.

Although the 1964 Civil Rights Act did not originally apply to federal employees, Presidents Kennedy, Johnson, and Nixon all supported affirmative action efforts during their administrations. In 1961, Kennedy said it was the policy of the executive branch to encourage "positive measures of equal opportunity for all qualified persons within the government." This was reaffirmed by Johnson in 1965 in Executive Order 11246. Nixon issued an executive order in 1969 that required each federal agency to develop an affirmative action program to overcome past discrimination. Then, the 1972 Amendments to Title VII extended to federal employees the same protections as private employees and gave the EEOC jurisdiction over enforcement efforts regarding the federal service.

Disparate impact and consent decrees
An important issue facing the Supreme Court has been what consti-tutes the bases for proving discrimination, which then can serve as a basis for affirmative action agreements. In *Griggs v. Duke Power Company*, 1971, the Court held that Title VII forbids ostensibly neutral employment practices that are unrelated to job performance. The Court accepted the doctrine of *disparate impact* as a basis for affirmative action remedies. Instead of a plaintiff having to show a discriminatory intent on the part of an employer, the Court ruled that the plaintiff had to present information showing that women or members of a minority group were disproportionately under-represented in a firm or job category within that firm. In this case, a group of African-American employees had charged job discrimi-nation against the company under Title VII, arguing that the requirement that applicants have a high school diploma made it less likely that blacks would be hired. The Court ruled that the burden of proof rested on the employer to prove that the criteria that were the bases for hiring were a legitimate business necessity and were clearly related to successful performance on the job. Even if the employer were successful in showing this, the plaintiff could still prevail by presenting other valid practices were available to the employer that had less disparate impact. However, in *Wards Cove Packing Company v. Atonio*, 1989, the Supreme Court, which by

then included several appointees of President Ronald Reagan, placed a greater share of the burden of proof on the plaintiff to demonstrate that particular job performance criteria specifically discriminate against minorities or women. Further, when the plaintiffs contended that several employment practices created a disparate impact, they had to show the disparity created by each separate practice. The Court also lessened the employers' burden in justifying the hiring practice. Congressional liberals quickly initiated legislative action to overturn *Wards Cove* and return to the *Griggs* criteria. This was accomplished in the Civil Rights Act of 1991.

During the same session in which the Supreme Court ruled on *Wards Cove*, it decided several other cases that had implications for affirmative action programs. One of the most significant was *Martin v. Wilks*. It had generally been assumed that "consent decrees" that resulted in affirmative action programs were not subject to court challenges based upon claims of reverse discrimination by those who had not been a party to the case. In *Martin*, the Supreme Court accepted the legitimacy of a suit filed by several white firefighters in Birmingham, Alabama, against a consent decree that had been accepted by the city, the black firefighters, and the federal government. It held that those who claimed reverse discrimination could challenge consent decrees as long as they were not participants in the original proceedings where the decrees were accepted. This decision was also overturned by the Civil Rights Act of 1991.

Government contracts
The federal government has focused affirmative action efforts on recipients of federal contracts. President Lyndon B. Johnson issued executive order 11246 in 1965 that prohibited federal contractors from discriminating on the basis of race, religion, or national origin. The Office of Federal Contract Compliance (OFCC) in the Department of Labor (reorganized in 1978 to become the Office of Federal Contract Compliance Programs) was established in 1966 to monitor these contractors. In 1968, OFCC mandated that all contractors with more than fifty employees and with contracts over $50,000 write affirmative action plans and in 1969 it required some contractors in the construction industry to set goals and timetables for minority hiring. The policy became known as contract compliance.

The Public Works Employment Act of 1977, which amended the Local Public Works Capital Development and Investment Act of 1976, was an important legislative step regarding affirmative action in minority contracting. It required that at least 10 percent of the federal funds that are grants for local public works projects must be used by the local or state government to purchase supplies or services from minority business enterprises. The Supreme Court in *Fullilove v. Klutznick*, 1980, rejected a challenge to this Congressional action.

The Court, however, in *Richmond v. J. A. Croson*, 1989, narrowed the grounds upon which local and state governments could establish set-aside programs for minorities in the absence of a federal legislative mandate. In this case, the Court invalidated a set-aside program of the city of Richmond for minority contractors. Richmond had reserved 30 percent of its public works money for minority-owned construction firms after a study had shown that only a small percentage of its construction contracts had been awarded to minority-owned businesses. The Court ruled that Richmond would have to show previous discrimination against minority contractors in order to implement its program. As a result, several cities that had adopted Minority Business Enterprise programs to ensure that disadvantaged groups benefit from governmental contracts for construction and for the procurement of goods and services have had to undertake extensive studies to show discrimination against particular groups and must carefully tailor their programs around the findings of the studies.

The Supreme Court made a similar ruling in a 5–4 opinion in *Adarand Constructors Inc. v. Peña* in 1995. This case involved a policy of the federal Department of Transportation that gave contractors a bonus if they hired "disadvantaged business enterprises," as subcontractors, and the policy presumed that minority contractors fitted into that category. The majority opinion ruled that federal affirmative action programs would be subject to "strict scrutiny by the courts," meaning that they must be "narrowly tailored" measures to advance a *compelling governmental interest*. The Supreme Court emphasized that affirmative action programs must be examined to ensure that they do not infringe upon the personal right to equal protection of the laws.

Education
In addition to employment, affirmative action efforts in education have also come before the Supreme Court. The most discussed decision in education has been *Regent of the University of California v. Bakke*, 1978. Paul Allen Bakke was successful in challenging the University of California Medical School's affirmative action program, which included the set-aside of several slots exclusively for

minorities. Bakke had applied for admission but was refused, despite holding better qualifications than some of the other candidates who were admitted as part of the school's quota. Although a deeply divided Supreme Court court ruled in favor of Bakke, a majority of the Justices also concluded that minority candidates could receive some degree of extra consideration in a university's admissions policy.

The issue of affirmative action has been one of the most fiercely debated public policy issues for the past two decades. The conservative Reagan administration used the issue to try to strengthen its political support within the white working class population and appointed members to the EEOC and the Civil Rights Commission who were unsympathetic to affirmative action programs that provided group benefits. The Clinton administration tried to strike a middle course regarding affirmative action efforts, suggesting that they were appropriate under some circumstances. However, in March 1996, the administration announced its intention to limit preferences for minority contractors.

Reading
Equality Transformed: A Quarter-century of Affirmative Action by Herman Belz (Transaction, 1991) charts the history of policies and programs.
Debating Affirmative Action: Race, Gender, Ethnicity and the Politics of Inclusion edited by Nicolaus Mills (Delta Books, 1994) examines the pros and cons.
Turning Back: A Retreat from Racial Justice in American Thought and Policy by Stephen Steinberg (Beacon Press, 1995) has an especially useful chapter 8.

See also: EQUAL OPPORTUNITY; INSTITUTIONAL RACISM; MERIT; LAWS: CIVIL RIGHTS U.S.A.

Robert Kerstein

Africa

The history of race and ethnic relations in Africa antedates the European colonial conquest by several millennia. The continent has been swept by numerous waves of migration and countless indigenous states conquered multi-ethnic empires. Indeed, the first European colonialism in Africa is over 2,000 years old: it began on a large scale with the defeat of Carthage by Rome in 146 B.C.E. Christianity entered Ethiopia in the fourth century; the Arabs conquered North Africa in the seventh, and Islam crossed the Sahara in the early years of the second millennium. The entire coast of East Africa has been in trade contact with Arabia, India, Indonesia, and China for at least 3,000 years. In the interior, a succession of large multiethnic empires rose and fell in the Sudan belt from Senegal to Ethiopia.

The states of central, eastern, and southern Africa were on the whole smaller, somewhat more recent and more ethnically homogeneous, yet a number of them were also ethnically stratified as a result of conquest. Some of them developed indigenous forms of racism, for example the kingdoms of Rwanda and Burundi where a Tuzi minority of some 15 percent of the population dominated Hutu peasants and Twa serfs. The Tuzi claim to superiority was based in good part on their towering stature.

The second half of the fifteenth century marks the Portuguese expansion along the coasts of Africa. The Portuguese were followed in the sixteenth and seventeenth centuries by every other maritime power of Western Europe, principally the English, French, Spaniards, Dutch, and Danes. The Dutch settlement at the Cape of Good Hope in 1652 marks the first sizable European colony in sub-Saharan Africa and was the embryo of contemporary South Africa.

During the 1500 to 1850 period, Europe's relationship to Africa was dominated by the slave trade, in order to supply with labor the European colonies of the New World. Contrary to common belief, the slave trade generally pitted Africans against Africans, and Europeans against Europeans, rather than Africans against Europeans. It was mostly Africans who waged war against their neighbors in order to enslave them, or to avoid being themselves enslaved, and then traded peacefully with European slavers on the coast. The Europeans, on their side, fiercely competed with each other for access to profitable markets and for control of the seas. In all, perhaps some fifteen million Africans crossed the Atlantic in chains, coming principally from West Africa, but also from the Zaire-Angola area, and, in the nineteenth century, increasingly from East Africa. The East African slave trade was centered in Zanzibar, and was largely the product of Arab entrepreneurship. The most massive trading took place during the last century of the traffic (1750–1850), with annual totals often exceeding 50,000.

After the abolition of slavery, the relationship between Africa and Europe entered a new phase. "Legitimate" trade continued, while the interior was gradually penetrated by "explorers," missionaries, and military expeditions. France conquered Algeria in 1830; the Boers and the British greatly extended their territorial encroachments in South Africa in the 1830s and 1840s. By the 1870s, the scramble was on; it consisted of a preemptive set of moves by competing colonizers (mostly the French, British, Belgians, and

Portuguese, and belatedly the Germans and Italians), to claim vast stretches of African real estate as theirs. The Berlin Conference of 1884–85 divided the spoils and established the ground rules for fighting over the African carcass. It was not until World War I, however, that European colonial rule was well entrenched over most of Africa (except for Ethiopia, Liberia, and Egypt). When one considers that World War II marked the beginning of the end of European colonialism, the ephemeral nature of European political domination over Africa is evident: it only achieved a measure of solidity for one generation.

Much has been written of the differences between the colonial policies of the various powers. The British and the Belgians were probably more racist and less assimilationist than the French and the Portuguese. The French, Portuguese, and Belgians had more centralized colonial administrations based on more direct rule, while the British favored indirect rule at least where they encountered large indigenous states as in Northern Nigeria and Uganda. However, the similarities between the European colonizers overshadow the differences. The basic ideology of colonialism was paternalism and the reality was domination and exploitation.

A distinction was often made between colonies of settlement and colonies of exploitation. The former (such as Algeria, South Africa, Zimbabwe, the Kenya highlands, and the Angolan plateau) were opened for European rural settlement and were anticipated to have a substantial contingent of permanent European settlers. (The less tropical areas of the continent were preferred for that purpose.) Today, only South Africa retains a substantial population of European settlers. Colonies of exploitation, on the other hand, were meant to be administered by a rotating cadre of European administrators and managers exploiting native labor for the production of minerals and tropical crops (such as cotton, coffee, and cocoa). The economic exchange between metropole and colony was based on unequal terms of trade: costly European finished products against cheap African raw materials (mostly in mining, agriculture, and forestry).

The winds of change brought about by World War II affected the colonial relationship in Asia first (principally in India, Indochina, and Indonesia), but by the 1950s, the rumblings of independence were beginning to be heard in Algeria, Ghana, Kenya, Guinea, and elsewhere. The Mau Mau movement in Kenya and the Algerian war of independence were the violent exceptions to a largely peaceful process of political evolution of power leading to the great wave of independence of 1960.

By the mid-1960s, only the southern third of Africa remained under colonial or white-settler rule. The independence struggle in the south took a violent turn as it became clear that independence was not going to be granted through peaceful negotiations. Angola and Mozambique had to fight the Portuguese for fifteen years before achieving their independence in 1975. In Zimbabwe, too, the struggle was violent, and freedom had to wait until 1981. Finally, Namibia became independent in 1990 and South Africa came under majority rule after the elections of 1994.

Since independence, African states have developed different relationships to Europe. Some ruling elites of African states have maintained close economic, political, cultural, and educational ties with Europe in general, and their former colonial power in particular, a relationship often characterized as neocolonialism. Countries such as the Ivory Coast, Senegal, and Kenya are examples. Others have taken a more militant course, and have sought to break their colonial ties, or, at least, to multilateralize their dependency. Tanzania, Guinea, Congo-Brazzaville, Ghana, and Nigeria might be put in that category. Some have sought alliance with communist states to achieve independence, only to fall into another form of dependency: Angola, Ethiopia, and Mozambique are cases in point.

Another interesting shift with independence has been one from race to ethnic relations. The accident of pigmentation differences between colonizer and colonized made the independence struggle to some extent a white-black conflict, even though many of the liberation movements stressed their non-racial and antiracist character. After independence, however, the racial issue receded into irrelevance, except for the expression of hostility against certain "middle-man minorities" such as Asians in East Africa. (Uganda, under Idi Amin, forcibly expelled its Asians, for instance.)

On the other hand, conflicts between indigenous groups for the spoils of independence quickly surfaced in many parts of Africa. Stigmatized as tribalistic, these movements were often, in fact, genuinely nationalist or irredentist. In some cases, ethnic conflicts led to open wars and massacres, as in the Sudan, Ethiopia, Rwanda, Burundi, and Nigeria. In other countries, the game of ethnic politics, while a constant reality, has remained relatively peaceful.

Terminological confusion reigns supreme in the analysis of ethnic relations in Africa. What is called nationalism in Africa is nothing like what the term has conventionally meant elsewhere. How can the concept of nationalism be applied to such multinational states as Senegal, Nigeria, or Zaire? Conversely, what is called tribalism in Africa is often genuine nationalism. The real nations of Africa are the Ibo, the Kikuyu, and the Ewe, not Nigeria, Kenya, and Togo. Only a few of these nations, like the Somali and the Swazi, have their state; the overwhelming majority are part of multinational states, or, even worse, are split between several states. It serves, of course, the interests of the ruling elites of these multinational states to stigmatize demands for national self-determination as tribalist, thereby also conforming to the old colonialist view of Africa as congeries of tribes.

Few African states show concrete signs of moving toward the creation of new nations coinciding with their geographical boundaries. Indigenous traditions and languages remain vigorous, and the official languages (French, English, Portuguese) remain tools of convenience of the ruling class, not the basis for the emergence of new national languages. Only Tanzania, with the effective spread of Swahili as a true national language, shows clear progress toward welding a multiplicity of ethnic groups into what may in time become a genuine new nation.

Reading
The African Slave Trade by Basil Davidson (Little Brown, 1961) is a fascinating account of the African-European partnership in slaving, by a radical British scholar.
Race and Ethnicity in Africa edited by Pierre L. van den Berghe (East African Publishing House, 1975) is a collection of articles on North, West, East, and Southern Africa, with several general analytical pieces.
Africa, the Politics of Independence by Immanuel Wallerstein (Vintage, 1961) is a brief treatment of the transition from colonialism to independence by a sympathetic American scholar.

See also: APARTHEID; COLONIALISM; PLURALISM; RACISM; SLAVERY; ZIMBABWE

Pierre L. van den Berghe

African Americans

The term African American refers to the approximately thirty-five million Americans of African descent living in the United States in the 1990s. This term was revitalized in the late 1980s. During the 1960s, a similar self-description was popular in the black community: "Afro-American." While African American is a popular term utilized by many Americans, the term "black" is the most preferred self-description according to one survey published by the Joint

Center for Political and Economic Studies, a black research think tank based in Washington, D.C.

While both terms are considered interchangeable, it has been pointed out by some observers that black is more appropriate because it reflects the broader African diaspora and longer history than that associated with African American. Others have also expressed a preference for black because it includes many African-descent groups living in the United States that do not use African American as a racial or ethnic self-description. One example of such a case are Haitians, who may identify themselves as black, but not necessarily African American. In fact, in the 1990 federal population count by the U.S. Bureau of the Census, black is defined as including persons who indicated their "race" as "black or Negro" or reported entries such as African American, black Puerto Rican, Jamaican, Nigerian, West Indian, or Haitian.

In the late 1980s two major national studies focusing on the status of African Americans were published. One study was commissioned by the National Academy of Science, and is titled *A Common Destiny: Black in America* (National Academy Press, 1988). This study represents a reexamination of the status of blacks in America within the framework of the classic study by the Swedish economist, Gunnar Myrdal, *An American Dilemma* (1944). The other major study was sponsored by a research think tank based at the University of Massachusetts, the William Monroe Trotter Institute. This study is titled *An Assessment of African Americans in the United States* (1989).

While there are important differences in how these two studies approached issues related to black life in the United States, there is at least one important similarity. Both studies concluded that, while blacks have realized important progress in many arenas such as education, politics, military, government, housing, and the economy, many blacks have yet to enjoy social equality with whites. In other words, while there has been some progress and improvement in matters related to race, there still exists an entrenched racial divide and hierarchy in the United States. While some, like Gunnar Myrdal in the 1940s have referred to this racial paradox as an American "dilemma," others like Malcolm X and Martin Luther King, Jr. in the 1960s, have described it as America's "hypocrisy."

Race relations
It cannot be denied that the United States has made enormous strides in improving relations between blacks and whites since the

Civil Rights Movement. Racial segregation, as the official policy of many states was abolished in the United States as a result of important civil rights legislation. It is also reported in numerous surveys that more whites than ever before are tolerant of interaction with blacks in the areas of housing, schools, and jobs. Individual blacks continue advancing as trailblazers in places once completely barred to blacks. For example, Colin Powell serves as the top military official in the U.S. government. Black sports figures like the basketball superstar Michael Jordan, and TV and media personalities like Bill Cosby and Oprah Winfrey, are embraced by white Americans enthusiastically.

Paradoxically, at the same time that this kind of progress is evident, there has been an increase in the number of incidents of racial harassment and violence across the nation. The Southern Poverty Law Center reported in 1989 that hate violence in the United States has reached a crisis stage. Between 1980 and 1986 approximately 2,900 racial incidents were reported across the United States including 121 murders, 138 bombings, and 302 assaults.

According to a major study focusing on police and community relations conducted by the National Association for the Advancement of Colored People in 1992, relations between predominantly white police forces and black neighborhoods continue to be potentially explosive. And, in the spring of 1992 the worse riot in the nation's history occurred in Los Angeles when a jury acquitted four white police officers in the brutal beating of a black male.

Several major studies suggest that in many ways the United States can still be characterized accurately as two societies, one black, the other white, as described in the Kerner Commission Report, a national study which examined the causes of disturbances in the nation during the mid-1960s. This is the conclusion of not only the two national studies cited earlier, but many other recent and scholarly studies as well. Such studies include Kevin Phillips's *The Politics of Rich and Poor* (1989); *Quiet Riots* (1988) by Roger Wilkins, Jr. and Fred Harris; Thomas and Mary Edsall's *Chain Reaction* (1990) and Andrew Hacker's *Two Nations* (1992).

Families
Historically, the family structure of African Americans has been different than that of whites in the United States. Many factors have been proffered as explanation for the differences in black and white family structure including slavery and its lingering effects, economic conditions, African American culture, the impact of social

welfare policies such as public assistance, and conditions that dampen the availability of marriageable black men such as prisons, wars, drugs, and persistent high levels of unemployment.

Currently, there are many different kinds of families among African Americans as there are in other racial and ethnic communities in the United States. There are several trends in the structure of families that are common to all families regardless of race and ethnicity. For example, there is an overall decline in the number of married couple families, and increase in the number of single female-headed families, as well as increasing rates of teenage pregnancies throughout society. Still, about one-half of all black families were a married couple family in 1990, compared to about 83 percent of all white families. Another difference between black and white families is the larger size of family households (2.6 persons), but smaller than the average family household size of Latinos in the United States (3.5 persons) in 1990.

Education

America's racial paradox is reflected in the nation's educational systems. The gap in school enrollment between African American and white children is rapidly disappearing. By 1980, less than one half year separated the median schooling levels of African Americans (12.6 years) and whites (13.0 years). The difference between the high school completion rates of these two groups is also much smaller than in previous periods. The scores on national, standardized tests such as the Scholastic Aptitude Test (SAT) and the National Assessment of Education Progress in the areas of reading, mathematics, and science continues to improve for black youth. And the number of blacks earning medical and law degrees has increased significantly in recent years.

Despite much progress in the arena of education many of the nation's public schools remain segregated as predominantly white, black, or Latino schools. Seldom can one find a public school in a major American city where black and white students have opportunities to interact as classmates in the same programs. Continuing disparities in educational experiences of black children and youth are taking place in a national context where the proportion of black children composing the entire public school population is about 16 percent, and increasing rapidly.

In higher education, blacks now attend colleges and universities that have been hostile to their presence in earlier periods. But many observers would contend that W. E. B. DuBois's assessment of

American higher education's posture toward black students in 1926 is still an appropriate description today. The attitude of the northern institution toward the Negro student is one that varies from tolerance to active hostility. In 1986, the National Institute of Prejudice and Violence, based in Baltimore, Maryland, reported that "an increasing number of colleges and universities are reporting incidents of cross burnings and other acts of blatant bigotry or racial violence." Calls for multicultural curricula that reflect the growing ethnic diversity of the society, as well as "black studies" are resisted by significant sectors of faculty, staff, and leadership of many of the nation's public and private institutions of higher education. Additional factors dampening the presence of blacks in American higher education include federal cuts in financial assistance at the same time that the costs for attending college and graduate schools have risen dramatically.

Poverty and employment
Poverty continues to be a major feature of black life in the United States. While there has been a decline in the proportion of African Americans in poverty from a rate of 55 percent in 1959 to 32 percent in 1989, this latter figure is still three times the poverty rate among whites in the United States. This kind of poverty gap between blacks and whites remains despite the particular family structure of blacks, according to figures reported by the United States Bureau of the Census. In other words, while black married-couple families had a much lower poverty rate than black female-headed families, blacks living in the former kinds of families were still more than twice as likely to be impoverished in 1990 than comparable whites in married-couple families. A large proportion of black youth and children, in particular, are mired in persistent poverty. In 1990, approximately half of all black children under six years of age in the United States were poverty-stricken.

Unemployment rates in black communities continue to be between two and three times greater than white unemployment regardless of the healthy or unhealthy state of the economy. In 1992 the official unemployment rate as reported by the U.S. government's Bureau of Labor Statistics was 6.3 percent for white workers, while for black workers it was reported at 13.9 percent. The unemployment rate for white teenagers was 19 percent, but for black teenagers it was 39.9 percent. In some parts of the nation the unemployment levels for young blacks are in crisis proportions. For instance, in 1988 the Joint Center for Political and Economic Studies conducted a survey and reported that a majority of working-age blacks were not in the labor force in many U.S. metropolitan areas where at least 100,000 blacks resided.

When comparisons on the basis of wealth are made between blacks and whites, wide disparities are also found between these two groups. The U.S. Bureau of the Census reported in 1988 that more than half (51.9 percent) of all black households had a net worth of $5,000 or less; but among white households only slightly more than one-fifth (22.6 percent) could be placed in this category. Only 15.5 percent of all black households had a net worth of $50,000 or more in 1988, compared to almost half (46.9 percent) of all white households in the United States.

Legal institutions and criminal justice
There is a general sense that some of the legal progress realized by blacks in the area of civil rights has been eroded under a conservative U.S. Supreme Court. Several cases decided by the U.S. Supreme Court in 1989 have included legal opinions and interpretations that represent a narrow and circumscribed view of pursuing social and racial equality in the United States.

Such cases include *Wards Cove v. Atonio* (109 S. Ct. 2115) which shifted the burden of proof of racial discrimination onto the alleged victim. The *Martin v. Wilks* (109 S. Ct. 2180) decision gave white male employees of the Birmingham, Alabama, Fire Department the right to challenge a 1974 consent decree to hire black firefighters, although these white firefighters were not employed at the time of the decree. The *Richmond v. Croson* (109 S. Ct. 706) outlawed a requirement for 30 percent construction contract minority set asides in the city of Richmond, Virginia. The program had been established because over a period of time blacks, comprising more than one third of this city's population, had received less than 1 percent of all construction contracts from the city. And in 1993, the Supreme Court declared unconstitutional congressional district boundaries drawn to facilitate black congressional representation.

Such state efforts have been based on the Voting Rights Act of 1965. *Shaw v. Reno* (113S. Ct. 2816) suggested that such efforts represented segregation even though aimed at situations where black voters have never been able to elect black representatives due to racial discrimination.

These decisions have been made by a U.S. Supreme Court dominated by the court appointments of Presidents Ronald Reagan (1980–88), and George Bush (1989–92). Together, these two appointed close to two-thirds of all the federal judges in the United States. What has been perceived by some as the taking over of the U.S. Supreme Court by conservative forces continued with the retirement of legal giant Thurgood Marshall in 1991. His retirement capped a distinguished career devoted to social and racial justice and equality. Marshall's replacement, Clarence Thomas – himself African American – appointed by Bush, was criticized by many in the legal community as a conservative ideologue, and lacking a distinguished legal career.

In the area of criminal justice there has been a significant increase in the number of blacks appointed to various positions, including judges, prosecutors, police officials, and police commissioners. Since 1960, however, the proportion of blacks in the nation's prisons has increased to a point where approximately half of all prisoners in the United States are black. In 1995, the Sentencing Project in Washington, D.C. reported that one third of all black males in their twenties are incarcerated or involved with the criminal justice system in the United States.

Some observers in the United States believe that such high rates reflect racial discrimination against black youth. This was one conclusion of a national report to be published by the National Association for the Advancement of Colored People, "Hearings on Police Conduct and the Community in Six American Cities (1992)." This report was based on hearing public testimony from a broad range of community representatives in several major cities.

Politics

The 1980s witnessed a black political explosion in the United States as blacks were elected mayors of Chicago and New York City for the first time; even in Boston, for the first time in its history, a black candidate won the mayoral preliminary election and qualified to run in the general election. The first black governor in this century was elected in the state of Virginia. And Jesse Jackson rocked the national political establishment by running for the Democratic party's presidential nomination in 1984 and 1988; in the latter year he amassed approximately one-quarter of the Democratic party delegates needed to clinch the nomination. The traditional gap between the proportion of blacks and whites registered as voters was closed considerably. The increased electoral muscle of the black community was critical in the election, or reelection of several U.S. Senators, especially some representing the Southern states. It was due to this new muscle that several U.S. Senators abided by the will of black voters and defeated President Ronald Reagan's nomination of conservative jurist Robert Bork as a justice to the Supreme Court.

As is the case with the other arenas of black life in the United States, however, many problems related to race persist despite important progress. African Americans were unable to elect another black mayoral candidate in the city of Chicago after the death of the city's first black mayor, Harold Washington. David Dinkins, the first black mayor of New York City, was defeated in his bid for a second term.

Important political victories for blacks have not yet been translated into major improvement for a large sector that remain unemployed and in poverty. And at the national level, presidents have been hostile to the political growth and development of the black community since 1980. There have been only two instances in the last 120 years of the nation's history when the President has vetoed civil rights legislation passed by the U.S. Congress. The first instance was when Reagan vetoed the Civil Rights Restoration Act of 1988; the second veto was cast by President Bush when the Civil Rights Act of 1990–91 was presented to him for his signature. Despite these kinds of political ups and downs for black America, the possibility of major impact on the nation's electoral institutions at all levels remain hopeful. The 1990s and beyond may witness the election of additional black governors, as well as blacks elected to the U.S. Senate, as was the first black woman U.S. Senator, Carol Moseley Braun. In 1992 blacks were elected to the U.S. House of Representatives for the first time since the 1860s and 1870s in the southern states of Florida, Alabama, North Carolina, South Carolina, and Virginia. The unfolding demography of the nation, furthermore, will continue to ensure that blacks remain a powerful, albeit potential, factor to consider in the nation's politics.

Reading
Quiet Riots by Roger Wilkins, Jr. and Fred Harris (Pantheon, 1988) is a series of essays that focus on changes in race and poverty in the U.S. since the Kerner Communion report in 1968.
Two Nations by Andrew Hacker (Scribner, 1992) offers a bleakly analytical picture of a society "separate, hostile, unequal." "Race has made America its prisoner," concludes Hacker.
Assessment of the Status of African-Americans, Vol. iv, edited by Winnie L. Reed, (William M. Trotter Institute, University of Massachusetts at Boston, 1990) is a comprehensive review of the status of African Americans in the areas of social relations, economy, politics, education and criminal justice.

See also: AFFIRMATIVE ACTION; EMPOWERMENT; MALCOLM X; KING; THOMAS

James Jennings

African-Caribbeans in Britain

The post-World War II movement of African-Caribbeans from their countries of origin to Britain, their routine experience of racism and discrimination in the metropolitan center and their eventual location at the subordinate levels of Britain's class-stratified society are phenomena of colonialism. That is, the system geared toward the raw exploitation of human labor and natural resources. This system was secured and justified by the belief in racial inferiority and inequality, a belief which has remained firmly embedded in the collective consciousness of the indigenous white British population. What is more, it had enormous and far-reaching implications for the economies of the metropolis and periphery and, crucially, for the economic and social relations between them. A. Sivanandan has emphasized this point in his argument that: "colonialism perverts the economy of the colonies to its own ends, drains their wealth into the coffers of the metropolitan country and leaves them at independence with a large labor force and no capital with which to make that labor productive" (in *A Different Hunger*, Pluto Press, 1982).

Migration

At the end of World War II, the British and other western capitalist nations embarked on a process of rapid economic growth which necessitated the import of migrant labor. This demand was only partially satisfied by the influx of workers from Poland and other parts of Europe and it was at this juncture that Britain, almost in desperation, turned to its colonies and ex-colonies in Africa, India and the Caribbean.

Migration from the Caribbean, especially Jamaica and Barbados, had been a fairly routine experience – a conventional means of escape from the twin problems of overpopulation and under/unemployment, phenomena that had been determined by colonial exploitation. Until 1952, the migrants, for a variety of economic and social reasons, had generally headed for the United States; however, the enactment of restrictive immigration legislation by the U.S. government in that year effectively blocked this route. Despite the reluctance of both Labour and Conservative parties to encourage black migrants to Britain, the economic situation demanded that this vast reservoir of cheap and alternative labor in the Caribbean could not be ignored. Especially as it could be attracted easily to the metropolitan center. The migrants, along with those who later arrived from India (and after 1947, Pakistan) collectively came to be known as "a reserve army of labor" to the British economy.

The nature of the work they were put to in the metropolitan center was also pre-determined by the colonial legacy. In a period of full employment, white indigenous workers inevitably moved into the higher echelons of the labor market. The vacancies which remained at the "cellar level" of the market were filled by the migrants: these were the low status, often unskilled positions in the textile and clothing industries, engineering and foundry works, hotels, hospital and transport services. Prevailing perceptions of blacks as inferior, fit only for menial tasks had originated in the colonial era; but their experiences of black migrants in the metropolitan center reinforced these stereotypes. In short, because blacks were compelled to accept undesirable, menial work in Britain and were seen to demonstrate the veracity of colonial stereotypes about them, they were inevitably caught in the most vicious of vicious circles.

Class profile
In profile, the migrants formed a fraction of the working class: they occupied similar positions in relation to the means of production and supplied labor not capital. Nevertheless, though their objective interests were basically those of the working class generally, the migrants were often seen as unwelcome competitors. This was consolidated as the post-World War economic boom began to recede in the late 1950s. As a corollary, hostility toward them increased. The outbreak of violence between blacks and whites in 1958 in the Notting Hill district of London and in Nottingham exemplified this growing trend. The increasing demands for selective immigration control, primarily to curtail the entry of nonwhite colonial and ex-colonial migrants can also be understood from this perspective.

It is difficult to establish with any precision the collective response of the African-Caribbean migrants to these circumstances, though research does indicate that there was widespread disillusionment with life in the "Mother Country." After all, they had not expected to compete with native workers for jobs, nor had they anticipated the individual and institutionalized discrimination and harassment which they habitually experienced in their day-to-day lives. Nor were they completely unmoved by these experiences: the manifestation of racist violence in 1958 highlighted the need for greater organization and militancy within the communities. It strengthened their fortitude and resistance and helped to set the scene for the publication of journals such as the *West Indian Gazette* and the establishment of the Standing Conference of West Indian Organizations in Britain. Despite these sporadic and important gestures of defiance however, it is difficult to disagree with the view that the energies of the African-Caribbean migrants were geared primarily to a process of social involution: the cultivation of separateness from the hostile society and the emergence of group solidarity and community-togetherness. The enormous growth of the Pentecostalist movement in Britain testified to the extent of this withdrawal process. In 1970, it was estimated, for instance, that one branch of this sectarian movement alone had a following of nearly 11,000 congregations.

This tendency to eschew more militant postures against the daily inequalities of British hostility derived from a variety of factors. Some African-Caribbeans adhered to what has been termed "the migrant ideology;" in other words, because their presence in Britain was based purely and simply on economic grounds, they saw themselves as transient workers who would return to their countries of origin once they had accumulated sufficient money. As such, they were prepared to tolerate conditions in Britain, because they regarded their stay as temporary. Others put up with what Nancy Foner, in *Jamaica Farewell* (Routledge, 1979), called "the pain of being black in Britain" largely because they believed that their children, born and brought up in Britain and therefore not encumbered with an immigrant culture, would not experience the debilitating effects of racial discrimination. They would, in effect, compete on an equal footing with their white counterparts in Britain's meritocratic education system.

The persistence of the colonial legacy ensured that this was false optimism, however. The disadvantages experienced by the African-Caribbean migrants in Britain were only tenuously related to their newness in the society; they were unlikely to diminish with the passage of time. It is precisely the fact that their disadvantaged positions are likely to be reproduced in the life patterns of their children that distinguishes the experiences of colonial migrants from those of other migrant workers. The result: citizens of African-Caribbean origin continue to occupy subordinate positions in the labor market, tend to earn less than white indigenous workers, and are more vulnerable to the risk of unemployment, especially in times of economic recession. Nor is this trend attributable in any significant measure to their alleged "underachievement" in school examinations. The proposition that, even in the midst of a severe recession, school leavers of equal merit stand an equal chance of getting a job simply cannot be sustained. Young unemployed blacks tend to be better qualified than their white unemployed peers.

Youth
Though there is always a risk of oversimplifying the issue, the uprisings in many multiracial areas in 1981 and 1985 give clues to the response of young black people to their situation. The recognition that their life chances are often determined not by their possession of educational qualification but by their skin color has generated the adoption of a more militant posture than their parents were willing to assume. Of course, black youths do not constitute a homogeneous group or undifferentiated social category: many black youngsters openly reject the oppositional stance taken in 1981 and 1985. At the same time, many of the youths involved in the 1980s uprisings retain a commitment to the work ethic and other features of British society. To characterize black youth as an alienated social group is simplistic and misconceived. It also serves to consolidate the invisibility of gender in this characterization. At the same time, it is difficult to deny that young people of African-Caribbean origin display a far greater and overt resistance to racism and discrimination than their parents did. Winston James reckons that the slogan "Here to stay, here to fight" now rings louder than ever. In the continued absence of a coherent and politically unified movement in Britain, comparable to, say, the Civil Rights movement in the United States, African-Caribbean resistance retains the potential to take the form of episodes such as those witnessed in 1981 and 1985. Though these may generate short-term, ameliorative action they are unlikely to bring about any substantial improvement in the life opportunities of the African-Caribbean communities.

Reading
Shattering Illusions by Trevor Carter (Lawrence Wishart, 1986) is an insightful analysis of African-Caribbeans in Britain since the 1950s. Written by an educationalist and political activist, himself of African-Caribbean origin, it looks at the emergence of black resistance to British racism, at collective and individual levels of organization.
Young, Female and Black by Heidi Safia Mirza (Routledge, 1992) redresses the imbalance of research by focusing on young black women aged between 15 and 19, charting their experiences in school and the labor market.
Staying Power by Peter Fryer (Pluto, 1984) remains a classic text. It is a

massive historical account of black presence in Britain, dating back to the sixteenth century.

Inside Babylon edited by Winston James and Clive Harris is subtitled "The Caribbean Diaspora in Britain" (Verso, 1993) and includes a series of useful, sometimes provocative essays on this theme.

See also: MIGRATION; PENTECOSTALISM; RASTAFARIAN MOVEMENT

Barry Troyna

Afrocentricity

A philosophical and theoretical perspective, as distinct from a particular system, based on the essential core of the idea that interpretation and explanation based on the role of the Africans as subjects is most consistent with reality. It became a growing intellectual idea in the 1980s as scores of African American, African Brazilian, Caribbean, and African scholars adopted an Afrocentric orientation to data. Afrocentricity is generally opposed to theories that "dislocate" Africans in the periphery of human thought and experience.

Afrocentricity argues that the Western dogma, which contends that Greeks gave the world rationalism, in effect marginalizes those who are not European. The Afrocentrists contend that the dogma is historically inaccurate and that the construction of the Western notions of knowledge based on the Greek model is a relatively recent construction beginning with the European Renaissance. In the standard Western view neither the Africans nor the Chinese had rational thinking. Only the Europeans had the ability to construct rational thought. Thus, the Afrocentrists contend that the Eurocentric view has become an ethnocentric view which elevates the European experience and downgrades all others. Afrocentricity is not the counterpoint to Eurocentricity, but a particular perspective for analysis which does not seek to occupy all space and time as Eurocentricism has often done. For example, to say classical music, theater, or dance is usually a reference to European music, theater, or dance. However, this means that Europeans occupy all of the intellectual and artistic seats and leave no room for others. The Afrocentrists agree for pluralism in philosophical views without hierarchy.

In the Afrocentric view the problem of location takes precedence over the topic or the data under consideration. The argument is that Africans have been moved off of social, political, philosophical, and economic terms for half a millennium. Consequently it becomes necessary to examine all data from the standpoint of Africans as subjects, human agents, rather than as objects in a European frame of reference. Afrocentricity has implications for fields as different as dance, architecture, social work, literature, politics, and psychology. Scholars in those fields have written extensively about the motifs of location and the constituents of de-centeredness in various areas.

Afrocentrists contend that human beings cannot divest themselves of culture, whether participating in their own historical culture or that of some other group. A contradiction between history and perspective produces a kind of incongruity which is called decenteredness. Thus, when an African American writes from the viewpoint of Europeans who came to the Americas on the *Mayflower*, or when literary critics write of Africans as "the Other," Afrocentrists claim that Africans are being peripheralized.

Metaphors of location and dislocation are the principal tools of analysis as events, situations, texts, buildings, dreams, and authors are seen as displaying various forms of centeredness. To be centered is to be located as an agent instead of as "the Other." Such a critical shift in thinking means that the Afrocentric perspective provides new insights and dimensions to the understanding of phenomena.

Contemporary issues in Afrocentric thinking have involved the explanation of psychological misorientation and disorientation, attitudes which affect Africans who consider themselves to be Europeans or who believe that it is impossible to be African and human. Severe forms of this attitude have been labeled extreme misorientation by some Afrocentrists. Additional issues have been the influence of a centered approach to education, particularly as it relates to the revision of the American educational curriculum.

Reading
Afrocentricity (Africa World Press, 1987), *The Afrocentric Idea* (Temple University Press, 1987), and *Kemet, Afrocentricity and Knowledge* (Africa World Press, 1990) by Molefi Kete Asanti form a trilogy of works looking at the origins, constituent parts and analytical methods of Afrocentricity.
The Africa Centered Perspective of History by Dona Marimba Richards (Africa World Press, 1992) covers the history of European dominated thought and how it enthroned racism.
Behind the Eurocentric Veils by Clinton Jean (University of Massachusetts Press, 1990) is an examination of how social and political institutions have been rationalized on a Eurocentric model and dislocated African institutions to the margins.
Journal of Black Studies (published by Sage) is a multidisciplinary forum related to issues concerning persons of African descent.

See also: ETHIOPIANISM; GARVEY; NATION OF ISLAM; NÉGRITUDE

Molefi Kete Asanti

Amalgamation
This describes the merging of two or more different groups to produce a new and distinct group. It can be simply expressed as A+B+C=Z, where A, B, and C are individual groups and Z is the outcome of their mixing. Originally, the term referred to biologically different groups. Brazil had an official policy encouraging the inter-marriage of its many distinct groups. More recently, the term is reserved for the fusion of cultural groups, whose mixing produces a new and unique culture. Contemporary Mexico combines elements of Spanish with native American culture and the result is distinct from either. Amalgamation is contrasted with assimilation in which one culture tends to dominate and absorb all others into a single culture i.e., A+B+C=A, in which A is the most powerful group.

Reading
"Race and ethnicity" by Richard Schaefer and Robert Lamm in their textbook *Sociology*, 4th edition, (McGraw-Hill, 1992) has a clear section on amalgamation with examples.

See also: ASSIMILATION; INTEGRATION; MULTICULTURALISM; PLURALISM

Ellis Cashmore

American Dilemma, An
See MYRDAL

American Indians
More than 40,000 years ago, the first groups of Mongolians made their way across a natural bridge of land called Beringia into present-day Alaska. Moving along ice-free corridors of what is now Canada and the northern United States, bands of these migrants went as far as 11,000 miles south to the tip of South America where their remains are to be found, dated as early as 8000 B.C.E. As they moved into the eight climatic zones that are included within North, Central, and South America, the migrants, or Native Americans, adjusted to the environment. The greatest progress was made in the area extending from central Mexico to Bolivia and Peru, where the cultivation of corn brought about wealth, creation of cities, complete with plazas, parks, public buildings, and extensive trade with other areas.

1492–1800: Conquest
Some Native Americans settled in what now is the United States and many of the advances initiated in Mexico and Guatemala, such as the cultivation of corn and building pyramids, began to be

introduced in the north. Communication between the tribes in the United States was difficult, for some 50 separate languages and dialects were spoken; but trade did flourish, especially in the Mississippi Valley, where conch shells and pearls from the Gulf of Mexico were taken to villages in Illinois and nearby areas and copper from the Great Lakes region distributed for hundreds of miles.

There were approximately two million Native Americans living within the bounds of the United States when the Europeans arrived in the fifteenth century. Native Americans had been relatively disease-free when they arrived from Asia, but after contact with Europeans, they began in large numbers to die of smallpox, malaria, measles, mumps, and other diseases because they developed no immunity. Between 1519 and 1540 – the main period of the Spanish Conquest – Aztec, Maya, and Inca populations were reduced by half. By 1560, up to forty million Native Americans may have died from contact with the Spanish.

Although Spaniards found gold in the Caribbean and Central and South America, they could not find it in what is now the United States, and signs of their entry into the region are marked by a few forts and many missions erected to convert the Native Americans. The French were more fortunate, for they came in search of furs and the Mississippi Valley contains many cities they developed from trading posts – i.e., Detroit, St. Louis, New Orleans, and Green Bay.

The greatest number of settlers were from England and these signed treaties with Native Americans for acquisition of land. As large numbers of families from the British Isles and mainland Europe intruded on the tribal lands, conflict arose. In 1763, Native American resistance to British settlement in the Middle West forced the English crown to declare the Proclamation Line. This remains the legal basis for the foundation of reserves, land claims and aboriginal rights in the United States and Canada to this day. The proclamation forbade settlement west of a line formed by the drainage divide of the Appalachians; all persons who had encroached beyond that boundary were to leave. Any future cession of Native American land had to be negotiated by representatives of the British crown with tribal leaders. One cause of the American Revolutionary War (1775–81) was the attempt by the British government to check the assumed right of colonists to expand unimpeded into native territories by guarding Native American lands from British subjects' incursions.

As the number of native born whites (Creoles) and mixed Indian-whites (Mestizos) increased in Central and South America, the fullblood natives revolted against high taxes and forced labor, but uprisings against the Spanish, such as the Incas in Peru in 1780, were failures and gradually the fullblood natives retreated into areas undesired at the time by the Creoles and Mestizos. Forced labor by the Mayans on the banana and coffee plantations in Guatemala continued for many years into the twentieth century.

After the colonies became independent as the United States, the natives' title to the land was respected and possession was taken by the government only by purchase or other legal means. In 1789, Henry Knox,the first Secretary of War, recommended that the federal government and not the states have the prime responsibility in Indian matters and any acquisitions of land be made under the authority of the federal government. His recommendation was adopted by federal authorities. Henceforth when one of the various tribes in the East rose against the settlers that had invaded their land and were defeated in a war against the whites, its members were sent to a reservation reduced in size in or near the earlier residence of the tribe. Such a transaction was authorized by a treaty signed by tribal leaders and representatives of the federal government.

1830–1935: Removal
The Indian Removal Act of 1830 led to the forcible "removal" of 100,000 Native Americans, mainly Cherokee, of North Carolina, and Seminole, of Florida, from their land. The Act stayed true to the spirit of 1763 Proclamation in the sense that separation was a guiding spirit. With the heavy movement of settlers to the West, there were other wars between the Native Americans and whites. Always the conflict ended with the tribe being confined to a reservation that was reduced in size, or removal to Kansas or Oklahoma where a reservation was assigned to it. Once on the reservation, the tribe was governed by the terms of the treaty that had been signed with the government regarding size of reservation, food, and money or annuities for ten or fifteen years. Agents represented the government and they in turn supervised staff which typically included a farmer, school teacher and interpreter. Although Native Americans were confined to the reservation under a threat of armed force by nearby troops, they endured periods of starvation when the government ignored terms of the treaty regarding food distribution. Much of the reservation land was unsuitable for farming and the quality of education in the one-room school was poor.

1936–present: Separate culture

During the period spent on the reservation, the teachers and agents did their best to change the dress of the Native Americans, have the men cut their hair, eradicate the native religion and lifestyle, and names were changed to include a first name and surname that could be pronounced by whites; a forced assimilation added to the emphasis of strict separation. Resistance to this process virtually ended in 1890 at the Battle of Wounded Knee in which 200 Sioux natives were massacred by U.S. forces. In 1887, Congress passed the General Allotment, or Dawes Act which provided for the division of most of the reservations into 160-acre tracts to be awarded to each adult male and the surplus land be available for sale to the general public. The vast majority of the reservations were liquidated but the Native Americans profited very little from their allotments, for when the owner died, the land was divided among several children and was too small for a successful farming or grazing venture. Much of the land was lost to the whites through inadequate laws that did not protect Native Americans. By 1935, some 100,000 had been dispossessed.

Nearly forty years after the passage of the Allotment Act, Lewis Merian was appointed by the Secretary of Interior to investigate conditions among the Native Americans. He found the majority of the Native Americans to be extremely poor, unable to adjust to white society; much of the land on which they lived could not support an experienced white farmer. In addition, their health was poor and quality of education rated in the same category. Alcohol contributed to poor health throughout the history of Native American–white relations, as traders, and whiskey dealers made a supply of liquor readily available to Native Americans and so initiated habits that persist to the present day.

As a result of the Merian Report, the Indian Reorganization Act was passed in June 1934. This allowed the Native Americans to write a constitution, form a government and borrow from a credit fund to establish business firms on the reservation. Under its terms, the elected tribal chair took the place of chiefs, and activities such as stockraising, farming enterprises, salmon canneries, and tourist facilities helped raise the average income of the Native Americans who worked in those enterprises. Native languages, religions, and crafts were encouraged and standards of education improved.

This program was aimed at reversing the effects of the earlier attempts to force assimilation: it recognized the cultural distinctness of Native Americans and eschewed any effort to alter this distinctness.

Contemporary Native American activism may have begun in 1961 in Chicago when 500 persons attended a conference which had as its goals a review of past policies and formulation of new ones. Young delegates to the conference formed the National Indian Youth Conference which sponsored demonstrations and protested state arrests of Indian fishermen who had fishing rights guaranteed under federal treaties. Congress began to pass numerous laws, including the 1975 Self-Determination Act, which benefited Native American education, social welfare, and civil rights and reinforced their legal status as a distinct ethnic group. In 1972, two members of the activist American Indian Movement were killed in a siege at Wounded Knee, indicating that resistance among Native Americans is still alive. In 1990, protesting Mohawks held an 11-week siege at Oca, Quebec.

A recent interpretation of federal law on reservations brought about the opening of cigarette shops, bingo halls, and casino gambling on the reservations and the infusion of more money for the tribal budgets. Since state tax laws and regulations were not operative upon the reservations, cigarette shops were opened that sold cigarettes for less than what was charged elsewhere in the state. With this success bingo halls came that offered much higher prizes than elsewhere and finally casino gambling opened. All of this additional money gave the tribes a chance to provide better housing and economic opportunities for the members. There are now as many Native Americans in the United States as when Columbus landed in 1492 (two million). But since many are counted as persons who have only a small amount of Native American blood, the number is probably relative.

Reading

Education for Extinction: American Indians and the Boarding School Experience, 1875–1928 by David Wallace (University of Kansas Press, 1995) shows how Indian children were removed from their homes and taken into government boarding homes so that white culture could take root and the "savage" culture of Indians could fade to extinction.

The American Indian: Prehistory to the Present by Arrell M. Gibson (D.C. Heath and Co., 1980) is a good basic text.

Custer Died For Your Sins: An Indian Manifesto by Vine Deloria Jr. (University of Oklahoma Press, 1988) is an outstanding history told from the Native American viewpoint.

See also: CONQUEST; CREOLE; CULTURE; EXPLOITATION; NATIVE PEOPLES

James A. Covington

Anti-Semitism

The adherence to views, attitudes or actions directed against the interests, legal rights, religious practices, or lives of Jews has been known, at least since 1870, as anti-Semitism (Ernest Renan was apparently the first to use the term). But the mythology supporting its justification derives from the image of Jews as demons "Christ killers" and the "devil incarnate" who used Christian blood for rituals. According to A. N. Wilson, in his biography *Jesus: A life* (Norton, 1992), early Christians, who were fearful of Roman persecution, blamed Jews for Jesus' death: they invented the idea that Jews had turned on Jesus for blasphemy. "Such a distortion of history would not have been so serious had it not been used as an excuse for 2,000 years of Christian antisemitism," writes Wilson. "Were Jesus to contemplate the fate of his own people at the hands of the Christians, throughout the history of Catholic Europe," adds Wilson, "it is unlikely that he would have viewed the missionary activities of St. Paul with such equanimity." Paul, unlike Jesus, advocated the abandonment of the Jewish Torah.

In eleventh-century Europe, the vast majority of Jews were economically impoverished and traditional in their beliefs. Their distinctive dress and lifestyle made them readily recognizable scapegoats in times of hardship. Voluntary migrations and forced expulsions in the thirteenth and fourteenth centuries gave rise to a Jewish diaspora. In 1492, 150,000 Jews were expelled from Spain.

Anti-Semitism has been viewed in terms of both religion and race. The most virulent expression of the latter is clearly the Holocaust of World War II, which was intended to eliminate the European Jewry. While anti-Semitism has declined sharply in the years since the war, it remains a potent force in Europe, in Arab states and in the United States, among other places.

Many racist organizations still cling to *The Protocols of the Learned Elders of Zion*, a notorious text, first published in Russia in 1903, which purports to be the minutes of a secret meeting of Jews held in the early years of the twentieth century in which plans for world domination are outlined. This added to the image of Jews: they were cast as organizers of an intricate conspiracy geared to take over society's major financial institutions. It was originally used by the Russian tsars as a rationale for the oppressive policies against Jews, but also, in the 1920s, by the industrialist Henry Ford, who owned a newspaper which issued constant attacks on Jews. Ford later apologized.

Reading
Anti-Semitism: The Longest Hatred by Robert Wistrich (Pantheon, 1992)
traces the phenomenon from its early beginnings, especially from the third
century B.C.E. (Before the Common Era), to medieval and contemporary
manifestations in Europe and the Middle East.
In Search of Anti-Semitism by William F. Buckley, Jr. (Continuum, 1992)
examines anti-Semitism in the U.S. conservative movement today.
Jewish Identity and Civilizing Processes by Steven Russell (Macmillan, 1996)
traces the Jewish experience in Western Europe from the Middle Ages to
the present, using a theoretical framework derived from Norbert Elias.

See also: DIASPORA; GENOCIDE; OTHERS; RACISM; ZIONISM

Ellis Cashmore

Apartheid

An Afrikaans word, meaning "apartness" or total separation. In
the context of South Africa, where it defined official policy, it
referred to the segregation of whites and those defined as "nonwhites." It was based on *baasscap*, a philosophy that asserted white
supremacy.

Apartheid has its roots in the white master/black slave relationships of the seventeenth-century colonialism. The Dutch developed
a small slave colony in Cape Town (on the Atlantic coast) in the
1650s and began to supply fresh produce to ships sailing from
Europe to Asia. In the eighteenth and nineteenth centuries, Dutch
settlers known as Boers (farmers) moved into the inner regions of
Southern Africa. The Boers' incursions brought them into severe
conflict with native peoples, such as the Khoikhoi (Hottentots, as
they were called by the Boers) from the Cape and Bantu tribes
from the southeast. The black native peoples were suppressed by
the 1870s and the Boers constructed a series of all-white republics
in the Orange Free State and the Transvaal.

The British interest in the areas grew after the discovery of gold
in Johannesburg and confrontation erupted into the Anglo-Boer
War, 1899–1902. Britain emerged victorious and established the
area as a colony, the Union of South Africa. This was declared a
self-governing state, or white dominion, in 1910, with blacks being
excluded from all areas of political influence.

The division between blacks and whites was continued by the
United Party under the leadership of Jan Smuts (1870–1950), who
took office as Premier in 1919. He lost the support of the white
working class and was defeated in a 1924 election. Returning to
power in 1945, Smuts, who had once declared himself against segregation, asserted: "It is fixed policy to maintain white supremacy in

South Africa." Between 1946 and 1948, Smuts pushed through a series of moves designed to remove blacks' already limited franchise and property rights. Apartheid was fully institutionalized in 1948 when the Afrikaner Nationalist Party won election.

Hendrik Verwoerd (1901–66) who, in 1948, became South Africa's Minister for Native Affairs and, from 1958, national leader, is acknowledged as the most important architect of apartheid. He was a Nazi sympathizer and reigned for eight years, his commitment to apartheid was strengthed by his belief that he was an instrument of god's will. Verwoerd's recognition of the need to maintain South Africa's social division influenced his decision to withdraw his country's application for continued membership of the Commonwealth. In 1961, South Africa became a republic.

The first plots of land for native peoples, called Bantu reserves, were officially set up in the Transkei in 1962. The South African state policy was that separate self-governing black states should be created with a view to their eventually becoming independent (a native reserve system had been started in the 1840s designed to restrict the natives' rural land to 13 percent of the total area of the country). Blacks constituted about 72 percent of the total population of nearly thirty million; they were allocated 12 percent of the land. Whites constitute about 17 percent of the population (the remainder being composed of "coloreds" and Asians).

In order to sustain the economy, the system had to allow blacks to migrate temporarily to white urban areas, or zones. Blacks were issued with pass books and required to carry them at all times; they were made to produce them on demand by the police; failure to carry or produce was made a punishable offence. Blacks, it was determined, were allowed to enter white areas only for the specific purpose of working; basically, they were needed to do menial jobs that whites refused to do with whites sometimes earning up to twelve times as much as nonwhites.

After working, blacks were legally required to return to their reserves. This arrangement had actually started in the nineteenth century, when a solution had to be found to the problem of maintaining a supply of cheap labor (then for the mines) without disrupting the essential white-black division. Black workers were made to stay in austere barracks for the length of their contract of labor, then forced to return to their reserves. Overstaying was made punishable by long prison sentences.

Verwoerd pursued his policies with Bantu Laws Amendment Acts in 1963 and 1964; these eliminated any semblance of blacks' employment security and effectively reduced them to the status of chattel.

Certain other elements of apartheid, such as the illegalization of sexual relations between whites and nonwhites, were in effect before 1948, but the implementation of the system served to cement the segregation legally and totally. To complement the whole system, blacks were denied any effective political rights. So the whole thrust of the apartheid system was to: (1) ensure legally strict geographical and social segregation in all spheres of life; and (2) maintain a rigid pattern of inequality in which blacks were effectively kept powerless and without wealth.

Needless to say, such a harsh system experienced periodic challenges, two of the most important coming from black organizations in 1960 (at Sharpeville) and 1976 (at Soweto). Both attempted coups were suppressed after horrific bloodshed. The South African army and police have, over the years, equipped themselves thoroughly to deal with uprisings, one of the common tactics being to torture and even kill suspected seditionaries. The death of Steven Biko in 1977 demonstrates this. Biko (1947–77) was, at the time, one of the most charismatic and influential leaders of the Black People's Movement, itself modeled on the American Black Power organizations of the 1960s. The 1976 atrocity at Soweto has marked a kind of watershed in South Africa's political history and Biko's death was part of a ruthless crackdown by the Police Security Force. Section 6 of the South African Terrorism Act was regularly invoked to detain suspected black leaders. Biko was, in fact, the forty-sixth black person to die in police custody. "A struggle without casualties is no struggle," Biko himself tragically anticipated.

In a technical sense, apartheid's dissolution began in 1990 when South Africa's Premier, F. W. DeKlerk, authorized the release of Nelson Mandela and announced the attempted transition from a fragmented and fractious society to a liberal, multiethnic, democratic nation. Agonizing resolutions between the ruling National Party and Mandela's Africa National Party yielded little obvious progress – only a decline in black living standards and a sharp rise in crime. The legacy of apartheid and the separation, isolation and poverty it created made nation-building a forbidding task.

In 1996, a critical court case ruled against the continuation of apartheid in education. Despite the technical elimination of apartheid, the Potgietersrus primary school, 160 miles north of Johannesburg, refused to admit black children on the grounds that it was safeguarding Afrikaans language, religion and culture. When three black children enrolled, white parents blockaded the school, in a manner reminiscent of the incident at Little Rock, Arkansas, where U.S. troops had to escort black pupils to a high school in 1957. South Africa's Supreme Court ordered the Potgietersrus school to admit black children and thus remove one of the last vestiges of apartheid.

Reading

Segregation and Apartheid in Twentieth Century South Africa edited by William Beinhart and Saul Dubow (Westview, 1995) is a collection of key texts that explore the historical and political origins of apartheid as well as its intellectual underpinnings.

Deconstructing Apartheid Discourse by Aletta J. Norval (Verso, 1996) analyzes apartheid during the transformative period during the 1970s and 1980s and its disarticulation from the mid-1980s. The author accentuates the specificity of the mode of social division instituted by apartheid which Norval calls "a failed hegemonic project."

The South African Mosaic by Normazengele A. Mangaliso (University Press of America, 1994) is a sociological analysis of the post-apartheid conflict.

See also: MANDELA; SMUTS; SOUTH AFRICA; VERWOERD

Ellis Cashmore

Aryan

From *āryas*, a Sanskrit word meaning noble (but apparently in earlier use as a national name), which was used in English primarily to denote the family of Indo-European languages related to Sanskrit. The word acquired greater currency when it was used in the 1850s and 1860s by Gobineau and Max Müller to identify a group of people who produced a particular, and higher, civilization. Gobineau maintained that there was a hierarchy of languages in strict correspondence with the hierarchy of races. He wrote: "Human history is like an immense tapestry. . . . The two most inferior varieties of the human species, the black and yellow races, are the crude foundation, the cotton and wool, which the secondary families of the white race make supple by adding their silk; while the Aryan group, circling its finer threads through the noble generations, designs on its surface a dazzling masterpiece of arabesques in silver and gold." Most of the authors, who in the late nineteenth century dilated upon the history of the Aryans, wrote less elegantly than this but often in almost equally general terms. Max Müller came to regret the extension in the use of the word and complained "To me an ethnologist who speaks of an Aryan race, Aryan blood, Aryan eyes and hair, is as great a sinner as a linguist who speaks of a dolichocephalic dictionary or a brachycephalic grammar. . . . We have made our own terminology for the classification of languages; let ethnologists make their own for the classification of skulls, and hair, and blood."

Reading
The Aryan Myth by Leon Poliakov (Chatto, 1974) is a comprehensive account of the concept.
Race: The History of an Idea in America by Thomas F. Gossett (Schocken Books, 1965) is a briefer treatment.

See also: CHAMBERLAIN; GOBINEAU; NEO-NAZISM; WHITENESS; VOLK
                                                        Michael Banton

Asian Americans

Asian Americans were among America's earliest settlers and have long been part of its history. Large-scale Chinese immigration began with the Gold Rush in 1849. For more than three decades, their labor contributed to the rapid economic development of the new nation. Between 1849–80, over 200,000 Chinese entered America. The gold they mined filled the coffers of the Treasury, and without their muscle, the transcontinental railroad that tied the country together and created a national economy would have been delayed for years. They tilled the soil and fed the settlers streaming West. However, when the economy faltered, the Chinese, despite being pioneer settlers, became victims of prejudice and persecution. They became the focus of an "anti-coolie movement." Exclusion laws introduced in 1882 prevented migration from China.

Migration
The continuing need for labor led to recruitment of the Japanese in 1884. Like the Chinese before them, they soon met with racial prejudice and demands for their exclusion. In 1908, male laborers from Japan were restricted entry, but Japanese women continued to travel to the United States, so that grounds were laid for a native-born Japanese American generation.

As each Asian group came in seriatim, they all met similar conditions. After Japanese immigration was restricted, alternative labor sources from Korea and India were tapped during the early 1900s. The Indians were excluded by law in 1917, and by 1924, all Asian immigrants were classified as "ineligible to [sic] citizenship", and therefore not permitted to enter the country. With immigration blocked, the Asian presence in the United States declined. Most Japanese by this time were native-born Americans. Nevertheless, when the United States entered World War II, these Americans of

Japanese descent were herded into relocation camps and detained for the duration of the war.

While legislation almost completely halted the immigration of Asians after 1924, Filipinos, being United States subjects, were afforded a special status. Filipinos filled the labor gap which was created by the exclusion of all other Asians. However, their eventual fate was to follow that of other Asian groups. In 1934 the federal government granted independence to the Philippine Islands in exchange for the curtailment of immigration. Thus, the attitude toward Asians in the United States was characterized by a pattern of tolerance when their labor was needed followed by racism and eventual exclusion.

Postwar experiences
After World War II some Asians were permitted to enter the country, but quotas governing their admission hovered in the area of about 100 per country per year. This was tantamount to exclusion. Whereas earlier immigrants were able-bodied males, many women from Japan, the Philippines, and Korea arrived as war brides of American soldiers, since they were not subject to the quota limitations. This added a new dimension to the Asian population: interethnic families and mixed blood offspring.

The tide turned in 1965 with enactment of a new immigration law. The national origins quotas were abolished and countries were allowed up to 20,000 immigrants each. The change in the law coupled with political unrest and the Communist threat in many of United States, caused Asian immigration to balloon. Asians presently make up one-third of legally admitted immigrants to the United States. The decade 1981 to 1990 saw more than two million Asians admitted with the following breakdown by country. China/Taiwan/Hong Kong: 445,000, India: 251,000, Japan: 47,000, Korea: 334,000, Philippine Islands: 549,000, Vietnam: 173,000. There are now eight million Asian Americans in the United States (3 percent of the total population).

The aftermath of the Vietnam War in 1975 brought a new category of Asians to the United States: refugees from Vietnam, Cambodia, Laos, Thailand, and even Burma. The United States felt a moral obligation to help these refugees seek asylum from danger and persecution and to help them get resettled in their homeland. By 1990, more than a million refugees from southeast Asia had entered the country through special refugee relief legislation. These numbers were in addition to the immigration quotas.

In 1990, the Census counted seven million Asians in the United States. Of these 23 percent are Chinese, 19 percent are Filipinos, 12 percent are Japanese, 11 percent Indian, 11 percent Korean, 8 percent Vietnamese and 16 percent others. Asians are only 3 percent of the U.S. population, but their numbers have more than doubled every decade since 1960.

The term Asian American may be misleading in that it implies a commonality of experience which does not exist. There is an enormous variety of races, religions, and languages and the nations from which they come are widely diverse in their culture, customs, and traditions. Although the use of the term is often expedient for political categorization, it does not account for the diverse experiences of the individuals and communities which it attempts to encompass. But, as a group Asians are considered to be one of the five major ethnic groups within the United States: White, Black, Hispanic, Asian, and Native American. In the 1980s and 1990s, Asians have been the fastest growing minority group in the nation.

Current profiles
Even within ethnic groups, Asians are not homogeneous. For example, Chinese immigrants come from mainland China, Taiwan, Hong Kong, Singapore, or Vietnam each with distinctive backgrounds. Some Asian Americans have roots in America that go back to the middle of the 1800s, but a large majority are recent immigrants. In fact, over 95 percent of the refugee population is foreign-born, as are a majority of Asians in the United States. Recent immigrants, such as Filipinos and Indians, Koreans, Taiwanese and Hong Kong Chinese are well educated and better off than their compatriots of the past. However, Chinese from the Mainland and refugees from Southeast Asia come from war-torn or politically disrupted backgrounds. These groups have greater problems trying to rebuild their lives. At one time, Japanese were the dominant Asian group; now immigrants from Japan are few.

Asian populations are concentrated along the East and West Coasts, the Hawaiian Islands and in urban centers. Approximately three out of five Asians live in the three states of California, New York and Hawaii. They have introduced their cuisine to the American palate, so that Chinese restaurants, Japanese sushi bars, and Indian food stores dot the urban landscape. Asians tend to value education, so parents push their children to achieve academically. The educational profile of Asians is high, but the language barrier and the recency of their immigration preclude them from getting jobs commensurate with their education. So they go into small businesses like restaurants, green groceries, newspaper stands, motels and garment factories.

Although the doors of America have been opened to Asians since 1965, and many Asians intend to put down roots in their adopted country, they are perpetually considered foreigners and associated with their mother country. An unfavorable trade balance with Japan will wreak hostility not only against Japanese Americans, but against all Asians. Asian Americans were blamed for the killings in Vietnam. Chinese Americans are suspected of having Communist sympathies because they have relatives in China. When the economy is weak, Asians are accused of taking jobs away from whites and blacks who are seen as 'American', while Asians are viewed as foreigners. Recent outbreaks of violence against Asians have been very disquieting. At the same time Asians are perceived as achievers in schools and in business. They are scapegoated in the classic "damned if they do, damned if they don't" way.

Reading

Asian Americans: An Interpretative History by Sucheng Chan (Twayne, 1991) takes a topical approach rather than dealing with each Asian American group separately.

Pacific Bridges: The New Immigration from Asia and the Pacific Islands edited by James Fawcett and Benjamin Carino (Center for Migration Studies, 1987) is a scholarly treatment of world-wide contemporary Asian immigration.

Strangers from a Different Shore by Ronald Takaki (Little Brown, 1989) makes an in-depth probe into the Chinese, Japanese, Filipino and Indian American experiences.

Adjustment Experience of Chinese Immigrant Children by Betty Lee Sung (Center for Migration Studies, 1987) shows how the schools, the community, and families help immigrant children in their adjustment to life in a new country. This may be read in conjunction with *Education and Class* by Yuan Cheng (Avebury, 1994) which compares the life chances of Chinese in Britain and the United States.

See also: ASIANS IN BRITAIN; DIASPORA; MIGRATION

Betty Lee Sung

Asians in Britain

The term "Asian" in a British context usually refers to migrants and their offspring from South Asia, that is, India, Pakistan, Bangladesh and Sri Lanka. It also includes those of Asian descent who previously lived in the East African countries surrounding Lake Victoria: Kenya, Tanzania, and Uganda. The former traveled to Britain as migrants mostly in the 1950s and, especially, the 1960s.

The latter were political refugees who fled to Britain following the expulsions of the 1970s. Collectively, South Asians make up 2.7 percent of Britain's total population of 54.8 million, Indians forming the single largest group (840,000), with 475,000 Pakistanis and 160,000 Bangladeshis. (There are also 157,500 Chinese, though these are not conventionally analyzed in the same frames of reference as South Asians.)

Migration
The South Asian presence in Britain can be traced back to the nineteenth century, when itinerant merchants and mountebanks traveled the country. Many held high office in colonial governments and played prominent parts in public life. Their profile was in stark contrast to South Asian migrants after the war, who traveled in search of work and often labored in menial jobs in the textile industries of such cities as Bradford, Leeds, and Manchester.

Research by Muhammed Anwar indicates that many migrants viewed their stay in Britain as temporary and were sustained by *The Myth of Return* (Heinemann, 1979). But the myth was exactly that and most settled permanently into what was, in the 1960s, a "reserve army of labor." South Asians, particularly Indians, have a strong cultural tradition of migration; so much so that there is a warrantable Indian diaspora.

Migration patterns were affected between 1960 and 1971 by legislation designed to restrict the flow of migration from Britain's former colonies, most specifically New Commonwealth countries (which included the South Asian nations). Many migrants who had intended to stay in Britain only temporarily hurriedly sent for relations so as to avoid the restrictive controls. Once families were reunited, permanent settlement followed.

Different circumstances preceded the arrival of other Asian groups in the late 1960s and early 1970s. Political refugee expulsions came from Kenya in 1967–68 and Uganda in 1973–73. The Kenyan situation prompted a blatantly selective – and, by inference, racist – piece of immigration in 1968.

Many East African Asians were business owners who had remitted capital in anticipation of forced migration. Their position on arrival in Britain was of a different order from those migrating from Asia. They had not arrived in desperate search of work, nor were they alone (many traveled in families); they also had some experience in business and, in some cases, had left solidly established enterprises. The entrepreneurial spirit traveled well and, by the late

1980s, a second generation of East African Asians had become a constituent part of Britain's ethnic business class.

At the other end of the class structure, Bangladeshis, who are mainly Muslims, slid towards virtual underclass status. They were overrepresented among the unemployed, had low property owner-ship rates compared to other South Asians and worked mostly in manual occupations. While other South Asian groups improved in terms of educational achievement, Bangladeshi children failed to improve.

Culture

Cultural differences are not enough to explain the differences in achievement levels. Other Muslim groups, from Pakistan and, to a lesser extent, India have successfully negotiated an accommodation for their cultures. Multicultural and antiracist education policies make provision for the teaching of English as a second language so that mother tongues such as Urdu or Gujarati would not be threatened. Sikhs were involved in a successful and important legal case, *Mandla v. Dowell Lee*, which resulted in their being recognized as a protected group under the terms of the Race Relations Act of 1976. This meant that their cultural distinctiveness, the most visible sign of which is the male's turban, was officially recognized.

Muslims have sought strenuously to preserve their Islamic tradition, initially through the building of grand mosques in most major British cities. Later, Muslim schools pressured for official recognition. The Educational Reform Act permitted this.

Conflict

South Asians have borne the brunt of some of the most brutal forms of racial harassment. The so-called "paki-bashing" episodes of the late 1960s became the almost ritualistic practice of white fascist youths. The minor surge of neo-Nazi political parties in the 1970s brought Asians to prominence once more as targets for physical attack. In one especially nauseous case in 1981, a Pakistani woman and her three children were killed after their house was set alight.

In 1992, two separate incidents in Blackburn, Lancashire, and Birmingham suggested a new pattern of interethnic violence, as gangs of youths clashed. The gangs were organized on the basis of region e.g., Punjabis, Bengalis, Bangladeshis, each group of which seems to have maintained its cultural identity in spite of almost two generations of the homogenizing and assimilating forces of urban life. The causes of the conflict were probably less cultural than economic as regional groups have progressed at different rates.

The conflict underlines the heterogeneity of Britain's South Asian population. There are at least fifteen Asian languages spoken, each with its own literature. Apart from the main religions, Islam, Hinduism and Sikhism, there are Jains, Zoroastrians, Christians, and a variety of other belief systems. In the 1990s, South Asians are spread throughout the class structure, many owning their own businesses and many more working in the professions. A sizable percentage remain in working class occupations.

Reading
South Asians Overseas edited by C. Clarke, C. Peach and S. Vertovec (Cambridge University Press, 1992) is a generic guide, as its title suggests and may be read in conjunction with *Migration: The Asian Experience* edited by Judith Brown and Rosemary Foot (Macmillan, 1994) which deals with the various facets of Asian migration and settlement.
Race and Politics in Britain by Shamit Saggar (Harvester Wheatsheaf, 1992) provides an overview of the various issues as they affect Asians.
"Political blackness and British Asians" by Tariq Modood (in *Sociology*, vol. 28, no. 4, 1996) rejects attempts to class Asians as black for the purposes of color-solidarity and political identity.

See also: ASIAN AMERICANS; HARASSMENT; INTERETHNIC CONFLICT; MIGRATION

Barry Troyna/Ellis Cashmore

Assimilation
The process of becoming similar. The primary sense of this word has been overlaid in sociology by one of its subsidiary meanings, that which denotes the absorption of nutriment by a living organism – as the body is said to assimilate food. The popularity of the organic analogy in early twentieth-century sociology increased the tendency to give assimilation this secondary meaning. So did the concern in the United States at that time about the influx of immigrants from Eastern Europe and the Mediterranean countries: these were suspected of being of inferior stock and less easily assimilable than immigrants from northwestern Europe. Thus under the pressures of the age, assimilation came to be equated with Americanization just as in Britain in the 1960s it was identified with Anglicization.

The confusions in this oversimplification were exposed by Milton M. Gordon who distinguished several different models employed in the United States. One he called Anglo-conformity; this was the process by which immigrants were brought – or should be brought

– to conform to the practices of the dominant Anglo-Saxon group. The second was the "Melting Pot," in which all groups pooled their characteristics and produced a new amalgam. The third model comprised two versions of pluralism: cultural and structural, according to whether the minority, while resembling the majority in many respects, retained elements of distinctive culture or could be distinguished by the way its members continued to associate with one another.

For sociological purposes, further distinctions are necessary. Assimilation can be seen as one kind of ethnic change in which people become similar, and contrasted with differentiation in which groups stress their distinctiveness, for example by observing food taboos or displaying distinctive signs and symbols. Members of a group who differentiate themselves in one respect (as, say, Sikhs wear turbans) may assimilate in another (like language use). So in discussing ethnic change it is necessary to specify particular items of culture and to examine the direction in which change occurs and the speed with which it takes place. Moreover, ethnic change at the local level may in the short term run in a direction opposite to that at the nation level. A group which is a numerical minority in the country may be in a majority locally, so that people belonging to the national majority may be under pressure to change towards the group which is the local majority. For example, in parts of British cities where there are substantial numbers of black children, it is not uncommon for white and Asian children to interest themselves in black music and adopt black speech patterns. In the 1960s, there were neighborhoods in which most black families came from Jamaica. Black children whose parents came from other countries tended to adopt forms of the Jamaican dialect and that dialect contributed more than others to the new black speech patterns.

Some minorities consciously adopt practices designed to resist the pressures toward assimilation that are generated within the national society, such as the advertising of consumer goods. Religious groups establish their own schools, while gypsies and travelers keep their children away from state schools if they fear that these threaten their family ties. In other circumstances, members of the majority may impede assimilation by withholding social acceptance, as white Americans have discriminated against black Americans although the latter were culturally much more Americanized than recent white immigrants. Sociologists should therefore be on their guard against the simple view of assimilation as a unitary process on the group level which assumes that the minority will conform to majority ways and that the majority, in absorbing them, will not itself change. The processes of assimilation are much more complex. They need to be studied on the individual and the group levels, with the focus on specific forms of behavior seen in their full political and social context.

Reading
Assimilation in American Life by Milton M. Gordon (Oxford, 1964) is a general discussion.
Racial and Ethnic Competition by Michael Banton (Cambridge, 1983); chapter 7 discusses the interrelation of processes at the individual and group levels.
Ethnic Change edited by Charles F. Keyes (University of Washington Press, Seattle, 1981) is a collection of essays analyzing the processes of change in a variety of situations.

See also: BOAS; ETHNICITY; INTEGRATION; PLURALISM

Michael Banton

Authoritarian personality, The
See PREJUDICE

Aztlán
A potent symbol of nationalist Mexican-American movements, *Aztlán* refers to an ancestral homeland, utopian promised land, and a political emblem. *Aztlán* first appeared in sixteenth-century records of Spanish missionaries. Aztec informants told of their ancestors' migration from a northern homeland to Tenochtitlan (now Mexico City). Missionary documents locate *Aztlán* in present day northeastern Mexico and southwestern Texas or immediately north of Mexico City. In the contemporary period, it is thought to be the land that Mexico ceded with the Treaty of Guadalupe Hidalgo in 1848.

In 1969, "El Plan Espiritual de *Aztlán*" was collectively authored at the Chicano National Liberation Youth Conference and endorsed by Rodolfo "Corky" Gonzales, and this served to revive interest in the territory. The document outlined a plan for the cultural self-determination and unity of Chicanos. Prior to the 1960s, the word Chicano was widely regarded prejoratively. But, as the term "black" – once used to disparage African Americans – was recoded, Chicano was elevated to a new status, intended to accentuate the restoration of Mexican-American uniqueness amid U.S. imperialism. The unifying force of the movement became known as Chicanismo.

As the nationalist agenda of Chicanismo gained impetus, the pragmatic efforts of César Chávez and the United Farm Workers'

Federation to unionize Mexican and Mexican-American agricultural labor seemed too limited in scope and *Aztlán* became something of a rallying cry for reappropriating the cultural unity and solidarity that had been dissipated in the U.S.A. Followers laid claim to full rights of citizenship by ancestral birthright in the southwest.

Klor de Alva has called *Aztlán* "the single most distinguishing metaphor of Chicano activism." Its potency in mobilizing Mexican-Americans points up the power of Promised Lands for diasporic peoples. As Africa and Zion have been transformed from actual or mythical homelands into signifiers of resistance and, in some cases political defiance, so *Aztlán* captured the hearts and minds of Mexican-Americans in uniting in a common cause. In fact, the very unity it fostered led to its downfall: as minority groups organized on the basis of gender, class and sexual orientation, the *Aztlán* movement was considered too artificial in its homogeneous ethic and the concept of one people lost credibility.

Reading

Aztlán: Essays on the Chicano Homeland edited by R. Anaya and F. Lomelí (University of New Mexico, 1991). The first collection of essays and political documents by scholars and artists on *Aztlán* from the 1960s through 1989.

"The Aztec Palimpsest: Toward a new understanding of *Aztlán* Cultural Identity and History" (in *Aztlán* vol. 19, no. 2, 1992) by Daniel Cooper Alarcón is an excellent survey of the Mesoamerican history and contemporary political uses of the term as well as the current critiques concerning the changing nature of Chicano identity.

Youth, Identity, Power: The Chicano Movement by Carlos Muñoz, Jr. (Verso, 1989) is the authoritative history of the Chicano movement by one of the key participants.

See also: CHÁVEZ; DIASPORA; LATINOS

Stephanie Athey

B

Black bourgeoisie in Britain

Britain's black bourgeoisie emerged in the late 1980s/early 1990s and comprised South Asian and African-Caribbean entrepreneurs who had turned to self-help as a guiding principle of "development," used here in the same sense as Shelby Steele: "the sum product of *individual* effort" (*The Content of Our Character*, St. Martin's Press, 1990).

The period marked a break with more traditional remedial social policies implemented by government and government agencies. Discouraged by over three decades of relative impoverishment, many ethnic minorities reassessed their position and opted for self-employment, leading to business ownership. South Asians' tradition of entrepreneurship has been a well-documented global phenomenon for many years, but the nature and scope of their enterprise changed and widened in the late 1980s. Margaret Thatcher's "enterprise culture" was intended to create a fertile environment for the growth of small businesses. During Thatcher's tenure as Britain's Prime Minister (1979–90) there was a series of policy reforms aimed at minimizing the role of the state and maximizing the responsibility of individuals. Ironically, few of the companies that started up in this period and went on to grow to at least medium-sized concerns were assisted by the various loans and incentive schemes offered in this period. By 1993, an estimated 7 percent of combined South Asian and African-Caribbean population (accounting for 4.5 percent of Britain's total) were involved in some kind of entrepreneurial activity. The service sector was most favored, but a small minority of both South Asians and African-Caribbeans were engaged in manufacturing.

Apart from the obvious difficulties facing ethnic minorities in a predominantly white society, Britain's black bourgeoisie faced three additional problems. The first was demonstrable: generating capital through bank loans. Banks have shown a reluctance to venture loans to ethnic groups. The second concerned expansion. Many companies traded in a niche market, specializing in products and services for particular ethnic minorities. Expanding into other sectors proved troublesome, especially in the recession of the early 1990s.

The third problem was less visible and operated in such a way as to prevent black-owned companies being genuinely equal opportunity employers. "Racism by proxy" was the term given to the practice whereby black owners were compelled to employ white people at senior and middle management levels. Agencies and organizations with which the black bourgeoisie maintained business relationships were found to communicate to the owners their preference for dealing directly with white personnel. The dilemma facing the owners was whether to rebuff the request and jeopardize what might be a lucrative business relationship, or cooperate and covertly practice racism by proxy. Many opted for the second alternative and, effectively, kicked away the ladder they had themselves climbed.

Reading

The Asian Petty Bourgeoisie in Britain by Shaila Srinivasan (Avebury, 1995) is based on a study in Oxford, England and addresses key questions: why so many Asians enter business? With what consequences? What are their class positions? Is business a vehicle for social mobility?

Middle-Class Blacks in Britain by Sharon Daye (Macmillan, 1994) carries its central question in its subtitle: "A racial fraction of a class group or a class fraction of a racial group?"

"The new black bourgeoisie" by Ellis Cashmore in *Human Relations* (vol. 45, no. 10, 1992) plots the growth of the ethnic business class and contains details of the various manifestations of racism by proxy.

See also: BLACK BOURGEOISIE IN THE U.S.A.; MIDDLEMAN MINORITY

Ellis Cashmore

Black bourgeoisie in the U.S.A.

This term generally refers to black individuals or families who are middle class in social and economic status. The term was popularized in the United States by sociologist E. Franklin Frazier in his class work, *Black Bourgeoisie*, published in 1957. (First published in 1955 under the French title, *Bourgeoisie Noire*.) A major theme of this work is that the behavior and actions of the black middle class as well as those who aspire to be considered in this social status in the United States are not responsive to the needs of poor or working-class sectors in the black community. Furthermore, the black middle-class sector described by this author concentrates on maintaining image of status, even if illusionary, rather than devoting time, energy, and collective resources toward the building of an independent black social and economic base in the United States.

In the 1960s, at the height of the Black Power movement, many in the black community used black bourgeoisie pejoratively. The term was used to describe those blacks with overly integrationist and accommodationist tendencies, as illustrated in manner of living style, attitudes toward the black poor and working class, and economic status. The term was also used to describe those black professionals not connected to the political and economic struggles of the black community.

Despite an increase in the number of scholarly and popular works focusing on the U.S. black middle class in the last twenty years, as pointed out by Bart Landry in *The New Black Middle-Class*, there is no consensus in the literature on the definition of this term. While he refers to a broad range of characteristics in order to define and pinpoint the U.S. black middle class, other observers have relied on income data. The U.S. Bureau of the Census has utilized an annual income of $50,000 or more per year as the basis for defining middle class status in the United States.

Sociologist William J. Wilson revived discussions regarding the nature and obligations of the black middle class in his work, *The Declining Significance of Race* (University of Chicago Press, 1978); Wilson argued that, in the 1960s, the black middle class started to become similar to the white middle class in terms of education and upward mobility. At the same time, however, a highly impoverished sector is growing in size in American cities and becoming increasingly separated in terms of social and even geographical distance from the black middle class. Wilson's contention that the black middle class is becoming more geographically distant from the black poor has been questioned by several social scientists studying this topic.

In *Introduction to Afro-American Studies* (Twenty-First Century Books, 1986), Abdul Alkalimat has pointed out that the black middle class has had a dual character in the history of black people in the United States. Due to the fundamental importance of race in American history, the black middle class has been a force for social change at the same time that it has been an instrument to maintain order among the poor and the working-class sectors in this community. The black middle class has struggled to weaken racial barriers in society in ways that would benefit the entire population, but as these same barriers are destroyed, it has not guaranteed that the interests of the poor and working class in the black community are being satisfied. Some observers, for example, have pointed to cities such as Atlanta or Los Angeles, where the black middle class have spearheaded successful political strategies that tend to tear down racial barriers; such victories have been important for the growth and development of black professionals in many arenas. But in many of these same cities, poverty and economic dislocation have increased significantly for many blacks.

Reading
The Black Bourgeoisie: The Rise of the New Middle Class by E. Franklin Frazier (The Free Press, 1957) is the original acerbic exposition.
The Black Middle Class by Bart Landry (University of California Press, 1987) takes a more empirical approach and distinguishes between Frazier's subject and the "new" version comprising professionals as well as entrepreneurs.
Behind the Mule: Race and Class in African-American Politics by Michael C. Dawson (Princeton University Press, 1994) is a general appraisal of the conditions of black Americans.
New Migrants in the Marketplace: Boston's Ethnic Entrepreneurs edited by Marilyn Halter (University of Massachusetts Press, 1995) examines the economic culture and small business activity of a range of migrant groups in the Boston area, including British Caribbeans, Dominicans, and Haitians.

See also: BLACK BOURGEOISIE IN BRITAIN; EMPOWERMENT; MIDDLEMAN MINORITY

James Jennings

Black feminism

This term is often used to designate an intellectual and political movement, referring specifically to the work of Black female scholars and activists who are rethinking Black experiences from a feminist perspective and revising white feminist politics from an Afrocentric perspective. This work draws on a long history of Black women's political consciousness and resistance, a history which demonstrates: (1) the simultaneous operation and interlocking nature of gender, race and other oppressions; and (2) the centrality of Black women's experience and knowledge to political struggle.

In defining the term, Patricia Hill Collins traces a tendency to equate "biology with ideology." Some texts adopt biologically deterministic criteria for the term Black and conflate woman with feminism, regardless of her ideology. Other scholarship narrows the scope of feminist inquiry to research and activism focused exclusively on women. Ironically, adherence to race and gender classifications may give further credence to the very categories Black feminism seeks to dismantle and redefine. Ann duCille, in "The occult of true Black womanhood" (*Signs*, vol. 19, no. 3, 1994), suggests any definition which grants "black women privileged access" to knowledge "rooted in common experience" actually "delimits and demeans" Black feminist discourse as it "restricts this work to a narrow orbit in which it can be readily validated only by those black and female for whom it reproduces what they already know."

However, definitions which promote a race or gender "blindness" to the background of Black feminist practitioners may further obscure the importance of Black women's experience and analysis. It is the insidious and pervasive suppression of Black women's knowledge and circumstance which necessitates Black feminist work in the first place.

When calls for a specifically Black feminist theory, criticism and activism emerged in the context of contemporary struggles, they stressed the suppression of Black women's experience in other liberationist discourses. As the title of the ground-breaking collection by Gloria Hull *et al.* expressed it, *All the Women are White, all the Blacks are Men, but Some of us are Brave* (Feminist Press, 1982).

Both Black liberation and white feminist organizations marginalized Black women's issues and analysis despite two facts: (1) Black women's labor was deemed indispensable to the Black liberation movement; and (2) Black women had organized and promoted many feminist causes together with and often prior to the white women's segregated organizations. Thus the historic Black Feminist Statement by the Combahee River Collective, of 1977, called for struggle against "manifold and simultaneous oppressions": "we are actively committed to struggling against racial, sexual, heterosexual, and class oppression, and see as our particular task the development of an integrated analysis and practice based upon the fact that major systems of oppression are interlocking."

Because of the history of racism within white feminist organizations and the eclipse of women of color within much white feminist theory, there is occasional hesitation about defining Black women's politics as "feminist" in any sense. In her *In Search of Our Mother's Gardens* (Harcourt Brace, 1983), Alice Walker advocated the term womanist – not feminist – to capture the unique perspective and strongly humanist vision she believed distinguished the activism of Black women.

For those who adopt the term, womanist thought deepens the hue and broadens the issues associated with white-oriented feminism. Womanist philosophy is alert to racial hierarchy and combines a strong affirmation of manhood with an equally strong ideological critique of gender oppression. Walker emphasizes the need for solidarity with Black men in the fight against racism as well as "patriarchy." In a similar vein Sherley Anne Williams in *Reading Black, Reading Feminist* (edited by H. L. Gates, Meridian, 1985), expands the province of Black feminism beyond the study of Black women's experience, she urges Black feminists to turn gender analysis to a study of Black men's self-representation as well.

Collins argues that Black feminist epistemology has been shaped by the traditional role of Black women as mothers, "othermothers" (adoptive-, foster-, community mothers), teachers and sisters. Black women were central to the retention and transformation of an Afrocentric worldview which survived within the all-Black rural and urban locations created by segregation. In the United States, for instance, Black women drew upon their grounding in traditional African American culture and thereby fostered the development of a distinctive Afrocentric women's culture. As Black women's labor was increasingly ghettoized in domestic work, this gender-inflected and racialized political economy ensured Black women a unique "outsider-within" perspective which demystified ideologies of white power through an "alien" insider's close observation of white households.

Through these contradictory locations Black women have produced a unique "standpoint" on self, community and society, yet at the same time that Black women's politicized thought protests these subordinate locations, the economic, political and ideological strategies of subordination work to suppress that thought. Because of this historic suppression, Collins and others maintain that Black women's experience – as interpreted and theorized by Black women – must form the core, but not the entirety, of Black feminist work.

Black feminist scholarship accordingly exhibits some persistent themes, including Black women's labor and role in the political economy, controlling images of Black women in racist ideology and empowerment through self-definition, Black women's health, the Black family, motherhood as community leadership, sexual politics in both the context of dominant society and the context of Black women's relationships.

Reading
Black Feminist Thought: Knowledge, Consciousness and the Politics of Empowerment by Patricia Hill Collins (HarperCollins, 1990) is a solid introduction to black feminism and may usefully be read in conjunction with *Theorizing Black Feminisms: The Visionary Pragmatism of Black Women* edited by Stanlie James and Abena P. A. Busia (Routledge, 1993).
"Multiple jeopardy, multiple consciousness: the context of a Black Feminist ideology" by Deborah King (*Signs*, vol. 14, no. 1, 1988) argues that Black

feminism is a multiple level engagement stressing Black women's self-determination and the "simultaneity of oppression" as a concept essential to this endeavor.

" 'Mama's baby, papa's maybe': An American grammar book" by Hortense Spillers (*Diacritics*, vol. 17, 1987) suggests that the "ungendering" of African captives through the course of the Middle Passage constituted entirely new social subjects, with which feminism has yet to reckon. The Black female stands outside of the bounds of "gender" and gender itself is a form of racial supremacy.

See also: AFROCENTRICITY; PATRIARCHY AND ETHNICITY; SUBALTERN

Stephanie Athey

Black Muslims
See NATION OF ISLAM

Black Power
The Black Power movement in the 1960s represented another period of cultural renaissance in black America, similar in some ways to the Harlem Renaissance of the 1920s. Many independent black cultural and educational institutions were founded during the Black Power movement which lasted from the mid-1960s to the early 1970s. The Black Power movement in the United States – also referred to in some writings as the Black Consciousness or Black Arts movement – was significant for the debates it generated regarding the appropriate political strategies that should be pursued by blacks.

The call for Black Power first caught the focused attention of the national media in the United States in the summer of 1966 when the chairman of the Student Nonviolent Coordinating Committee, Stokely Carmichael, used it several times in a speech at a civil rights rally in Mississippi; since then, it was enunciated and endorsed in speeches by other civil rights activists during this period.

This term has not been defined precisely; it has remained vague in its meaning and use. As a concept, Black Power has been utilized differently by activists and organizations representing a broad ideological spectrum. During the late 1960s and 1970s many books and articles were written on this topic.

One of the first attempts to define this concept was a book co-authored by Stokely Carmichael and Charles V. Hamilton, *Black Power: The Politics of Liberation in America* (Vintage, 1967). These authors implied that Black Power was quite an American concept in that it basically called for black people to act on the basis of organized group power. While for some in the civil rights movement the term was to be derided and avoided as racially divisive, eventually it become acceptable by many black organizations and activists; as a matter of fact, even President Richard M. Nixon implicitly endorsed this term in the early 1970s, when he called for black capitalism as an appropriate response to the needs of blacks in the United States.

The Black Power movement helped to propel the first black mayors of major cities into office. Several congressional representatives were elected to the U.S. Congress as a result of the Black Power movement. Additionally, this period gave rise to ideological debates within the black community that were muffled during the earlier Civil Rights Movement as a result of the focus on racial desegregation.

Reading
Black Power: The Politics of Liberation in America by Stokely Carmichael and Charles V. Hamilton (Vintage, 1967), introduced the concept and fused it with relevance.
The Black Revolt: A Collection of Essays edited by Floyd Barbour (Extending Horizons, 1968) brings together several different perspectives.
"Race, class and conflict: intellectual debates on race relations research in the United States since 1960" by Manning Marable (Sage *Race Relations Abstracts*, 1981) discusses and critiques some of the major writings on the subject.

James Jennings

Blues

Blues was the first genre or musical expression that was universally acknowledged as being an integer of black culture. William Barlow, in his *"Looking Up at Down": The Emergence of Blues Culture*, argues that: "The blues . . . were an amalgam of African and European musical practices – a mix of African cross-rhythms, blue notes, and focal techniques with European harmony and ballad forms. There are many alternative histories of the music's formation and development (see, for example, James Cone's *The Spirituals and the Blues*, Orbis, 1991; Stanley Booth's *Rhythm Oil*, Pantheon, 1992).

While interpretations differ, all agree that the music grew out of the collective work of the first generation of African Americans after emancipation. They had not directly experienced slavery, but their lives remained oppressively harsh and unpromising. The music they played embodied hopelessness and depression; the topics they sang about were sickness, imprisonment, alcohol, drugs, work, and the segregation forced by Jim Crow.

Blues was a secular music: it avoided the churches' spiritual music which gloried in God's salvation and ecstatically encouraged the journey to the promised land in terms that generally avoided the more unpleasant aspects of life on earth. "Negro spirituals," which in the 1930s were displaced by gospel as the dominant religious music, conveyed the kind of hope offered by the church, particularly the Baptist church. Blues offered no such thing – only realism. Lawrence Levine provides a nice distinction by quoting the singer Mahalia Jackson, who refused to give up gospel music even though blues music would have given her a better living: "Blues are the songs of despair, but gospel songs are the songs of hope. When you sing them you are delivered of your burden."

Musically, the blue notes were the neutral or flattened pitched occurring at the major and minor points of the third and seventh degrees of the scale. But, the connotations of depression and despair were much more resonant. As such, it had specific relevance to blacks: it documented a distinctly African American secular experience.

It was also highly individualized. Unlike, early African American musical forms, blues was usually performed solo and without antiphony (i.e. a choral response). This suggests to Levine "new forms of self-conception." These features distinguished blues as what Levine describes as "the most typically American music Afro-Americans had yet created." As such, it "represented a major degree of acculturation to the individualized ethos of the larger society." West African influences may be there for some to detect, but there can be no denying that blues was very much part of an American consciousness, an adjustment of individuals to the here-and-now.

Muddy Waters and Howlin' Wolf are often credited with being the great modernizers of blues. Waters migrated from the Mississippi Delta to Chicago and replaced the acoustic folk blues with a sharper electric sound. By contrast, John Lee Hooker, who has continued to tour as a septuagenarian in the 1990s, maintained a more traditional approach.

Reading
"Looking up at Down": The Emergence of Blues Culture by William Barlow (Temple University Press, 1989) begins its analysis from the premise that blues has deep roots in West African musical traditions.
Blues People by LeRoi Jones (Payback Press, 1995; originally published 1963) argues that both blues and jazz have a "valid separation from, and

anarchic disregard of Western popular forms." "Blues," he adds, is "the most important basic form in Afro-American music."

Black Culture and Black Consciousness by Lawrence W. Levine (Oxford University Press, 1978) traces the history of African American culture, giving particular emphasis to the role of music.

See also: CREOLE; PENTECOSTALISM; RAP; REGGAE

Ellis Cashmore

Boas, Franz (1858–1942)

A United States anthropologist who was born and educated (in physics and geography) in Germany. His research on racial variation illustrates the transition from the pre-Darwinian concern with morphology to the statistically based approach later established in population genetics. Boas's study of "Changes in the Bodily form of Descendants of Immigrants" (1912), carried out on behalf of the immigration authorities, attracted particular attention. In it the stature, weight and head-shape of 18,000 individuals were measured, comparing United States-born children with their European-born parents and with children born to such parents prior to immigration. He found that the round-headed ("brachycephalic") East European Jewish children became more long-headed ("dolichocephalic") in the United States, whereas the long-headed South Italians became more round-headed. Both were approaching a uniform type. Moreover the apparent influence of the American environment made itself felt with increasing intensity the longer the time elapsed between the immigration of the mother and the birth of her child. Boas was puzzled by his findings. They were measures of phenotypical variation and anthropologists at this time were ignorant of the causes of the variation which had to be sought in the genotype.

The physical changes Boas documented were not of great magnitude but they brought into question the assumption to which most anthropologists were then committed, that the cephalic index (the ratio of the breadth to the length of the skull when seen from above) was a stable measure of genetic history. Boas was an influential teacher, respected for his industry and devotion to objective analysis, who was willing publicly to challenge the racial doctrines propagated by the anti-immigration campaigners. Thomas F. Gossett, a historian of racial thought, was so impressed by Boas's record that he concluded "what chiefly happened in the 1920s to stem the tide of racism was that one man, Franz Boas, who was an authority in several fields which had been the strongest sources of racism, quietly asked for proof that race determines mentality and temperament."

Reading
Race, Language and Culture by Franz Boas (Macmillan, 1912) is the classic text.
The Anthropology of Franz Boas edited by Walter R. Goldschmidt (American Anthropological Association Memoir 89, 1959) is an appraisal of Boas's work.
Race: The History of an Idea in America by Thomas F. Gossett (Shocken Books, 1963) has sections on Boas's analyses and his overall contribution to the field of research.

See also: ASSIMILATION; CULTURE; GENOTYPE; PHENOTYPE

Michael Banton

Brazil

The arrival of the Portuguese in 1500 marks the historical beginning of Brazilian race relations. The most salient characteristic of that history is the gradual elimination of Brazil's indigenous populations, both physically and culturally, and their replacement by populations of African and European origin.

The Portuguese encountered "Indian" groups of thinly settled, small-scale, semi-nomadic, stateless, classless, tropical horticulturists. These native societies, numbering, in most cases, only a few hundred to a few thousand individuals each, were not only organizationally and technologically unable to resist the encroachments of the colonizers; their lack of immunity to diseases imported from Europe (especially measles, smallpox, and influenza) made them vulnerable to disastrous pandemics.

Attempts to enslave the Indians proved mostly abortive, as they either withdrew into the less accessible parts of the interior, died of disease, or escaped. This secular process of retreat into the Amazonian jungle continues to this day, as the Brazilian frontier gradually encroaches over the last pockets of Indian populations. The latter now number well under 1 percent of Brazil's 120 million people, although perhaps 5 to 10 percent of Brazilians have some Indian ancestry, especially in the interior states. (People of mixed Indian-European descent are often referred to as *caboclos*.)

This process of displacement of Amerindians in Brazil has sometimes been called genocidal. There has, of course, been sporadic frontier warfare between Indians and colonists, resulting sometimes in small-scale massacres, and there have been numerous allegations of deliberate spreading of epidemics through sale or distribution of contaminated blankets. It is untrue, or at least unproven, that the Brazilian government in this century has deliberately sought to exterminate Indians, although the effects of policies of frontier development and Indian resettlement have often been disastrous for the Indians, and continue to be so. As autonomous cultures, Amazonian Indians are fast disappearing, although surviving individuals become assimilated and interbreed with the encroaching settlers. The clash is more an ecological one between incompatible modes of subsistence than a "racial" one, and the process is better described as one of gradual "ethnocide" rather than as genocide.

The other main feature of Brazilian race relations is, of course, the relationship between people of European and African descent. Extensive interbreeding between them, particularly during the period of slavery, has created a continuum of phenotypes, described by an elaborate nomenclature of racial terms. Conspicuously absent from Brazilian society, however, are distinct, self-conscious racial groups. Nobody can say where "white" ends and "black" begins, and indeed, social descriptions of individuals vary regionally, situationally, and according to socioeconomic criteria, as well as phenotype. In Brazil as a whole, perhaps 40 percent of the population is of partly African descent and might be classified as "black" in, say, the United States. In northeastern Brazil, the heart of the sugar plantation economy, and hence of slavery, perhaps as many as 70 to 80 percent of the population is distinctly of African descent.

Much discussion has centered on how racially tolerant Brazil is. Brazilian slavery has been described as more humane than in the United States or the British Caribbean, and the Catholic church has been seen as mitigating the harshness of the owners. It is probably true that the Portuguese were less racist and more relaxed and easygoing in their relations with blacks, and thus created a less rigid, caste-bound society than did the British and North Americans in their slave colonies. Thus, emancipation was more frequent and easier, and freedmen were probably freer than their counterparts in the U.S. South, for example. On the other hand, the physical treatment of Brazilian slaves was undoubtedly inferior to that meted out to slaves in the United States. Mortality rates were extremely high, especially in the mines, which, next to the sugar plantations, were the main destination of Brazilian slaves.

A century after their emancipation, Afro-Brazilians continue to be overrepresented at the bottom of the class pyramid, but substantial numbers are found in the middle class, and conversely, many white Brazilians, especially first- and second-generation European immigrants, are also quite poor. Afro-Brazilians have never been subjected to the institutionalized racism, segregation, and discrimination characteristic of, say, South Africa, or the United States.

They do not constitute a self-conscious group, because Brazilians do not classify themselves into racial groups. This is not to say that they are not race conscious. Indeed, they are often very conscious of racial phenotypes, so much so that they commonly use a score or more of racial labels to describe all the combinations and permutations of skin color, hair texture, and facial features. Indeed, racial taxonomies are so refined that members of the same family may well be referred to by different racial terms.

Paradoxical as it sounds, it was probably this high degree of racial consciousness at the level of the individual phenotype which, combined with a high level of marital and extra-marital interbreeding, prevented the formation of self-conscious, rigidly bounded racial groups in Brazil. To be sure, blackness has pejorative connotations, but more in an aesthetic than in a social or intellectual sense. Courtesy calls for ignoring an individual's darkness, using mitigating euphemisms (such as *moreno*, "brown"), and "promoting" a person racially if his or her class status warrants it. "Money bleaches" goes a Brazilian aphorism. Thus, it is certainly not true that Brazil is free of racial prejudice, but it is relatively free of *categorical discrimination* based on racial group membership.

To be sure, class and race overlap to some extent, but there are no *institutional* racial barriers against upward mobility for blacks. Intermarriage between the extremes of the color spectrum are infrequent, but not between adjacent phenotypes. Race, or better, phenotype, is definitely a component of a person's status and attractiveness, but often not the most salient one. In many situations, class is more important. Indeed, race relations at the working-class level are relatively free and uninhibited, compared to the United States, for example, and residential and school segregation is based almost entirely on class rather than race.

In short, Brazil may be described as a society where class distinctions are marked and profound, where class and color overlap but do not coincide, where class often takes precedence over color, and where "race" is a matter of individual description and personal attractiveness rather than of group membership. Brazil is definitely a race conscious, but not a racial caste society. It is not a racial paradise, but neither is it a racially obsessed society like South Africa or the United States.

Reading
The Masters and the Slaves by Gilberto Freyre (Knopf, 1964) is the classic account of Brazilian slavery by a distinguished Brazilian scholar of psychoanalytic orientation.

Brazil by Ronald M. Schneider (Westview, 1995 examines the historical development of Brazil from 1500 to independence in 1822, the middle class revolution of 1930, the military takeover in 1964 and the return to democracy after 1984.

Race and Racism, by Pierre L. van den Berghe (Wiley, 1978), especially Chapter 3, is a summary of Brazilian relations.

"Residential segregation by skin color" by Edward Telles in *American Sociological Review* (vol. 57, no. 2, April, 1992) analyzes patterns of geographical division.

See also: CASTE; COLOR LINE; FREIRE, FREYRE; PHENOTYPE; WHITENESS

Pierre L. van den Berghe

British Movement

An organization started in 1968 with 150 members, that came to prominence in the late 1980s after a recruitment strategy aimed at disaffected youth. Its membership was bolstered by the reborn skin-head movement, which had terrorized British Asians in the 1960s. British Movement rallies were typically violent affairs.

The roots of the movement go back to 1957, when a fascist group called the White Defence League was started and became a contributory factor in ethnic violence. In 1960, it amalgamated with another group to become the British National Party, with Colin Jordan as its head. Jordan left to form the National Socialist Party, which he later relaunched as the British Movement. No more than a marginal organization with a commitment to antisemitism and other forms of racism, it only started to acquire significance with the skinhead renascence.

It recruited at soccer stadia, rock concerts, and openly on the streets, appealing to white British youth who were persuaded of the "threat" posed by ethnic minorities. By the early 1990s, the BM had receded from prominence and the skinheads had all but faded and its role as the main youth-oriented organization was taken up by the British National Party (BNP) which had been formed in 1960 by Colin Jordan and John Tyndall. The BNP committed itself to what it called "a homogeneous community."

Reading

"Racist violence and political extremism" is the theme of a special issue of *New Community* (vol. 21, no. 4, 1995). It includes essays on this theme in relation to Britain and mainland Europe.

"New-age nazism" by Matthew Kalman and John Murray (*New Statesman & Society*, June 23, 1995) looks at the way neo-nazi groups have aligned themselves with green and new age movements.

The Extreme Right in Europe and the U.S.A. edited by Paul Hainsworth (Pinter, 1992) is a country-by-country analysis of neo-nazi groups.

See also: FASCISM; NATIONAL FRONT; NATIONALISM; POLITICS AND RACE; SKINHEADS

Barry Troyna

Busing

In 1954, in the *Brown v. Board of Education, Topeka, Kansas* case, the US Supreme Court ruled that segregated education was unconstitutional and in violation of the 14th Amendment. By this ruling, schools had to be desegregated and special buses were to transport black and Latino students to schools in the suburbs. There, they would receive the same educational provision as white students. It was contended that the process of desegregation, or busing, would ensure that students would be treated first and foremost as individuals and not as members of a caste. Desegregation was based on a number of seductive, if not empirically tested assumptions. First, it was anticipated that busing would equalize educational opportunities. Subsequent research, however, showed that this was little more than wishful thinking. The effect of desegregation on educational performance was erratic. Under optimal conditions, it was likely to be effective. But as James Coleman pointed out, most school changes under optimal conditions have this effect.

Second, it was assumed that busing would help counteract the historically divisive nature of perceived racial difference and facilitate the emergence of a more tolerant society. This proposition was based on what is known as the contact hypothesis. This holds that enhancing interracial contact (in schools, residential areas, the workplace) is bound to improve relations between members of different groups. Once again, however, this is a romanticized view – a fiction that only under highly contrived conditions translated into an empirically verifiable scenario. Despite these profound reservations, busing in the United States was conceived as a liberal practice and its opponents, and their arguments, were generally characterized as racist.

Nine years after the *Brown* decision, a similar attempt was made in Britain to ensure a greater ethnic mix in schools. This, however, provoked the opposite reaction. Busing was seen as racist, a denial of equality of opportunity to colonial migrants and their children. Black and white liberals up and down the country vehemently opposed both its principle and practice. How do we account for these contrasting reactions?

In the United States, legally sanctioned school segregation embodied "a persisting badge of slavery", as David Kirp has put it

(1982). Schools in black neighborhoods were generally old and run-down and tended to be the last repaired, worst funded and under-staffed. Because education is conventionally viewed from the liberal democratic perspective as the gateway to social and occupational advancement, the provision of inferior education to black students was seen as a legally sanctioned instrument which endorsed and perpetuated black subordination in the United States. Not surprisingly then, the initiative for desegregation derived from the black American communities.

In Britain, on the other hand, there was no clear educational justification for the introduction of busing. The initiative had come from a group of white parents in the Southall district of London who had complained to the Minister of Education, Edward Boyle, that the educational progress of their children was being inhibited in those schools containing large numbers of nonwhite, mainly South Asian pupils. Boyle subsequently recommended to government that the proportion of immigrant children should not exceed 30 percent in any one school. In 1965, "Boyle's Law," as it came to be called, received official backing from the Department of Education and Science. As a result, a few local education authorities followed the steps already taken in Southall and West Bromwich and formally implemented busing procedures.

The main imperative for this action was clear: to assuage the anxieties of white parents. The fact that skin color was used as the sole criterion for deciding which students were to be bused vividly demonstrated this point. But, as opponents of busing pointed out, these fears were largely unfounded in any case. Research carried out in primary schools in London had shown that the ethnic mix of a school had a minimal influence on the level of reading ability attained by pupils. Opponents also insisted that busing was premised on the racist assumption that schools with a large proportion of nonwhite students are inherently inferior to those in which white students are the majority.

By the late 1970s, most of the local education authorities that had introduced busing had been persuaded by the efficacy of these arguments (if not by the threat of intervention by the Commission for Racial Equality) and abandoned the procedure. In the United States, the slow process of desegregation continues despite the contention that it has encouraged "white flight" and has only slightly, if at all, led to educational or inter-personal benefits. Nevertheless, the different reactions to busing of the black and other nonwhite communities in the United States and Britain highlight its symbolic importance. On one side of the Atlantic, it is seen as a catalyst for equality of opportunity; on the other, it is an instrument designed to undermine that ideal.

Reading

Just Schools by David Kirp (University of California Press, 1982) begins with a brief but critical discussion of the relationship between the Brown decree and equality of opportunity, then considers the experiences of five Bay Area communities in the twenty-five years since the introduction of desegregation.

Equality and Achievement in Education (Westview, 1990) by James Coleman who, in the 1960s advocated busing as a means of social engineering to enhance equality of opportunity. In this book he revisits some of his earlier assumptions and lays bare their weaknesses.

Contact and Conflict in Intergroup Encounters (Blackwell, 1986) comprises a series of critical essays on the contact hypothesis. The introduction by editors Hewstone and Brown and the essay by Steven Reicher are especially incisive.

See also: LAW: CIVIL RIGHTS (U.S.A.); DISPERSAL; EDUCATION AND CULTURAL DIVERSITY

Barry Troyna

C

Capitalism

This refers to a particular type of socioeconomic structure bounded by a particular historical period. However, there are substantial disagreements between Marxists and non-Marxists, and between various strands of Marxism over the defining features of the socio-economic structure and historical period.

Non-Marxists tend to define capitalism in one of the following ways. First, it is conceived as any society characterized by the presence of exchange or market relations. Thus, the defining characteristic is individuals bartering or exchanging products for money. Second, as any society in which production occurs for the purpose of profit. Thus, the defining characteristic is the intention on the part of a group of people to organize the production and distribution of goods in order to realize more money at the end of the process than the sum they started with. Third, as any society in which production is carried out by means of industry. In this instance, it is the specific use of power-driven machinery that is identified as the defining characteristic of capitalism.

The first two definitions imply that capitalism has existed over very large areas of the world since the earliest times of human activity. Proponents of these positions often also argue that this demonstrates that capitalism is a natural and inevitable form of socioeconomic organization. This conclusion is less likely to be accepted by some advocates of the market as the defining characteristic if they then wish to draw a distinction between market and nonmarket forms of socioeconomic organization (the latter being defined as some form of state socialist society). The third is more historically specific, locating the development of capitalism in the later eighteenth century in Europe from where it has spread to characterize large areas of the world in the twentieth century.

Of these various positions, the most influential within sociology in the past two decades has been the identification of capitalism with the existence of market relations, as in the work of Max Weber. It is upon this tradition of theorizing that much of the sociology of "race relations" has drawn in its attempts to analyze "race relations" in some form of historical and structural context.

Similarly, within Marxism, there is a long-established debate over the origin and nature of capitalism. There are two main positions, although both are premised on the acceptance of Marx's method and labor theory of value. Thus, both accept that all previously existing societies are characterized by class exploitation which takes the form of one class living off the surplus product produced by another class. Despite other similarities with non-Marxist analyses, the acceptance of this claim makes the following two positions quite distinct.

The first position identifies capitalism with a system of production for the market which is motivated by profit. Thus, for advocates of this position, the appearance of markets and the development of trade, particularly international trade, marks the origin of capitalism in Europe in the fourteenth and fifteenth centuries. This position has been developed to the point that capitalism is seen to be synonymous with the development of a world market of exchange relations, in which Europe stands at the center of a series of dominant/subordinate relations with South America, the Caribbean, India, Africa and Southeast Asia. These analysts typically employ the following dualisms: center/periphery, metropolis/satellite, development/under-development. It is argued that the development of the center metropolis is both product and cause of the underdevelopment of the periphery/satellite. In its most extreme form, it is claimed that capitalism refers to this system of international relations rather than to any national unit or units which participate in those relations.

The second position identifies capitalism as a mode of production sharing the following characteristics: (1) generalized commodity production, whereby most production occurs for the purpose of exchange rather than for direct use; (2) labor power has itself become a commodity which is bought and sold for a wage. On the basis of these characteristics, the origin of capitalism is located in England in the seventeenth century, from where it has spread out beyond Europe as nation-states have formed themselves around generalized commodity production utilizing wage labor. Advocates of this position place primary emphasis upon the character of the production process, to which the process of exchange is viewed as secondary. It accepts that the origin of capitalism lies partly in the accumulation of capital by means of colonial exploitation, but adds that this only led to capitalist production once a class of free wage laborers had been formed.

Both Marxist positions maintain that capitalism developed out of feudalism and that the development marked the beginning of a world division of labor and a world process of uneven development. They therefore suggest a determinant relationship between capitalism and colonialism and this forms the backdrop to various Marxist accounts of historical and contemporary "race relations."

Reading
General Economic History by Max Weber (Transaction, 1981) is a general
account of Weber's analysis of the nature and origins of capitalism.
Capital, vol. 1 by Karl Marx (Penguin 1976), especially Parts 2, 3, 5, 7 and
8, is Marx's analysis of the nature and origins of capitalism.
The Transition from Feudalism to Capitalism edited by Rodney Hilton
(Verso, 1978) has an outline of the essentially contested issues in the
debate over the origin and nature of capitalism among Marxists.

See also: COLONIALISM; EXPLOITATION; MARXISM AND RACISM

Robert Miles

Caste

The concept of "caste" has been applied to a wide variety of social institutions, both human and nonhuman. Entomologists have used it to describe the functionally and anatomically discrete morphs (workers, soldiers, etc.) of many species of eusocial insects, especially ants, bees, and termites. Social scientists have spoken of castes in societies as different as those of Spanish American colonies until the nineteenth century, the Indian subcontinent, twentieth-century South Africa and the United States, and precolonial West Africa.

In the social sciences, there have been two main traditions in the use of the term caste. There have been those, mainly Indianists, who have reserved the term to describe the stratification systems of the societies influenced by Hinduism on the Indian subcontinent. The other tradition has extended the term to many other societies that lacked some of the features of the Hindu caste system, but nevertheless had groups possessing the following three characteristics:

- endogamy, ie. compulsory marriage within the groups;
- ascriptive membership by birth and for life, and, hence, hereditary status;
- ranking in a hierarchy in relation to other such groups.

These three characteristics have been called the minimal definition of caste, and such a definition has been extensively applied by Lloyd Warner, Gunnar Myrdal, and many others to white–black relations in the United States and in other societies, like South Africa, with a rigid racial hierarchy.

There is a double irony in the position of those who want to reserve the term for India and related societies. First, caste is not a term indigenous to India at all; it is a Spanish and Portuguese word (*casta*), first applied to racial groupings, mostly in the Spanish American colonies. The *casta* system of the Spanish colonies, however, was not a caste system in either the Indian or the extended sense. There was little group endogamy, and extensive racial mixtures gave rise to a proliferation of "half-caste" categories like *mestizos*, *mulatos*, and *zambos*. As a result, *casta* membership became rather flexible, negotiable and subject to situational redefinitions based on wealth and prestige.

Second, the term "caste," far from helping to understand the Indian situation, actually confuses it. It has been applied, often indiscriminately, to refer to two very different groupings: *varna* and *jati*. The four *varnas* (brahmins, kshatriyas, vaishyas, and sudras) are broad groupings subdivided into a multiplicity of *jati*. The effective social group in most situations is the *jati* rather than the *varna*. Yet most Hindu scriptural references are to *varnas*. Little seems gained by using a single exotic term such as "caste" to refer to two such different types of groups.

Beyond use of the term caste in Indian society and in racially stratified countries such as South Africa and the United States, the word has also been applied to certain specialized occupational groups, especially low-status endogamous pariah or outcaste groups in a range of other societies. For example the Eta or Burakumin of Japan, and the blacksmiths and praise-singers of many African societies have been called castes.

There is little question that the Hindu caste system has a number of unique characteristics, but that is no reason to restrict to India the use of the concept to designate rigid ascriptive, stratified and endogamous groups. A useful distinction should be made, however, between genuine caste societies where the whole population is divided into such groups, and societies with some caste groups, where only a minority of the people belong to pariah groups. Perhaps only India and South Africa until 1994, each in its own special way, could be described as caste societies, while many more societies, both past and present, have endogamous groups of pariahs and outcastes.

Reading
Homo Hierarchicus by Louis Dumont (Weidenfeld & Nicholson, 1970) is probably the best recent account of the Hindu caste system.
Caste and Race edited by Anthony de Reuck (Little Brown, 1967) is a collection of essays by leading authorities, covering many societies.
The Ethnic Phenomenon by Pierre L. van den Berghe (Elsevier, 1981), especially Chapter 8, gives a more extensive discussion of the issues above.

See also: COX; MYRDAL; RACE

Pierre L. van den Berghe

Caucasian

A name introduced by J. F. Blumenbach in 1795 to designate one of the "five principal varieties of mankind." Europeans were classified as Caucasians. The name was chosen because Blumenbach believed the neighborhood of Mount Caucasus, and especially its southern slope, produced the most beautiful race of men, and was probably the home of the first men. He thought they were probably white in complexion since it was easier for white to degenerate into brown than for a dark color to become white. The other four "principal varieties" were the Mongolian, Ethiopian, American, and Malay races.

Caucasian has continued to be used as a designation for white people into the twentieth century, although there is no longer any scientific justification for the practice. The distinctive characteristics of white populations need nowadays to be expressed statistically in terms of the frequency of particular genes, blood groupings, etc. Apparent similarities in appearance may be the basis for social classifications but are of little use for biological purposes.

Reading
Racial Theories by Michael Banton (Cambridge University Press, 1987) traces the development of ideas that have influenced thinking about race and racism.
The Anthropological Treatises of Johann Friedrich Blumenbach edited by Thomas Bendyshe (Longman, Green, 1865) is the original source.

See also: ARYAN; PHENOTYPE; RACE; WHITENESS

Michael Banton

Causes célèbres

Legal cases or lawsuits that attract widespread attention. In race and ethnic relations, *causes célèbres* typically refer to cases that have been transformed theatrically by the mass media so that they display some of the cleavages and conflicts affecting culture. The term was used in 1893/4 to describe the Dreyfus Case in France which was a crucible of antisemitism. Recent history has produced a number of *causes célèbres* in which racial issues have been brought to the fore. They may be grouped as: (a) a legal action prompted by an alleged crime or incident seemingly driven by a racist motive; (b) a case that has consequent actions that disparately affect different ethnic groups; or (c) a publicized case or trial that embodies racist themes, moods or feelings. The exemplars are:

(a) The Central Park jogger

In April 1989, a young white female who worked on Wall Street, was raped and beaten by at least nine young working-class African American and Latino men, aged 15–17, while jogging in New York's Central Park. She was beaten and left alone. The young men, from Harlem were found guilty of raping and assaulting the woman and each was given a sentence of 5 to 10 years, the maximum term for juveniles in New York State.

Within hours of the attack, the police had six suspects, accused of what was later described as "wilding." The internationally reported case provoked an almost hysterical reaction, which, critics argued, contributed to an unfair trial. While all but one of the accused made videotaped confessions of their involvement in the attack, DNA testing did not link any of the five to the rape. Physical evidence connected two to the beating.

Amsterdam News, the community newspaper, insisted that a "legal lynching" had taken place. It argued that the police were under severe pressure to "find a target" for the nation's anger and that the men were virtually coerced into making confessions. It also pointed out that the woman's name was withheld, though in comparable cases involving black victims, names had been released. The case both disclosed the intersecting fault lines of sex and race and prompted the specter of an attack motivated by racism.

(b) The Rodney King case

In March 1991, Rodney King, an African American male, was stopped for speeding by Los Angeles police officers. The four white officers administered a brutal beating, which was videotaped by a member of the public and later broadcast worldwide. In 1992, the four police officers were acquitted, a verdict that sparked off three days of violent unrest in LA and elsewhere in the United States. While ostensibly the uprising was in protest at the acquittal, there were other contributory factors. Cornel West wrote that the "riot" was "the consequence of a lethal linkage of economic decline,

cultural decay, and political lethargy. . . . Race was the visible catalyst, not the underlying cause" (in "Learning to talk of race" – see
below).

The King verdict was extraordinary in the sense that it seemed
to contradict the available evidence – a tape showing him receive
fifty-six baton blows, punches and kicks. But, its power to provoke
a fullscale riot may have lain in the fact that it dramatized what is
a quotidian feature of blacks' relationships with the police in Los
Angeles.

The aftermath of the verdict forced the "race" issue to the fore,
after a period of relative "tranquillity" in which "universal programs" of reform were advocated over group-targeted policies. The
view was inspired by the groundswell of scholarly opinion predicated
on the idea that racial inequality had nonracial origins; that the
impersonal forces of the market economy explained more about the
impoverishment of innercity blacks than notions of racial discrimination. The King decision seemed vividly to remind the nation –
indeed, the world – that assumptions that racial discrimination had
faded were ill-founded.

(c) Barry, Tyson, and Simpson

Three cases in which high-profile African American males have
stood accused of offenses have acquired resonance far beyond the
circumstances of the cases. In 1990, Marion Barry, the Democrat
Mayor of Washington, D.C. where about 80 percent of the population is black, was convicted and imprisoned for possession of
cocaine. For over two decades, Barry had been part of a civil rights
offensive on the notoriously conservative capital city. During his
third consecutive term, a female friend lured him into a police
drugs sting. At their assignation in an hotel room, hidden cameras
captured them smoking crack cocaine. At the end of a six-week
trial that seemed to have disgraced and possibly destroyed him
politically, Barry went to jail for 180 days. The videotape was shown
on a courtroom monitor.

Barry did not take the stand himself, but accounts of his drug
binges and sexual propensities, backed by evidence from a collection
of pimps and pushers, were relayed to homes across the United
States via television. To many whites, Barry was a venal demagogue
who betrayed the trust of the most needy of his own people and
whose character deficiencies should have disqualified him from ever
holding public office again. But to many African Americans
(especially among D.C.'s electorate), Barry was a heroic and

defiant, if flawed, figure who was punished for confronting a white power structure. Three years after his release, he was reelected Mayor.

The suspicions harbored by many blacks about the criminal justice system were in evidence once more in 1991 when Mike Tyson was indicted by a Marion County, Indiana, grand jury of raping Desiree Washington, a contestant at a Miss Black America pageant; she claimed Tyson had forcibly had sex with her in an Indianapolis hotel room. Washington later alleged that Tyson had given her a venereal disease. Tyson was released from prison in March 1995, and resumed his professional boxing career five months later under the guidance of Don King.

Unlike the reaction to Barry, there was a less forgiving response to Tyson and a celebratory function following his release was stymied by protests from women's groups. But for many, Tyson remained an icon of black masculinity; and with that came the inescapable burden of being a visible target. He was a contemporary example of the "uppity nigger" who needed to be put in his place. Doubts lingered for long after Tyson had been imprisoned: had he been a white sports star – like Troy Aikman or Larry Bird – accused of raping a black woman, would the verdict have been the same?

There were similarities with the O. J. Simpson case: a conspicuously successful black sports performer-turned-movie star accused of a heinous crime. In June 1994, he was charged with the murder of his estranged wife, Nicole Simpson and her friend Ronald Goldman. Simpson's defense, led at great cost ($4–5 million) by celebrity lawyer Johnnie Cochrane, revolved around the charge that the Los Angeles Police Department (LAPD) had planted evidence. In the wake of the King case, it was not unreasonable to suppose that racism was a motive in some LAPD actions and Cochrane skilfully played the "race card."

Further dimensions were lent to the case by research shortly before the verdict that indicated that a majority of African Americans believed the accused to be innocent, while a majority of whites thought him to be guilty. Simpson was acquitted of the charges in 1995.

All three cases elicited cynicism, mistrust, and a feeling that perhaps historical patterns were repeating themselves: black men were being punished for being successful.

Reading

Unequal Verdicts: the Central Park Jogger Trials by Timothy Sullivan (Simon & Schuster, 1992) lacks analytical bite, but provides a good description of the case.

Reading Rodney King, Reading Urban Uprisings edited by Robert Gooding-Williams (Routledge, 1993) is devoted to an analysis of the case and its effects; it contains the West chapter cited above.

"The influence of racial similarity on the Simpson, O. J. trial." by K. D. Mixon, L. A. Foley, and K. Orme (*Journal of Social Behavior and Personality*, vol. 10, no. 3, September 1995) is based on research indicating that ethnic background strongly influenced perceptions of guilt or innocence. This may be read in conjunction with *Reasonable Doubt: the Simpson Case & the Criminal Justice System* by Alan M. Dershowitz (Simon & Schuster, 1996).

"Racially based jury nullification: Black power in the criminal justice system" by Paul R. Butler (*Yale Law Journal*, vol. 105, no 3, 1995) proposes "jury nullification" whereby African American jurors can consider race when acquitting black defendants; the authors argues that, as most black crime has its origins in poverty and oppression, jurors are morally justified in releasing nonviolent black criminals under some conditions.

See also: MEDIA AND RACISM; POLICE AND RACISM; RIOTS

Ellis Cashmore

Chamberlain, Houston Stewart (1855–1927)

"The Nazi Prophet," as he came to be called, was the son of a British naval admiral, who studied zoology under Carl Vogt in Geneva. He later moved to Dresden where he developed a theory that would influence world history. Published in 1899, Chamberlain's work was a gigantic exploration of what he called *The Foundations of the Nineteenth Century*. He traced them back to the ancient Israelites, locating the critical year as 1200, the beginning of the Middle Ages, when the *Germanen* emerged "as the founders of an entirely new civilization and an entirely new culture."

A large section of the work was intended to downplay the parts played by Jews, Romans and Greeks in the development of European culture. Yet Chamberlain was careful to note the increasing influence of Jews in the spheres of government, literature and art.

Inspired by the older theories of Gobineau and the newer work of Darwin, Chamberlain speculated that the indiscriminate hybridization, or mixing of races, was undesirable, though he remained convinced that the strongest and fittest race could, at any moment, be able to assume its dominance and impose its superiority and thus curb the degeneration process caused by racial mixing.

For Chamberlain, that race derived from the original peoples of

Germany, created "physiologically by characteristic mixture of blood, followed by interbreeding; psychically by the influence that long-continued historical-geographical circumstances produce on that particular, specific physiological disposition." Interestingly, however, he was rather imprecise on the exact definition of race. The term *Germanen* referred to a mixture of northern and western European populations which were said to form a "family," the essence of which is the *Germane*.

Chamberlain's importance was not so much in his adding new knowledge to the concept of race itself, as in his general argument about the inherent superiority of one group over all others. There was a clear complementarity between Chamberlain's version of history and, indeed, the future and what was to become National Socialist philosophy.

Although he played no active part in the rise of Nazism (he died in 1927 before the Nazis came to power in Germany) his work was used selectively to support theoretically many of the atrocities that accompanied the Nazi development.

Reading
The Foundations of the Nineteenth Century, 2 vols, by Houston Stewart Chamberlain (Fertig, 1968) is the infamous work translated by John Lee from the 1910 edition, but with a new introduction by George Mosse.
Race by John R. Baker (Oxford University Press, 1974) explores many aspects of the concept of race, and gives close attention to Chamberlain's treatment.
Race: A Study in Superstition by Jacques Barzun (Harcourt, Brace & Co., 1937) is a relatively early, but significant, overview of the concept of race and its often bewildering uses.

See also: FASCISM; GOBINEAU; RACE; RACISM; VOLK

Ellis Cashmore

Chávez, César (1927–93)

As King had adopted Gandhi's nonviolent civil disobedience as a means of furthering the struggle of blacks, so César Chávez did with Mexican-Americans. Chávez became synonymous with the Chicano movement: his principal achievement was the creation of the United Farm Workers' Union (UFW) which attracted a considerable proportion of California's agricultural labor force and led to improvements in wages and working conditions for Chicanos.

UFW tactics were modelled on King's boycotts, strikes, mass demonstrations and pushing for new legislation. When violence did threaten to upset his tactics, Chávez, like Gandhi, went on an extended fast in protest.

Before going further, a profile of Mexican-Americans might be useful. About 85 percent are born in the United States (approximately half of these being born to American parents). The vast majority are under thirty. Most speak Spanish as well as English and belong to the Roman Catholic church. Since the 1950s, there has been a fairly rapid movement from rural areas into the cities, though this geographical mobility has not been accompanied by any upward social mobility.

Educationally, there have been improvements from one generation to the next, but the average Mexican-American child has less education than his or her white American counterpart and tends to achieve less. Thus, the children demonstrate little evidence for predicting an improvement in status and material conditions and remain a predominantly poor people with limited education.

During the 1950s, Mexican-American war veterans founded the GI Forum, which became quite an important force in fighting discrimination against them, but out of the social upheavals of the 1960s grew the Chicano movement which was committed to changing the impoverished circumstances of Mexican-Americans. The idea was to promote economic changes through uniting people. And the unity was achieved through the restoration of Mexican culture by making people of Mexican origins recognize the commonness of their background and current conditions; it was hoped to mobilize them for political action, and thus produce constructive change.

Chávez had many obstacles to overcome, including the apathy of many Mexican-Americans, the resistance of agricultural businesses and their influential supporters and also the opposition of the formidable Teamsters' Union which, until 1976, challenged the UFW's right to represent Californian farm workers. Though his main success came in California, Chávez spread his efforts to unionizing agricultural workers elsewhere and became the single most important figure in the Chicano movement.

Beside Chávez, other Chicano leaders emerged in the period, some, like Jerry Apodaca and Raul Castro, opting for party politics. José Anger Gutiérrez in 1970 founded the Partido de la Raza Unida organization in south Texas and successfully fought school board, city council, and county elections.

In addition to the visible successes of Chávez in employment, Chicano groups have striven with some success for important educational objectives such as the reduction of school dropout rates, the improvement of educational attainment, the integration of Spanish language and Mexican culture classes into curricula, the training of more Chicano teachers and administrators, and the prevention of the busing of Chicano schoolchildren.

After the impetus of the 1960s, Chicanos became more fiercely ethnic, establishing their own colleges and universities, churches, youth movements. More recently, the movement has spawned Chicano feminist organizations. A further development came in 1967 with the Brown Berets, a militant group fashioned after the Black Panthers. As the Panthers reacted to the nonviolent working-the-system approach of King *et al*, so the Berets reacted to the Chicano resistance as led by Chávez. This wing of the Chicano movement was perhaps inspired by the incident in New Mexico in 1967, when, led by Reies Lopez Tijerina, Chicanos occupied Forest Service land and took hostage several Forest Service Rangers. Tijerina and others were arrested, but escaped after an armed raid on a New Mexico courthouse. Several hundred state troopers and national guardsmen were needed to round them up.

Although the Chicano movement does not reflect the general experience of Mexican-Americans, it demonstrates the effectiveness of militant ethnicity in the attempt to secure advancement. Chávez, in particular, created a broad base of support from a consciousness of belonging to a distinct ethnic group that was consistently disadvantaged, and thus pointed up the importance of ethnicity as a factor in forcing social change.

Reading
César Chávez: A Triumph of Spirit by Richard Griswold del Castillo and Richard A. Garcia (University of Oklahoma Press, 1995) is a biography of the farm worker-cum-labor organizer who was launched by events into a maelstrom of *campesino* strikes.
The Mexican-American People by Leo Grebler, Joan W. Moore and Ralph C. Guzman (Free Press, 1970) is the most comprehensive source on the whole subject while *The Chicanos: A History of Mexican Americans* by Matt S. Meier and Feliciano Rivera (Hill & Wang, 1972) traces Chicano history and developments through the 1960s.
Race and Class in the South-west by Mario Barrera (University of Notre Dame Press, 1979) is an economic approach to the Mexican presence in the United States.

See also: AZTLÁN; CIVIL RIGHTS MOVEMENT; LATINOS

Ellis Cashmore

Civil rights movement
On 1 December 1955, Rosa Parks, a black seamstress, refused to give up her seat to a white man on a bus in Montgomery, Alabama. Her action was to prompt changes of monumental proportions in

the condition of blacks in the United States. It provided the impetus for the most influential social movement in the history of North American race and ethnic relations.

Six months before the incident, the U.S. Supreme Court had, in the *Brown v. Board of Education* case, reversed the 58-year-old doctrine of "separate but equal" after a campaign of sustained pressure from the National Association for the Advancement of Colored People (NAACP), which believed the issue of social equality rested on desegregating schooling.

Parks's refusal to surrender her seat resulted in her arrest and this brought protest from black organizations in the South. The immediate reaction to the arrest was a black boycott of buses in Montgomery. So impressive was this action that it led to the formation of the Southern Christian Leadership Conference in 1957. This loosely federated alliance of ministers was the central vehicle for what became known collectively as the civil rights movement, or sometimes just "the movement." It was led by the Reverend Dr. Martin Luther King (1929–68), a graduate of Boston University, who became drawn to the nonviolent civil disobedience philosophies of Gandhi. King was able to mobilize grassroots black protest by organizing a series of bus boycotts similar to the one in Montgomery which had eventually resulted in a Supreme Court ban on segregated public transportation.

Securing desegregation in education and obtaining black franchises, however, were more difficult and King was made to mount a sustained campaign of black protest. Two laws in 1957 and 1960 aimed at ensuring blacks' right to vote in federal elections were largely negated by the opposition of southern states which actually made moves to reduce the number of black registered voters. Legal actions to desegregate schools were also foundering at state level as federal executive power was not widely available to enforce the law. By 1964 (ten years after the *Brown* case), less than 2 percent of the South's black students attended integrated schools.

At this point, King's movement was in full swing: boycotts were augmented with sit-ins (in streets and jails) and mass street rallies. As the campaign gained momentum, so did the Southern white backlash and civil rights leaders and their followers were attacked and many killed. By now John F. Kennedy was president, elected in 1960 with substantial black support. The first two years of his administration brought circumspect changes, but in 1963 Kennedy threw his support behind the civil rights movement calling for comprehensive legislation to: (1) end segregation in public educational institutions; (2) protect the rights of blacks to vote; (3) stop discrimination in all public facilities. A show of support for the proposed legislation came on 28 August 1963, with a demonstration staged by some 200,000 blacks and whites. It was at this demonstration that King delivered his famous "I have a dream" speech.

The movement's campaign saw its efforts translated into results in the two years that followed. Following Kennedy's assassination, President Lyndon B. Johnson's administration passed acts in 1964 that extended the powers of the attorney general to enforce the prohibition of discrimination in public facilities and in 1965 to guarantee the right to vote (regardless of literacy or any other potentially discriminatory criteria). The latter piece of legislation significantly enlarged the black vote in the South and, in the process, altered the whole structure of political power, especially in southern states.

But it was the former, the 1964 Civil Rights Act, that marked a dividing point in the U.S. race relations. Among its conditions were: (1) the enlargement of federal powers to stop discrimination in places of public accommodations; (2) the desegregation of all facilities maintained by public organizations (again with executive power to enforce this); (3) the desegregation of public education; (4) the extension of the powers of the Civil Rights Commission; (5) the prohibition of discrimination in any federally assisted program; (6) the total illegalization of discrimination in employment on the grounds of race, color, sex, or national origin; (7) the establishment of an Equal Employment Opportunities Commission to investigate and monitor complaints.

The Act was a comprehensive legal reformulation of race and ethnic relations and was due, in large part, to the sustained, non-violent campaigns of the civil rights movement and the ability of King to negotiate at the highest political levels. The leader's assassination in Memphis on 4 April 1968 symbolized the end of the era of the civil rights movement, though, in fact, there had been a different mood of protest emerging in the years immediately after the 1964 Act. Whereas King and his movement brought, through peaceful means, tangible gains and a heightening of self-respect for blacks, the new movement was based on the view that no significant long-term improvements could be produced through working peacefully within the political system – as King had done. The alternative was to react violently to the system. For many, Black Power replaced civil rights as the goal to be aimed for.

78   *Colonial discourse*

Reading
Freedom Bound: A History of America's Civil Rights Movement by Robert
Leeisbrot (Plume, 1993) is exactly what its title suggests.
Eyes on the Prize: America's Civil Rights Years, 1954–1965 by Juan Williams
(Viking, 1987) is a companion volume to the brilliant Public Broadcasting
System's television series of the same name.
The Making of Martin Luther King and the Civil Rights Movement by Brian
Ward and Tony Badger (Macmillan, 1995) is an original reassessment
of the movement, digging into the 1930s for its ancestry, evaluating its
contemporary effects and making comparisons with the South African and
British experiences.

See also: AFRICAN AMERICANS; JIM CROW; KING; LAW: CIVIL RIGHTS
U.S.A.; SEGREGATION

Ellis Cashmore

Colonial discourse

A concept employed as an alternative to forms of humanistic study,
the colonial discourse accentuates the role of domination, exploitation and disenfranchisement that are involved in the construction of
any cultural artifact, including knowledge, language, morality, or
attitude. Its sense derived from Foucault's analysis of power as
exercised through discursive practices (speech, writing, knowledge
– texts) as opposed to coercive force. So, the discourse is constituted
by communicative and representational practices which are a form
of power in themselves.

Interrogating the discourse reveals history as a palimpsest – as
something on which original impressions are effaced to make room
for further engravings, rather than a single narrative that describes
reality. Discourse analysts are wont to examine or "read" the arts
of description, in particular literature. There is more involved than
reading a text as a "reflection" of the discourse: in a sense, the text
is made possible by the existence of the discourse. As Said writes:
"References to Australia in *David Copperfield* or India in *Jane Eyre*
are made because they can be, because British power (and not
just the novelist's fancy) made passing references to these massive
appropriations possible" (in *Culture and Imperialism*).

Colonial discourse redefines boundaries so as to "problematize"
the ownership of the discourse. Fanon sought to treat metropolitan
and colonial societies together, as discrepant but interconnected
entities. And, following him, Bhaba asserts the unity of the "colonial
subject," which includes both colonized and colonizer. This alerts
us to conflictual conqueror/native relationship, a Manichean
struggle, in Fanon's phrase, and invites an investigation of how the

discourse is held together with rules and codes that are observed by all.

JanMohamed distinguishes between "dominant" and "hegemonic" phrases of colonialism, the former characterized by the imposition of European military and bureaucratic control over native populations and the passive consent of natives. By contrast, the hegemonic phase involves the native population's internalization of the colonizers' entire complex of values, attitudes, and institutions. While the Europeans' covert aim was to exploit colonies' natural resources, the overt aim is to "civilize" the Other via subjugation. This is articulated in literature which is a representation of a world at the boundaries of civilization.

A central idea informing colonial discourse analysis is that: how we formulate or represent the past shapes our understanding of the present. By elevating the importance of the role of discourse in extending the imperial reach and solidifying colonial domination, we are better able to clarify the role played by culture (including aesthetics, ideas, values, and other items that have relative autonomy from the spheres of politics and economics) in perpetuating different kinds of domination in the postcolonial era.

Reading
Orientalism (Pantheon, 1978) and *Culture and Imperialism* (Vintage, 1994) by Edward W. Said luminously show how colonialism is not just an act of accumulation and acquisition: it is supported and perhaps impelled by ideological formations that include notions that certain territories and people *require* domination.
"The economy of the Manichean allegory" by Abdul R. JanMohamed in *Race, Writing and Difference* edited by Henry L. Gates (University of Chicago Press, 1986) is one of several discussions or colonial discourses in the same book and may profitably be read in conjunction with another reader, *Colonial Discourse and Post-colonial Theory* edited by Patrick Williams and Laura Chrisman (Harvester Wheatsheaf, 1993).
Power/Knowledge by Michel Foucault, edited by Colin Gordon (Harvester Press, 1980) is a selection of interviews organized around the theme suggested by the title; it is a useful primer for the Foucauldian approach.

See also: DIASPORA; HYBRIDITY; OTHERS; POSTCOLONIAL; SUBALTERN
Ellis Cashmore

Colonialism
From the Latin *colonia* for cultivate (especially new land), this refers to the practices, theories and attitudes involved in establishing and maintaining an empire – this being a relationship in which one state controls the effective political sovereignty of another polity, typically of a distant territory. Among the several meanings of imperialism,

from the Latin *imperium* for command or dominion, is the belief in the desirability of acquiring colonies and dependencies.

It is not possible to understand the complexities of race and ethnic relations without considering the historical aspects of colonialism, for many contemporary race relations situations are the eventual results of the conquest and exploitation of poor and relatively weak countries by metropolitan nations.

Following conquest, new forms of production were introduced, new systems of power and authority relations were imposed and new patterns of inequality, involving people of different backgrounds, languages, beliefs, and, often, skin color, were established. These patterns of inequality persisted for generation after generation.

In the colonial system, the more powerful, conquering groups operating from the metropolitan center, were able to extract wealth from the colonized territories at the periphery of the system by appropriating lands and securing the labor of peoples living in those territories. In extreme instances, this took the form of slavery, though there were what John Rex calls "degrees of unfreedom" less severe than slavery.

It was characteristic of colonialism that the conquering powers regarded the colonized peoples as totally unrelated to themselves. Their assumption was that the colonized were so different in physical appearance and culture that they shared nothing; they were Others. Racist beliefs were invoked to justify the open exploitation, the reasoning being that natives were part of a subhuman species and could not expect to be treated in any way similar to their masters. Even the less racist colonizers, such as Spain and France, held that, although the natives were human, they were so far down the ladder of civilization, that it would take them generations to catch up. Racism, therefore, was highly complementary to colonialism (though it should be stressed that there are instances of racism existing independently of colonialism and vice versa, so there is no causal relationship between the two).

Colonization, the process of taking lands and resources for exploitation, has a long history. The great imperial powers (the countries acquiring colonies) were, from the sixteenth century, Spain, Portugal, Britain, France, and, to a much lesser extent, Holland and Denmark. These were quite advanced in navigation, agricultural techniques, the use of wind and water power and the development of technology, so they had the resources necessary for conquest.

By 1750, all of South and Central America and half of North

America were divided among these powers, with Britain the paramount force in North America. Britain's military might enabled it to conquer vast portions of India also, making its empire supreme; its conquests were successfully completed by white men with supposedly Christian ideals.

The interior of Africa remained for several hundred years untouched by the European empires because of the control of its northern coast, including Egypt, by dependencies of the Turkish empire and because of the prevalence of tropical diseases such as malaria in the center and south of the continent. The more accessible west coast of Africa, however, was comprehensively exploited, with western Europeans establishing forts for slave trading right from Dakar to the Cape (Arabs had done similarly on the eastern coast). There was a triangular trade route involving Europe, West Africa, and the Americas (including Caribbean islands), so that a slave population was introduced to the Americas to supplement or even replace native Indian labor. An estimated fifteen million Africans were exported to the Americas, mostly from West Africa, but some from the east, in the late nineteenth century when the continent was divided up among France (which controlled 3.87 million square miles), Britain (2 million square miles), Belgium, Germany (both 900,000 square miles), Italy (200,000 square miles), Spain (80,000 square miles), and Holland (whose republic of Transvaal was subsumed by 1902 in British South Africa), leaving a mere 400,000 square miles of uncolonized territory.

European domination extended also to Australasia. The French, Portuguese, Spanish, and, especially, the Dutch made incursions in the sixteenth and seventeenth centuries and the voyages of Captain Cook in the 1770s led to the British occupation of Australia, New Zealand and Tasmania. Later, the Pacific islands of Fiji, Tonga, and Gilbert were absorbed in the British empire; other islands were taken by France and Germany, with some of Samoa, Guam, and Hawaii later being taken by the United States.

By about 1910, the "Europeanization" of much of the world was complete, with colonial rule extending over most of the globe – Russia held territories in Central and East Asia. Outside the zones of direct European control, the Turkish and Chinese empires were inhabited by paternalist European officials and merchants. Only Japan, Nepal, Thailand, Ethiopia, Liberia, and the rebel Caribbean island of Haiti were without European political direction.

The colonial structures of empire were maintained as they had been established: by military might. Despite this, it would be wise to recognize the pivotal parts played by missionaries in disseminating Christian ideas that were highly conducive to domination; for example, the basic concept of salvation encouraged colonized peoples to accept and withstand their domination and deprivation in the hope of a deliverance in the afterlife, thus cultivating a passive rather than rebellious posture. This is not to suggest that the missionaries or their commissioning churches were deliberately engaging in some vast conspiracy. They were guided by the idea of a civilizing mission to uplift backward, heathen peoples and "save" them with Christianity. This was, indeed, as Kipling called it, the "white man's burden." Colonialism operated at many levels, crucially at the level of consciousness.

World War I did little to break European colonial grip: Germany lost its African and other colonies, but to other European powers. After World War II, however, the empires began to break up with an increasing number of colonies being granted independence, either total or partial. Britain's empire evolved into a Commonwealth comprising a network of self-governing nations formerly of the empire; social and economic links were maintained, sometimes with indirect rule by Britain via "puppet" governments.

Colonialism worked to the severe cost of the populations colonized. For all the benefits they might have received in terms of new crops, technologies, medicine, commerce, and education, they inevitably suffered: human loss in the process of conquest was inestimable; self-sufficient economies were obliterated and new relationships of dependence were introduced; ancient traditions, customs, political systems, and religions were destroyed. In particular, Islam suffered inordinately: the military conquests of Africa simultaneously undermined the efficacy of the Islamic faith.

(The great imperial power of modern times was Russia: the Soviet area of control, whether through direct or indirect means, spread under communism to encompass countries in Eastern Europe, Cuba, and Afghanistan. Soviet systems did not, of course, operate slavery, but evidence suggests that their regimes were extremely repressive. The manipulation of consciousness, or "thought control," so integral to earlier colonial domination, was equally accentuated in Soviet systems.)

The basic assumption of human inequality that underlay the whole colonial enterprise has survived in the popular imagination and manifests itself in what has been called the "colonial mentality" (see *Introduction to Race Relations*, Chapter 1). The belief in the inferiority of some groups designated "races" has been passed down from one generation to the next and remains beneath modern race relations situations. The colonial mentality which structures people's perceptions of others is a remnant of colonialism, but is constantly being given fresh relevance by changing social conditions.

Reading
Introduction to Race Relations, 2nd edition, by E. Cashmore and B. Troyna (Falmer, 1990) is an approach to the subject area that emphasizes the historical importance of colonialism and the persistence of the colonial mentality.
Race Relations by Philip Mason (Oxford University Press, 1970) is a shorter interpretation of the author's main thesis, *Patterns of Dominance* (Oxford University Press, 1970), which chronicles the imperial expansions and the resulting race relations situations.
An Unfinished History of the World by Hugh Thomas (Pan, 1979) has a chapter called "Empires" which provides a readable, historical account of the European conquests.

See also: COLONIAL DISCOURSE; CONQUEST; OTHERS; SLAVERY; THIRD WORLD

Ellis Cashmore

Color line

The color line is that symbolic division between "racial" groups in societies where skin pigmentation is a criterion of social status. It is, of course, most clearly and rigidly defined in the most racist societies, that is in societies that ascribed different rights and privileges to members of different racial groups. If access to social resources (such as schooling, housing, employment, and the like) is contingent on race, racial classification must be maintained and racial membership must be kept as unambiguous as possible. This is true even when racial discrimination is supposedly benign, as with affirmative action in the United States, for instance.

The simplest systems of racial stratification are the dichotomous ones, in which one is classified as either white or black, white or nonwhite, white or colored. An example is the United States, where any African ancestry puts one in the social category of "Negro," "Black," "Colored," or "Afro-American" (to use different labels applied at different times to the same people). More complex systems have three groups, as do some Caribbean societies, with distinctions drawn between whites, mulattos, and blacks. South Africa under Apartheid officially recognized four racial groups (whites, Coloreds, Indians, and Blacks), but often lumped the three subordinate groups into the blanket category nonwhite.

The color line may be more or less rigid. In some countries, like some states of the United States until 1967, interracial marriage was forbidden by law. In South Africa, both intermarriage and sexual relations between whites and nonwhites were criminal offences subject to stiff penalties (up to seven years of imprisonment). To prevent "passing" (i.e. the surreptitious crossing of the color line), the South African government passed the Population Registration Act, providing for the issuance of racial identity cards, and the permanent racial classification of the entire population.

Especially in societies that are virulently racist and attempt to maintain a rigid color line, the incentives for "passing" are great enough to encourage those whose phenotype is sufficiently like that of the dominant group to cross the color line. Even extensive "passing" does not necessarily undermine the color line. Indeed, "passing," far from defying the racial hierarchy, is a self-serving act of individual *evasion* of the color line. The very evasion implies acceptance of the system, a reason why "passing" is often resented more by members of the subordinate group to whom the option is not available, than by members of the dominant group who are being infiltrated by racial "upstarts."

At the other end of the spectrum are societies where racial boundaries are so ambiguous and flexible that, even though they exhibit a good deal of racial consciousness, one may not properly speak of a color line. Brazil is an example of a country lacking any sharp breaking points in the continuum of color. Nobody is quite sure where whiteness ends and blackness begins.

Reading
Race Relations by Michael Banton (Tavistock, 1967) is a classic text on the subject, from a comparative sociological perspective.
Race Relations by Philip Mason (Oxford University Press, 1970) is a shorter account from a more historical point of view.
South Africa: A Study in Conflict by Pierre L. van den Berghe (University of California Press, 1967) is a detailed account of apartheid in South Africa.

See also: AFFIRMATIVE ACTION; APARTHEID; BRAZIL; ETHNIC MONITORING; PHENOTYPE; SEGREGATION

                                                        Pierre L. van den Berghe

Conquest

From the Roman *conquerere* (seek or get), this refers to the acquisition and/or subjugation of a territory by force. Military conquest is the commonest origin of plural societies (societies composed of distinct ethnic or racial groups). It is also the most frequent origin of inequality between ethnic and racial groups. The other principal origin of plural societies is peaceful immigration, whether voluntary, semi-voluntary (e.g. indenture), or involuntary (e.g. slavery and penal colonies). Conquest, of course, is also a form of immigration, namely one in which it is the dominant group which comes in and disperses to establish control over the natives. What is commonly meant by immigration, however, is a situation in which the dominant group is indigenous, and in which immigrants move in peacefully and disperse to assume a subordinate position. Conquest and peaceful immigration lead to very different situations of race and ethnic relations.

Plural societies originating in conquest are frequently dominated by racial or ethnic minorities who exert their control through superior military technology and organization rather than numbers. Being often ruled by minorities, such societies are typically highly despotic and characterized by sharp ethnic or racial cleavages and a large degree of legally entrenched inequality between ethnic groups.

Unlike in countries that owe their pluralism to peaceful immigration, conquest leads to relatively stable or slowly changing ethnic boundaries, largely because the conquered groups typically retain a territorial basis and remain concentrated in their traditional homeland. In contrast to immigrant groups who often disperse on arrival in their host countries, conquered groups, by staying territorialized, find it easier to retain their language, religion, and culture. Furthermore, the dominant group often does not even seek to assimilate the conquered. So long as the conquered remain submissive and pay taxes, they are commonly left relatively undisturbed in running their daily affairs at the local level. They may even retain their native elite, under a system of indirect rule.

Two principal types of conquest can be distinguished, depending on the level of technology of the conquered. Where the natives belong to small-scale, stateless, thinly settled, nomadic groups of hunters and gatherers or simple horticulturists, the outcome is often their displacement by the invaders. Sometimes there is a definite policy of genocide, but often epidemic diseases, frontier warfare, and loss of a territorial basis for subsistence combine to bring about the destruction of native cultures as functioning groups, and the relegation of the remnants of their population to native reserves. In these "frontier" situations, which characterized countries such as Canada, the United States and Australia, the conquerors essentially replaced the indigenes, both territorially and demographically. The aboriginal societies were not only fragile and defenseless; their small numbers and their resistance to subjection made them virtually useless to the conquerors as a labor force.

Whenever the conquerors encounter a settled peasant population belonging to a stratified, state-level, indigenous society, however, the situation is very different. Initial resistance may be stronger, but, once control is achieved, the conquerors find an easily exploitable labor force (which often continues to be under the direct supervision of the collaborators from the former ruling class of the conquered groups). The result is exploitation rather than displacement. Examples are most traditional empires of Europe, Asia, Africa, and precolonial America, as well as most Asian and African colonies of Europe.

Reading
Ethnic Groups in Conflict by Donald Horowitz (University of California Press, 1985) is a study incorporating many case studies of ethnic conflict all over the world.
Interethnic Relations by E. K. Francis (Elsevier, 1976) is a broad sociological treatment of ethnic and race relations, especially strong on Europe and North America.
Patterns of Dominance by Philip Mason (Oxford University Press, 1970) is much like the above, but more historical, and strongest on Asia and Africa.

See also: COLONIALISM; NATIVE PEOPLES; RACE; SLAVERY

Pierre L. van den Berghe

Conservatism

As a political doctrine conservatism begins from a skepticism about the ability of human beings, acting within the constraints of consciousness, to understand the complexities of society. It follows that the only guide to governing society is *caution* in interfering with what is already established. This does not imply a hostility to change: conservatism accepts that societies must continually respond to circumstances; but the response should be anchored in custom, tradition, and established norms and values.

While this avoidance of change of a radical kind might be regarded as a timeless part of human disposition, conservatism acquired coherence as an intellectual doctrine in 1790 with Edmund Burke's critique of the French Revolution and the rationalism (particularly the authority of individuals over privileged bodies such as church or government) it extolled. Burke's *Reflections on the Revolution in France* countered the rationalist insistence on rebuilding entire societies in the spirit of innovation, as a break with the past: the present is never free from the past, Burke argued.

Fundamental constituents of society, such as the state's legitimacy, are the product of traditions that stretch back for several generations.

This reverence for persistent structures, habits, and prejudices that have passed through generations has been a constant theme in conservative thought to the present day. (For Burke, "prejudice" refers positively to the wisdom and commonsense understandings that lie in tradition and which should not willingly be given up.)

Burke admired Adam Smith's *Wealth of Nations*, especially its arguments about the most effective means of preserving individual and communal liberties. The opposition to central governments' intercession and the respect for the free market as a "natural" mechanism continue to dominate conservative thought. Clearly, the free market generates inequalities and conservatives believe this is an inevitable consequence of protecting liberty. The inherent objective of equality is in a redistribution of unequally shared resources. According to conservative thought, this is not possible without violating individual (or familial) liberty, epitomized in the ability to own and protect property. Conservatives over the years have prioritized liberty over equality and have spurned any attempt to make the values seem compatible.

The state's role, as seen by conservatives, is to facilitate an environment that permits and even encourages freedom of competition, while protecting individual choice and freedom. One immediate consequence of this is a suspicion of state-initiated rules designed to regulate or control human behavior. In race and ethnic relations, this has prompted troublesome dilemmas. Civil rights, or race relations, legislation introduces norms intended to govern action. Affirmative action extends such government. But, while few doubt the necessity of the former in creating and protecting liberties, many remain mindful of Burke's remark, "Those who attempt to level, never equalize," when resisting affirmative action. Individual inequality and social hierarchy are vital to autonomy and, ultimately, a prosperous society. Removing such barriers to movement as segregation facilitates the freedom of opportunity so dear to conservatives. Yet, to reward on the basis of anything but merit is anathema.

Modern scholars, particularly Charles Murray and Thomas Sowell, have pointed out the baleful consequences of state policies to alleviate the condition of the poor – a group in which African Americans and Latinos are overrepresented. "We tried to provide more for the poor and produced more poor instead," Murray reflects on welfare programs, which, he argues, have destructive long-term effects in the shape of a chronically dependent underclass. In a similar vein, Sowell discounts all antidiscrimination laws and policies, instead blaming an alleged deficiency in African Americans for their continued impoverishment.

Support for moderate black political leaders (such as Douglas Wilder) and a disaffection with activists like Jesse Jackson have led to the suspicion that ethnic minorities may be shifting towards conservatism. A study by the Center for Media and Public Affairs in 1986 reported a gap between blacks and organization-based leaders on several policy issues. Whether such a disillusionment will convert into conservatism is uncertain.

Modern black conservatives believe so. Gary Franks, the first black Republican to be elected to the House of Representatives since 1937, invoked Booker T. Washington to support the claim that "black economic nationalism" (as Washington called it) translates in practical terms to individual initiative, or self-help. Franks belongs to a faction of the black caucus that endorses home ownership and entrepreneurial endeavor. The faction stresses the important distinction between desegregation, which was a matter to be tackled by social policy, and integration, which is a personal matter to be pursued by individuals.

The British Conservative party fielded seven ethnic minority candidates in the 1992 General Election (compared to the Labour party's eight) and made an effort to woo the upwardly mobile and entrepreneurial elements of the ethnic minority population with its central values, expressed by Asian politician Andrew Popat as: "Work, ambition, thrift, determination and the opportunity to get as far as your ability will take you."

Reading

Conservatism by Robert Nisbet (Open University Press, 1986) is a neat, clear, and resonant summary of the origins and tenets of conservative philosophy.

Black Politics in Conservative America by Marcus Pohlmann (Longman, 1990) looks in part at African Americans' allegiance to conservative politics.

Losing Ground by Charles Murray (Basic Books, 1984) and *Ethnic America* (Basic Books, 1981) by Thomas Sowell exemplify the intellectual conservatism in North American race relations, a trend roundly criticized by Thomas Boston in his *Race, Class and Conservatism* (Unwin Hyman, 1988).

"Songs of the new blues" by Ellis Cashmore in *New Statesman and Society*, vol. 44, No. 165 (1991) reviews the British Conservative Party's ethnic minority candidates and their perspectives.

See also: AFFIRMATIVE ACTION; JACKSON; POLITICS AND "RACE"; RACE; THOMAS

Ellis Cashmore

Cox, Oliver C. (1901–74)

He was born in Trinidad and died in the United States. He studied law at Northwestern University and then continued these studies for a higher degree in law at University of Chicago. While there, he contracted polio and the subsequent physical disabilities persuaded him that he would not be able to practice law. He chose to take a Master's degree in economics and then completed a PhD in Sociology in 1938. Thereafter he became Professor of Sociology at Lincoln University, Missouri and, later, at Wayne State University.

Quantitatively, his main area of interest and writing was on the nature of capitalism as a system. This is evident in his following major publications: *The Foundations of Capitalism* (New York: Philosophical Library, 1959) and *Capitalism as a System* (New York: Monthly Review Press, 1964). The nature of capitalism and its evolution from the feudal system of Europe was the subject matter of one of his later articles, "The problem of social transition" (in *American Journal of Sociology*, 1973, 79, pp. 1120–33). However, his name is known primarily through the renewed interest in the 1960s and 1970s in his earlier book *Caste, Class, and Race* (New York: Doubleday, 1948; reprinted in 1959 and 1970 by Monthly Review Press). This became both the object of attack by radical "black" sociologists in the United States and of admiration by Marxist and leftist writers in Britain. The former regarded Cox as an assimilationist on the strength of some of the claims made in this text. The latter interpreted the text as the "classic" Marxist analysis of the origin of racism and of the relationship between class and "race." Both groups were referring to a text which was a product of an earlier time and set of concerns. Moreover, Cox's claims and predictions from that earlier time were contradicted by the events of the 1960s, leaving him, so others have observed, a lonely and disillusioned man.

Much of Cox's work was influenced by the writings of Marx and this is clearly evident in *Caste, Class, and Race*. In this text, he defends two main contentions. First, he argued that "race relations" cannot be reduced to caste relations and so the text develops an extensive critique of W. Lloyd Warner and John Dollard. Second, he argued that what he preferred to define as "race prejudice" (he rejected the term racism) was not a natural phenomenon but was a direct consequence of the development of capitalism, from which he concluded that a solution to the "race problem" could be found only in the transition from capitalism to a democratic and classless society. It was in developing this second argument that Cox attempted to set out a detailed theoretical and historical account of the relationship between class and "race."

When viewed historically, Cox's text, published in 1949, was significant because it attempted to reassert the significance of Marxist categories of analysis in a context which was, to say the least, unfavorable to Marxism. This should be recognized, even when one goes on to argue that Cox's use of some of the Marxist categories was grounded in what would now be regarded as a very limited selection of Marx's work. Indeed, the way in which the concept of class is defined and employed has led others to argue that the work cannot easily be regarded as being within the Marxist tradition. Cox's tenuous relationship with Marxism is confirmed by the aforementioned article in the *American Journal of Sociology* of 1973, which is concerned with the transition from feudalism to capitalism and which makes no reference to the new classic Marxist contributions of M. Dodd and P. Sweezy, let alone volume 1 of Marx's *Capital*.

Reading
Caste, Class, and Race by Oliver C. Cox (Monthly Review Press, 1970), despite later criticisms, remains a challenging contribution when viewed historically.
The Idea of Race by Michael Banton (Tavistock, 1977) locates Cox's later work and criticizes it in the context of an analysis of the tradition of "race relations" analysis.
"Class, race, and ethnicity" by Robert Miles in *Ethnic and Racial Studies* (1980, vol. 3 no. 2, pp. 169–87) is a critical analysis of Cox's attempt to theorize a relationship between class and "race."

See also: CAPITALISM; CASTE; MARXISM AND RACISM

Robert Miles

Creole
A distinct culture produced as the result of the merging of two or more other cultures. It was originally taken from the Portuguese *crioulo*, meaning a slave brought up in the owner's household; the word became *criolli* in Spanish and *creole* in French, and came to take a particular meaning in the state of Louisiana in the early 1800s. After the Louisiana Purchase of 1803, those of French and Spanish descent called themselves creoles as if to distinguish themselves culturally from Anglo-Americans who began to move into

Louisiana at the time. The creoles evolved their own distinctive styles of cuisine, music and language. The term later came to refer to the group of "coloreds," that is, the products of miscegenation (black and white mixture). They were a self-conscious ethnic group who regarded themselves as different and separate. Based in New Orleans, they spoke French and developed their own educational institutions, such as Xavier University.

In a Caribbean context, creole referred to the descendants of Europeans who were both born and lived in the Caribbean; it was also used to distinguish a West Indian-born slave from an African one. Those born in the islands developed their own dialects, musics and culture and the word creole came to mean anything created anew in the Caribbean (it probably stemmed from the Latin *creara* for "created originally"). So particular dishes, dialects, art forms, etc. were known as creole and this denoted something very positive and original. Nowadays, the term creole describes homegrown qualities exclusive to ethnic groups, particularly in language and dialect.

Reading
Ten Generations by Frances J. Woods (Louisiana State University Press, 1972) is the life story of an extended family of American creoles, who were something of an elite.
West Indian Societies by David Lowenthal (Oxford University Press, 1972) defines creole culture as based on a past history of slavery and a present legacy of color, and covers the whole development of creole culture. Less impressive, but still useful in this context, is Eric Williams's *From Columbus to Castro: The History of the Caribbean, 1492–1969* (Deutsch, 1970). *Jamaica Talk* by Frederic G. Cassidy (Macmillan, 1969) is an interesting study of possibly the most important element of creole cultures: language.

See also: AMALGAMATION; HYBRIDITY; KINSHIP; MULTIRACIAL/BIRACIAL
Ellis Cashmore

Culture

Defined by Sir Edward Tylor in 1871 as, when "taken in its wide ethnographic sense," being "that complex whole which includes knowledge, belief, art, morals, law, custom and any other capabilities and habits acquired by man as a member of society." Since then, definitions have proliferated with little if any increase in precision. Sir Raymond Firth has written that "If . . . society is taken to be an organized set of individuals with a given way of life, culture is that way of life. If society is taken to be an aggregate of social relations, then culture is the content of those relations. Society emphasizes the human component, the aggregate of people and the relations between them. Culture emphasizes the component of accumulated resources, immaterial as well as material."

In the United States in particular, culture is regarded as possibly the most central concept of anthropology as a discipline, but it has not been built into the sort of theoretical structure which can cause it to be defined more sharply for use in the formulation of testable hypotheses. Whereas it may be convenient to refer to, say, "Japanese culture" and its characteristics, and to recognize subcultures within such a unit, it is usually impossible to conceive of cultures as having clear boundaries. It is therefore impracticable to treat them as distinct and finite units that can be counted. Cultures tend to be systems of meaning and custom that are blurred at the edges. Nor are they usually stable. As individuals come to terms with changing circumstances (such as new technology) so they change their ways and shared meanings change with them.

It is important to bear in mind these limitations to the explanatory value of the culture concept when considering its use in the educational field. It is argued that the curricula for all subjects should be reviewed to ensure that schools make the maximum possible contribution to the preparation of children for life in a multiracial world, and in a society which includes groups distinguished by race, ethnicity and culture. At present there is a tendency to use the name "multicultural education" as an official designation for programs directed to this end, though the names multiracial and multi or polyethnic education are favoured by some people. All these names are open to the objection that there is no finite number of stable constituent units. The use of "culture" in this connection is questionable since advanced technology is so readily identified with culture of the First World, the west. The culture of people living in India and Trinidad has many features in common with the culture of England: cars, radios, books, and so on; but the things taken to represent the cultures of Indians and Trinidadians tend to be festivals, songs, and recipes. This trivializes the culture of the people who live in those societies as much as it would were English children told that their culture was exemplified by Guy Fawkes Night, Morris dancing, and custard. It might be better to talk of education for cultural diversity were it not so difficult to know how much is desired in comparison with the traditional educational aims of literacy and numeracy.

Reading
Elements of Social Organization by Raymond Firth (Watts, 1952) on page 27.

Culture: a Critical Review of Concepts and Definitions by A. L. Kroeber and Clyde Kluckhohn (Peabody Museum Papers, 1952) has a systematic review of definitions.

See also: AMALGAMATION; BOAS; ETHNICITY; KINSHIP; PLURALISM

Michael Banton

D

Darwinism

Darwin's influence upon the history of racial thought was profound. His demonstration of the mutability of species destroyed the doctrines of the racial typologists who assumed the permanence of types. He showed the debate between the monogenists and polygenists to be scientifically unproductive. He introduced a new conception of "geographical races, or sub-species" as "local forms completely fixed and isolated." Because they were isolated they did not interbreed and so "there is no possible test but individual opinion to determine which of them shall be considered as species and which as varieties." Darwin (1809–82) made no attempt to classify human races, observing that the naturalist has no right to give names to objects which he cannot define. As is to be expected, there are weaknesses in Darwin's work: he thought that acquired characteristics might be inherited; he believed that inheritance was an equal blending of parental characters, etc. Such problems were resolved when the scientific study of genetics became possible. As Jacob Bronowski once wrote, "The single most important thing that Charles Darwin did was to force biologists to find a unit of inheritance." Not until the statistical reasoning of population genetics had taken the place of the typologists' dream of pure races were the implications of Darwin's revolution for the understanding of race fully apparent.

Darwin's thought can be better understood if it is seen as combining several strands. Ernst Mayr distinguished five. In the first place, by assembling and ordering so much evidence of continuous change in the natural world, Darwin advanced a more convincing case for evolution than his predecessors had done. Secondly, he was the first author to postulate that all organisms have descended from common ancestors by a continuous process of branching; this constituted a theory of common descent. Thirdly, he insisted that evolution was a gradual process producing many forms intermediate between geographical varieties and species. Fourthly, he maintained that evolution is the result of natural selection, supplemented in some species by the process of sexual selection.

The theory of evolution proper does not depend upon acceptance of Darwin's argument about selection as its cause, or upon any assumption that evolution is gradual, or that selection is sufficient to explain speciation. It is a general theory which can be used to generate falsifiable hypotheses.

Darwin's theory was at first the less convincing because it did not account for the origin of life and for the genetic code. Since then many gaps have been filled, particularly by new knowledge about the workings of viruses. Under the influence of population genetics, the Darwinian argument was developed into a mathematical theory of differential reproduction. Natural selection came to mean that some individuals were fitter because they left more offspring than others, without explaining which individual would leave more. The idea that it was the individuals best adapted to their environment which left more offspring was assumed, but it had no explicit place in the theory. So, in the words of C. H. Waddington, a geneticist writing in the late 1950s, "The whole guts of evolution – which is, how do you come to have horses and tigers and things – is outside the mathematical theory." That gap also is now much smaller.

The evolution of the transition from reptiles into mammals, with the loss of some bones and the acquisition of others, is now so well documented that it is virtually impossible to draw a dividing line between reptile and mammal. The evolution of flight, showing the contribution of gliding and soaring to the development of flapping flight has been exemplified through studies of gliding lizards and flying foxes. The evolution of horses is the better understood because there is now an almost unbroken fossil record over 60 million years of a succession of genera and species. It shows that there have been both gradual changes and sudden jumps, the latter supporting the theories of "punctuated equilibria" in evolution.

"Darwinism" is not an expression much used by specialists, but "Neo-Darwinism" is sometimes employed to designate Darwin's original theory as modified by the genetical laws of inheritance first stated by Mendel. For readers interested in racial and ethnic relations in the late twentieth century, it is important to appreciate that the use of "race" as a social construct in ordinary English-language speech derives from pre-Darwinian science, and fails to allow for what has since been learned about the sources of variation in human as in other species.

Reading
Darwin by Adrian Desmond and James Moore (Penguin, 1991) is a much-praised account of his life and work.

The Growth of Biological Thought by Ernst Mayr (Harvard University Press, 1982) locates Darwin's work in ths history of biology.
Evolution by C. Patterson (1978) and *Mammal Evolution* by R. J. G. Savage and M. R. Long (1986, both British Museum – Natural History) are more general texts.

See also: EUGENICS; HERITABILITY; SOCIAL DARWINISM; SOCIOBIOLOGY

Michael Banton

Development

The elevation of the concept of development to its current status as a loosely defined but ubiquitously accepted definition of means and goals for socioeconomic advancement has been a comparatively recent phenomenon, although it has roots in such earlier concepts as Social Darwinian notions of evolutionary societal progress and Marxist notions of phased sequences in history. The phenomenon is closely associated with the growth of bureaucratic and technocratic modes in government, and the assignment to state structures of a central role in the planning and implementation of programs of social betterment. Thus discussions on development characteristically take as their focus contexts where state bureaucratic vanguardism typifies government, either in the formerly planned economies of Eastern Europe or in the "developing" societies of the Third World. Here "five year development plans" and "development ministries" abound, to a degree not found in the industrialized societies of the West.

Socioeconomic conditions in the postcolonial states of the Third World have provided a particular locus for development thinking. First, Third World nationalism, as Young has pointed out, has played a major role in placing development at the centre of the state's agenda. In its anticolonial phase, nationalism was primarily concerned with political and cultural liberation. This phase having been successfully concluded, nationalism has turned its attention to concomitant goals of material well-being, social equity and national integration, all subsumed under the rubric of development. Secondly, the notion of development has an important comparative dimension. With their colonial histories, Third World states have suffered from an exploitative location in a global economic system which has inhibited the growth of structures of self-sufficiency. On a number of economic performance indicators they compare unfavorably with the industrialized world of the West. "Development" for these countries thus has often carried the inference of improved performance as measured by these indices.

This inference informs both of the two major perspectives in development thinking which emerged after World War II. The first, dominant during the 1950s and 1960s, saw development as a linear path in economic growth marked by stages through which all countries had to pass. Strongly influenced by neoclassical economics, this perspective placed emphasis on capital formation and employment generation through the creation of economic/technological enclaves which would act as "engines of progress" for entire economies. Such progress was to be measured primarily by economic indices, the assumption being that economic growth would "trickle down" to create diffused societal benefits. In following this path Third world countries would be emulating the stages of growth of Western industrial societies; in this mode the perspective is often termed the Modernization theory.

A second perspective, which came to prominence during the 1970s, also starts from the premise that economic growth constitutes the main criterion for development but differs radically in its analysis of the obstacles to its achievement. This perspective holds that the development of the industrialized former colonial powers was historically and reciprocally linked to the underdevelopment of the colonial periphery in a system of global economic exploitation. Little change has been effected in this system by political decolonization. Through transnational investment, trade and technology, abetted by the complicity of local elites, the system remains largely in place. Capital and resource flows continue to the benefit of the developed societies at the expense of the underdeveloped, which cannot develop until the system is either destroyed or radically modified. Generally termed the Underdevelopment theory, in some of its forms this perspective sees the global economy as presenting a zero-sum situation in which the development of the Third World inevitably implies redistributive costs to the other participants in the system.

Theoretical debates between the proponents of these two perspectives have during the 1980s tended to modify the sharp contrasts suggested, the attempt being to identify and synthesize valid points made by each. More important, however, is their continuing influence as rationalizations for the policies of major actors on the international politico-economic scene. Many of the activities of international aid and technical assistance agencies continue to draw on assumptions rooted in Modernization theory; the international political stances of many Third World countries continue to be informed by perceptions embedded in the underdevelopment theory.

A third perspective on development has evolved since the early 1970s which challenges the centrality assigned to economic growth indicators as a measure of development. From this perspective these indicators, with their implication that Western patterns of production and consumption constitute a standardized objective, are an incomplete definition of human and social good. Furthermore they can be dangerously misleading in that they set goals which, given resource/demand ratios in the Third World, are unattainable. In some of its forms referred to as the "Basic Needs" approach to development, this perspective accepts an economic dimension to development objectives in the production of the food, shelter, and commodities required for the necessities of life. Development also concerns access to basic educational, health and welfare services; equity issues therefore form an important aspect of this approach. Finally, an emphasis is placed on progress toward the growth of cultural and moral values, participatory involvement by all members of society and the evolution of a sense of national identity within the framework of viable, representative, and integrative political structures.

Within the Third World this perspective has gained considerable currency, not as a substitute for the first two but rather as a component in a spectrum of development definitions which is selectively evoked in given contexts. Its emphasis on equity, cultural identity, and national integration provide a useful link for the analysis of the ethnic factor in development. Given the multiethnic composition of most Third World states, ethnicity is clearly an important variable when issues of national integration are addressed and is often seen as obstructive to integrative objectives. On the other hand, the emphasis placed on cultural identities introduces a different value perspective, and some analysts have argued that "ethnodevelopment" must be an important component in larger developmental schemes. Popular national slogans such as "Unity in Diversity" reveal an awareness of the contradictions raised by the ethnic issue and also frequently disguise the lack of coherent programs for dealing with them. The debate over assimilationist or pluralist policies is only infrequently made explicit in Third World politics, not because the issue is considered unimportant but because its sensitivity is regarded as requiring covert, *ad hoc* policy shifts. That this is a critical gap in development planning is demonstrated by the recent and largely unanticipated eruptions of ethnic conflict in "developing" countries such as Fiji and Sri Lanka.

The intersection of ethnic and development issues in the economic arena has also been largely neglected both by analysts and by policy-makers. More consideration is required of the notion of ethnic identity as social capital. Some recent analyses of peasant modes of agricultural production in the Third World, based on affective principles of economic reciprocality, have shown how these can create rational and functionally beneficial structures for the peasant populations involved but which also frustrate the macroeconomic objectives of state development. The affective affinities involved include ethnicity and the "economy of affection" hypothesis is a useful corrective to approaches which can only see ethnicity through the prism of political action, opening up a search for its salience in a broad spectrum of affectively informed behavioural loci within the structures of economic development.

Reading
Culture and Development by K. C. Alexander and K. P. Kumaran (Sage, 1992) investigates the uneven developments in regions of India after 40 years of planning.
The Sociology of Developing Societies, 2nd edition, by Ankie M. M. Hoogvelt (Macmillan, 1978), has a broad survey of issues and perspectives.
Development Perspectives by P. Streeten (Macmillan, 1981) is an essay collection by one of the subject's foremost analysts.
"Ethnicity and third world development" by Marshall W. Murphree in *Theories of Race and Ethnic Relations*, edited by J. Rex and D. Mason (Cambridge University Press, 1986), is a more extended discussion of the ethnic factor in development.
The Sociology of Development edited by Bryan Roberts, Robert Cushing, and Charles Wood (Edward Elgar, 1995) is a colossal (1,232 pages) two-volume collection of essays on such themes as dependency, modernization, and the global economy; its focuses include Africa, Latin America, China, and Mexico.

See also: AFRICA; COLONIALISM; CONQUEST; EXPLOITATION; THIRD WORLD

Marshall Murphree

Diaspora
Drawn from ancient Greek terms *dia* (through) and *speirō* meaning "dispersal, to sow or scatter," diaspora and its adjective diasporic have been utilized in recent years in a variety of ways. Among these uses – some rather new, all inherently related – three approaches to the notion of diaspora emerge and a fourth unrelated approach reacts to them.

As a social category

"The Diaspora" was at one time a concept referring almost exclusively to the experiences of Jews, invoking their traumatic exile from an historical homeland and dispersal throughout many lands. With this experiences as reference, connotations of a "diaspora" situation were negative as they were associated with forced displacement, victimization, alienation, and loss. Along with this archetype went a dream of return. These traits eventually led to the term's application comparatively to populations such as Armenians and Africans.

Now, however, "diaspora" is often used to describe practically any community which is transnational, that is, whose social economic and political networks cross the borders of nation-states. Such current overuse and under-theorization – which sees the conflation of categories such as immigrants, guestworkers, ethnic minorities, refugees, expatriates, and travelers – threatens the term's usefulness. More rigorous theoretical work germane to the category, however, is being developed contiguously (as witnessed in academic journals such as *Public Culture*, *Cultural Anthropology* and *Diaspora*).

As a form of consciousness

Here, with a direct allusion to W. E. B. Du Bois's notion of "double consciousness," diaspora refers to individuals' awareness of a range of decentered, multi-location attachments, of being simultaneously "home away from home" or "here and there." It is in this sense that Paul Gilroy (in *The Black Atlantic*, Verso, 1993) both presents stimulating ideas surrounding the exposition of a people's historical "roots and routes" and passes on the proposition (originally made by rap artist Rakim) that "It don't matter where you're from, it's where you're at."

As a mode of cultural production

In this approach, the fluidity of constructed styles and identities among diasporic people is emphasized These are evident in the production and reproduction of forms which are sometimes called "cut'n'mix," hybrid, or "alternate." A key dynamic to bear in mind, according to Stuart Hall, is that cultural identities "come from somewhere, have histories" and are subject to continuous transformation through the "play of history, culture and power" ("Cultural identity and diaspora" in *Identity: Community, Culture and Difference* edited by J. Rutherford, Lawrence & Wishart, 1990). For Hall, diaspora comprises ever-changing representations which provide an "imaginary coherence" for a set of malleable identities.

As a new kind of problem

According to this line of thinking – typically associated with right-wing groups – transnational communities are seen as threats to state security and potential sources of international terrorism. In this view too, people's links with homelands and with other parts of a globally dispersed community raise doubts about their loyalty to the "host" nation-state. Hybrid cultural forms and multiple identities expressed by self-proclaimed diasporic youths, too, are viewed by "host-society" conservatives as assaults on traditional (hegemonic and assimilative) norms. Such appraisals are countered by persons who see strong transnational networks as unsurprising features of globalization (particularly involving the enhancement of telecommunications and the ease of travel) and who welcome the construction of new compound identities and hybrid cultural forms by way of valuing cosmopolitan diversity.

Reading

"Diasporas in modern societies: myths of homeland and return" by William Safran (in *Diaspora*, vol. 1, no. 1, 1991) describes common characteristics of diaspora groups and outlines a future agenda for research.

"Diasporas" by James Clifford (in *Cultural Anthropology*, vol. 9, no. 3, 1994) provides a superb overview of theoretical issues surrounding diasporas and related social and cultural topics.

"Rethinking 'Babylon': iconoclastic conceptions of the diasporic experience" by Robin Cohen in (*New Community*, vol. 21, no. 1, 1995) looks beyond images associated with the historical Jewish experience to offer a general typology of diasporas in an age of globalization.

See also: AFRICAN AMERICANS; AFRICAN CARIBBEANS; ASIAN AMERICANS; ASIANS IN BRITAIN; HYBRIDITY; IRISH AND COLONIALISM; ROMA; ZIONISM

Steven Vertovec

Disadvantage

A euphemism for the result of discrimination and exploitation, the term "disadvantage" conveniently hides the causality of status differences and is, thus, currently fashionable in Western capitalist states, especially in the United States. Indeed disadvantage implicitly puts the burden of explanation for inferior status on supposed disabilities of the victims. Underprivilege is an equally convenient obfuscation of the sources of inequality.

The concept of "disadvantage" has been central to a set of ameliorative strategies devised in the United States, supposedly to redress ethnic and racial differences, mostly in income, education, and access to employment and schools. Certain minorities are defined as disadvantaged or underprivileged, and, therefore, qualified for affirmative action. Existing differences are principally ascribed to racial or ethnic factors, to the nearly complete exclusion of class. Minorities are alleged to be in a "disadvantaged" position partly because of ethnic or racial discrimination against them, and partly because of unfortunate failings of their own which they must be helped to overcome (e.g. lack of education, lack of a work ethic, hedonism, "externality," or the latest psychologistic fad).

Social remedies for disadvantage consist mostly of making supposedly benign exceptions for minorities rather than in changing the class structures which perpetuate inequalities. Affirmative action, or positive discrimination, takes the form of racial and ethnic quotas in university admissions and in hiring, remedial courses for minorities, racial busing for school "integration," and the like. The common denominator of some fifteen years of these policies has been their lack of success, or even their boomerang effect (in the form of white backlash, increasing salience of racial consciousness, and devaluation of credentials of all minority group members).

Long before the United States, the government of India, both under British rule and since independence, adopted similar policies to relieve the disadvantage of the "backward" castes. The results were quite similar: far from reducing the significance of caste status, a political incentive was created for people to organize along caste lines, and to claim "backward" status for economic or political advantage. In Israel, too, the government has initiated policies of benign discrimination in favor of Oriental Jews, though not toward Arabs, whose position is far worse, and who suffer from much more blatant discrimination.

Reading

Affirmative Discrimination by Nathan Glazer (Basic Books, 1975) is a critique of the policy and of its impact in the United States, by an American sociologist.

Minority Education and Caste by John Ogbu (Academic Press, 1978) is a lucid analysis of the source of educational "disadvantage" for minority groups in the United States, Britain, India, Nigeria, and elsewhere, by a Nigerian anthropologist.

See also: AFFIRMATIVE ACTION; RACIAL DISCRIMINATION; MINORITIES; RACISM

Pierre L. van den Berghe

Dollard, John (1900–80)

A United States psychologist who, having undergone psychoanalysis in Berlin, became the first writer to apply Freudian interpretations to black–white relations in North America. According to Freudian doctrine, social living and human culture require a degree of orderliness and discipline which conflict with the desires of the young human. Socialization entails frustration. The basic reaction to frustration is the aggressive response designed to reassert mastery, but a child finds it unprofitable to attack a parental figure who is responsible for his or her socialization. The child must either turn the aggression in on itself or store it up, waiting for a convenient opportunity to discharge it on a suitable scapegoat. The first key concept is therefore that of generalized or "free-floating" aggression held in store; the second, that of social permission to release this aggression on a particular target group; the third, that scapegoats must be readily identifiable (as the Negro's skin color served as a sign telling the prejudiced person whom to hate). According to this view racial prejudice was always irrational. In a later article, Dollard distinguished between direct and displaced aggression according to whether it was discharged against the agent of the frustration (direct) or a scapegoat (displaced); he stressed that in a situation of direct aggression some displaced aggression would also be released, adding an emotional element which might be responsible for the irrational behavior often observable in situations of rational conflict. Dollard's main contribution is his book *Caste and Class in a Southern Town* (1937), which brings together the Freudian interpretation and a description of black–white relations in the Mississippi town of Indianola. In it, blacks and whites are presented as separate castes after the manner of W. Lloyd Warner, though without carrying through the sort of analysis Warner's students, Allison Davies, B. B. Gardner, and M. Gardner, achieved in their book about another Mississippi town published a little later under the title *Deep South*.

Reading
"Hostility and fear in social life" by John Dollard, *Social Forces*, vol. 17 (1938), is a short but comprehensive statement of Dollard's views about prejudice.

See also: MYRDAL; PREJUDICE; RACIAL DISCRIMINATION; SCAPEGOAT

Michael Banton

Drugs and racism

It is important at the outset to draw a distinction between drug usage and drug dealing. One who uses illicit drugs recreationally may not trade in illicit drugs professionally, and vice versa. It is unclear how sharply the distinction should be drawn. For, even though drug use and drug dealing are not coextensive, it cannot be gainsaid that a small percentage of drug users trade in drugs as a means of supporting their drug habit.

Some would argue that the cry of racism is given as a convenient excuse for those who wish to engage in illicit drug use or dealing or both. They see no other connection between drugs and racism and, in fact, would argue that drug users or dealers would pursue their private crusades even in the absence of racism. Along these lines, others would argue that it is a kind of reverse racism even to attempt to place the blame of drug use or drug dealing on racism.

On the other hand, it is argued that there is a definite relationship between drugs and racism. For example, in the United States, racism contributes to both drug use and drug dealing in at least two ways. First, past racism – two centuries of slavery and nearly a century more of government-sanctioned racism under the Jim Crow system that ended only in the late 1960s – left black communities with tremendous social and economic disadvantage: less well-paying jobs, inadequate housing, and lower quality education than that in white communities. Second, present-day racism that motivates racial discrimination in employment, housing, and education exacerbates the dismal living conditions today's black Americans have inherited from past racism. Both forces – past racism and present-day racism – have converged on generations of black families living in racially isolated communities.

Caught in an intergenerational cycle of poverty and despair, it is not surprising that black Americans use or deal in drugs at disproportionately high rates. The recreational use of drugs offers temporary relief (if not the only relief) from the pain and frustration of trying to succeed against insurmountable social and economic odds. While some might be able to fathom this connection, they have a more difficult time comprehending the nexus between these conditions or racism and drug dealing.

They, like society as a whole, tend to view drug dealing strictly as a form of criminal activity. In contrast, black Americans who live in poverty and deal in drugs view drug dealing as "an important career choice and major economic activity." Beepers hanging from the belt and briefcase swinging from the hand; drug dealing is what they do for a living. It is not simply their job (they view themselves as "capitalists," not as laborers), it is their business. Indeed, studies have shown that, not unlike those formally educated in Harvard Business School principles of finance, these drug dealers consciously seek to establish the optimum level of risk and return. Another study has concluded that: "The structure of drug-dealing organizations is complex and contains many roles with approximate equivalents in the legal economy." In racially isolated communities, drug dealing is sometimes the only business in town.

Reading
"Drug abuse in the inner city: impact on hard-drug users and the community" by Bruce D. Johnson, Terry Williams, Kojo A. Dei, and Harry Sanabria (in *Drugs and Crime*, edited by Michael Tonry and James Q. Wilson) (University of Chicago Press, 1990, pp. 1–67) is a sophisticated discussion of drug use and drug dealing in the inner city.
Life with Heroin: Voices from the Inner City by Bill Hanson, George Beschner, James M. Walters, and Elliot Bovelle (Lexington Press, 1985) gives the inner city drug user's perspective.
Pipe Dream Blues by Clarence Lusane (South End Press, 1993) proposes that racism motivates government policy on drugs; not to be confused with *The American Pipe Dream: Crack Cocaine and Inner City* by Dale Chitwood, James Rivers and James Inciardi (Harcourt Brace, 1996) which examines the impact of crack on city populations.
Malign Neglect by Michael Tonry (Oxford University Press, 1995) argues that racial bias is built into the mandatory sentencing laws.

See also: AFRICAN AMERICANS; BLACK BOURGEOISIE; GHETTO; UNDERCLASS

Roy L. Brooks

E

Education and cultural diversity

Studies of the educational response to cultural diversity have explored a number of substantive themes against a bewildering backcloth of contradictory understandings of key conceptual and theoretical themes. If researchers tend to be out on a definitional limb when they grapple with the protean concept, multicultural education (and cognate terms such as multiracial education, multi-ethnic education, intercultural education, polytechnic education, antiracist education, and education for prejudice reduction) this is not surprising. After all, they derive from concepts which, burdened with the weight of ideological baggage in the disciples of sociology, anthropology, philosophy, psychology, and politics, fail to travel well either within or between these disciplines. The result: they remain diffuse, complex and, above all, contested terms.

Some educational researchers have admonished their peers for failing to explicate the denotative and connotative meanings of multicultural education (and its variants) when used as explanatory or analytical tools. It is easy to see why. On some occasions, terms such as multicultural, multiethnic and multiracial education are used synonymously and interchangeably. On others, particular concepts are assigned privileged status in the design, execution, and dissemination of research, but remain ill-defined.

In Britain, this debate has tended to be structured around an intensive exploration of the distinction, if any, between multicultural and antiracist education. For some writers, the distinction is more apparent than real. They argue that despite protestations to the contrary, antiracists have tended to mobilize concepts, pedagogical strategies and policy imperatives which bear more than a passing resemblance to those associated with the (discredited) multicultural education paradigm. Antiracists maintain that their conception of racism and their strategies to combat its reproduction in education differ in profound ways from those which are operationalized by advocates of multicultural education.

There are other researchers, however, in Britain and elsewhere who show their impatience with efforts to consolidate conceptual clarity. For them, such enterprises are self-indulgent; displacement activities which distract attention away from the formulation and implementation of concrete policies to mitigate racial inequality in education.

There is further complication, especially for those researchers and practitioners involved in comparative studies. This relates to the limited exportability of terms across national and cultural boundaries. In Britain, for instance, the discourse is heavily racialized with terms such as "black," "racism," and "antiracism" naturalized in the literature and associated practices. This contrasts sharply with, say, the discourse in other Western European contexts. Similarly, terms such as "immigration" and "integration" have assumed a specific denotative and connotative status in Britain which is not necessarily shared in other national contexts.

This conceptual muddle is paralleled in the debate surrounding multilingualism. There, phrases such as mother tongues, community languages, and home languages are often used interchangeably without explanation or precision.

In spite of this terminological and conceptual confusion, there is some common ground. Above all, multicultural education assumes a view of an ethnically and culturally diverse society to which the education system should respond in a positive manner. In this sense, it may be distinguished from monocultural education and its attendant ideology of assimilation. It is also generally accepted that multicultural education embraces two distinct but complementary objectives. First, meeting the particular educational needs of ethnic minority children. Second, preparing all children for life in a multicultural society.

Of particular interest is the level of articulation between these particularistic and universalistic idioms of multicultural education and their relative contribution to the realization of equality of opportunity in education. If the "multicultural society" is interpreted as social description then it could be argued that *de facto* structural assimilation offers the most fruitful route to equality of opportunity. It assumes the preeminence of a transmissionist education, primarily concerned with endorsing cultural hegemony and conserving the organization of the school, pedagogy, assessment, and curriculum accordingly.

Alternatively, the perception of the "multicultural society" in prescriptive terms demands the legitimation of cultural pluralism through transformative education. In this scenario, educational structures and experiences are reconstituted to ensure that cultural pluralist and antiracist ideals are normalized in administrative, pedagogical, curricular, and appraisal procedures. The dilemma facing educational systems in culturally diverse societies is both real and demanding. Too little allowance for diversity can lead to alienation, unrest and loss of control; too much, to fragmentation and loss of control.

Reading
Racism and Education: Research Perspectives by Barry Troyna (Open University Press, 1993) illuminates the role played by education policy and provision in the reproduction of racial inequality in education. It also considers the status and value of research in this field.
"Race" Identity and Representation in Education is edited by Warren Crichlow and Cameron McCarthy (Routledge, 1993). It is a comprehensive series of essays, drawing on contributions from the United States, UK, Canada, and Australia, who give centrality to the issue of racial inequality contexts.
Racism and Education: Structures and Strategies, Race, Culture and Difference and *Racism and Antiracism* are all published by Sage Books (1992). They provide a careful and detailed insight into the complex issues associated with this contentious theme.
Diversity and Multicultural Education by Lois Foster (Allen and Unwin, 1988) offers a sociological perspective on the evolution of this orthodoxy in Australia.
Antiracism, Culture and Social Justice in Education (Trentham Books, 1995) is edited by Morwenna Griffiths and Barry Troyna. It comprises a range of new empirical and theoretical insights into racism and antiracism in education.

See also: MULTICULTURALISM; UNDERACHIEVEMENT; WHITE FLIGHT
Barry Troyna

Emancipation

In Roman Law, *emancipare* meant literally "to transfer ownership," specifically the release of a child from paternal authority. By extension, emancipation came to mean the freeing of slaves, and, in an even broader sense, the lifting of legal restrictions on certain groups, as when we speak of the emancipation of Jews in eighteenth- and nineteenth-century Europe, of serfs in nineteenth-century Russia, or of women in twentieth-century Europe.

In the context of race relations, "emancipation" usually refers to the collective manumission of slaves in specific countries or colonial territories, especially in the Western Hemisphere. France was the first to issue an emancipation proclamation of its slaves, in 1794, but the edict was rescinded by Napoleon in 1802, and actual emancipation only took place in 1848. Britain legally abolished slavery in its empire in 1833, with a five- to seven-year transition period of "apprenticeship." Most Spanish American colonies emancipated

their slaves within a few years of achieving independence from
Spain in the 1820s. In the United States, the first Emancipation
Proclamation was issued in 1862, but it only became effective in
1865. Brazil was the last major country of the Americas to abolish
slavery in 1888, only a couple of years later than in the remaining
Spanish colonies of Cuba and Puerto Rico.

The late eighteenth century saw the rise of an abolitionist movement in Europe and America, especially in Britain, France, the
United States, and Brazil. The movement achieved its first major
success when Britain and the United States outlawed the trans-
atlantic slave trade in 1807. However, it was not until the early
1860s that the trade was effectively abolished. Rates of manumission
of individual slaves during the slavery period differed widely from
territory to territory. Some countries that were late in abolishing
slavery, such as Brazil and Cuba, had much higher rates of manumission than countries where final abolition came earlier (e.g. the
British colonies and the United States).

Whether slavery is considered extinct in the world at present is
largely a matter of definition. A number of traditional forms of
serfdom and clientage subsist in parts of Africa, Asia, and even
Latin America, which are difficult to distinguish from domestic
slavery. As for massive, chattel slavery, the Soviet and Nazi concentration camps would seem to qualify as modern revivals of slavery.

Reading
Slave and Citizen by Frank Tannenbaum (Random House, 1946) is a classic
account of differences between the slave regimes in various parts of the
Western Hemisphere.
Race and Class in Latin America edited by Magnus Mörner (Columbia
University Press, 1970) especially Part 1 on "The abolition of slavery and
its aftermath."
Slavery and Social Death by Orlando Patterson (Harvard University Press,
1982) is an impressively detailed sociological study.

See also: BRAZIL; RACE; RACISM; SLAVERY
Pierre L. van den Berghe

Empowerment
In the United States, the term "empowerment" has not been defined
specifically and analytically in the social sciences: it has been used
in different, even contradictory ways. In some discussions, it refers
to a sort of psychological liberation; that is, someone has been
"empowered" to act on his or her own behalf. In other discussions
it may refer to the capacity of individuals or a group to pursue an
economic agenda free of interference from excessive government.

This is how one conservative black Republican U.S. senatorial candidate for the state of Maryland in 1988 used the term in his campaign.

This word is not found in the Central Intelligence Agency's "World Factbook" (Quanta Press, 1990), or in the *Academic American Encyclopedia* (1991). As a descriptive term, however, empowerment has become increasingly used and popularized in discussions focusing on race and poverty. Empowerment is utilized with increasing frequency especially in policy and political circles.

The United States federal government, as have a range of public agencies at the local and state levels, have started to use this term without clearly defining it. A recent "Empowerment Task Force" was established by the White House staff of President George Bush. The U.S. Secretary of Housing and Urban Development (HUD), Jack Kemp, has utilized this term many times to describe the general strategy of the national administration in the area of urban public housing. But as far as this national administration is concerned, it seems that empowerment simply implies enabling public housing tenants to buy their housing units, thereby turning over the management of public housing to the residents.

Mack H. Jones used the word empowerment to describe the electoral victories and accomplishments of blacks in Atlanta, Georgia from the late 1960s to the mid-1970s. As used in this particular article, therefore, empowerment is a description of blacks gaining electoral office. Jones does add, furthermore, that the empowerment of the black community will not be adequate for improving living conditions due to the fact that the agenda for public policy is determined by the hierarchical relationship between white power and influence, and black political life. The major quality of this relationship is "the subordination of blacks by whites and the concomitant institutionalized belief that white domination is a function of the inherent superiority of white."

Lawrence J. Hanks uses the term empowerment as does Jones. He suggests that black political empowerment reflects three components: proportional distribution of electoral positions based on the number of blacks in the total population, development and enactment of public policies benefiting blacks, and improvement in the social and economic status of the black community (p. xi). For both Jones, and Hanks, empowerment refers primarily to the electoral victories of blacks in various settings. Thus, the black community becomes empowered as it gains electoral office.

But Jones and Hanks, however, critique this process by pointing out that merely gaining political office by blacks does not necessarily mean that public policies more favorable to black social and economic needs will be pursued. Both authors see other political and economic limitations on the potential for empowerment – as they use this term – to improve drastically the living conditions of blacks.

Roberto Villareal *et al.*, attempt a slightly different, and concrete definition of political empowerment by writing that this term refers to "an increasing capacity to win value satisfaction through the organization of aggregation of individual resources and through the skill of organizational leadership in striking mutually beneficial bargains with other participants in the coalition-building process." Like Jones and Hanks, however, Villareal *et al.* state that electoral progress must be an integral part of a group's empowerment.

I have used the term empowerment to mean specifically political mobilization aimed at challenging relationships of wealth and power in American society. The winning of electoral office by blacks or Latinos, therefore, is not enough to justify a descriptive term suggesting that a group has "empowered" itself. Though winning electoral office is one critical component of an empowering process, by itself, such victories do not guarantee that a group is capable of challenging the relationships of economic and social hierarchy that Jones described in Atlanta, Georgia.

Reading

The Struggle for Black Political Empowerment in Three Georgia Counties by Lawrence J. Hanks (University of Tennessee Press, 1987) focuses on how blacks have attempted to mobilize themselves politically in three locations in the Southern region of the United States. His study seeks to answer how political empowerment of blacks does or does not translate into public policy benefit for blacks.

Latino Empowerment by Roberto E. Villareal, N. G. Hernandez, and H. O. Neighbor (Greenwood Press, 1988) describes empowerment as the ability to successfully bargain for group demands. Such bargaining is not confined to the electoral arena. Two critical elements for empowerment of Latinos, according to these authors, are aggregation of individual and community resources and the quality of leadership.

"Black political empowerment in Atlanta: myth and reality" by Mack H. Jones (*Annals*, no. 439, September 1978) discusses black empowerment in terms of the first wave of city-level electoral victories in urban America. He uses Atlanta, Georgia, as a case study to argue that electoral victories will not be enough to significantly improve the living conditions of masses of blacks.

The Politics of Black Empowerment by James Jennings (Wayne State University Press, 1992) examines the complex political processes that neeed to be negotiated en route to black empowerment.

See also: AFRICAN AMERICANS; CONSERVATISM; POLITICS AND "RACE"; RIOTS

James Jennings

Environmental racism

This term has its origins in a 1987 report by the U.S. Commission on Racial Justice, which found a pattern of "environmental racism" in the siting of toxic waste dumps and incinerators, and concluded that most of the largest and most dangerous landfills were in communities with majority black or Latino populations. Now, it refers more generally to the various ways in which minorities fare badly in relation to the quality of the built environment; poor housing quality (and the failure to secure renovation grants), poor location, high noise and chemical pollution levels, and so on.

A key issue is residential settlement patterns: ethnic segregation is a common feature of many, perhaps most, contemporary societies; differing only in degree. This is not a problem *per se*: those sharing a common heritage may clearly wish to share residential space. But, majority and minority communities differ in the extent to which this desire can be actualized in the context of what those involved would regard as a "desirable" environment. In other words, for a variety of reasons such as those outlined at the end of the previous paragraph, minorities tend disproportionately to live in environmentally poor neighborhoods; poor, in this context, meaning neglected and decaying urban infrastructure, high pollution levels and lacking inward investment and therefore employment opportunities.

Urban policy, certainly in Britain and the United States, has tended over the past few decades to take a "color-blind" approach in dealing with these problems of urban decay. For example, a 1994 report by the U.S. Environmental Protection Agency concluded that, although ethnic minorities were likely to be more exposed to hazardous chemicals, the pattern was determined less by race than by poverty. The policy implication was that poverty in the general sense should be targeted. An exception to this was the set of guidelines prepared by the Clinton administration in 1994: this required federal agencies to make sure that their programs did not inflict an unfair degree of environmental damage on poor white or ethnic minorities.

One of the key problems in the inner urban areas relates to the levels of unfitness and disrepair in the older housing stock. In Britain in the 1960s the central policy was one of clearance, i.e. the poorest housing was razed to the ground to make way for new developments. Rex and Moore, in their seminal research on Birmingham, showed how policy decisions led to the exclusion from clearance plans of areas with large numbers of Black residents; local policy makers using the pretext that the statutory obligation to rehouse those displaced would provoke anger from white residents who did not benefit in this way. When policy moved away from clearance to renewal (in the mid-1970s), the question for researchers shifted to one of assessing the impact on minority populations of more localized investment within designated Housing Action Areas or General Improvement Areas. The investment was more likely to benefit white residents. All of these matters have significant implications for health, given the established links between poor housing and certain sources of high morbidity (and mortality) levels.

Reading
Race, Community and Conflict by John Rex and Robert Moore (Oxford University Press, 1967) spells out very clearly both how and why minority populations in Birmingham were located in areas which suffered from environmental decay.
"Renewal, regeneration and 'race': issues in urban policy" by Peter Ratcliffe appeared in *New Community* (vol. 18, no. 3, 1992) and shows how urban policy has consistently failed to improve the position of minority residents.
Environmental Health and Racial Equality (Commission for Racial Equality, London, 1994) presents a review of attempts to undermine discriminatory practices, but concludes that local authorities in Britain have in general done little to control "environmental racism."

See also: GHETTO; INSTITUTIONAL RACISM; PRUITT-IGOE; SEGREGATION
Peter Ratcliffe

Environmentalism
Environmentalist explanations of racial diversity were first developed in the eighteenth century. The Bible presented all mankind as descended from Adam and Eve. How then could differences of physical appearance have arisen? The French naturalist Buffon maintained that originally there was one species of man which, after being dispersed, changed "from the influence of climate, from the difference of food, and of the mode of living, from epidemical distempers, as also from the intermixture of individuals." The attainment of civilization depended on a society's ability to develop a social organization appropriate to its environment. The environment of tropical West Africa was seen as a particularly adverse one so that one strand in the defense of the slave trade was the belief that it provided an opportunity for Africans to attain human fulfillment

in a more favorable setting. The natural humanity of West Africans was denied neither by the slave traders nor by the contemporary books of geography. Some eighteenth-century writers assumed that the prevailing adaptation to environment had been achieved over a long period and that it was dangerous for people to migrate to a region with a different kind of environment. The implication of Voltaire's *Candide* was that it was best for people to remain and cultivate the gardens of their own country. Europeans who settled in North America were expected to degenerate, and biblical support was found for the view that God had determined the bounds of each nation's habitation (*Acts* 17: 26).

The high point of eighteenth-century environmentalism in its application to race relations was the 1787 *Essay on the Causes of the Variety of Complexion and Figure in the Human Species* by Samuel Stanhope Smith (later president of Princeton College). Smith insisted that the Bible showed all men to be of one species. There was a general association between skin color and the degree of latitude marking out a people's habitat once allowance had been made for the "elevation of the land, its vicinity to the sun, the nature of the soil, the state of cultivation, the course of winds, and many other circumstances." Color, he wrote, might well "be considered as a universal freckle." Races could not be clearly distinguished from each other and it was therefore impossible to enumerate them with any certainty. All that stood in the way of the advancement of Negroes and other peoples of non-European origin was their removal to a better environment. If Negroes "were perfectly free, enjoyed property, and were admitted to a liberal participation of the society, rank and privileges of their masters, they would change their African peculiarities much faster."

Environmentalist explanations of racial diversity were under sharp attack during the first half of the nineteenth century from writers who stressed hereditarian causes of difference. Both kinds of explanation were brought together in Darwin's theory of natural selection. With the establishment of genetics as a field of scientific research, it became possible to examine the relative importance of environmental and hereditarian explanations of particular observations. It is quite reasonable, however, to describe as environmentalists those writers who stress the relative importance of social, cultural, economic, nutritional, and similar factors in the differential performance of individuals of different socioeconomic status or different ethnic group membership when, for example, taking intelligence tests.

Reading
The Image of Africa by Philip D. Curtin (Macmillan, 1964) is a historical
study of environmentalist thought.
Mirage in the West by Durand Echevaria (Princeton University Press, 1957)
is another historical study.
White Over Black by Winthrop D. Jordan (University of North Carolina
Press, 1968) is a study of the type of thought in the U.S.A.

See also: AFRICA; DARWINISM; HEREDITARIANISM; HERITABILITY;
SOCIOBIOLOGY

Michael Banton

Equal opportunity
Originally advocated by the U.S. civil rights movement, this principle was appropriated by conservatives in the late 1970s and used
as an alternative to policies that emphasized equality of results, as
opposed to opportunities. As such, it was a perfect complement to
the conservative egalitarianism that was preeminent in the United
States and Britain through the 1980s and 1990s. The components of
equal opportunity were:

- The adequacy of the market place in the fair distribution of
  rewards appropriate to ability, innovation and endeavor.
- The need to encourage the elimination of discrimination at the
  point of entry into the job market.
- The absence of state responsibility for racism in history.
- The standardization of merit-oriented criteria in employment; as
  embodied for example, in typical equal opportunities employers'
  job advertisements ". . . encourage applications for all suitably
  qualified candidates irrespective of ethnic origin, race, sex, . . .
  etc."
- The undesirability of government interference in protecting
  groups that, for historical reasons, have been disadvantaged or
  rendered vulnerable.
- The need for only finetuning in the matters of professional expert-
  ise and job proficiency to give presently disadvantaged groups
  the skills and values necessary to be competitive in the job
  market; and correspondingly the essential soundness of present
  structural arrangements.
- The dire consequences of policies designed to improve the conditions of specific groups by favor, preferment or protection.
  Dependence on the state, it was thought, was the most likely
  result.

Equal opportunity was perfectly consonant with the ideological frameworks erected by Ronald Reagan in the United States and Margaret Thatcher in Britain in the 1980s. The appeal to market forces, absence of government in the expansion of opportunities, and the opposition to the granting of special privileges or rights made it a successful weapon with which to challenge some forms of modern liberalism. In contrast to policies that urged an active role for government in the advancement of disadvantaged groups, conservative egalitarianism emphasized laissez-faire and "supply-side" economic theory as the way to correct glaring inequities in the distribution of resources.

While the moral legitimacy of the concept has been established on both sides of the Atlantic, equal opportunity has been limited in practical results, primarily because it ensures no discrimination in appointments. Managing its implementation in promotion or transfer has proved more difficult and has lessened its potency.

Reading
Equal Opportunity Theory by Dennis E. Mithaug (Sage, 1996) addresses the discrepancy between the concept of a human right and the experience of self-determination.
Chain Reaction by Thomas and Mary Edsall (Norton 1991) contains a chapter on "Race, rights, and party choice," which examines the symmetry between equal opportunity and Republican ideologies.
Taking Sides, 7th Edition, edited by Kurt Finsterbausch and George McKenna (Dushkin 1992) has a series of arguments including one entitled "Is black self-help the solution to social equality?" in its Part Three.

See also: AFFIRMATIVE ACTION; LAW: CIVIL RIGHTS, RACE RELATIONS: MERIT

Ellis Cashmore

Ethiopianism

The expression of black nationalistic-messianic movements organized around the vision of an Africa redeemed and liberated from colonial rule. Its sources derive from nineteenth-century chiliastic Christianity, missionaries, and black nationalism and its origins lie in the sixteenth century, as Jenkins points out in his *Black Zion*: "From the first day on which an African was captured then blessed by some swaggering Portuguese cleric and consigned to a terrible Atlantic crossing, there have been two distinct Africas. There is the geographical entity with its millions of social realities, and there is the Africa of the exiled Negro's mind, an Africa compounded of centuries of waning memories and vanquished hopes translated into myth."

Jenkins notes how slaves being transported to the Americas threw themselves overboard still locked in irons in vain attempts to swim home. In the early 1830s, Samuel Sharpe, a Jamaican slave, organized a rebellion based on the belief in a messianic deliverance to Africa. Sharpe used a combination of Christian concepts, particularly the idea of "second coming," and African beliefs, to generate enthusiasm for his uprising. Before him, slave preachers from America had traveled to the West Indies to establish what was called Native Baptism, again a fusion of Christianity and African beliefs.

At the turn of the nineteenth century, Paul Cuffee, a black sea captain living in Massachusetts, attempted a migration program, but succeeded in returning only thirty-eight people to Sierra Leone. After Cuffee, the vision of a mass migration of blacks to Africa was sustained, albeit with some modifications, by various leaders, one of whom, Bishop Henry M. Turner, succeeded in settling an estimated 500 people in Liberia.

One of the most vivid expressions of Ethiopianism came in the 1920s with the Universal Negro Improvement Association (UNIA) under the leadership of Marcus Mosiah Garvey, whose slogan "Africa for the Africans" captured the philosophy of the movement. Blacks in the United States and the West Indies were implored to abandon hopes of integration into white society and turn their sights towards Africa.

Garvey adopted the national colors of Ethiopia for the UNIA and constantly referred to the Ethiopian empire as a source of inheritance and ancestry in counterposition to the imperial dominance of western powers. "We negroes believe in the God of Ethiopia," insisted Garvey. "He shall speak with the voice of thunder that shall shake the pillars of a corrupt and unjust world and once more restore Ethiopia to her former glory." Like other similar movements, the UNIA identified the whole African continent as "Ethiopia," the idea being that, in ancient times, there was just one vast nation called Ethiopia; the conquering Europeans found it expedient to split up the continent into separate countries because it facilitated domination – the "divide and rule" principle.

Elements of Ethiopianism can be found in many twentieth-century messianic movements, such as those led by Daddy Grace, Father Divine, J. Arnold Ford, and W. D. Fard, who started the movement which became today's Nation of Islam.

Perhaps the most universal manifestation of Ethiopianism is rastafari. This movement emerged in the 1930s, taking the basic ideas of the UNIA but grafting them on to an apocalyptic vision of the future in which the whites' political control of the west would be loosened and all black peoples would be returned.

In Europe the movement called *négritude* became a cultural counterpart to the more obviously political movements. This gave artistic expression to what were taken to be distinct African modes of thought. One of its leading proponents, Leopold Senghor, told his followers to attempt to rid their minds of "white" thoughts, reject white values and immerse themselves in Ethiopia, which he used synonymously with Africa.

Reading
Black Zion by David Jenkins (Wildwood Press, 1975) is a clear exposition of the various manifestations of Ethiopianism since the early slave days, showing how they are sometimes purely religious. This may be read in conjunction with *Black Exodus* by Edwin S. Redkey (Yale University Press, 1969) which covers much the same ground, but gives more emphasis to the American movements, particularly southern slave rebellions, such as Nat Turner's.
Black Nationalism by E. U. Essien-Udom (University of Chicago Press, 1962) is essentially a study of the Nation of Islam, but with interesting sections on its forerunners, such as the Moorish Science Temple of America and Father Divine's Peace Mission.
Black Messiahs and Uncle Toms, revised edition, by Wilson J. Moses (Pennsylvania State University Press, 1993) chronicles the extraordinary continuity in Ethiopianist themes among African American social and religious movements.

See also: AFROCENTRICITY; DIASPORA; GARVEY; NATION OF ISLAM; *NÉGRITUDE*; RASTAFARI; WHITENESS

Ellis Cashmore

Ethnic cleansing
See GENOCIDE

Ethnic monitoring
A method of assessing the effectiveness – or lack of effectiveness – of affirmative action, or analogous programs, by recording the ethnic background or origin of the recruits or existing personnel of an organization. Applicants or members would be asked to describe themselves according to specified criteria, a typical case being the British National Union of Journalists' application form which lists: "A – Black (Afro-Caribbean, including Black British whose forebears originate in or recently came from Guyana or an island in the West Indies). B – Black (African including Black British whose forebears originate in or recently came from Africa). C – Black (Asian, including Black British whose forebears originate in or

recently came from the Indian sub-continent). D – White (UK); or E – Irish."

Proponents of such procedures (such as the Commission for Racial Equality) argue that this is the only means of either measuring the progress of organizations in creating equal opportunities in recruitment, selection and promotion, or of exposing discrimination over periods of time. Opponents (who include personnel managers of employers and many ethnic minority groups) contend that the questions asked are, at best, impertinent and, at worst, racist in that they encourage the perpetuation of differences in areas where ethnic differences are irrelevant. There is an additional fear over the uses to which such data can be put.

Frank Reeves has called the procedure a "benign form of discursive racialization," meaning that "racial characteristics" are identified in policy, albeit for benign purposes – the elimination of racism being the primary one. This is in contrast to malevolent forms, for example when fascists delineate populations in terms of their alleged race.

Reading
The Manufacture of Disadvantage edited by Gloria Lee and Ray Loveridge (Open University Press, 1987) has many selections covering ethnic monitoring and its problems: in particular, chapters by Lee, Jenkins, and Miles.
Racism and Equal Opportunities Policies in the 1980s edited by Richard Jenkins and John Solomos (Cambridge University Press, 1987) addresses the problem of equal opportunity and methods of ensuring its maintenance.
British Racial Discourse by F. Reeves (Cambridge University Press, 1983) explores the use of racial evaluations in political discourse, suggesting that this may be overt or covert and geared to either benign or racist ends.

See also: AFFIRMATIVE ACTION; LAW: CIVIL RIGHTS; LAW: RACE RELATIONS

Barry Troyna/Ellis Cashmore

Ethnicity

The actual term derives from the Greek *ethnikos*, the adjective of *ethnos*. This refers to a people or nation. In its contemporary form, ethnic still retains this basic meaning in the sense that it describes a group possessing some degree of coherence and solidarity composed of people who are, at least latently, aware of having common origins and interests. So, an ethnic group is not a mere aggregate of people or a sector of a population, but a self-conscious collection of people united, or closely related, by shared experiences.

Those experiences are usually, but not always, ones of deprivation; for example, characterizing immigrants and their descendants. The original migrants might have left their homelands to seek improvements elsewhere or maybe they were forcibly taken from their lands, as were African slaves. Conversely, the deprived peoples might have been the natural inhabitants of lands that were invaded and then alienated from them. North American Indians and Australian Aborigines would be apposite examples of this. Whatever the circumstances, the people coming under the total or partial domination of either a hostile indigenous population or a conquering group of intruders go through experiences of deprivation. They may be materially deprived, culturally denuded, politically neutered; quite often all of these.

After they become aware of their common plight, their response may be to generate stability, support and comfort among others who undergo similar experiences. By emphasizing the features of life, past and present, they share, they define boundaries inside which they can develop their own particular customs, beliefs, and institutions – in short, their own cultures. The ethnic group, then, is a cultural phenomenon, even though it is based originally on a common perception and experience of unfavorable material circumstances.

Some have argued for the replacement of the word "race" with "ethnic group," although this argument seems to stem from a fundamental confusion. Ethnic groups do prosper in times of adversity and quite frequently there is a relationship between a group that is considered a distinct "race" by the dominant population and the group that considers itself a unified people sharing a common experience. But whereas "race" stands for the attributions of one group, ethnic group stands for the creative response of a people who feel somehow marginal to the mainstream of society. There is no necessary relationship between the two concepts, though, in actuality, there is often a strong overlap in the sense that a group labeled a race is often pushed out of the main spheres of society and made to endure deprivations; and these are precisely the conditions conducive to the growth of an ethnic group. These are the very people likely to band together to stress their unity or common identity as a way of surviving. Michael Banton has summed up the essential difference between an ethnic group and a "race": "the former reflects the positive tendencies of identification and inclusion where the latter reflects the negative tendencies of dissociation and exclusion."

Floya Anthias writes that: "A common experience of racism may act to 'ethnicize' diverse cultures, as in the case of the 'Black' category in Britain" (in "Connecting 'race' and ethnic phenomena," *Sociology*, vol. 26, 1992). Anthias goes on to point out that ethnicity can militate against, as well as promote the advancement of, political goals, in particular goals related to class and gender. "Ethnicity can be a vehicle for diverse political projects," she argues, adding that often ethnicity is antithetical to "the notion of emancipation," and supportive of gender inequalities. Her bracing argument cautions against championing ethnic pluralism as a tool in the fight against racism.

Ethnicity, then, defines the salient feature of a group that regards itself as in some sense (usually, many senses) distinct. Once the consciousness of being part of an ethnic group is created, it takes on a self-perpetuating quality and is passed from one generation to the next. Distinct languages, religious beliefs, political institutions become part of the ethnic baggage and children are reared to accept these.

The ethnicity may, of course, weaken as successive generations question the validity of the ethnic group. An example of this would be the responses of many children of South Asian migrants in the UK; the "second generation" found the cultural demands (ranging from arranged marriages to dress restrictions, etc.) excessive and in sharp contrast to the culture they were associated with when away from their families. Whereas the original migrants found the maintenance of their culture highly necessary, their sons and daughters found it irrelevant. Yet the ethnic affiliation cannot be freely dropped as if a cultural option; frequently, it is deeply embedded in the consciousness through years of socialization within the ethnic group. The ethnic boundary is difficult to break out of.

On the other hand, ethnic awareness can be actively promoted to serve immediate purposes. The development of the Chicano movement attests to this. Disparate groups of Mexicans and people of Mexican descent were made aware of their own common plight, principally through the efforts of people like César Chávez (1927–1993) who galvanized agricultural workers into a strong ethnic-based labor union. In this case, ethnicity was used quite openly as a resource to promote the feeling of "we" and "them" (the white business-owners who exploited them) in the achievement of both short-term and long-term tangible goals. The generation of this "we-ness" prompted confrontation in the form of strikes, sit-ins, boycotts, and demonstrations. The Chicano ethnicity was not a mere spontaneous rearing of a new awareness, but a deliberate manipulation of people's perceptions of their own situations. In this sense, ethnicity can be used as an instrument in the effort to achieve clearly defined ends. The Italian-American Congressman Vito Marcantonio (1902–54) successfully drew on strong ethnic support to hold him in power in the 1934–40 period and his attempted reforms included ethnic progressive programs.

In other situations, ethnicity may be, as Sandra Wallman put it, "an utter irrelevance or a crippling liability." Emphasizing or exaggerating cultural differences may not only distinguish a group from the rest of a population, but also incur the wrath of the wider society. Witness, for example, the experiences of Yosif Begun (1932–   ), one of countless Russians sentenced to Siberian exile for the "crime" of sustaining Jewish ethnicity through the teaching of Jewish language, history and culture. Western anti-Semitism still prevails, possibly sustained by the view that "Jews keep themselves to themselves . . . they like to think of themselves as superior." Despite the social mobility of Jews, their progress is still, to a degree, inhibited by such postures.

Situations such as these mean that the ethnic group is widely recognized by other nonethnics. The group has a significance quite apart from the members of the group. This does not make the group any more or less "real" in an objective sense. The whole point about ethnicity is that it is as real as people want it to be. The group may have no significance at all outside the perceptions of the group members themselves; yet it is real to them and their subjective apprehension of the group motivates them to organize their lives around it. Ranger, Samad, and Stuart favor the term "imagination of tradition" to explain how ethnicities can become "concretized" (in *Culture, Identity and Politics*, Avebury, 1996).

For instance, it might be possible to expose many of the beliefs on which the rastafari movement is based as ill-founded. Rastas themselves feel united by a common ancestry as well as current material circumstances. The bonds that hold the "brotherhood" together have their origins in a conception of an ancient Africa, united and glorious in a "golden age." The fact that many of the ideas held by rastas may be erroneous does nothing to weaken the ethnic bonds, for rastas themselves find them meaningful and structure their day-to-day lives around them. The strength of ethnicity lies at source in the subjective relevance it has for the group members.

There is a clear parallel between the rastas' ethnic response and that of black Americans in the 1960s. Previous generations of blacks had attempted to imitate the lifestyles of middle-class whites, attempted – perhaps vainly – to move physically and intellectually away from the ghetto life and all its associations with the past. Pale skin and straight hair symbolized the attempt to remove the "taint" of blackness and aspire to white standards. Young blacks in the 1960s reversed this. They plunged back into history in a search for their roots, and, to signify this, grew their hair into "Afros" and changed their names to African equivalents, at the same time declaring "black is beautiful." For the blacks themselves, they were "discovering" their past and, therefore, themselves. For others, they were creating ethnicity anew. True, they were basing that ethnicity on the conception of a common ancestry, but the way in which they reformulated it was a product of their imaginations. Thus the ethnicity was a subjective phenomenon that was lent credibility by the many thousands of members it attracted.

Ethnic growth, then, can emerge from a number of sources. It can be a defensive mechanism, as with, say Italians, who moved to America, faced antagonism and hardship and so turned in on themselves to recreate their own Italian culture in the new context. The basic characteristics of the culture were carried over and given fresh relevance. On the other hand, the Afro ethnicity of young blacks was a new construction.

Underlying these and other responses is the theme that ethnicity is basically reactive: it is elicited and shaped by the constraints and limits on opportunities imposed on the people who seek to be ethnic. Those people perceive that they are up against something and organize themselves (survive) or advance themselves (achieve). But the ethnic group is always a reaction to conditions rather than a spontaneous stirring of people who suddenly feel the urge to express themselves through the medium of a group. As stressed before, ethnicity appears as a cultural phenomenon, but it is a response to material conditions.

The "ethnic revival," as it is sometimes called, has prompted some writers, such as Nathan Glazer and Daniel Moynihan, to theorize that ethnicity has already displaced social class as the major form of cleavage in modern society. Ethnicity, they conclude, is "a more fundamental source of stratification." While it seems untenable to dismiss class as the critical factor in all forms of social conflict, there is certainly sufficient material to predict that ethnicity and ethnic conflict will be, in the future, at least as significant as class conflict. Having stated this, it would be unwise to separate the two forms, except for analytical purposes, for there is often a very intimate connection between class position and ethnic response.

Ethnic groups are more often than not fractions of the working class, an underclass that is especially vulnerable to the kinds of exploitation that capitalism is based on. This is not to suggest that ethnic groups must stay anchored in this position. The actual fact of organizing ethnically is often instrumental in furthering the interests of the members and some groups, like Irish Catholics and Jews in the United States, overcome material deprivations and aspire to elites. Quite often the ethnic impulse spills over into political realms and strong political organizations are built up to represent the ethnic groups' interests. But nearly always the group starts life from a low-class position of marginality.

To sum up: (1) ethnicity is the term used to encapsulate the various types of responses of different groups; (2) the ethnic group is based on a commonness of subjective apprehensions, whether about origins, interests or future (or a combination of these); (3) material deprivation is the most fertile condition for the growth of ethnicity; (4) the ethnic group does not have to be a "race" in the sense that it is seen by others as somehow inferior, though there is a very strong overlap and many groups that organize themselves ethnically are often regarded by others as a "race;" (5) ethnicity may be used for any number of purposes, sometimes as an overt political instrument, at other times as a simple defensive strategy in the face of adversity; (6) ethnicity may become an increasingly important line of cleavage in society, though it is never entirely unconnected with class factors.

Reading

Theories of Ethnicity: A Classical Reader edited by Werner Sollors, Henry Cabot and Anne Cabot (Macmillan, 1996) draws together a wide range of essays written on conceptual and practical facets of ethnicity.

Racialized Boundaries by Floya Anthias and Nira Yurval Davies (Routledge, 1992) extends the provocative argument that ethnicity should be properly understood as a political instrument and should not be warmly embraced as a cultural phenomenon.

Ethnic Identity: Creation, Conflict and Accommodation, 3rd edition, edited by Lola Romanucci-Ross and George de Vos (Sage, 1995) is a wide-ranging examination of ethnicity in areas such as the former Yugoslavia, the Baltic States and Sri Lanka, with the themes of language and nationalism linking the analyses.

American Mosaic edited by Young Song and Eugene Kim (Prentice Hall, 1993) is a selection of readings on North American patterns of ethnicity in history and contemporary society.

See also: CULTURE; KINSHIP; MULTICULTURALISM; PLURALISM; POLITICS AND "RACE;" RASTAFARI

Ellis Cashmore

Ethnocentrism

See PREJUDICE; XENOPHOBIA

Eugenics

A social movement originated by Francis Galton (1822–1911), the author of *Hereditary Genius*. It is currently defined as an applied science directed toward the improvement of the genetic potentialities of the human species. Its history, particularly with respect to questions of racial relations, has been punctuated by controversy.

Galton argued that mental ability was inherited differentially by individuals, groups, and races. He showed that this ability, like the physical trait of height, followed a normal curve of distribution within the population and that the relatives of outstandingly able individuals tended to be very able themselves. Galton drew on his own money to create a research fellowship, and a eugenics laboratory at University College, London, which was directed by his friend Karl Pearson. Later he bequeathed funds to endow a chair of eugenics for Pearson. A Eugenics Education Society was founded in London in 1908 and similar societies followed in many other countries.

In Darwin's theory, a race is a line of individuals of common descent. A race which transmits more of its characteristics to future generations is fitter than other races and therefore is likely to predominate over them in the future. This gives rise to the same sort of controversy as other theories (such as Marx's) which claim to predict the course of future development. Those who adopt a "naturalistic" stance contend that ethical decisions should be based on the knowledge of what is going to happen anyway. Antinaturalists insist that "what is good" and "what the future will bring" are questions requiring different kinds of answer. Their objections are expressed with humor in C. S. Lewis's "Evolutional Hymn" (reprinted in *The Oxford Book of Light Verse*). Another position is that humans are different from other forms of life in having the ability to direct the course of their future evolution. A government can enact legislation to prevent unfit persons (mental defectives, persons suffering from hereditary diseases, etc.) from having children; this is called negative eugenics. Equally, it can take action (through tax incentives, special allowances, etc.) to encourage persons considered to be of the best stock to have more children; this is called positive eugenics. The eugenics movement had a limited success when its campaign for the institutional segregation of the mentally backward led to the Mental Deficiency Act of 1913, but its political program ran into massive opposition and petered out. Genetic counseling is currently available to persons who fear that any children they might have would suffer from hereditary defects. This is not normally provided under the name of eugenics but it can be seen as an example of a eugenic measure.

Reading
"Galton's conception of race in historical perspective" by Michael Banton, pp. 170–9 in *Sir Francis Galton FRS: The Legacy of his Ideas* edited by Milo Keynes (Macmillan, 1993) examines Galton's influential ideas.
Eugenics and Politics in Britain, 1900–1914 by G. R. Searle (Woordhoff, Leyden, 1976) describes the establishment of eugenics in its social context.

See also: DARWINISM; HEREDITARIANISM; HERITABILITY; SOCIAL DARWINISM

Michael Banton

European racism

During the early 1990s, one of the key phenomena of contemporary political reality in both Western and Eastern Europe was the growth of racism and growing public debate about immigration. This trend was in West European countries as diverse as France, Germany, Austria, Belgium, and Italy. In the post-Communist societies there was a veritable flowering of racist and nationalist movements in Hungary, Romania, Poland, Czech Republic, and the components of the ex-Soviet Union. The disintegration of Yugoslavia was accompanied by organized attempts to move whole ethnic and religious groups by means of "ethnic cleansing" and terror. Given these trends it is perhaps not at all surprising that the question of racism was increasingly a subject of political concern and that many people were openly worried by the growth of neofascist political movements.

From the mid-1980s, there was mounting evidence of growing racism and hostility to migrants, with neofascist and right-wing political parties using immigration as an issue on which they could attract support. There were also numerous forms of policy and political intervention to deal with the social and economic position of minority communities. In such a sociopolitical environment, there seemed no doubt that the racist movements were an important political force across Europe.

In the context of Western Europe, two immediately conjunctural factors are often singled out as helping to shape developments. First, it is argued that developments in Eastern Europe and the former Soviet Union helped to create "fears" about the likelihood of mass immigration from the former Communist states in countries as diverse as Germany, Italy, and Austria. Second, the issue of immigration from North Africa became a key political issue in France and other societies. It is argued that political instability and demographic changes were likely to lead to pressures to migrate in the North African region as a whole and that this was likely to have a major impact on countries such as France and Italy, and hence the rest of Europe.

In Eastern Europe, the collapse of communism created a political vacuum and brought to the surface the disastrous economic situation in many countries. This resulted in massive social and economic dislocations which have highlighted the disjuncture between the expectations created by political reforms and the everyday deprivations faced by large sections of society. In this context extreme nationalist and racist movements were able to attract support by blaming minorities, such as Gypsies and Jews, for economic and social ills. In multiethnic societies such as the Czech Republic, Romania, and the former Yugoslavia, such movements were able to mobilize support by manipulating ethnic divisions and boundaries.

In both Eastern and Western Europe, there was widespread confusion in the early 1990s about the boundaries of national identity, and the role of cultural, religious, and linguistic differences. This meant that a variety of political and social movements mobilized support with the help of symbols and ideologies that reflected a resurgence of both old style and new forms of racism. The *Vlaams Blok* in Belgium and the *Front National* in France both used immigration and anti-Semitism as key symbols in their political mobilizations. In Germany, groups such as the *Republikaner* and the *Deutsche Volksunion* used a similar platform and drew support on the basis of opposition to migration from Eastern Europe. The traditional Nazi slogan of *judenfrei* was transformed into the call for Germany to become *ausländerfrei*, free of foreigners.

One of the most pernicious aspects of this renewal of racist movements was the growth of attacks on foreigners and the use of terror tactics by neofascist groups. Though much of the publicity about this phenomenon was concerned with Germany, the growth of attacks on racial and ethnic minorities was a much broader trend that affected countries across the whole of Europe. The political climate which produced a resurgence of electoral support for racist movements was accompanied by a wave of physical attacks and violence. The targets of such attacks were not only migrant groups, such as the Turks in Germany, but national minorities, such as the Gypsies in Hungary and Romania.

Apart from the proliferation of racist social movements there was an intensification of ideological and political struggle around the expression of racism that often claims not to be a racism. While many groups openly used racial symbols, others presented themselves as defenders of "national" interests and attempted to dissociate themselves from racism as an ideology of superiority of biological difference.

There is no easy model that we can use to explain the power and role of such types of racism in contemporary Europe. We need to be aware that simplistic notions of racism, or notions derived from one specific sociohistorical context, cannot be used to explain the role of racist ideologies and movements in the "New Europe." Part of the problem is that the role of the *Front National* in France and similar movements in Belgium, Germany, Austria and elsewhere needs to be contextualized against the background of developments in particular national political settings *and* trends in European societies more generally. Researchers have generally not been good at combining these two levels of analysis and ensuring that they explain as well as describe the development of new forms of racism.

But perhaps the most glaring issue that faced European societies in the 1990s was the lack of serious debate about the best ways to tackle growth of racism and the articulation of appropriate antiracist initiatives. This was certainly a difficult aspect of policy in this field, as we can see by the confused and conflicting accounts of antiracism.

It should be noted that the recent wave of attacks on migrants and minorities has also helped to mobilize a sizable response by antiracists and minority communities themselves. This has been evident in the growing mobilizations in Germany and France against the extreme right and in the attempts by minority communities to organize self-defense strategies. In the aftermath of the violent attacks on foreigners in Germany massive demonstrations organized by antiracist groups took place all over the country. These have helped to increase popular awareness of the dangers posed by the activities of the racist movements.

It is also clear that governments are under strong pressure to crack down on the more violent extreme right movements and parties. In December 1992 the German government initiated legal measures designed to curb the activities of some of the neo-Nazi groupings that had been involved in attacks on migrants and refugees. Banning orders against some groups have already been issued and other groups are likely to be banned in the near future. What is also interesting, however, is that nongovernmental bodies also began to take action. For example, the German football (soccer) federation organized all the clubs in the Bundesliga to tackle the attempts by the neo-Nazi groups to mobilize support among young football supporters.

Reading
Racism and Migration in Western Europe edited by John Wrench and John Solomos (Berg, 1993) discusses the changing forms of political debates about race and immigration.
The Age of Migration by Stephen Castles and Mark Miller (Macmillan, 1993) provides an overview of the politics of immigration in the current period.

See also: ANTI-SEMITISM; MIGRATION; NATIONALISM

John Solomos

Exploitation
This has both a narrow and a more broad usage. The narrow usage is found within Marxist writing to refer to the process by which a class of non-producers are able to live without working by extracting a surplus from a class of direct producers. This process of exploitation takes a number of different historical and structural forms. Within a feudal society, the serfs produced crops and other items both for themselves and for the various levels of the aristocracy, either by directly working the lord's land (and handing over to him all the product), or by handing over a proportion of the product from their activity on their customary land. Despite variations in the specific form that the transfer of surplus took, what characterized the process was a legal/customary constraint upon the serfs to produce directly for the dominant class.

By way of contrast, for Marxists the process of exploitation in a capitalist society is obscured by the very form that it takes. Within capitalism, the worker sells labor power for a wage to a capitalist. The capitalist uses the labor power, in combination with raw materials and machinery, etc., to produce commodities which are then sold. By virtue of the fact that the worker receives a given sum of money for every hour worked or item produced, it appears that he or she is fully rewarded for the time spent laboring for the capitalist. In fact, the value received by the worker in the form of wages is less than the value of the commodities that are produced as a result of the employment of his or her labor power. Profit originates in the difference between these two values (in the sphere of production) and not in the difference between the combined price of all the "factors of production" and the price of the product as paid by the purchaser (in the sphere of exchange).

In both these instances, exploitation is being used to refer to the extraction of surplus value at the point of production. The process is, however, not simply an "economic" one. Rather, it occurs within supporting political and ideological relations. Hence, in feudal societies, there were customary/legal definitions of the amount of time that the serf should spend laboring for the lord. And, in a capitalist society, the relationship between worker and capitalist is surrounded and linked by a wide range of legal provisions and ideological notions concerning a "just wage" and "acceptable" working conditions, etc. This integral political/ideological dimension to exploitation within Marxist analysis provides the bridge to broader and, ultimately, non-Marxist uses of the concept of exploitation.

To illustrate this point, we can take two examples, those of slave labor and contract, migrant labor. In the case of slave labor, the slave is owned as a thing by a master who receives the total product of the slave's labor, but in return for which the slave has to be provided with food, clothing, and shelter. However, the ownership of a human being as a thing requires that the human being be divested partially, or completely, of humanity. Thus, one can identify a historical, *ideological* process by which those human beings who were enslaved were defined as less than human by virtue of their condition of "heathenness" and, later, by their supposed "race." In the case of a contract, migrant worker, the entry into the society where capital employs his or her labor power in return for a wage is legally and ideologically structured in such a way that the conditions under which this exchange occurs are inferior to those applying to indigenous labor. Hence, the contract worker may have no permanent residence or voting rights.

These political and ideological processes are, in both cases, integral to the process by which a surplus product is obtained from the utilization of labor power. In other words, in Marxist analysis, they are integral to the process of exploitation. However, it is common for the notion of exploitation to be used to refer directly to these ideological and political processes in themselves, and without reference to the appropriation of surplus value. This broader usage tends to arise from theoretical perspectives that regard wage labor as a natural or acceptable form of appropriation of labor power, against which other forms are then evaluated and analyzed. Thus, in the case of slave labor, exploitation is used to refer to both the harshness of the treatment of the slave and the way in which the slave is dehumanized, as assessed relative to the "freedom" of the wage labor. And in the case of contract, migrant labor, exploitation is located in the comparative legal/political disadvantages of the worker when compared with "indigenous, free" labor.

We find parallels in the way in which writers analyze the position of New Commonwealth migrants and their children in Britain. This is judged to be the sole or primary product of racism and discrimination and therein, it is argued, lies their exploitation. In other words, racism and discrimination are forms of exploitation in and by themselves, as measured by the fact that "white" people are not the object of such experiences and processes. In this usage, exploitation loses any direct connection with production relations and comes to refer to any process by which one group is treated less equally than some other. Thus, the many ways in which men treat women, "whites" treat "blacks," and parents treat children, can all fall within the rubric of exploitation. This move towards extreme generality, and the analytical problems that it causes, is evident in the way in which the notion of exploitation is increasingly qualified by a descriptive adjective as in racial exploitation, sexual exploitation, and parental exploitation.

Reading
Capital, vol. 1, by Karl Marx (Penguin, 1976), where, in Parts 3, 4, and 5, he details his analysis of the nature of exploitation in a capitalist society through the concepts of absolute and relative surplus value.
Ethnic Minorities and Industrial Change in Europe and North America edited by Malcolm Cross (Cambridge University Press, 1992) provides comparative data on the scale of persisting exploitation of minority workers.
Racial Oppression in America by Robert Blauner (Harper & Row, 1972) is an example of an analysis which tends towards a broad utilization of the notion of exploitation.

See also: CAPITALISM; DISADVANTAGE; MARXISM AND RACISM
Robert Miles

F

Fascism

Refers to a political movement which aspires to a particular form of authoritarian class rule within a capitalist society. It emerged in Western Europe in the period after World War I, although its ideology has much deeper roots in European political action and political thought. As a form of class rule, it is characterized by an acceptance of a form of capitalism as an economic structure and process, by the elimination of all independent working-class and other political organizations and by authoritarian forms of political rule and administration. The latter is evident in the rejection of bourgeois liberal conceptions of party organization and representation in favor of the establishment of a permanent political elite, and in the establishment of a corporate state. As an ideology, it is characterized by an extreme nationalism (which commonly but not characteristically becomes racism) and an "irrationalism," which asserts that the interests of "the nation" must always predominate over all other interests. Although fascist movements have existed in all European countries since the 1920s, only in Germany, Italy, and Spain have they attained political power.

Fascist movements of the early twentieth century represented a revolt against bourgeois society and the liberal state as well as against the growing working-class political and trade union organizations. The early support for these movements came from sectors of the population excluded from both financial and political bourgeois privilege, and working-class organizations, notably petit-bourgeois, clerical and professional strata, and the peasantry. Such strata were facing extreme political pressure from "above" and "below" in a context of the major social and economic dislocation in Europe after 1918, and so any explanation must take full account of both the nature of the strata that gave support to fascism and the structural conditions that permitted fascism to become a solution. Fascism represented a solution insofar as it constituted a new route to political power and promised through national reorganization a new and radically different political and economic future. This revived support from sections of both the petit-bourgeoisie and the working class, but the political and financial support of monopoly capital became the decisive factor in ensuring the attainment of political power. The route to political power was based upon only tactical support for electoral activity, combined with paramilitary organization and activity, not only for "self-defense" but also for a coup d'état. Its vision for the future was a national state purged of all forms of internationalism (from finance capital to communism) and bourgeois privilege in which the ordinary man (and sometimes woman) would have his (and her) rightful place as a member of a national community. The explicit political subordination of women to the task of biological reproduction of the nation, with all its implications, has received particular attention in more recent analyses of fascism. It also aimed at dispensing with bourgeois parliamentarianism as a form of government, to be replaced by the rule of the fascist party which would embody all national interests.

The routes to power in Italy, Germany, and Spain differ in important ways. However, in all three cases, the support of important sections of the ruling capitalist class became crucial, both in terms of political credibility and financial support. The emphasis on national regeneration and suppression of working-class political organization promised greater economic and political rewards to sections of the dominant class, faced with economic crisis and a strong and politically conscious working class, than did bourgeois parliamentarianism. It is in this sense that fascism, once in power, is to be understood as a form of class rule.

The relationship between fascism and racism is a particularly controversial issue. It was only in Germany that racism came to play a predominant part in political ideology and strategy and this has led some commentators to conclude that a firm distinction be drawn between fascism and nazism. It is certainly the case that the fascist movement in Germany explicitly reproduced a notion of German nationalism which was biologically based and excluded the Jews as an allegedly distinct and inferior "race" which threatened biological extinction if allowed to remain. An explicit biological nationalism was not as important in Italy or Spain but it does not follow that the resulting treatment of the Jews makes German fascism a special case. Not only, in all three cases, was fascism an alternative form of class rule which guaranteed a modified capitalism, but, moreover, the historical coincidence of the generation of the ideas of "nation" and "race" as means of political mobilization in the nineteenth century means that nationalism contains within it the potential of becoming expressed by means of an explicit racism. This is not simply a matter of historical coincidence but also of the nature of nationalism per se, characterized as it is by the belief in the historical/natural existence of populations sharing a common heritage and culture which must receive expression and organization in a territorial state. The notion of natural, cultural distinctiveness can, in particular historical circumstances (given the predominance of the commonsense idea of "race"), easily come to be expressed in terms of "race."

The defeat of the fascist powers in World War II has not led to the elimination of fascist movements in Western Europe. Although the political ideology and strategy of fascism was discredited in defeat and in the discovery of the activities of nazism against the Jews and other sections of the German and other European populations, small fascist parties have been allowed to continue to exist and have, since the mid-1970s, shown signs of increasing support and activity throughout Europe. In some cases, particularly in Britain, this has been on the basis of the articulation of an explicit racism in reaction to the presence and settlement of migrant labor. But this should not be allowed to obscure the more general, common features of fascist movements, in particular their tactical support for bourgeois democracy combined with paramilitary, repressive activity of various kinds.

Reading

Fascism and Dictatorship by N. Poulantzas (New Left Books, 1974) contains a challenging and influential re-interpretation of fascism from a Marxist perspective.

Fascism: A History by Roger Eatwell (Chatto, 1995) is a wide-ranging survey that provides a general history of fascism; it is complemented by *Fascism* edited by Roger Griffin (Oxford University Press, 1995) which offers more than 200 extracts on fascism written by its precursors, practitioners, and critics, including one by the nineteenth-century composer Richard Wagner. Both books argue that fascism constituted a serious intellectual alternative to socialist or liberal progress.

See also: BRITISH MOVEMENT; EUROPEAN RACISM; NATIONALISM

Robert Miles

Freire, Paulo (1921–   )

A Brazilian educator and philosopher, Freire is best-known for his work on critical literacy which was first articulated in his landmark volume, *Pedagogy of the Oppressed* (first published in English in 1970). In this book, Freire developed a revolutionary pedagogy for liberation, arguing that the act of reading is a politically transformative event. In the ensuing years and up to the present, Freirean literacy programs designed for both developing and postindustrial countries around the world have attempted to free the oppressed from the powerlessness resulting from illiteracy and pre-critical literateness under the system of "banking education" where subjects are regarded as passive "receptacles" of information.

For Freire, the act of reading is simultaneously an act of reading the world. In other words, subjects exist *with* the world rather than merely living in it. Thus, one of his central ideas is that humans come to know the world as beings-for-themselves-and-others and have the capacity to transform concrete everyday lives and the lives of others. Through critical literacy, people read both the word and the world, and consequently become critically empowered to make their own history.

An important concept in Freire's writings is that of *reflection*. By critically interrogating the objective reality in which individuals and groups find themselves, people become reflectively aware of the relations that oppress and dehumanize them. Reflection is a necessary but not sufficient act of liberation: pure introspection results in what Freire calls "verbalism," while acting, when unaccompanied by critical reflection, degrades into mere "activism." Together, critical reflection and action create what Freire refers to as *praxis* (theory linked with practice).

Praxis is accomplished partly by acting with others in order to collectively transform the material conditions of existence. As such, Freire's pedagogy is *dialogical* and establishes the conditions of learning an act of knowing between subjects. The goal of this act of knowing (dialogical communication) is freedom from oppressive material and social conditions. Becoming literate is not just a cognitive process of decoding signs, but requires living one's life in relation to others. Friere's (essentially phenomenological) literacy method invites learners to examine the concrete lived conditions of their existence. Such conditions come to be understood as social, political, and economic "codifications" through which everyday reality for the oppressed has become naturalized and made into an inevitable and presumably inescapable part of their situation.

Further, these codifications are made into a "knowable object" by the oppressed through a process of "decodification" in which the codified totality is broken down and "retotalized' through a form of ideology critique. Freire's goal is to create *epistemic shifts* in the consciousness of the oppressed through a focus on "action-object wholes" and "forms of orientation in the world" that eventually leads to concrete goals, strategies, and programs. In other words, such epistemic shifts lead to the creation among the disenfranchised of political subject positions and forms of collective subjectivity. In this way, Freire's literacy method enables the disenfranchised to alter their structural condition in Brazilian society through challenging the coercive power relationships of the dominant social order that support the privileging hierarchies of race, class, and gender.

In this conception, reading is already social. In order to liberate oneself and others from the kind of dehumanization experienced by subordinated groups under colonialism, subjects must criticize their lived context, or "limit situations." True dialogue among subjects is realized when they speak to one another as authentic human beings, as subjects free from oppression.

Reading
Pedagogy of the Oppressed (Continuum Press, 1970) is Freire's influential text and may fruitfully be read in conjunction with *Pedagogy of Hope* (Continuum Press, 1994).

See also: BRAZIL; EDUCATION AND CULTURAL DIVERSITY

Peter McLaren/Zeus Leonardo

Freyre, Gilberto (1900–87)

Brazilian social anthropologist and member of the Brazilian parliament (1946–50), Freyre is best-known for his work, *The Masters and the Slaves* (first pub. 1933), a detailed analysis of plantation society which re-established the positive contribution of Africans in shaping Brazilian character and culture. The book punctured the myth of a cordial Brazilian democracy, or melting-pot culture, where ethnic groups and classes had dissolved racism and prejudices.

Sexual contact between white masters and black slaves was the key to Freyre's concepts of racial informality and flexibility: the mulatto offspring was considered the symbol of racial democracy, transcending class barriers and integrating cultures and ethnic identities – an idea expressed as *mesticismo*. But, Freyre argued, the democracy always assured the supremacy of white European culture as the goal towards which the process of integration was to advance. The vision of a "meta-race" of brown Brazilians only camouflaged the location of class power and domination.

Mass migration and the proletarianization of Brazil in the twentieth century brought a sharpening of class conflict and an end to traditional sexual intimacy, which was a legacy of the oppressive patriarchal relations of plantation economies. Freyre was jailed in the reign of Getúlio Vargas before World War II.

Reading
The Masters and the Slaves by Freyre (Knopf, 1964) is the influential text.

See also: BRAZIL; CONQUEST; CREOLE; FREIRE; WHITENESS

Ellis Cashmore

G

Gandhi, Mohandas Karamchand (1869–1948)

Leader of the Indian nationalist movement which successfully repelled British colonial rule, Gandhi was born in Porbandar on the western coast of India and had an arranged marriage in the customary Hindu way at the age of thirteen. His wife Kasturbai was his lifelong supporter. At nineteen, he went to England to study law and graduated as a barrister before returning to India in 1891. There his lack of self-confidence led him to accept a post in South Africa, where he felt professional demands were less stringent.

It was in South Africa that he first encountered racialism, a pivotal experience being when he was ejected from a Pretoria-bound train despite holding a first-class ticket – Indians were allowed only in third-class compartments. His ejection was based solely on his color. After this, he committed himself to campaigning for the rights of Indians in South Africa through the vehicle of the Natal Indian Congress, formed in 1894.

To attain his objectives, Gandhi came to formulate his central method of nonviolent civil disobedience, or passive resistance, which later became known as *Satyagraha*, meaning "truth force"; for example, whenever he or his followers were beaten or imprisoned, there would be no retaliation, only a refusal to comply with others' demands. In the years that followed, the method was adopted by movements the world over, particularly by Martin Luther King's Southern Christian Leadership Conference.

During his twenty-one-year stay in South Africa, he edited an influential publication, *Indian Opinion*, which was distributed throughout South Africa. He became internationally renowned for his campaigns. His intermittent imprisonments served only to elevate his status. During the Anglo–Boer War, 1899–1902, Gandhi organized an ambulance corps in support of the British government. At this stage, he believed in the virtues of British colonial rule. The reversal of this opinion was to feature centrally in his subsequent operations in south Asia. After the war, the civil disobedience continued, culminating in a massive protest march in 1913 which resulted in the granting of many of Gandhi's demands for Indians.

His growing reputation in South Africa was constantly relayed to

India, thus producing an invitation by the Indian National Congress (INC) for him to return to India to help his own country win *swaraj*, that is self-rule. He took up the invitation in 1915, taking over the unofficial leadership by 1921. The INC was formed in 1885 mainly as a liberal middle-class movement dedicated to reviving interest in traditional Indian culture; it later developed a political edge when it campaigned for greater freedom from British political control. Gandhi was responsible for transforming the INC from a more or less elitist organization into a mass movement with the support of the Muslim League and other smaller movements. Instead of constitutional lobbying, the INC opted for mass direct action in the form of nonviolent civil disobedience.

Gandhi was able to unify and mobilize the movement to such measures because his leadership was premised on charisma; in Gandhi, Indians saw not only a leader, but a person endowed with supernatural powers. This he acknowledged: "Men say I am a saint losing myself in politics. The fact is I am a politician trying my hardest to be a saint." He came as a messiah, bringing images of sainthood with his severe dietary restrictions, his vows of celibacy, his insistence on wearing only homespun *khaddar* and his utopian vision of an independent, agrarian India freed of the modern science and technology, which, he argued, were instruments of Western domination.

At the outbreak of World War I, at Gandhi's insistence, India offered support to Britain in anticipation of a stronger elected element in government led by the Indian National Congress and the Muslim League. This was provided in the Montagu-Chelmsford Reforms of 1919, but was insufficient to stem the tide of postwar dissatisfaction. The British government, in its concern for the maintenance of order, passed the Rowlatt Acts, which gave the government greater powers to punish Indian dissidents.

Gandhi implemented a massive campaign of civil disobedience and urged his followers to withdraw from all schools and government positions. Whenever violence erupted, Gandhi embarked on extended fasts as if to blackmail his followers into ceasing their violence. This invariably succeeded. One such incident was when nearly two thousand villagers burned alive twenty-one Indian policemen in their station in Chaura Chaura in the United Provinces in February 1922.

One of the nonviolent protests against the reforms of 1919 turned into an atrocity when General Dyer ordered British troops to fire on a crowd of unarmed Indians at Amritsar, the result being 379 people killed and 1,137 injured. General Dyer himself said, after the massacre: "It was no longer a question of merely dispersing the crowd, but one of producing a sufficient moral effect. My intention was to inflict a lesson that would have an impact throughout all India."

During the events leading to the Amritsar incident, Gandhi's attitude toward the British colonialists changed completely: he became convinced that "the British government today represents satanism." This change led him into alignment with some factions of the INC who were strongly anti-British, and served to win him the leadership of the organization.

There were three decades of turmoil in India before the country won its independence from the British in 1947. Although Gandhi's influence was in decline in the years immediately preceding independence, it was his charismatic leadership which gave the Nationalist movement its impetus on a mass basis, for which he became known as the *Mahatma*, "the great soul." In 1948, he was assassinated by a Hindu extremist.

Martin Luther King acknowledged Gandhi as his inspiration and used the INC as the model for his own movement. King, like Gandhi, demanded great, almost inhuman self-discipline of his followers in restraining themselves when subjected to violence. As Gandhi strove to acquire independence and equality for Indians, King strove for freedom and equality for black Americans.

Reading
M. K. Gandhi: An Autobiography (Penguin, 1982) is the Mahatma's own account of his experiences and philosophy translated from the original Gujerati.
Gandhi's Political Philosophy by Bhiku Parekh (University of Notre Dame Press, 1989) is a scholarly attempt to systematize the leader's thoughts.
Gandhi: Prisoner of Hope by Judith Brown (Yale University Press, 1989) sets Gandhi in historical, colonial context.

See also: CHÁVEZ; CIVIL RIGHTS MOVEMENT; POWER; SMUTS

Gita Jairaj

Garvey, Marcus (1887–1940)

One of the enduringly influential black leaders of this century. His actual achievements do not compare with those of King, Washington, or even Du Bois, but his general thrust to elevate black people by forcing them to recognize their African ancestry was to have a lasting impact.

Born in Jamaica, Garvey traveled throughout the Caribbean and Central America before starting his organization in the United

States. His Universal Negro Improvement Association (UNIA) went strongly against the grain of other black American movements. As his biographer E. David Cronon puts it: "Garvey sought to raise high the walls of racial nationalism at a time when most thoughtful men were seeking to tear down these barriers." Whereas leaders such as W. E. B. Du Bois and his National Association for the Advancement of Colored People (NAACP) were campaigning for the greater integration of blacks and whites (principally through legislation), Garvey declared integration impossible and implored his followers to make a sharp break with whites. His simple aim was to restore all blacks to what he considered their rightful "fatherland," Africa. "If you cannot live alongside the white man, even though you are his fellow citizen; if he claims that you are not entitled to this chance or opportunity because the country is his by force of numbers, then find a country of your own and rise to the highest position within that country," was Garvey's message and he summed it up in his slogan, "Africa for the Africans."

To show that this was no empty slogan, Garvey made efforts to realize his ambition by buying a steamship line, called "Black Star," and even entered into what were ultimately abortive negotiations with the Liberian government to make possible a mass migration. Garvey, at the peak of his popularity, claimed four million followers all willing to forsake America and migrate to Africa to start a new life as what Garvey called "The New Negro."

This concept of the New Negro was pivotal in Garvey's movement. Blacks were told to rid themselves of any notions of inferiority and cultivate a new sense of identity; they were urged to take pride and dignity in the fact that they were truly Africans. Their subordination was the result of whites' attempts to control them not only physically, but mentally too. One method used by whites was religious instruction: blacks were taught to believe in conventional Christianity and worship whites' images. But Garvey augmented his UNIA with a new, alternative religious movement called the African Orthodox Church. Its leader, George Alexander McGuire, instructed UNIA members to tear up pictures of white Christs and Madonnas and replace them with black versions. Garvey explained: "Our God has no colour, yet it is human to see everything through one's own spectacles, and since white people have seen their God through white spectacles we have only now started to see our own God through our own spectacles."

Often, Garvey would fuse his practical policies with biblical imagery, sometimes hinting at the inevitability of the exodus to Africa:

"We have gradually won our way back into the confidence of the God of Africa, and he shall speak with the voice of thunder that shall shake the pillars of a corrupt and unjust world and once more restore Ethiopia to her ancient glory." Messages like this and continual reference to Ethiopian royalty helped generate the kind of interest that eventually turned into the Rastafarian movement, members of which even today regard Garvey as a prophet.

At a time when black organizations, particularly in the United States, were assiduously trying to implement gradual integrationist policies, Garvey's program was an outrage. He was vigorously condemned by Du Bois *et al.* and there were assassination attempts. Further notoriety came when Garvey entered into negotiations with the Ku Klux Klan; in a bizarre way, both harbored the same ideal: the removal of blacks.

Throughout the 1920s, Garvey's influence spread in the United States and in the Caribbean and he cultivated a mass following. The steamship line failed and negotiations for a migration to Africa broke down, so his following eventually faded. A spell in Jamaican politics ended after a series of clashes with the law and Garvey left for England where he died in 1940.

Yet his influence amongst blacks continued; as his wife was to express it, "Garvey instilled in them *new concepts* of their rightful place on earth as God's creation." Garvey had instigated what he called "a second emancipation – an emancipation of the minds and thoughts." He identified the evil not so much in whites who controlled blacks, but in the minds of blacks themselves: they accepted their own inferiority and so failed to recognize their own potential. Garvey provided a blueprint for banishing the sense of inferiority with his conception of the New Negro. Even in the 1990s, Garvey is revered by a great many blacks as one of the most important leaders not in terms of practical achievements, but in terms of transforming consciousness.

Reading

Philosophy and Opinions, 3 vols, by Marcus Garvey (Cass, 1967), is a collection of speeches and essays edited by Garvey's wife Amy Jacques Garvey; the best account of the complex, sometimes contradictory, patterns of Garvey's thought.

Black Moses by E. David Cronon (University of Wisconsin Press, 1974) is a well-researched biography of the man and his movement with attention given to the social contexts of the times.

Marcus Garvey: Anti-Colonial Champion by Rupert Lewis (Africa World Press, 1988) is an appreciation of Garvey's contribution.

See also: BLACK POWER; ETHIOPIANISM; NATION OF ISLAM; RASTAFARI

Ellis Cashmore

Genocide

The term *genocide* is of recent derivation; etymologically, it combines the Greek for group, tribe – *genos*, with the Latin for killing – *cide*. In 1933, at a time when neither the extensiveness nor character of the barbarous practices carried out under the auspices of the Third Reich could have been envisaged, the jurist Raphael Lemkin submitted to the International Conference for Unification of Criminal Law a proposal to declare the destruction of racial, religious, or social collectivities a crime in international law. In 1944 he published a monograph, *Axis Rule in Occupied Europe*, in which he detailed the exterminatory and other practices and policies pursued by the Third Reich and its allies. He went on to argue the case for the International regulation of the "practice of extermination of nations and ethnic groups," a practice which he referred to now as *genocide*. Lemkin was also instrumental in lobbying United Nations officials and representatives to secure the passage of a resolution by the General Assembly affirming that "genocide is a crime under international law which the civilized world condemns, and for the commission of which principals and accomplices are punishable." The matter was referred for consideration to the UN Economic and Social Council, their deliberations culminating with the signing of the 1948 United Nations Convention on Genocide (UNCG).

The starting point of most discussions of genocide is with the definition of the term under Article II of the UNCG:

In the present Convention, genocide means *any* of the following acts committed *with intent* to destroy, *in whole or in part*, a national, ethnical (*sic*), racial or religious group as such.

(a) Killing members of the group;
(b) Causing serious bodily or mental harm to members of the group;
(c) Deliberately inflicting on the group conditions of life calculated to bring about its physical destruction in whole or in part;
(d) Imposing measures intended to prevent births within the group;
(e) Forcibly transferring children of the group to another group.

I have placed in emphasis those parts of this Article which have been interpreted by others, particularly lawyers, human rights organizations, social scientists, and functionaries operating in international organizations, as being especially difficult of interpretation and/or application.

Experts, both academic and nonacademic, rarely agree that a specific complex of behaviors merits the designation *genocide*. The reasons for this are threefold. First, like any other legal instrument, it was the outcome of negotiations between parties that held conflicting views as to the appositeness of its constituent parts. Although Article IX allows for disputes between parties to be adjudicated by the International Court of Justice, for obvious reasons this has never occurred; consequently, there is no body of case law to clarify its parameters. Second, as the term was evolved to single out a particularly reprehensible complex of behaviors which have been the object of universal condemnation, the term has acquired a very high moral loading. This gives rise to an unedifying competitiveness to designate specific instances of behavior, usually involving mass killings, as genocidal in order to claim the moral high ground. This practice is not confined to politicians, media commentators, writers, perpetrators or victims, but is one which some academics have been prone to as well.

Thirdly, it is quite apparent that the "ideal-typical" genocidal complex which Lemkin had in mind was the destruction of European Jewry. The destruction of European Jewry was quite clearly also uppermost in the minds of those who drafted and negotiated the UNCG. It unequivocally falls under the terms of Article II, and subclauses (a) to (d). Precisely because this particular case was so important in the genesis of the term, and its normative specification in the UNCG, its application to other situations has been problematic. Although the massacre of Armenians by the Turks during World War I, the slaughter of the Ibo during the Nigerian Civil War, and the death by starvation of the Kulaks in the 1930s in the Ukraine, to mention only a few "genocidal-type" examples, share some elements with the destruction of European Jewry, there are also important differences which make their subsumption under Article II problematic. Some of these difficulties arise because Lemkin was insufficiently rigorous in codifying the behaviors he wished to see outlawed. Although his focus was on "extermination" of nations and ethnic groups, he illustrated what he meant by genocide by reference to such policies as the "destruction of institutions of self-government and imposing a German pattern of administration," "by substituting vocational education for education in the

liberal arts," or "shifting wealth to Germans." Some of these policies are only tangentially related to "extermination."

The intimate cognitive linkage between the concept genocide and
the fate of European Jewry during the Nazi era, accounts also
for the conceptual connection between the concepts genocide and
holocaust. However, whereas the origins of the term genocide are
associated with the fate of other European peoples during the same
period, the concept holocaust in its early usage in connection with
these matters was tied uniquely to that of Nazi-occupied Europe's
Jewish population.

The term holocaust is biblical in origin, referring to a sacrificial
offering "wholly consumed by fire in exaltation of God" (from the
Greek *holos*, whole, and *kauston*, burnt). In the context of the
policies directed, first at German Jews, and later the Jews of all
those countries occupied by the Third Reich in the years 1938–45,
the term holocaust is specifically employed to refer to the physical
liquidation of European Jews under German control, a policy
referred to as *die Endlösung*, or *Final Solution* of the Jewish question. The program of routinized, assembly line killings of Jews in
specially constructed extermination centers, the most well known
and notorious of these being Auschwitz, Treblinka, Majdanek, and
Sobibor, is what is implicitly or explicitly referred to when employing the term Holocaust, a concept many writers capitalize when
used in this context.

A significant number of authorities also employ the term more
broadly to designate the wide range of policies specifically targeted
on Jews which were applied by the authorities of the Third Reich,
not merely those evolved to secure their physical destruction. From
1933 onward, many laws and regulations were passed which impacted on the whole way of life of German Jews. Similar laws were
introduced in countries under German occupation. Many Jews died
in the ghettos of malnutrition and associated diseases, on route to
the ghettos, concentration camps and extermination centers, and at
the hands of the special action groups, *Einsatzgruppen*, which operated in the occupied areas of the U.S.S.R.

The term Holocaust has gradually been applied more diffusely,
to designate massive programs of physical destruction which have
befallen people other than Europe's interwar Jews. The most obvious reason for this being that genocidal programs were applied to
other groups during the same period in the same geographical
region. As many Polish Christians were victims of Nazism as Polish
Jews. Gypsies were exterminated in Auschwitz as well. Millions of

non-Jewish citizens of the U.S.S.R. were liquidated systematically after the German invasion. Seventy thousand German citizens who were physically or mentally handicapped were victims of the To or euthanasia program. When other peoples' experiences come to be identified with policies similar to those which it is believed were applied to European Jews, it follows that the terminology used to conceptualize it will merge. Consequently the terms genocide and holocaust have been applied very widely.

The inevitable consequence is that for purposes of comparative study neither term has been sufficiently analytically pure to further the development of useful theoretical perspectives. Instead of discussing the substantive characteristics, causal complexes, and consequences associated with all the too common occurrences of mass killings, academics have spent much time on definitional quibbles. Definitions proliferate but understanding advances little. As each expert proffers an alternative/modified definition, comparisons of findings and explanations become unproductive.

In nonacademic usage both terms are applied to subsume a vast range of phenomena and case studies. Virtually every large scale massacre is referred to as a holocaust, including the demise of red squirrels in Britain. The term genocide is also often used profligately. Its most recent, partially justified, attributions have been in connection with the civil conflicts in the former Yugoslavia and Rwanda. Even in these cases, however, the employment of the term genocide by scholars betrays a lack of understanding of the origins or meaning of the concept.

The brutal civil war in the former Yugoslavia has been accompanied by widespread massacres, rapes, and forcible evacuations and deportations. The policy of forcible evacuation, more commonly referred to as ethnic cleansing, led, at its peak, to more than two million refugees in various European countries, and a massive redistribution of the population in terms of its demographic characteristics relative to geographical location. Massive movements of population resulting from civil wars and international conflicts, are not, of course, a new phenomenon, in either Europe or elsewhere. The Versailles Treaty at the conclusion of the First World War led to the redistribution of population groups in Eastern/Central Europe, as did Stalin's nationalities policies. Successive Israeli administrations have overseen the ethnic cleansing of Arab populations following the 1948 War of Independence, and the June War of 1967. Idi Amin "cleansed" Uganda of its Asians during the 1960s.

There was nothing new about "ethnic cleansing" in the former

Yugoslavia. All forced migrations are invariably accompanied by tragic violence and brutality. The perception of there being something "special" about what transpired in Bosnia-Herzegovina arose from its evocation of only partially submerged cultural memories. Although the concepts genocide and holocaust are, like most social science concepts, amorphous they, nonetheless, resonate always with a particular configuration of events, events which Lemkin sought to subsume under the concept genocide, and which witnesses to the fate of Europe's Jews designated as a Holocaust.

Reading
The Holocaust: The Jewish Tragedy by Martin Gilbert (Collins, 1986) is comprehensively descriptive and may be read in conjunction with *Why Did the Heavens Not Darken*, by Arno J. Mayer (Verso, 1990) which is both insightful and controversial.
The History and Sociology of Genocide: Analyses and Case Studies edited by F. Chalk and J. Jonassohn (Yale University Press, 1990) is a theoretical introduction with useful case studies and complements Gill Elliott's *Twentieth Century Book of the Dead* (Allen Lane, 1972).
Ordinary Men: Reserve Battalion 101 and the Final Solution in Poland by C. R. Browning (Harper Perennial, 1993) is a masterpiece.

See also: ANTI-SEMITISM; FASCISM; ROMA; UNESCO

Stuart D. Stein

Genotype

The underlying genetic constitution of an organism in respect of a particular trait or traits, as opposed to the phenotype or appearance of that organism. All people with brown eyes have the same phenotype in respect of eye color, yet some of them may carry a recessive gene for blue eyes and therefore have a different genotype. For predicting inheritance, it is the genotype that is important.

Genes control enzymes and in that way control the nature of physical characteristics. They are located on chromosomes and since all chromosomes exist in pairs, so do genes. The two members of a gene pair may be either identical or different. A person who carries blue-eye genes on both chromosomes is said to be homozygous for that characteristic; someone with a blue-eye gene on one chromosome and a brown-eye gene on the other is heterozygous in that respect. If a man who is homozygous for brown eyes and a woman who is homozygous for brown eyes have children they will all be brown-eyed. If a man who is homozygous for blue eyes has children with a woman who is homozygous for brown eyes the outcome is more complicated. Every egg cell the mother produces will contain one brown-eye gene; every sperm cell the father produces will contain one blue-eye gene. No matter which sperm fertilizes which egg, the fertilized ovum will be heterozygous, containing one blue-eye and one brown-eye gene. Each child will be brown-eyed since the brown-eye gene forms more of the chemical (tyrosinase) that colors the eye; it is therefore said to be dominant, whereas the blue-eye gene is recessive; although it is part of the genotype it cannot be seen in the phenotype.

If the father and mother are both heterozygous with respect to blue and brown-eye genes, they will form sperm and egg cells with one blue and one brown-eye gene. When these cells interact, three combinations are possible for the ovum: two brown-eye genes; one gene of each; two blue-eye genes. Since the one of each combination is twice as likely as either of the others, and since the brown-eye gene is dominant, the probability is that of four children three will have brown eyes and one blue.

This example oversimplifies the inheritance of eye color because, as everyone can see, there are eyes of other colors than blue and brown. Possibly other genes at other places in the chromosomes or other kinds of eye-color genes are involved in the production of the relevant chemicals, but the example serves to clarify the differences between phenotype and genotype. It also illustrates Mendel's laws: first, that inheritance is particulate, resulting from the interrelation of distinctive genes rather than from the blending of hereditary elements to produce a mixed character; and, second, that characters are independently inherited, so that a child's inheritance of his or her father's eye color does not indicate the likelihood of the inheritance of his or her father's hair or skin color.

Reading
The Race Concept by Jonathan Harwood and Michael Banton (David & Charles, 1975) examines the often confused theorizing over "race."

See also: HERITABILITY; PHENOTYPE; RACE

Michael Banton

Ghetto

The congregation of particular groups who share common and ethnic cultural characteristics in specific sectors of the city often takes the form of a segregated area and is described as a ghetto. The concept, ghetto, however, is notoriously imprecise and, in popular usage, it has assumed pejorative connotations. Areas such as Bel-Air in Los Angeles, Hampstead in London, and Solihull in the English city of Birmingham, are rarely considered as urban ghettos despite their homogeneous nature: after all, their residents are overwhelmingly white and upper-middle-class. In contrast, areas in those cities such as Watts, Brixton, and Sparkbrook – which contain relatively large black populations – are frequently characterized as ghettos. Clearly then, the term, ghetto, is not simply a descriptive term which refers to areas of ethnic and cultural homogeneity. It has highly potent connotations, symbolizing all that is negative about city life: high crime rates, pollution, noise, poor quality housing, bad sanitation, and so on.

On the whole, most commentators agree that, technically, a ghetto should comprise a high degree of homogeneity, all residents sharing similar backgrounds, beliefs, and so on. They should also be living amid poverty, in relation to the rest of the city's population. By these two criteria, then, New York's Harlem and the Watts district in Los Angeles can be defined legitimately as ghettos. In Britain, however, the term, ghetto, is wholly inappropriate even to areas such as Brixton, Notting Hill, and Sparkbrook. Despite the concentration of colonial migrants and their descendants in these and other districts within the major urban centers of Britain, they are nowhere approaching all-black areas. On the contrary, whites continue to constitute the majority of residents in these areas, with the presence of blacks and South Asians largely confined to a few streets. But, despite its technical inappropriateness, the term, ghetto, continues to be popularly applied to these areas. In short, "ghetto" is emotive and racist in its connotation.

The origins of the term, ghetto, can be traced back to Europe in the Middle Ages when it described how Jews voluntarily established corporate areas within the city, largely for protective purposes. The voluntaristic nature or otherwise of the "ghettoization" process, however, is a contentious issue. Some writers adopt a "choice" model of interpretation in which they focus on the attitudes and behaviors of ghetto residents themselves. Those who put forward the "constraint" theory tend, in contrast, to adopt a broader perspective, which engages more directly with social and political processes. In other words, theirs is a more deterministic account of ghetto formation. Not surprisingly, these different interpretations of the process lead to contrasting appraisals of their function. Louis Wirth, for instance, presented a romantic version of ghetto life in Chicago in the 1920s, in which he stressed its voluntaristic nature, and hence, its positive community features. On the other hand, Robert Blauner saw ghettos as an "expression of colonized status" and a means by which the white majority is able to prevent blacks dispersing and spreading discontent. He argued that black ghettos in America are controlled by white administrators, educators, and police who live outside the ghetto but in effect administer its day-to-day affairs. In other words, they exert "direct rule" over the black communities, a relationship which Blauner termed internal colonialism. Under this system, blacks in the ghetto are subject people, controlled from outside: the "burn, baby, burn" episodes of the 1960s, therefore, represented an attempt by the ghetto dwellers "to stake out a sphere of control by moving against (U.S.) society and destroying the symbols of its oppression."

In Britain, a similar debate surrounds the pattern of ethnic segregation in the cities: some writers stress the discriminatory practices of the housing market as the determinant of migrant residence; others insist that clustering is actively sought by the migrants and occurs independently of such discriminatory practices.

All in all, then, the term, ghetto, tends to lack conceptual clarity and provides limited analytical precision. While its connotative powers continue to remain intact, its value as a social scientific concept is limited.

Reading
The Ghetto by Louis Wirth (Chicago University Press, 1928) is an account of ghetto life in Chicago in the 1920s by a student and colleague of Robert Park, co-developer of the "urban ecology" theory.

Racial Oppression in America by Robert Blauner (Harper and Row, 1972) presents the theory of internal colonialism among a number of other essays designed to reveal the inadequacy of existing theoretical analyses of American race relations.

The Politics of Race and Residence by Susan Smith (Polity, 1989) looks at the processes behind spatial concentration and segregation in the contemporary city.

The Ghetto and the Underclass by John Rex (Gower, 1988) is a series of essays on "race" and social policy. Although Rex refers on occasion to ghettos and the process of ghettoization he does not provide a clear-cut definition of the terms.

Racism, the City and the State edited by Malcolm Cross and Michael Keith (Routledge, 1993) explores the relationship between racism, the city and the state by addressing urban social theory, contemporary cultural change and racial subordination.

See also: DISPERSAL; INTERNAL COLONIALISM; KERNER REPORT

Barry Troyna

Gobineau, Joseph Arthur de (1816–82)

A Frenchman born into a bourgeois family with aristocratic pretensions, who claimed the title "Count." Educated in German as well as in French, Gobineau earned a living from journalism until 1849, after which he obtained a succession of diplomatic appointments up to 1877. It would seem that in the Paris salons Gobineau obtained an acquaintance with contemporary anthropological speculations, notably with those of Victor Courtet de l'Isle, author of *La Science politique fondée sur la science de l'homme*. These were important to his four-volume *Essay on the Inequality of Human Races*, the first two volumes of which appeared in 1853 and the last two in 1855. The question of racial inequality receives little attention in Gobineau's remaining writings (which included twenty-six other books).

Some sections of the *Essay* are unequivocal in asserting a philosophy of racial determinism, but there are ambiguities and inconsistencies, so that different commentators emphasize different themes of the work. If anything can be seen as the book's central problem, it is probably the assertion that "the great human civilizations are but ten in number and all of them have been produced upon the initiative of the white race" (including, apparently, those of the Aztecs and the Incas, though their civilizations are never examined). What explains the rise and fall of civilizations? Alongside this problem, and at times overshadowing it, is the author's desire to lament the breakdown of the old social order and to insist that the process of degeneration has advanced so far as to be irreversible. To answer the historical question Gobineau contends that races differ in their relative worth; and that "the question on which the argument here turns is that of the permanence of type." Whereas the whites are superior in intellect they are inferior in the intensity of their sensations so that "a light admixture from the black species develops intelligence in the white race, in that it turns it towards imagination." Mixtures of blood seem to be necessary to the birth of civilizations but mixtures, once started, get out of control and the "historical chemistry" is upset. Thus there is a subsidiary theme in the book which stresses the complementarity of races as well as their hierarchical ordering. Logically there is no reason why the inability of racial types to lose their fundamental physical and moral characteristics, plus the idea that "ethnic workshops" can be built to diffuse a civilization, should not lead to the birth of an eleventh. The prophecy of decline ("what is truly sad is not death itself but the certainty of our meeting it as degraded beings") therefore has its origin not in Gobineau's borrowed anthropology but in his personal pessimism.

One message that the book conveyed is the impotence of politics: nothing that men do can now affect the inevitable outcome. Nor does it lend support to nationalism, since Gobineau's "German" and "Aryan" are not to be equated with *die Deutsche* but include the Frankish element among the French population. The country which has best preserved Germanic usages and is "the last centre of Germanic influence" is England, though in some degree the leadership of Aryan-Germanism has passed to Scandinavia. Gobineau emphasizes status differences as well as racial ones ("I have no doubt that negro chiefs are superior," he writes, "to the level usually reached by our peasants, or even by average specimens of our half-educated bourgeoisie"). If it had been taken seriously, therefore, the *Essay* would not have appeared of ideological value as a basis for German nationalism or for claiming European racial superiority. But because of its ambiguities and its pretensions as a comprehensive philosophy of history, its political potential was greater than that of other works in the typological school. The first volume was quickly translated into English because it appealed to white supremacists in the South of the United States. The Wagnerian movement in Germany cultivated Gobineau's ideas and in 1894 a Gobineau Society was formed to give them publicity. In Hitler's Third Reich, the *Essay*, suitably adjusted, became a popular school reader. Michael Biddiss states that in the political literature of Nazism there are many phrases and conceptions echoing Gobineau's work: "above all, there is in the *mode* of thinking every similarity."

Reading
Father of Racist Ideology: The Social and Political Thought of Count Gobineau by Michael D. Biddiss (Weidenfeld & Nicolson, 1970) is a biographical treatment.
Gobineau: Selected Political Writings by Michael D. Biddiss (Cape, 1970) is a particularly useful anthology.

See also: ARYAN; CHAMBERLAIN; HAECKEL; HEREDITARIANISM; RACE

Michael Banton

H

Haeckel, Ernst (1834–1919)

A famous German zoologist, academic entrepreneur, and popular-
izer of science, who built a vacuous philosophy of life called
"Monism" on a Darwinian foundation. He coined a variety of new
terms, some of which have survived; among them was the "biogen-
etic law" that ontogeny recapitulates phylogeny. This doctrine had
been discussed in biology since the 1820s and appears in Robert
Chambers's anonymously published *Vestiges of Creation*. All
embryos were supposed before birth to pass through the earlier
stages of evolution so that European babies passed through Ethiopian and Mongolian stages in the womb.

Haeckel's significance for the study of racial thought lies firstly in
his decisive influence upon the development of the Volkish movement, a special kind of romantic German nationalism. Haeckel and
the Monists were an important source and a major inspiration for
many of the diverse streams of thought that later came together
under the banner of National Socialism. Secondly, he publicized a
distorted version of Darwinism in which racial differences were
fundamental. Haeckel wrote of "woolly haired" negroes, "incapable
of a higher mental development" and of Papuans and Hottentots
as "fast approaching their complete extinction." One of his major
theses was that "in the struggle for life, the more highly developed,
the more favored and larger groups and forms, possess the positive
inclination of the certain tendency to spread more at the expense
of the lower, more backward, and smallest groups." In this way,
Haeckel and the Monists became the first to formulate a program
of racial imperialism and *lebensraum* for Germany. Haeckel himself
supported the Pan-German League, one of that country's most
militant, imperialistic, nationalistic, and anti-Semitic organizations.

Haeckel had a direct and powerful influence upon many individuals important to the rise of racial anthropology and National
Socialism. One of them was Ludwig Woltmann, a member of the
Social Democratic Party who attempted to fuse the ideas of Haeckel
and Marx, transforming the latter's concept of class struggle into
a theory of worldwide racial conflict. Another was Adolf Hitler.
According to Daniel Gasman, Hitler's views on history, politics,

religion, Christianity, nature, eugenics, science, art, and evolution, however eclectic, coincided with those of Haeckel and were more than occasionally expressed in very much the same language. At least two significant ideological contacts can be established between Hitler and the Monist League that propagated Haeckel's doctrines. Among many Nazi scientists and intellectuals there was a general acclaim for Haeckel as an intellectual ancestor and forerunner, but he was never lauded as a major prophet of the movement (as was Houston Stewart Chamberlain). Chamberlain's conception of race derived from the pre-Darwinian theory of racial typology which permitted enthusiasts to regard the Aryans as being of distinctive origin and permanently superior. Darwinism was included in the German curriculum in biology but the Nazis were suspicious of a doctrine which attributed an inferior anthropoid ancestry to all men and was incompatible with their belief that Aryans had been racially superior from the very beginning.

Reading
The Scientific Origins of National Socialism by Daniel Gasman (Macdonald, Elsevier, 1971).

See also: ARYAN; CHAMBERLAIN; DARWINISM; SOCIAL DARWINISM; VOLK
Michael Banton

Harassment: racial and racist
Harassment of the black populations in Britain has a long history. From the clashes in the dockland areas of London, Cardiff, Liverpool and South Shields between 1919 and 1948 involving attacks on colonial seamen; through the "Nigger-hunting" campaigns of the Teddy Boys in the 1950s and the "Paki-bashing" episodes in the 1960s; to the murders of Gurdip Singh Chaggar in Southall in 1976 and Altab Ali in Whitechapel two years later, harassment is "a way of life" for black citizens in Britain.

Associated with this spectacular evidence in Britain's "tradition of intolerance" have been two significant and insidious trends. First, in contrast to the attacks on black people in Britain in the earlier part of the twentieth century (and before) in Nottingham and Notting Hill in 1958, it has been possible to discern a move from collective to individualized violence. Second, assailants have tended to depersonalize their victims. "Doing a Paki" has, for instance, endured as a resonant theme since the emergence of Skinhead cultures in the late 1960s.

By the early 1980s it had become clear that these acts of violence were not "just a hiccup" in British race relations, as they had been characterized by the Minister of State at the Home Office on the occasion of Chaggar's death in 1976. No: they constituted a pervasive and corrosive influence on the quality of life experienced by black citizens in modern-day Britain. As a 1989 Home Affairs Committee report put it, harassment constitutes one of the "frightening realities" for black citizens and their children.

The 1980s and early 1990s witnessed a flurry of activity in this area. Initiatives crystallized around a (belated) attempt to document the incidence of harassment, tease out its discernible patterns, if there were any, and to develop strategies to preempt its occurrence, deal with its perpetrators, and support its victims. Despite the increasing concern shown by national and local politicians, the police, educationalists, community relations and activists and antiracist campaigners, the emergent material remains strong on description, weak on definition. In short, a stipulative definition of what constitutes "racial harassment" (and cognate terms such as racial incidents, racial bullying, racial attacks, racial violence, inter-racial conflict) remains elusive. But definitions are important. Why? Because they help in constructing the parameters of empirical research and in clarifying some of the myths, assumptions and stereotypes which prevail in this area.

The operational definitions of a racial incident that currently prevail in statutory agencies, the police force, central and local government, and monitoring groups leads to broad interpretations. That is, whether the perpetration of violence is expressly motivated, or is perceived by the victim as motivated, by "racial" considerations. This is unsatisfactory for three reasons.

To begin with, a racial incident tends to be equated with an overt attack on an individual or group and their property. That is, an easily observable incident that is amenable to monitoring and recording. But this behavioristic definition fails to take into account more subtle, but no less intimidatory expressions of harassment which also define and confine the experience of blacks in Britain: racist graffiti or other written insults; verbal abuse; disrespect toward differences in music, food, dress, or customs; deliberate mispronunciation of names; mimicry of accent; exclusionism and so on.

The other major shortcoming of these definitions is their tendency to conflate "racial" with racism. As a result, they fail to provide the analytical tools for clarifying and interpreting the incidence and direction of conflict between black and white adults and their children. At the level of empirical analysis the broad characterization of conflict between blacks and whites as "racial" constrains us

156   *Hegemony*

from accounting for the two dominant patterns which have emerged
from research in this field. Namely, that black people are more
likely to experience "racially" motivated harassment than their
white counterparts; and that black children are more frequently
subjected to abuse aimed at their perceived "racial" origins than
white youngsters.

There is, however, another and more serious weakness with the
interchangeable use of "racial" and racist conflicts. Racist attacks
(by whites on blacks) are part of a coherent ideology of oppression,
which is not true when blacks attack whites, or indeed, when there
is conflict between members of different ethnic minority groups.

What is omitted from the most popular operational definitions of
these incidents is a recognition of the asymmetrical relations
between black and white citizens (and their children) and sensitivity
of the extent to which the harassment and abuse of blacks by whites
is expressive of the ideology which underpins that relationship:
racism.

Reading
Beneath the Surface of Racial Harassment (Avebury, 1992) by Barnor Hesse
   and colleagues offers a theoretical exposition of "racial harassment" linked
   to an empirical research study into its incidence and forms in an outer
   London borough.
Racism in Children's Lives (Routledge, 1992) by Barry Troyna and Richard
   Hatcher explores the salience of racist name-calling in the lives of young
   children growing up in predominantly white neighborhoods.
Traditions of Intolerance edited by Tony Kushner and Kenneth Lunn (Manchester University Press, 1989) deals with the history of harassment.
A special issue of *New Community* (vol. 21, no. 4, 1995) focuses on racist
   violence and political extremism in Western Europe.

See also: INTERETHNIC CONFLICT; RACIAL DISCRIMINATION; REVERSE
RACISM; SKINHEADS

                                                            Barry Troyna

Hegemony

From the Greek *hegemon*, meaning leader or ruler, this term has
become associated with a particular brand of twentieth-century
Marxism, especially that espoused by the Italian Antonio Gramsci
(1891–1937). Hegemony describes the total domination of the
middle class (bourgeoisie) not only in political and economic
spheres, but also in the sphere of consciousness. Marx theorized
that the dominant ideas of any age are the ideas of the ruling class
and this is taken as a central point in Gramscian interpretations of
capitalist societies. What is accepted as common sense, the obviously

correct way things are, is not a neutral perception of the world, but a particular way of grasping reality which fits in neatly with the existing social order. In other words, the bourgeoisie's leadership extends from the material world into people's minds.

For Marx, consciousness was not separable from material existence; this means that what goes on in our heads can never be divorced from how we live the rest of our lives; so practices such as how we feed and clothe ourselves, our place in the social order, and how we work, are all influences on our consciousness. People have a certain view of reality and, for the most part, they believe in the legitimacy or "rightness" of that reality. Under capitalism, the working class (proletariat) live in a social order which works against their true interest: they are systematically exploited. However, and this is crucial, they do not oppose that order because they believe in its legitimacy; so they accept their own subordination. They believe it is part of common sense.

The actual mechanisms through which common sense is disseminated and transmitted from one generation to the next (thus ensuring the perpetuation of capitalism) are complex, but the Algerian philosopher Louis Althusser (1918–90) has offered an influential version using the concept of an Ideological State Apparatus (ISA). An ideology is a way of viewing reality; for Althusser (and other Marxian theorists), ideologies distort or mask true reality and serve ruling-class interests (i.e. enable them to keep control). Through schooling, going to church, attending to the media, people piece together a picture of reality. By accepting this common-sense picture of reality, people make themselves available for exploitation by those who dominate (and therefore control agencies like education, the media, etc.). One of the critical features of this is that the people accepting the common sense remain unaware of their exploitation. Hence there is a hegemonic control and the bourgeoisie maintains its leadership without having it seriously questioned.

According to Gramsci, hegemonic control and the consent it yields is never totally secure and must continually be sought; there is always room for resistance through subversive – or counterhegemonic – cultural work.

The relevance of all this to race and ethnic relations became apparent in the early 1980s, particularly through the theoretical work of the University of Birmingham's Centre for Contemporary Cultural Studies (England). Racist ideologies are seen as components of common sense: ideas about the inferiority of blacks and

Asians have deep roots in history, but they are "reworked" over and over again and serve to divide working-class people. "Problems" connected with so-called racial groups are interpreted as "pathological" because these groups are seen as somehow different. This kind of common-sense thinking operates at local levels (for example in riots and unemployment) and at international levels, as Errol Lawrence points out: "The relative 'under-development' and poverty of many 'Third world' countries is of course not viewed as the outcome of centuries of imperialism and colonial domination, but rather is thought to be expressive of a *natural state of affairs*, in which blacks are seen as genetically and/or culturally inferior."

Images of primitiveness, backwardness and stupidity are associated with blacks and Asians and these are unquestioningly accepted as part of common sense. They are integrated elements of a wider ideology, however, and the ideology's strength rests on people's failure to unmask it and examine alternative ways of viewing reality. So racism, in this Gramscian interpretation, is not a peculiarity of extreme right-wing forms of society, but part of everyday common-sense knowledge in modern society. The continued subordination of blacks and Asians is as much the result of ideology as it is to do with the more easily identifiable form of inequalities in work, housing and education.

Reading
"Just plain common sense: the 'roots' of racism" by Errol Lawrence in *The Empire Strikes Back*, edited by the Centre for Contemporary Cultural Studies (Hutchinson, 1982), is a strongly argued case for understanding racist ideologies within a Gramscian framework; this article uses interesting historical material to show how imperialist regimes created racist images that have been transmitted from one generation to the next and have gained purchase in the context of the "organic crisis" of capitalist societies.
Policing the Crisis by S. Hall, T. Jefferson, C. Critcher, J. Clark and B. Roberts (Macmillan, 1978) is an old but influential analysis which traces the processes through which race came to be recognized as a social problem. Hall developed the approach in a paper, "Race articulation and societies structured in "dominance,"" in *Sociological Theories* (UNESCO, 1980).
Hegemony by R. Bocock (Tavistock, 1987) is a short, accessible introduction to the concept.
White on Black by Jan N. Pieterse (Yale University Press, 1992) examines how blacks have been represented in Western culture over the past 200 years.

See also: IDEOLOGY; MARXISM AND RACISM; MEDIA AND RACISM; POWER; RACISM

Ellis Cashmore

Hereditarianism

The argument that racial differences are hereditary arose in opposition to the belief that, since all mankind is descended from Adam and Eve, diversity must be a product of adaptation to environment. In 1520, Paracelsus maintained that peoples "found in out-of-the-way islands" were not descended from the sons of Adam; early hereditarian theories followed this thesis by claiming that racial differences had existed from the beginning of humanity. At the start of the nineteenth century, the influential French anatomist George Cuvier classified *Homo sapiens* as divided into three subspecies, Caucasian, Mongolian, and Ethiopian, each of which was further subdivided on geographical, linguistic and physical grounds. He represented the races as constituting a hierarchy and contended that differences in culture and mental quality were produced by differences in physique. This line of reasoning was developed into an international school of racial typology as expressed in Britain by Charles Hamilton Smith (1848) and Robert Knox (1850), in France by Arthur de Gobineau (1853), in the United States by Josiah Clark Nott and George Robbins Gliddon (1854), and in Germany by Karl Vogt (1863). This school has more often been referred to as that of "scientific racism." Its adherents maintained that racial types were permanent forms, at least for the period for which evidence was available, and might have been separately created. The stricter typologists, such as Knox and Nott, believed that the various human types were adapted to particular zoological provinces. Just as marsupials were peculiar to Australia, so Australian Aborigines exemplified the kind of men who belonged in that province. Other animals would not long survive there. It was the height of foolishness for Europeans to attempt to colonize North America, Australia, or tropical regions because they were not suited to these environments; if they attempted it their descendants would degenerate and die out. The typological theory of racial differences appeared some three decades before the main phase of European imperial expansion and its doctrines provided little, if any, support for imperialist campaigns.

Whereas environmentalist theories offered explanations for the diversity of racial forms and hereditarian theories for the stability of these forms within particular environments, both kinds of explanation were brought together in Darwin's theory of natural selection. With the establishment of genetics as a field of scientific research, it became possible to examine the relative importance of hereditarian and environmental explanations of particular observations. It is quite reasonable, however, to describe as hereditarians those writers who stress the importance of genetic inheritance relative to environmental influences in the differential performance of individuals of different socioeconomic status or different ethnic group membership when, for example, taking intelligence tests.

Reading
The Leopard's Spots by William Stanton (University of Chicago Press, 1960) is a historical study of hereditarian thought.
The Black Image in the White Mind: The Debate on Afro-American Character and Destiny, 1817–1914, 2nd edition by George M. Frederickson (Wesleyan University Press, 1987) is another historical account.
Racial Theories by Michael Banton (Cambridge University Press, 1987) explains the origins and some of the consequences of early theories of race.

See also: ENVIRONMENTALISM; GOBINEAU; HERITABILITY; RACE
Michael Banton

Heritability

A measure of genetic inheritance. More technically, a heritability estimate for a particular trait expresses the proportion of trait variation in a population which is attributable to genetic variation. Suppose, for example, that in a certain population individuals vary in stature. If the variation can be traced to genetic differences the heritability estimate for stature will be 1; if it can all be traced to differences in the environments of individuals the estimate will be 0.

Every organism is the product of both inheritance and environmental influence. A hereditary trait (like skin color) may be modified by environment (e.g. sun tanning). Equally a trait sensitive to environmental modifications (like weight in humans) may be genetically conditioned. Geneticists speak of genes being "switched on and off" by environmental stimuli. The difficulties involved in studying the interactions between heredity and environment can be illustrated by the inheritance of genes for yellow or colorless legs among certain kinds of chicken. If they are fed on white corn they all have colorless legs. If they are fed on yellow corn, or on green feed, some have yellow legs. If those belonging genetically to the yellow-leg variety are fed, some on white and others on yellow corn, the former have colorless and the latter yellow legs, so that the difference can be attributed to an interaction between environmental factors (i.e. nutrition) and genetic ones. This is why heritability has to be estimated for particular populations and the estimates for different traits in the same population vary substantially.

There was an angry debate in the early 1970s about the heritability of intelligence as measured by IQ tests. Studies in the United States had consistently recorded an average of about 15 percentage points difference in the scores of black and white samples, while Asian Americans regularly scored better than whites. It was not in question that environmental factors could account for individual IQ differences of 20–30 points, or that U.S. blacks and whites differed in several IQ-relevant environmental respects. The dispute centered upon whether environmental differences could account for all the differences between groups. Hereditarians such as A. R. Jensen maintained that since heritability estimates for IQ can be as high as 0.8, the intergroup difference is likely to be in part genetic. However the available heritability estimates only expressed the relative importance of environmental factors for IQ differences within the white population, and no reliable estimates were available for the blacks. The hereditarian argument was blocked by the lack of evidence that environmental differences operated between the groups in the same way as within the white population. Moreover, if discrimination against blacks in the United States was itself an intellectual handicap this made intergroup comparison impossible because like was not being compared with like.

Reading
The Race Concept by Michael Banton and Jonathan Harwood (David & Charles, 1975) is an elementary exposition.
The Bell Curve: Intelligence and Class Structure in American Life by Richard Herrnstein and Charles Murray (Free Press/Simon & Schuster, 1994) is a statement of hereditarian views.
The Science and Politics of I.Q. by Leon J. Kamin (Penguin, 1977) gives a critique of the evidence about intelligence; the opposition of views is analyzed in "The race-intelligence controversy" by Jonathan Harwood in *Social Studies in Science* (vol. 6, 1976 and vol. 7, 1977).

See also: ENVIRONMENTALISM; HEREDITARIANISM; INTELLIGENCE AND RACE

Michael Banton

Holocaust
See GENOCIDE

Humor and ethnicity
Ethnic humor, as defined by M. L. Apte (in *American Behavioral Scientist*, vol. 30, no. 3, 1987), is "a type of humor in which fun is made of the perceived behavior, customs, personality, or other traits of a group or its members by virtue of their specific socio-cultural

identity." To this we might add that those groups have, historically, been powerless and usually unable to resist the attributions of the humor.

Jokes, in particular, reflect social attitudes. For example, Jews are the most universal butt of ethnic humor and their treatment illustrates what Zijderveld (in *Social Research*, vol. 35, 1968) calls "joking-down" and "joking-up," i.e. making fun of (and with) groups either above or below oneself in terms of status or class position as a way of corroborating power relations. This constitutes a form of control and has spawned countless aggressive anti-Semitic jokes, which in turn reinforce the feeling of superiority of the jokers. The concept of the Wandering Jew in the Western diaspora has given rise to a serviceable stereotype, in which Jewish achievements have been reinterpreted as negative characteristics (e.g. wealthy Jews are wealthy not because they are successful, but because they are miserly and mean). In dehumanizing Jews to the level of stereotypes, the joke not only conveys the racism of the teller, but actually encourages further racism.

Joking-up, by contrast, has created a distinctive Jewish humor and wit originating in self-deprecation – joking about one's own marginality. In this sense, the humor serves as a resistance. The wit of retaliation and the comedy of revenge function similarly, as symbolic victories of minorities over majority groups. The humor is a source of cohesion in the minority group. Once established, however, the self-derogating humor is frequently appropriated by the majority and given approval. The humor works to remind the majority what they *aren't* (not miserly or mean, in this instance).

Blacks have also been targets for ethnic humor. In his early study (in *American Sociological Review*, vol. 2, 1946), Burma differentiated between "anti-Negro" humor as expressed by whites to reflect their alleged supremacy and control, and anti-white humor, in which Southern whites were depicted as being outsmarted by cunning blacks. In the former, the Jim Crow stereotype of the nineteenth century was employed and this was later transmuted into the Sambo character, dull-witted and always trying unsuccessfully to imitate white culture with humorous consequences. In the latter, blacks made use of a corruption of Sambo: in the late nineteenth and early twentieth centuries, the central character of black humor was a city slicker and conman who mocked the features ascribed to him by exposing the prejudices of whites. Thus, Jess Simple and Slim Greer are symbols of the ridicule of whites' values and lifestyle by means of role reversal, parodies of white society. This tradition, which plays on the realities of street life and self-mockery, has been continued by such contemporary comedians as Godfrey Cambridge, Dick Gregory, Red Foxx, and Richard Pryor. (*Note*: Eddie Murphy's rise has been less an extension of this tradition, more a modification of "anti-Negro" humor, merely substituting homosexuals, women, and other minority groups in place of blacks.)

Davies (in the volume by Powell and Paton) argues that, in the West, orally communicated jokes about ethnic groups, such as Irish or "Pakis" (South Asians), are the most popular kind. The attribution of ignorance and stupidity serves the cause of efficiency and rationality by denigrating their opposites and defusing the anxieties of those living in the "joyless economy" of modern times. By joking about the failure of stereotyped groups to fit into the modern world, ethnic humor acts as a benign social control, inculcating in both the jokers and the ethnic butts a sense of "what is right": deficient minorities should be more like the adequate and rational majorities.

A growing area of interest is the way the mass media have confirmed or modified ethnic stereotypes in expressions of humor. Obvious examples are *Love Thy Neighbour*, *Till Death Us Do Part* and *All in the Family*, which presumably intended to ridicule prejudice, but more probably validated it on TV. The most outrageous display of racism in a TV show came in the British-produced *Mind Your Language* about a polyglot language class, every member of which was a grotesque caricature. While confirming the norm enforcement function of the media or reflecting society's ambivalence about ethnic minorities, the humorous depiction of minorities can also provide the social analyst with a barometer to the changing situation and status of a particular group vis-à-vis the wider society.

One seeming breakthrough in status-conferral challenging the stereotype of African Americans is the ratings success of *The Cosby Show*, the most popular American sitcom between 1984 and 1992. Bill Cosby, in pioneering shows about African Americans as multidimensional black characters, also exemplifies their recent acquisition of power positions as TV executive producers and directors in the United States, enabling them to present for the first time their cultural viewpoints in a non-clichéd way. Despite this, Cosby's portrayal of a middle-aged professional black father with three children, an expert on child-rearing who is "full of pious views and good intentions" (Grassin), does little more than reaffirm the more benign ways the white middle class perceives black participation in American society, viz. "The black male should be individualistic, racially invisible, professionally competent, successful, and upwardly mobile. Expressions of racial conflict and black collectivity are absent" (Crane, D. *The Production of Culture: Media and the Urban Arts*, Sage, 1992).

A further dimension of humor and ethnicity accompanying the burgeoning study of women's humor is the case of African American women who are traditionally attributed with employing verbal wit denied their white sisters until comparatively recently. This is evidenced by the man-and-wife stage acts developing out of the older minstrelsy from the early 1890s. Thus Jackie "Moms" Mabley played the lewd widow in standup comedy routines for much of this century, working within the joking frames of folk humor recognized by her predominantly black audiences.

Classic female blues singers, such as Lucille Bogan and Clare Smith, in the 1920s and 1930s challenged male sexual potency in the raunchy epithets and double entendres of their songs. In all these comic formats, the black woman played the antagonist to the man. Zora Neale Hurston (1903–60), one of the first widely acclaimed African American women novelists, assimilated folk tradition into modern literature. She dramatized verbal duels of mock courtship and postcourtship routines in the south. Munroe observes that she "played out in the liminal land of the porch." The singularity of her comic achievement is seen as advancing, however indirectly, a pioneering feminist agenda.

Reading
Ethnic Humor Around the World: A Comparative Analysis by Christie Davies (Indiana University Press, 1990) examines the origins of such jokes from every continent, explaining with a profusion of examples how, why, and about whom people everywhere tell ethnic jokes.
Humour in Society edited by C. Powell and G. E. C. Paton (Macmillan, 1987) is a pioneering collection of articles, including several on aspects of ethnic humor, the central argument being that humor is employed by and within certain groups to manage tension in conflictual relations, especially those concerning ethnic groups.
"Courtship, comedy, and African-American expressive culture in Zora Neale Hurston" by B. Munroe, in *Look Who's Laughing: Gender and Comedy* edited by G. Finney (Gordon & Breach, 1994), examines some key twentieth century female comics and genres in African-American comic expression.

See also: BLACK FEMINISM; JIM CROW; MEDIA AND RACISM; STEREOTYPE
George Paton

Hybridity
The term hybrid has developed from biological and botanical origins to become a key term in contemporary cultural criticism. "Wherever

it emerges it suggests the impossibility of essentialism," writes Young. In Latin *hybrida* originally meant to the offspring of a tame sow and a wild boar, though in the nineteenth century, it became a physiological phenomenon, referring to a "half-breed" (as the Oxford English Dictionary expresses it) or a "mongrel or mule" (according to Websters). Theories of racial typologies warned of the dangers of hybridization and degeneration that would result from the mixing of distinct races which occupied different hierarchical positions. Anxiety about hybridity served to keep "races" separate.

More recently, hybridity has been appropriated by cultural critics and deployed against the very culture that invented it to justify its divisive practices of slavery and postcolonial exploitation. Rowe and Schelling refer to hybridization as "the ways in which forms become separated from existing practices and recombine with new forms in new practices" (in *Memory and Modernity*, Verso, 1991). So, while hybridity originally denoted an amalgamation or mixture, it now describes a dialectical articulation. For example, in Hall's work on the black experience in Britain, he recalls a moment of homogenization in which "blackness" contests dominant representations of black people. Out of this awareness of commonality (of being black), comes an awareness of heterogenity, of diffuseness, of being part of a dispersed population – what Hall calls "diaspora-ization".

In this sense, hybridity describes a *culture* composed of people retaining links with the territories of their forbears but coming to terms with a culture they inhabit. They have no wish to return to their "homeland" or of recovering any ethnically "pure" or absolute identity; yet they retain *traces* of other cultures, traditions and histories and resist assimilation.

Bakhtin uses hybridity in another way, to describe a language's ability to be simultaneously the same and different: "An utterance that belongs . . . to a single speaker, but actually contains mixed within it two utterances, two speech manners, two styles . . . the division of voices and languages takes place within the limits of a single syntactic whole, often within the limits of a single sentence." The application of this to colonial settings, through the work of Bhaba, reveals hybridity to be a moment of challenge and resistance against a dominant cultural power: "Hybridity . . . is the name for the strategic reversal of the process of domination through disavowal (that is, the production of discriminatory identities that secure the 'pure' and original identity of authority)."

In this perspective, colonialism has actually produced hybridization: in establishing a single voice of authority or dominion over *others*, it *in*cludes the *ex*cluded others in its discourse (i.e. by representing them) and simultaneously estranges the basis of its authority. Hybridity is the antidote to essentialist notions of identity and essentialism: the colonial authority and other are locked into the same historical narrative, their cultures and identities contingent on each other.

Reading

Colonial Desire: Hybridity in Theory, Culture and Race by Robert J. C. Young (Routledge, 1995) connects old racial theories with present cultural criticism by showing how we retrospectively construct old notions of race as more essentialized than they actually were: "Culture and race developed together, imbricated within each other."

The Location of Culture by Homi Bhaba (Routledge, 1994) is a dense and sometimes perplexing text on what the author calls "beyond theory." "Hybridity is the sign of the productivity of colonial power, its shifting forces and fixities . . . [it] represents that ambivalent 'turn' of the discriminated subject into the terrifying, exorbitant object of paranoid classification – a disturbing questionning of the images and presences of authority."

The Post-Colonial Studies Reader edited by Bill Ashcroft, Gareth Griffiths, and Helen Tiffin (Routledge, 1994) pulls together a wide range of writings by, among others, Fanon, Spivak, and Said; all united by postcolonial theory and criticism.

See also: COLONIAL DISCOURSE; CREOLE; DIASPORA; POSTCOLONIAL; OTHERS; SUBALTERN

Ellis Cashmore

I

Ideology

This concept is the object of continuing debate and argument, although all uses of it suggest that it refers to a complex of ideas. This reflects the origin of the term in the late eighteenth century when it was used to refer, in a technical sense, to the science of ideas. It took on another meaning around the same time, one of which is still predominant in common-sense discourse and in conservative political thought. This uses the term in a pejorative sense to refer to impractical or fanatical theory, to ideas which are abstract and which ignore "the facts." Neither of these two uses are of any direct relevance to the way in which the concept is employed analytically now.

Contemporary analytical usage reflects the different ways in which the concept was employed by Marx. In Marx's own writings, one finds two distinct usages. The first is his use of the concept to refer to false and illusory descriptions of reality, a meaning that is synonymous with the notion of false consciousness. This usage is found clearly expressed in *The German Ideology*, written by Marx and Engels in 1846. This notion of ideology is used by both Marxists and critics of Marxism in combination with a mechanical interpretation of the base/superstructure metaphor. This is evident in arguments which claim that ideology is the reflection and product of ruling-class interests and has the function of obscuring from the working class the "real" nature of its domination and exploitation by capital.

The second use of ideology in Marx's writings is to refer to the complex of ideas that correspond to particular sets of material interests and experiences. This usage is found in Marx's later work, notably in the *Grundrisse* and *Capital*. However, this usage itself fragments into two different emphases. On the one hand, ideology is used to refer in a general sense to the content of the forms of consciousness which come into being and are reproduced in the course of the reproduction of material life. On the other, it is used to refer to the structural fact of consciousness: in this sense, ideology is used to refer to a particular level or dimension of a social formation. However, both usages are usually associated with a further distinction between ideology and science, which implicitly (if not explicitly) returns us to an elaboration on the theme of illusion. The introduction of the concept of science as a polarity is necessary in order to permit a critical evaluation of the nature and content of ideology in these two second senses.

The work of Althusser and Poulantzas has been the site of much of this recent debate, from which have emerged some important clarifications and developments. One of these is pertinent to an analysis of racism and nationalism as ideologies. It has been argued recently that although ideologies refer to accounts of the world that are, in totality, false, they must be analyzed and understood in such a way as to allow for the fact that people who articulate them can nevertheless make sense of the world through them. This means that ideological generation and reproduction cannot be understood simply and solely via some notion of false perception or ruling-class domination. The latter may be empirically the same in particular instances but this is not the complete substance of ideology. Rather, it is more important to explain why and how ideologies "work" in relation to the essential relations of the mode of production, thus allowing a certain autonomy to the formation and reproduction of ideology. Thus, ideologies are mistaken, not so much because of false perception or indoctrination, but because of the determinate forms in which production relations can be experienced and expressed phenomenally.

The other important clarification to emerge from recent debates is consequent upon renewed interest in the work of Gramsci, from which has emerged the concept of common sense. This refers to the complex of ideas and perceptions, organized without coherence, which are a consequence of both historical tradition and direct experience and by which people negotiate their daily life. The term ideology can refer to this common sense which is characterized not only by its "matter-of-factness" but also by its internal disorganization. Ideology can therefore refer not only to a complex of ideas that are the product of "systematic" thought, but also to the internally contradictory and incoherent set of ideas through which daily lives are lived.

These general debates are refracted in the ways in which racism is analyzed as ideology. One classic, Marxist tradition has been to argue that racism is an ideology created by the ruling class in a capitalist society to justify the exploitation of colonial populations and to divide the working class. This clearly reproduces the notion of ideology as an illusory creation of the bourgeoisie. More recently, drawing upon the second general notion of ideology found in Marx, racism has begun to be analyzed as an ideology (complex of "facts" and explanations) which refracts a particular experience and material position in the world capitalist economy. It has independent conditions of existence, although those conditions are not themselves fully independent on the material parameters of the social formation. From this perspective, what is significant is that the ideology of racism allows sections of all classes to intellectually interpret and understand the world in a way which is consistent with their experience. Although the illusory nature of the ideas is openly acknowledged (on the basis of analytical historical analysis of the idea of "race," i.e. science), it has been argued that they nevertheless provide at one level a relatively coherent explanation of the world as perceived and experienced. In its extreme form, in this argument, racism becomes one further dimension of the ideological level of the social formation. Within this level of the social formation one can therefore identify an ideological struggle and conflict, between racists and antiracists, which is not assumed to be between purely proletarian and bourgeois forces.

Reading

On Ideology by Centre for Contemporary Cultural Studies (Hutchinson, 1978) is a detailed account of recent developments within Marxist analysis in the debate about the nature of ideology.

Marxism and Historical Writing by P. Q. Hirst (Routledge & Kegan Paul, 1986) is a critical discussion of contemporary Marxist theorists, with a view to assessing the materialist science of history.

Marx's Method by Derek Sayer (Harvester, 1979) is an analysis of the nature and place of ideology in Marx's historical materialism which explicitly rejects the notion of ideology as a conspiratorial creation.

See also: HEGEMONY; MARXISM AND RACISM; NATIONALISM; RACISM

Robert Miles

Institutional racism

While racism in one sense may describe the beliefs, or ideas, of individuals, in its institutional sense it refers to the anonymous operation of discrimination in organizations, professions, or even whole societies. It is anonymous in that individuals can deny the charge of racism and absolve themselves from responsibility. Yet, if a pattern of exclusion persists, then the causes are to be sought in the institutions of which they are part, the unspoken assumptions on which those organizations base their practices and the unquestioned principles they may use.

The term itself was introduced in 1967 by black activists Stokely

Carmichael and Charles V. Hamilton in *Black Power: The Politics of Liberation in America* (Penguin). Racism is "pervasive" and "permeates society on both the individual and institutional level, covertly and overtly," they wrote. Later writers, such as Douglas Glasgow, sought to restrict the use of the concept to express the fact that, in the 1960s and 1970s, "The 'for colored' and 'whites only' signs of the thirties and forties had been removed, but the institutions of the country [United States] were more completely saturated with covert expressions of racism than ever" (in *The Black Underclass*, Jossey Bass, 1980). Glasgow wrote further: "Institutional racism (which involves ghetto residents, inner-city educational institutions, police arrests, limited success models, undernourished aspirations, and limited opportunity) does not only produce lowered investment and increased self-protective maneuvers, it destroys motivation and, in fact, produces occupationally obsolete young men ready for underclass encapsulation."

On these accounts, institutional racism is to be camouflaged to the point where its specific causes are virtually undetectable, but its effects are visible in its results. The racism itself is concealed in the procedures of industries, political parties, schools, etc. Defining it as inclusively as this makes institutional racism a resonant term and one which has gained currency of late. But its generic status has invited criticism about its lack of specificity and, therefore, its limited usefulness as a tool of analysis. Jenny Williams, for instance, calls institutional racism "a bridging concept, linking and blurring the distinction between the material and ideological."

The strength of institutional racism is in capturing the manner in which whole societies, or sections of society, are affected by racism, or perhaps racist legacies, long after racist individuals have disappeared. The racism that remains may be unrecognized and unintentional, but, if never disclosed, it continues uninterrupted. But, its strength is, from a different viewpoint, its source of weakness: an accusation of institutional racism may allow everyone to escape; only the abstract institution is blameworthy. Critics insist that institutions are, when all is said and done, the product of human endeavors and it is a category mistake to suppose that *institutional* racism is a *cause* (i.e. terms from uncombinable categories are put together).

Conceptual criticism apart, institutional racism has demonstrated practical value in highlighting the need for positive, continuous action in expunging racial discrimination rather then assuming it will fade. Even organizations committed to "worthy" causes, which would

seem to complement the efforts of civil rights and equal opportunities, are bound to introspect, as a case in 1990 in Washington, D.C.,
indicates. Eight major national environmental organizations, including the Natural Resources Defense Council, the Wilderness Society,
and the Sierra Club, were charged by civil rights group with racism in
their hiring practices. None of the leaders of any of the organizations
were African American or Latino and few of the middle managers
were from minority groups; of 315 staff members of the Audubon
Society, three were black. Friends of the Earth's staff of 40 included
five minority workers. The Natural Resources Defense Council had
five ethnic minority staff out of 140. The Sierra Club had one Latino
among 250 staff.

The accused organizations' reaction was typical; there was a scarcity of black or Hispanic people among the pool of trained environmental specialists, it was claimed. The organizations added that they
were not aware of the "whiteness of the green movement" and
would implement a "concerted effort" to remedy the imbalance
(*New York Times* 1 February 1990).

In none of the attacks on the organizations were individuals
singled out, nor were any motives imputed. No one was actually
accused of refusing to appoint or promote anyone on racist grounds.
Criticisms were based on clinical analysis of figures, with the result
that institutional racism was found, in this case, in unlikely settings.
This was an example of how accusations of institutional racism
can crystallize awareness and promote more aggressive attempts to
discourage it. Other examples of institutional racism that have come
to light in recent years include:

- The credit policies of banks and lending institutions that prevent
  the granting of mortgages to people living in neighborhoods
  densely populated by ethnic minorities.
- Seniority rules when applied to jobs historically occupied by
  whites, that make more recently appointed ethnic minorities (and
  females) more subject to dismissal ("last in, first out" policies)
  and least eligible for advancement (the "glass ceiling").
- Restrictive employment leave policies, coupled with prohibition
  on part-time work or denials of fringe benefits to part-timers that
  make it difficult for the heads of single-parent families, most of
  whom are women and a disproportionately high amount of them
  of African descent, to get and keep jobs and maintain families.
- Implementing height requirements that are unnecessarily and

unintentionally geared to the physical proportions of white males and so exclude certain ethnic minorities from jobs.

• Using standardized academic tests or criteria that are geared to the cultural and educational norms of middle class white males and are not relevant indicators of the ability to perform a job successfully.

Institutional racism has become central in the contemporary race and ethnic relations vocabulary and, despite its conceptual elasticity, has shown utility in analyzing how institutions can operate along racist lines without acknowledging or even recognizing this and how such operations can persist in the face of official policies geared to removal of discrimination.

Reading
Race, Class and Gender, 2nd edition, by Paula Rothenberg (St. Martin's Press, 1992) contains a section on "The economics of race, gender and class in the United States," which has studies of institution-based inequalities.
Rethinking the American Race Problem by Roy Brooks (University of California Press, 1990) is full of law cases in which institutions have been accused of racism, but in which they have escaped prosecution because of the problem of having to prove intention and causation; institutional racism, as a concept places no relevance on intention, but centers only on results.
White Racism by Joe R. Feagin and Hernan Vera (Routledge, 1995) concentrates on the "everyday character" of racism and provides ample illustrations.

See also: AFFIRMATIVE ACTION; EQUAL OPPORTUNITY; ETHNIC MONITORING

Ellis Cashmore

Integration

This describes a condition in which different ethnic groups are able to maintain group boundaries and uniqueness, while participating equally in the essential processes of production, distribution and government. Cultural diversity is sustained without the implication that some groups will have greater access to scarce resources than others. For a society to be fully integrated, it must remove ethnic hierarchies, which permit differential access and it must encourage all groups' contributions to the social whole.

In Britain, integration has been a policy ideal since 1966, when the then Home Secretary, Roy Jenkins, defined it as "not a flattening process of assimilation, but as equal opportunity accompanied by cultural diversity in an atmosphere of mutual tolerance." The contrast with assimilation is important: far from facilitating an absorption of one culture by another, integration entails the retention or even strengthening of differences of ethnic groups. The popular metaphor for assimilation has been the melting pot; for integration, it is the salad bowl, with each ingredient, separable and distinguishable, but no less valuable than the others. (Canada has favored the concept of an ethnic mosaic, with the different pieces of society joined together in one arrangement.)

In the United States, integration is used synonymously with pluralism, specifically "equalitarian pluralism" as Martin Marger calls it, in which balance and cohesion are maintained among the various groups and there are no ethnic minorities because there are no ethnic hierarchies. In a sense, ethnic groups become political interest groups that compete for society's rewards. But these competitive differences do not lead necessarily to conflict: they are dealt with by "reasonable give and take within the context of the consensual mores of society," according to Marger (in *Race and Ethnic Relations*, 2nd edn, Wadsworth, 1991). Group differences are never threatened because mutual respect for such differences is an essential part of the social order and there need only be an agreement about the governing framework in which the production and distribution of scarce resources is fairly handled and in which the law is operated.

In some societies, such as Belgium, Canada, and Switzerland, institutional provisions are made to ensure an ethnically proportionate distribution of resources, thus protecting cultural differences while keeping groups integrated into the whole. Integration means more than coexistence: it implies an active participation of all groups and an agreement on the appropriate methods of organizing the allocation of power, privileges, rights, goods, and services without compromising cultural differences.

In both Britain and the United States, integration remains more of an ideal than a reality. Despite a plethora of culturally distinct groups, there has been slow progress toward involving them in mainstream politics, commerce, professions and other key areas. While persistent racism has retarded the progress of integration in both contexts, groups have mobilized around their ethnic identity to force some measure of integration. The Indian Workers' Association and Pakistan Workers' Association in Britain and the American Indian Movement and Congress of Racial Equality in the United States are examples of groups that have brought political pressure to bear. The official recognition they receive may be grudging and short-term, but it might also facilitate a fuller participation in society long-term.

Reading
Diversity in America by Vincent N. Parrillo (Sage, 1995) analyzes the possibilities of integration amid diverse ethnicities.
Majority and Minority, 5th edition, edited by Norman Yetman (Allyn & Bacon, 1991) has a section comprising nine essays on "Patterns of ethnic integration in America."
The Disuniting of America by Arthur Schlesinger (Norton, 1991) is a polemical essay criticizing attempts to integrate different ethnic groups into the USA as futile and undesirable.

See also: AMALGAMATION; ASSIMILATION; MULTICULTURALISM; PLURALISM

Ellis Cashmore

Intelligence and race

The issue of racial differences in intelligence has raged for well over a century, especially in relation to people of African descent. Blacks have long been regarded in the West as intellectually inferior to whites and Asians, and, starting in the nineteenth century, the racist doctrines of Arthur de Gobineau, of Houston Stewart Chamberlain (an intellectual mentor of Adolf Hitler), and others, have sought to give the stamp of scientific approval to theories of mental differences by race. With World War I, when IQ tests began to be widely applied to army recruits, school pupils, and other groups in the United States, interest in racial differences in intelligence was given another boost. Test results were used to "prove" the inferiority not only of blacks, but also of eastern and southern European immigrants.

In more recent times, the work of Arthur Jensen and other psychometricians has kept the controversy alive, especially Jensen's 1969 article in the *Harvard Educational Review*, and his *Bias in Mental Testing* (1980). For the last thirty years, however, the great weight of scientific opinion has been cast on the environmentalist side of the interpretation of group differences in IQ test performance. Jensen has been repeatedly attacked for asserting that black Americans were innately inferior in certain intellectual abilities, and that some 80 percent of the variance in IQ performance is due to heredity.

Jensen's "hereditarian" position has two principal components, which are, theoretically, separable. One consists of stating that the heritability of *individual* intelligence is high; and the other is to ascribe *group* differences in intelligence to genetic factors. The second statement in no way follows from the first. It is the consensus of most geneticists that human intelligence is determined by many genes, and that any assessment of such a complex set of abilities by an IQ test is suspect. Even if one accepts the validity of the test, to make statements of heritability concerning such a polygenic trait goes well beyond the scope of modern genetics. Finally, to transpose a guess on heritability of the individual phenotype to the level of group differences represents another giant leap beyond the data.

Indeed, any assessment of heritability is always time- and situation-specific: it only holds under a precise set of environmental conditions. The heritability of a given trait differs widely from group to group if environmental conditions vary (as they clearly do for white and black Americans). In short, Jensen's conclusions are not only based on unwarranted assumptions; they have absolutely no standing in human genetics.

There is much evidence that Jensen is wrong in attributing "racial" differences in IQ scores to differences in native intelligence. Similarly disadvantaged groups, quite unrelated to Afro-Americans, have also shown an IQ score gap of about 10–15 points (the average white–black gap in the United States). This includes such disparate groups as European immigrant groups in the United States in the earlier decades of the twentieth century, and Oriental Jews in contemporary Israel. Conversely, some subgroups of Afro-Americans in the United States, notably people of recent West Indian extraction, do considerably better than old-stock continental Afro-Americans (who, like West Indians, come principally from West African populations).

Scarcely anyone denies that there is an important genetic component in phenotypic intelligence, but our rudimentary knowledge of human genetics does not permit even an informed guess as to degree of heritability. Perhaps the safest conclusion is that intelligence, like other behavioral phenotypes, is 100 percent heredity and 100 percent environment. Even if heritability of intelligence in one group could be ascertained, it would not be the same in another group, and within-group heritability would not be a valid base for explaining between-group differences.

It is, of course, possible that significant differences in frequencies of genes affecting intelligence exist between human groups, but no such differences have yet been found, nor is it plausible to infer any from existing data. The weight of evidence points to an environmental explanation of intergroup differences in IQ scores. In any case, mean differences between groups are much smaller than individual differences within groups. Individual differences in IQ performance are probably attributable to a mixture of genetic and environmental factors, in unknown proportions. Most problematic of all is the extent to which IQ tests are a meaningful measure of intelligence.

Reading
"How much can we boost I.Q. and scholastic achievement", by Arthur Jensen, in *Harvard Educational Review* (vol. 39, 1969, pp. 1–123), is the most scholarly treatment of the hereditarian position.

Inequality by Christopher Jencks (Basic Books, 1972) argues for 45 percent heritability of IQ test score phenotype, plus or minus 20 percent.

The I.Q. Controversy edited by N. J. Block and Gerald Dworkin (Pantheon, 1976) is a collection of essays on IQ testing and its implications for social policy; it may profitably be read in conjunction with chapter six of *Race and Culture: A World View* by Thomas Sowell (Basic Books, 1994).

The Bell Curve: Intelligence and Class Structure in American Life by Richard Herrnstein and Charles Murray (Free Press/Simon & Schuster, 1994) is a controversial statement on the relationship between intelligence, race, class, and various other social characteristics such as crime, occupation, and education.

See also: DARWINISM; ENVIRONMENTALISM; GENOTYPE; HEREDI-TARIANISM; HERITABILITY; PHENOTYPE

Pierre L. van den Berghe

Interethnic conflict

This refers to the struggle between two or more ethnic minority groups in the same society. It involves more than competition for scarce resources: the aims of the group typically include eliminating, neutralizing or, at least, injuring rivals. While the nature of the conflict often appears to be ethnic, that is based on the incompatibility of cultures, the source is usually to be found in relative deprivation.

Relative deprivation describes the negative emotion, variously expressed as anger, resentment or dissatisfaction, which groups, or individuals, experience when they compare their situations with some standard or outside reference points. These may include other groups in the immediate environment. Interethnic conflict, as opposed to ethnic conflict (which includes clashes between ethnically different groups none of which is necessarily a political or economic minority) typically occurs when one ethnic minority compares its position to that of another ethnic minority and experiences deprivation. In absolute terms, the group may not be the most deprived or disadvantaged group: it is sufficient that the group feels deprived relative to other ethnic minorities.

Antecedents to the conflict need not be closely related to the interethnic resentment. For example, the conflict between African Americans and Cubans in Miami, Florida, in 1980. Cuban migration to Florida began in earnest in late 1965 and through the 1960s and 1970s, migrants competed with blacks for jobs. While the uprising in 1980 was triggered by the death of Arthur McDuffie, a black male, at the hands of police officers, much of the African American anger was vented against Cubans, many of whom had started their own businesses. Cuban-owned shops were destroyed when competition converted into outright conflict.

Interethnic conflict is not usually an adaptation of historical memory to fit a wholly new conflict. But there are exceptions and history and tradition can be powerful weapons to fire new mobilizations. Sporadic violence between South Asian groups in Britain in the late 1980s recalled traditional Sikh–Muslim conflicts. This inter-Asian violence changed character to regional-based violence in the early 1990s when youths affiliated with the origin of their parents (Bangladesh, Punjab, Pakistan, etc.) engaged in violence against each other.

Reading
Bridges and Boundaries edited by Jack Salzman (Braziller, 1993) addresses the tension-filled relations between African Americans and American Jews.
The Miami Riot of 1980 by Bruce Porter and Marvin Dunn (Lexington Books, 1984) is a full and detailed account of the uprising.
Relative Deprivation and Social Justice by W. G. Runciman (Routledge & Kegan Paul, 1966) is a treatment of the concept originally formulated by S. A. Stouffer *et al.*

See also: AFRICAN AMERICANS; ASIANS IN BRITAIN; RIOTS: U.S.A. (MIAMI) 1980

Ellis Cashmore

Internal colonialism
A term first used by Robert Blauner to describe the situation of minorities in contemporary America. In classic colonialism, a country's native population is subjugated by a conquering colonizing group. In internal colonialism, by contrast, the colonized groups are minorities under white bureaucratic control; they have been conquered and forcibly taken to the United States, in the process having their culture depreciated or even destroyed. North American Indians and Mexicans were forced into subordinate statuses in much the same way as Asians, Africans, and Latin Americans were conquered by Europeans. White Americans treated native populations

(Indians and Mexicans) as colonizers treated the groups they colonized.

According to Blauner, blacks, although they were not conquered and enslaved on their own land, were nevertheless conquered and forced into subordinate status in America. This experience of lack of voluntary entry into the country marks blacks, Native Americans and Mexicans off from all other migrant groups. Europeans who enter the United States voluntarily (whatever their motives) form an immigrant minority.

The groups conquered and colonized undergo unique experiences in the process of becoming a colonized minority: (1) they are forcibly made to exist in a society that is not their own; (2) they are subjugated to the extent that their social mobility is limited and their political involvement restricted; (3) their own culture is depreciated or even extinguished. As a result, the colonized group becomes trapped in a caste-like situation. This, in turn, affects that group's self-conception: it accepts the "superior" ways of life of the colonizing group and tends to view itself as inferior.

Specific areas, likened to internal colonies, were the basis of segregation in all areas of urban life: politics, education, occupations, and virtually every other area of social interaction. This spatial segmentation ensured that certain groups were herded together and were therefore easier to control by white bureaucracy.

By examining how the various minority groups first came into contact with white American society, Blauner contends, we can understand their differential treatment in the generations that followed. So: colonized minorities' positions are structurally quite different from those of immigrants. Whereas Irish, Italians, Poles, and others have advanced socially (albeit in a restricted way), blacks, Native Americans, and Mexicans have not. The latter groups remain disadvantaged with an almost lawlike persistence. Similarly, the institutions and beliefs of immigrants were never brutalized in the way colonized groups were. Underlying this is the fact that white racism is much more virulent when directed against colonized minorities than against immigrant groups.

Taxonomically, Blauner's thesis has many problems, not the least of which is: where do groups such as Puerto Ricans, Chinese, and Filipinos fit? The experience of these groups leads to a more fundamental conceptual problem of defining forced and voluntary migration. As Blauner's argument rests on this distinction, it may be asked whether so-called voluntary movement to America might not be precipitated by a complex of circumstances that severely limit the emigrants' alternatives. It may well be the case that the migrants' conditions are so intolerable that a migration is imperative – if only in the interests of survival. Even more extreme would be cases in which political situations actually motivate the migration. Such instances weaken the notion of an involuntary movement.

Nevertheless, Blauner's model of internal colonialism has been an influential contribution to theories of race relations and has at least directed attention away from current circumstances and toward history as a starting point for investigation.

Reading
Racial Oppression in America by Robert Blauner (Harper & Row, 1972) is the text in which the author sets out his important thesis.
Internal Colonialism by M Hechter (University of California Press, 1975) accounts for the causes of nationalism in Britain between the years 1536 and 1966 by using the internal colonialism model.

See also: COLONIALISM; GHETTO; MIGRATION; PLURALISM; POWER; SLAVERY

Ellis Cashmore

International Convention

The International Convention on the Elimination of All Forms of Racial Discrimination (ICERD) is a treaty prepared under the auspices of the United Nations and adopted by the General Assembly in 1965. By August 1995, some 143 states (including all the major powers except Japan) had acceded to it. By accession, states undertake to fulfill the obligations of the Convention and to report every two years on what they have done in fulfillment to a committee of eighteen individuals who they themselves elect. This body, the Committee in the Elimination of Racial Discrimination (CERD) reports to the General Assembly on the outcome of its examination of state reports and there is an annual debate, usually in October. CERD started its work in 1970.

By August 1995, 143 states had made declarations under article 14 of ICERD permitting persons within their territories to petition CERD if they consider that the state has failed to provide them with the protections promised under the Convention; CERD issues opinions on such petitions. This is of importance to European States because ICERD, unlike the European Convention on Human Rights, offers protections against racial discrimination in the exercise of economic rights.

Reading
International Action Against Racial Discrimination by Michael Banton
(Oxford University Press, 1996) discusses the provisions made by inter-
national law for the suppression of racialism.
*The First Twenty Years: Progress Report of the Committee on the Elimin-
ation of Racial Discrimination* (United Nations HR/PUB/91/4, 1991).

See also: LAW: CIVIL RIGHTS (U.S.A.); LAW RELATIONS (BRITAIN); LAW:
RACIAL DISCRIMINATION (INTERNATIONAL)

Michael Banton

Irish and colonialism

The Irish emigrant experience can only be understood by recognizing the dramatic impact that centuries of British colonialism has
had for the Irish people. As a result of its geographical position
and internal political feuds Ireland became the first English colony.
Although the Normans established settlements in the twelfth century
it was not until the sixteenth century that systematic colonization
took place under the Tudors and their successors. While the Normans had been eventually assimilated into traditional Gaelic society,
the sixteenth-century invaders were not. As a result of England's
break with Catholicism the common link between the two countries
was finally broken. Consequently, religion became the mechanism
whereby colonizer was distinguishable from colonized. This was
exacerbated by the fact that significant numbers of Scottish and
English Protestant settlers were subsequently given the lands of the
native Catholics by the English Crown, particularly in Ulster. The
native Irish were depicted as savage heathens who were "more
uncivill, more uncleanly, more barbarous and more brutish in their
customs and demeanours, than in any other part of the world that
is known." Consequently, it was justified, through military conquest
and legislation such as the 1697 Penal Laws, to deprive the native
population – "the uncivilized Other" – of their religious, civil, and
land rights. By the beginning of the eighteenth century almost 90
percent of the land was in the hands of non-Catholics of foreign
origin. Virtually the only legal way that Catholics could retain ownership of their land was through renouncing their religion.

Destitution and migration

For the majority of the Irish population, the peasantry, colonialism
brought destitution. An English agricultural reformer, Arthur
Young, compared the position of the peasantry in the late eighteenth century to that of slavery. They subsisted on one crop, the

potato, while the rest of the crops they produced were exported. When the crop failed between 1845 and 1851, 1.5 million died of disease and starvation. The Prime Minister of the time, Lord Russell, stated, "it must be thoroughly understood that we cannot feed the people." There can be little doubt that the famine resulted from the nature of the economic system fostered by colonialism. Of all the countries in northwestern Europe, only in Ireland did such a large percentage of the population depend on one crop for their daily survival.

The famine had dramatic consequences for Irish society. Military force and repressive legislation had never resulted in the acceptance of colonialism by the Irish. However, the sheer magnitude of the disaster undermined the infrastructure of a distinctive Celtic culture. For example, the Gaelic language, the medium of that culture, was virtually wiped out because the famine impacted so severely in the geographical areas where it had been extensively used.

Mass emigration also became part of the Irish experience. Although migration to Britain had existed for centuries it had been seasonal; and the migration of Scottish-Irish to North America had been relatively small in scale. Many Irish had been taken to Australia, as convicts. But, between 1841 and 1861 half a million Irish settled in Britain. Of even more significance was the fact that between 1846 and 1850 approximately 900,000 migrated to North America and by 1860 the Irish American population had leapt to one and a half million. Many Irish never survived their desperate journey across the Atlantic in the "coffin ships." In 1848, for example, of the 100,000 who left for Canada, 17,000 died on the journey and 20,000 died soon after their arrival. On Grosse Island, an immigrant landing station in Quebec, an inscription reads: "In this secluded spot lies the mortal remains of 5,294 persons, who flying from pestilence and famine in Ireland in the year 1847, found in America but a grave." This tragic Irish diaspora lasted until 1921.

In both Britain and North America the Irish endured anti-Catholic Anglo-Saxon and Anglo-American hostility and were accused of taking jobs, undercutting wages, and being political troublemakers. Anti-Irish cartoons in magazines such as *Punch*, supported by respectable writers such as Thomas Carlyle, Elizabeth Gaskell, and Charles Kingsley, depicted them as being a less evolutionarily developed race. Kingsley stated that, "to see white chimpanzees is dreadful; if they were black, one would not feel it so much, but their skins, except where tanned by exposure, are as white as ours." The American historian, Edward A. Freeman, commented that,

"This would be a grand land if only every Irishman would kill a negro and be hanged for it." It is in this context of Irishphobia that the racist caricature of the drunken, violent, ignorant Paddy was established. Their supposed "wildness" and "unpredictability" meant that writers questioned whether they could ever be assimilated into civilized society.

Adaptation, assimilation and reaffirmation

However, the Irish in America did adapt and did find a mechanism for assimilation, something they did not manage to do in Britain. Because of their urban concentration, their domination of municipal services such as the police and fire service, their transition to an urban proletariat, and their mastery of the Anglo-Saxon democratic political process, they were able to build powerful political machines in many cities. These Democratic party machines, from the 1870s onwards, provided the means by which the Irish were able to gain respectability in American society, challenge their WASP opponents and establish their superiority in relation to other racial and ethnic groups. It is argued that the election of John F. Kennedy indicated the final assimilation of the Irish into American society. This election finally removed any lingering sense of social inferiority and insecurity. But many still believe that President Kennedy, and his brother, were assassinated precisely because they were Irish Catholics.

Throughout this complex process of generational transition, adaptation and assimilation many Irish never forgot their homeland. These reluctant exiles carried with them a lasting sense of colonial banishment, a hatred of the English, and a romanticization of Ireland. It is hardly surprising that the Irish communities in America provided recruits, money, and support for successive revolts against the English presence in Ireland. In many respects notions of "Irishness," as a clear ethnic identity in America, were constructed in opposition to "Englishness." However, just as many decided to "forget" the "old country" and the "old ways." They carried with them (1) "shame" that they had arrived in the New World as paupers and dispossessed; (2) "guilt" they had abandoned family and friends to a tragic fate; (3) "denial" of their origins to overcome widespread prejudice and discrimination; (4) a sense of themselves as "survivors" who had no choice but to look to the future rather than dwell on a humiliating past.

Perhaps it is this ambivalent problematic of "memory" and "forgetting" that explains why it was not until the 1980s that millions of Americans felt curious and confident enough to recover, remember, and reimagine their "Irish" roots.

Ireland continues to be affected by its colonial experience. In 1922, as a result of the war of independence, the country was partitioned. This seriously damaged the national psyche, hindering both the process of decolonization and the construction of postcolonial national identity. In six counties of Ulster the descendants of the seventeenth-century settlers created a Protestant state for a Protestant people. The Catholic minority were deprived of their basic civil rights and suffered from considerable discrimination. In the late 1960s, using methods borrowed from the American civil rights movement, Catholics challenged the status quo and since that period there has been a violent sectarian struggle over the continued existence of Northern Ireland.

The partition had considerable consequences for the rest of Ireland. The Ulster crisis has always threatened its stability because of the possibility of violence spreading south of the border. Economically, partition deprived the Republic of Ireland of its most industrialized region and successive governments have had to deal with the consequences of the colonial underdevelopment of the rest of the country. As a result the only constant product that the country exports is successive generations of its young people. During the 1980s, and 1990s, tens of thousands left for Britian and mainland Europe. There is evidence to suggest that this new diaspora has revitalized existing Irish communities in both countries. However, the reemergence of mass emigration has decimated Irish towns and villages because only the very young and old remain.

Reading
The Irish World Wide: History, Heritage, Identity edited by P. O'Sullivan (St. Martin's Press, 1994) is the "state of the art" interdisciplinary treatment of the Irish abroad. There are six separate volumes:
Volume 1: Patterns of Migration
Volume 2: The Irish in New Communities
Volume 3: The Creative Migrant
Volume 4: Irish Women and Irish Migration
Volume 5: Religion and Identity
Volume 6: The Meaning of the Famine.
Emigrants and Exiles by K. Miller (Oxford University Press, 1985) remains one of the most important books on the Irish migration to North America.
From the Ward to the White House: The Irish in American Politics by G. E. Reedy (Charles Scribners and Son, 1991) is a good overview of the impact of the Irish on the development of the U.S. political party system.
The Great Calamity: The Irish Famine by C. Kinealy (Gill and MacMillan,

1994) is the most comprehensive analysis of what the Great Famine meant for Irish people.

See also: DIASPORA; ETHNICITY; MIGRATION; MINORITIES

Eugene McLaughlin

J

Jackson, Jesse (1941–   )

An active member of the Southern Christian Leadership Conference in the crucial 1966–71 period when he was in his late twenties, South Carolina-born Jackson developed into an extraordinarily energetic and flamboyant leader and spokesman for black Americans. He claimed to have been a close confidante of Martin Luther King and reflected on how the leader had died in his arms – a claim disputed by many present at the leader's death. In 1969, he led the Active Black Coalition for United Community Action, but, more significantly, in 1971, created People United to Save Humanity (Push), based in Chicago. This pressure group had an ingenious repertoire of strategies, one based on the threat of mass black boycotts of companies' products, should the companies in question fail to implement a set of Push demands, such as hiring or promoting to senior positions more black employees.

Reverend Jackson was unsuccessful in his bid to become the presidential nominee of the Democratic party in 1984, but his sometimes controversial campaign drew much attention. He ran against Michael Dukakis in 1988. He continually stressed the "multicultural" nature of U.S. society with his concept of the "Rainbow Coalition," a call for the political unity of all groups traditionally marginalized in electoral politics, including ethnic minorities, women, the poor, and environmentalists. Jackson tried to move beyond an ethnic interests-based agenda, eschewing the questionable title of the "black candidate" and appealing to a wider spread of groups – an attempt which was not wholly successful as his antagonizing of the Jewish community indicates.

After 1988, Jackson eschewed attempts at securing political office, even when strenuously urged to do so (as in the mayoral race for Washington, D.C., in 1990). Despite having no official government position, Jackson retained prominence and several polls in the early 1990s confirmed that he was among the most widely recognized figures in North American public life. In 1989, he visited the then Soviet Union and Africa in a series of high-profile international travels. Such was his prominence that he was able to meet and negotiate with heads of state. In 1990, he hosted a television panel discussion series. The Push strategy, which had brought success in the 1980s, suffered a reverse in 1991, when the sports goods manufacturer Nike, which contracts many blacks to endorse its products, refused to negotiate. Jackson's boycott faltered and Nike was unscathed.

In the midst of the Gulf War of 1991, Jackson flew to Iraq to try to persuade Saddam Hussein to release hostages. Despite strong speculation in 1992, Jackson refused to run for the presidency, claiming "the basis of my strength and credibility is not in any office or position, but my relationship with people." He added that those who assumed government office "ended up conservative and cautious."

Reading
"Profiles: Jesse Jackson" by Marshall Frady is an 89-page, 3-part article in *The New Yorker* (February 3, 10 and 17, 1992), while "Jesse Jackson and the new black political power" by William Strickland in *Black Enterprise* (vol. 21, no. 1, August, 1990) is another profile.
The Jackson Phenomenon by Elizabeth Colton (Doubleday, 1989) is a series of reflections by Jackson's press secretary during early 1988.
The Jesse Jackson Phenomenon by A. L. Reed (Yale University Press, 1986) argues controversially that Jackson's campaigns have hurt rather than helped the American black political movement.

See also: CIVIL RIGHTS MOVEMENT; KING; POLITICS AND "RACE"

Ellis Cashmore

Jim Crow

"Jim Crow" was a common slave name used as a song title by nineteenth century entertainer Thomas Rice (1808–60) who ridiculed blacks as amusing fools, congenitally lazy but with an aura of childlike happiness. The name was applied to legislation that provided for the practice of segregating whites and African Americans.

The conclusion of the Civil War brought about the 1863 Thirteenth Amendment to the U.S. Constitution, the Emancipation Proclamation that provided for the freedom of all slaves. It also prompted the question of whether the whites' responsibilities toward blacks should end with the prohibition of physical bondage: should the federal government provide protection and economic resources for freed ex-slaves? In formulating answers to this, the federal government attempted to reconstruct the South on a new basis of equality.

So, when eight southern states tried via legal means, known as the "Black Codes," to deny blacks access to desirable, well-paying work, the federal government introduced two additional amendments to provide: (1) equality of protection for all under the law; (2) equality of voting rights for all men (not women).

Reconstruction had barely begun when the military occupation of the South ended in 1875. The belief was fostered that blacks would prosper through their own initiative and application and without federal intervention. The Civil Rights Bill of 1875 was designed to grant equal access for all citizens to all public facilities. But only limited government aid was provided; economic security and political equality were matters of individual enterprise. Hostility toward blacks was rife, especially in the South, and resentment surfaced whenever blacks did show enterprise. The Thirteenth Amendment ended slavery, but did nothing to erode the racist beliefs that underpinned slavery.

In 1883, the US Supreme Court ruled that the 1875 Bill did not apply to "personal acts of social discrimination." Effectively, this meant that state laws requiring segregated facilities for blacks and whites were constitutional. The feeling was that the federal government had done too much to help blacks in their transition to free men. So the U.S. Supreme Court deprived the previous legislation of its cutting edge and restored the determination of civil rights to state rather than federal levels. What followed became known as the "Jim Crow" era: Southern states enacted a series of statutes that provided for the segregation of blacks and whites in such spheres as education, transport, marriage, and leisure.

The *Plessy v. Ferguson* case of 1896 was a legal milestone: the Supreme Court upheld the state of Louisiana's requirement that seating on trains be segregated. The doctrine emerging from this decision was that blacks and whites were "separate but equal." Mr. Plessy was, he claimed, seven-eighths "white," yet he was, for all intent and purposes, a "negro" and therefore not allowed to travel in "whites only" railroad cars. The doctrine of "separate but equal" spread throughout the South and, by 1910, there was a virtual caste system in practice. It served to maintain blacks in their subordinate positions by denying them access to reasonable educations and jobs; sharecropping was their principal means of survival.

"Jim Crow" was a type of *de jure* segregation, a separation required by law. When the law was not available to support segregation, the forces of the Ku Klux Klan were invoked. Hence, lynchings were widespread and largely overlooked by legal authorities. Blacks were thus inhibited from challenging the segregation and were more or less forced into accepting their inferiority. In other words, blacks were provided with no facilities for improving their education, for showing skillful application, nor for protesting aggressively their conditions (at least, not without fear of violent reprisals); so they were virtually made to conform to the whites' popular "Jim Crow" image of them.

The court decision that brought an end to the Jim Crow era came in 1954 with the *Brown v. Board of Education* case. Segregated schools were declared unconstitutional; the principle was then extended to buses, restaurants, parks, etc. Over the next decade the Jim Crow laws were gradually overturned, their total dissolution coming with the 1964 Civil Rights Act.

Reading
Race, Ethnicity, and Class in American Social Thought 1865–1919 by Glenn C. Altschuler (Harlan Davidson, 1982) is a historical monograph detailing developments in this crucial period in American race relations.
The Shaping of Black America by Lerone Bennett, Jr. (Penguin, 1993) charts African American history from 1619.
The Color Line: Legacy for the Twenty-first Century by John H. Franklin (University of Missouri Press, 1994) argues that the "color line" instituted by Jim Crow still holds in education, housing, health, and the legal system.

See also: CIVIL RIGHTS MOVEMENT; LAW: CIVIL RIGHTS U.S.A.; MYRDAL; SEGREGATION; SLAVERY

Ellis Cashmore

K

Kerner Report, The

The shorthand name for the report of the National Advisory Commission on Civil Disorders chaired by Otto Kerner. The commission was set up by President Lyndon Johnson in 1967 with the aim of investigating the causes and consequences of a series of uprisings that had occurred in many U.S. cities over the previous two years.

The first of these started on August 11, 1965. A confrontation between white police and young blacks in Watts, Los Angeles' largest black ghetto, marked the end of the period of nonviolent protest at black oppression in the United States and presaged the start of a series of "race riots." By the end of 1968, the catchword, "burn, baby, burn" had been heard in virtually every major U.S. city, coast to coast, north to south. In 1967 alone, over 150 "race riots" were recorded during the "long hot summer," the most serious taking place in Newark and Detroit. By the end of 1968, police had reported 50,000 arrests and more than 8,000 casualties.

Black and white left-wing radicals characterized the "riots" as revolutionary insurrection, comparable to the colonial rebellions in Africa and Asia. White reactionaries, while agreeing with this description, maintained that the episodes had been inspired by foreign agitators and black communists and urged the authorities to meet fire with fire. President Johnson, on the other hand, tended to agree with moderate black leaders that the relatively small caucus of young troublemakers had acted against the will of the vast majority of black Americans.

In his address to the nation on July 27, 1967, Johnson announced his intention to set up an investigation to determine the causes of the riots, to examine the characteristics of the areas affected and people who participated, to appraise the media's presentation and treatment of the riots and its effects, and, most importantly, to pinpoint strategies which would avert the possibility of further disorders.

The more speculative accounts of the "burn, baby, burn" disorders were largely repudiated by the wealth of statistical and documentary material presented by Kerner and his colleagues in their 1968 report. Not surprisingly perhaps, in view of the significance and authority with which the Commission was endowed, some of the Commissioners' results and research methodology have since been subject to careful scrutiny by social researchers and, in some instances, found to be flawed. Even so, the profile of "the typical rioter" sketched out by the Commissioners has generally been accepted: a young, single black male who had been born and brought up in the state and who shared a comparable economic position to blacks who had not participated in the disorders. He tended to be slightly better educated than other ghetto residents, though he was positioned in the lower echelons of the labor market, rarely worked full-time and was frequently unemployed. Although he was slightly more likely than nonparticipants to have been brought up at home in the absence of an adult male, the statistical difference was insignificant and its impact marginal. The evidence adduced by the Commission, and subsequently verified by other research, suggested that the motives of the "rioters" were primarily political: they were not responding to their own particular disadvantage nor indeed that of their local communities, but to the more general disadvantaged and oppressed position of the entire black community in the United States.

The most fundamental of the "underlying forces" which had precipitated the disorders was, in the words of the Commissioners: "the accelerating segregation of low-income, disadvantaged Negroes within the largest American cities." As they put it in their conclusion to the report: "Our nation is moving toward two societies, one black, one white – separate and unequal." They identified three paths along which government policies could proceed: the first was the "present policies choice" which, the Commissioners warned, carried the "highest ultimate price" of an even greater likelihood of further civil disorders, perhaps surpassing even the scale of the "burn, baby, burn" incidents. An "enrichment" policy, or "gilding the ghetto," constituted the second strategy. This recognized some of the positive aspects of ghetto life and was premised on the notion of separate but equal communities. Although a similar strategy had been advocated by many Black Power leaders, the Commissioners pointed out that "gilding the ghetto" to enhance its status would require a considerable deployment of national funds.

The preferred course of ameliorative action combined "gilding the ghetto" policies with "programs designed to encourage integration of substantial numbers of Negroes into the society outside the ghetto." In other words, the enrichment policy would be an interim measure: the goal was dispersal. This, they contended, would not only improve the educational and social standards of American blacks, but would also facilitate social integration and help secure social stability. Put simply, dispersal constituted the most effective means of crisis-management.

Despite its many limitations, the Kerner Commissioners made a deliberate attempt to present the disorders in a sociological perspective rather than one which dealt exclusively in a "law and order" framework. Although the report tended to overlook the more insidious and ultimately more wide-reaching forms of institutional racism as an instrument of oppression in the United States, it highlighted the central role that white racism (and the modes of action that this impels) played in the outbreak of the disorders. In this sense, alone, it presented a far more sophisticated appraisal than its UK counterpart, the Scarman Report, though, like that document, it evoked a sporadic and highly selective response from central government.

Reading
Report of the National Advisory Commission on Civil Disorders (Kerner Report) has an introduction by Tom Wicker (Bantam Books, 1968).
Prevention and Control of Urban Disorders by the U.S. Department of Justice (U.S. Government Printing Office, 1980) is a more up-to-date assessment of the riots.
"Parameters of British and North American racism" by Louis Kushnick (*Race and Class*, vol. 23, nos 2/3, 1982) argues that despite its liberal pretensions, the Kerner Commission advocated coercion and co-option. Its recommendations for more effective police control, for instance, were most enthusiastically and expeditiously implemented.

See also: BLACK POWER; GHETTO; RIOTS: BRITAIN, 1981; RIOTS: U.S.A., 1965–7; SCARMAN REPORT

Barry Troyna

King, Martin Luther (1929–68)
Born of a middle-class Atlanta family, King was educated at Morehouse College (Atlanta), Crozer Theological Seminary (Pennsylvania), where he was ordained into the National Baptist Church, and Boston University, where he received his doctorate in theology in 1955.

Almost a year after receiving his doctorate, King was serving as a Baptist pastor in Montgomery, Alabama, when he heard of Rosa Parks's refusal to give up her seat in the "whites only" section of a municipal bus. This historic action was to provide King with the opportunity to initiate a series of boycotts that eventually jelled into a movement of national importance, designed to secure civil rights for blacks, at that time still suffering from the vestiges of the "Jim

Crow" era, despite the technical ending of racial segregation brought about by the *Brown* decision of 1954.

King worked with black civil leaders, Ralph Abernathy, E. D. Dixon, and Bayard Rustin, to promote a boycott of Montgomery's buses. Throughout 1956, about 95 percent of the city's blacks refused to use public buses. In November 1956, a Supreme Court ruling declared the bus segregation laws of Montgomery unconstitutional. During the eleven months preceding the decision, King had emerged as a leader of substance, but the tangible success of the campaign transformed him. As Marable, in his book, *Race, Rebellion and Reform* (Macmillan, 1984), observes: "Overnight, King became the charismatic symbol of the political aspirations of millions of coloured people across the world."

The effect of the Montgomery success was to spark a series of isolated boycotts, though no coherent mass campaign materialized until the 1960s. King had, in 1957, formed the Southern Christian Leadership Conference (SCLC), of which he was president and which was to become his vehicle for civil rights reform. Influenced by the teachings of Thoreau and especially Gandhi, King employed the tactic of nonviolent disobedience, staging street demonstrations, marches, sit-ins and even jail-ins. After 1960, the sit-ins became more frequent and were used to particularly good effect by black students to protest against lunch-counter segregation at educational institutions.

King and his followers had to endure violent attacks from whites and even from some blacks who were fearful of reprisals. King himself was sentenced to four months imprisonment after leading a protest in Atlanta. Charges were dropped, but King was imprisoned for violating his probation on a traffic offense conviction. John F. Kennedy used influence to obtain King's release, a strategic move which undoubtedly played a part in Kennedy's election to President in that same year (in most cities and states, three-quarters of all votes cast by blacks were for Democratic nominees).

King enjoyed fruitful associations with both John and Robert Kennedy, negotiating civil rights reforms, the most important of which were the two laws passed in 1964 and 1965. The latter, which was signed by Kennedy's successor, Lyndon B. Johnson (whose presidential candidacy was endorsed by King), ensured voting rights for blacks and was preceded by a 4,000-strong march from Selma to Montgomery. In December 1964, King received the Nobel Peace Prize.

In his book, *Martin Luther King, Jr.*, W. R. Miller describes his subject's most remarkable achievement as his success in making middle-class blacks the "backbone" of his crusade. When King began to mobilize his organization in the Southern United States, one-fifth of the population in that region was black and, of these, at least one-in-three was above the poverty line. The import of this is that there was a sizable proportion of blacks who were beyond worrying about sheer physical survival and were ambitious enough to become the "backbone" of a mass movement for reform. King's association and support with the emergent black middle class was one of the keys to his success in leading a movement of great scale and force. But, it was also the reason why, even as early as 1960, when he was 31, "he seemed rather remote from the mind and mood that simmered across black college campuses," as Marable puts it.

By 1963, the "mood" had spread. For example, in that year, he delivered his famous "I have a dream" speech to an audience of 250,000 and several million television viewers. In content, it was a relatively mild speech, incorporating passages from many other, older deliveries and lacking any reference to the violent white backlash his sympathizers were having to endure. Also in 1963, he gave another speech in Harlem, before an audience of 3,000, many of whom jeered and chanted "We want Malcolm [X]!" to signal their discontent with King's gradual and moderate programs.

The same sentiment was articulated more aggressively from 1965 when Black Power spurred rioting in many major U.S. cities. King remained steadfast in his condemnation of violence, but was clearly troubled by both dissension within his own movement and external pressures from militants. From this point, King seems to have been drawn toward a more extreme position. In 1966, he admitted that his policy of "a little change here, a little change there" was an idea he had, as he put it, "labored with." His departure from this was heralded by his criticism of the Vietnam War; in particular, the disproportionate number of blacks involved in military action. Many blacks disapproved of King's position and turned sharply against him. Thus the final years of his life were spent struggling not only against the reactionary forces of white America, but against the radical demands of militant blacks who advocated violent solutions to the problems King addressed.

In April 1968, King traveled to Memphis to support a strike by black sanitation workers. Here he was assassinated. Following this, 70,000 troops were needed to quell violence that broke out in 125 American cities.

Reading
And the Walls Came Tumbling Down by Ralph Abernathy (Harper & Row,
1989) is a biography by the slain leader's confidante and adviser, which
discloses hitherto neglected facets of King's personal life.
King: a biography by D. C. Lewis (University of Illinois Press, 1978),
Martin Luther King by K. Slack (SCM Press, 1970) and *Martin Luther
King Jr* by W. R. Miller (Avon Books, 1968), are all good quality bio-
graphies.
Orders to Kill by William Pepper (Carroll & Graf, 1995) alleges that King
was killed by the U.S. intelligence agencies; written by a London-based
attorney, it dismisses the lone assassin (James Earl Ray, who was sentenced to 99 years) theory and argues that King was killed because it was
thought that his crusade for blacks was turning into a campaign against
involvement in Vietnam.

See also: AFRICAN AMERICANS; BLACK POWER; CIVIL RIGHTS MOVEMENT;
GANDHI; MALCOLM X

Ellis Cashmore

Kinship

To be distinguished from affinity (a relationship traced through
marriage) and descent. It is also important to differentiate kinship
as a personal network, as a means of recruiting corporate groups,
and as a sentiment of identification. Sir Raymond Firth wrote in
1958: "The way in which a person acquires membership of a kinship
group is termed descent. The way in which he acquires rank and
privileges is termed succession, and the way in which he acquires
material property after the death of its former owner is termed
inheritance." Descent may be traced (i) from a male ancestor
through males (patrilineal); (ii) from a female ancestor through
females (matrilineal); (iii) through both simultaneously but for different purposes (double unilineal); or (iv) through a mixture of lines
(variously called omnilineal, cognatic, or bilateral). Two persons
are kin when one is descended from the other (lineal kin, as with
grandparent and grandchild) or when they are both descended from
a common ancestor (collateral kin, as with a man and his brother
or uncle). Any table of kinship requires a reference point, that of
ego, from whom relationships are reckoned. When kinship is a basis
for claiming rights it is also necessary to establish a boundary to the
range of degrees of relationship (as the medieval German kinship
group included kin only up to the sixth cousins). It will be apparent
that only some of ego's kin will be of the same unilineal kinship
group as ego, so that kinship reckoning comprehends more persons
in the present generation than unilineal descent reckoning, whereas
descent lines can list large numbers of ancestors who would be

outside the range of recognized kin. The rights of kinship can be created, as by adoption, and they depend upon the social recognition of relationships, not upon genetic relationships (or consanguinity).

Most men and women grow up in families and therefore experience relationships of kinship as principles organizing the social world. They are therefore apt to organize their perceptions of the natural world according to similar principles, seeing family resemblances and relationships in animals, plants, etc. They also utilize the sentiments of identification generated within the kinship network as norms for judging social relations. For example, fraternity is considered an important value on the assumption that brothers support and care for one another, ignoring the frequency with which, in some social systems, brothers struggle with one another for primacy. Sentiments of kinship are extended in many ethnic movements to comprehend a much wider network (for example, the use of "brother" and "sister" in the African American revitalization movement). Relationships of descent are also replicated in the organization of ethnicity. Just as someone can be a MacDonald over against a Campbell, a Highlander in opposition to a Lowlander, a Scot and not an Englishman, but a Briton or a European when overseas, so an immigrant may be able to utilize a series of ethnic identities of different magnitudes according to the social situation in which he finds himself. One identity nests inside another in an order of segmentation.

Reading
Introduction to Social Anthropology 2nd edition by Lucy Mair (Clarendon Press, 1972) is a textbook on the subject of anthropology which is clear; the other literature is extensive and, in some cases, very technical.
Human Types by Raymond Firth (New English Library, 1958) is the source of the quotation on page 170.

See also: BOAS; CULTURE; ETHNICITY; PATRIARCHY

Michael Banton

Ku Klux Klan

A racist organization, originating at the end of the American Civil War in 1865, taking its name from *Kuklos*, Greek for circle or band, and Klan, from the Scottish clan, denoting common ancestry. At first intended as a secret society, the Klan opposed the new social and legal rights granted to four million blacks after the abolition of slavery. At various stages in its development, the KKK terrorized blacks, Jews, Catholics, Mormons, and communists, while retaining one constant imperative: to uphold white supremacy. The Klan was and, indeed, still is one of the most vigorous white racist organizations in the United States and, to a much lesser extent, Europe. Throughout its history, the Klan has fought to maintain the supposed purity of the white Anglo-Saxon Protestant – the WASP.

As with neo-Nazi organizations, the KKK philosophy was based on a vision in which the white race (its term) reigned supreme. For two hundred years of its history, America had housed a majority of Protestants of English descent, Anglo-Saxons. According to Klan philosophy, it was obvious that God constantly looked over, protected and designated whites as the supreme, ruling group. It was demonstrated by their material well-being compared to the other two main groups: (1) American Indians were subhuman savages fit only for mass extermination; (2) blacks were also less than human and were to be used as a form of property to relieve whites of harder forms of labor.

The Klan believed that there was a divine plan in which the WASP was to dominate; this plan had been violated by the freeing of slaves and the growing presence of Catholics. William Randel quotes from a KKK manifesto: "Our main and fundamental objective is the MAINTENANCE OF THE SUPREMACY OF THE WHITE RACE in this republic. History and Physiology teach us that we belong to a race which nature has endowed with an evident superiority over all other races, and that the Maker, in thus elevating us above the common standard of human creation, has to give us over inferior races a dominion from which no law can permanently derogate."

The Klan chose an assortment of methods to achieve its aim. At the respectable extreme it ventured into national politics, both independently and through the mainstream parties. At the other extreme, it simply annihilated whole groups of people. Just after its formation, the Klansmen used to clothe themselves in white robes and hoods and terrorize blacks: there were regular lynchings, castrations, and destruction of blacks' properties. But, even as recently as 1978, in Greensboro, the Klan ambushed a meeting and killed five people; though perhaps the Klan's most famous atrocity of recent times was in 1963 when a church in Birmingham, Alabama, was bombed, killing four black girls.

The KKK has gained momentum since the 1920s when it acquired an organizational structure, principally through the influence of William Mason. Ostensibly, it took the form of a secret society, much like Freemasonry, with a hierarchy of lodges and a network of communciations. The head of this "invisible empire," as the Klan called itself, was the Imperial Wizard, and under his command were Grand Dragons, Grand Titans, Lictors, and so on.

In the 1920s, racism was rife in the United States, and there was growing hostility to the new immigrants from Europe. Charles Alexander wrote of the southern branches in this period: "The Klan was only doing what the regional majority wanted – preserving the American way of life as White Southerners defined it." Randel estimates that, at this time, about five million people were in some way affiliated to the Klan. In some respects, it was regarded as a positive moral force and this image was fostered by philanthropic enterprises and churchlike rituals. Support was gained through charity appeals.

Its membership today is impossible even to estimate if only because the Klan carefully preserves its status as a secret organization. It has international linkups with other fascist groups and has branches in Britain, where it established a base in the mid-1960s. Its presence in England was signaled by a spate of burning crosses either nailed to or laid at the foot of doors of selected persons, usually black or Asian.

Bill Wilkinson, an Imperial Wizard, illegally entered Britain in 1978 with the expressed intention of generating support, but it seems his impact was nugatory. The British scene at that stage was full of neofascist groups ranging from the "respectable" National Front, through the virulent League of St. George to the paramilitary Combat 88. But, the Klan has maintained its principal strength in the United States and remains one of the most potent racist underground organizations.

Reading
The Ku Klux Klan by William P. Randel (Hamish Hamilton, 1965) is a detailed account of the growth of the organization in America, though this doesn't cover many aspects of the modern Klan or its activities in Britain.
The Ku Klux Klan in the Southwest by Charles C. Alexander (University of Kentucky Press, 1965) is a specific case study of one segment of the KKK in the United States.
The Fiery Cross by W. Craig (Simon Schuster, 1987) argues that the KKK is "an American institution."

See also: ARYAN; BRITISH MOVEMENT; NATIONAL FRONT; NEO-NAZISM; SKINHEADS; WHITENESS

Ellis Cashmore

L

Language, race and ethnicity

The study of the ways in which language is affected by race and ethnicity raises questions related to nationalism, multilingualism, colonialism, language planning, and the emergence of distinct varieties of black English in the United States and Britain.

As classifications of race based on phenotypical differences developed during the nineteenth century, evidence in support of such theories was sought from the study of language. Scholars sought to reconstruct language "families" on the basis of linguistic evidence. The European languages and the languages of India were classified together into the Indo-European group of languages. At the same time, the myth was established of a long-lost Indo-European or "Aryan" race who had spoken a proto-language from which Indo-European descended and who were the ancestors of the Slavs, Romans, Germans, and other European races. The proposition that race, culture and language are isomorphic is patently false, but has frequently had a strong appeal to the politicians and populations of many nations. Hitler's *Ein Volk, Ein Reich, Eine Sprache* is an example.

The way in which "race" as an analytical construct is subject to indeterminacy and insufficiency on close examination, however, is paralleled by the problems we encounter when we attempt to subject a "language" to a similar scrutiny. The term "language" can be seen to have a number of associated meanings: it can refer to the individual's "mother tongue;" the descriptions of language behavior by linguists as typified by dictionaries and grammatical descriptions; or the language of a particular community and its literature, especially the "standard" language of a particular nation. Finally, it can also refer to the language that people actually speak or write; and, interestingly enough, it is only in this last sense that the term is used in a non-idealized (and thus non-stereotyped) sense. The term "language," like "race," derives many of its broader meanings from the symbolism that attaches itself to the mental concept, however blurred that image might be.

Within sociolinguistics, it is axiomatic that the term "language" cannot be adequately explained by reference to linguistic criteria alone. There are many examples in the world, e.g. in Scandinavia, where dialect continua have been segmented almost arbitrarily by political or social forces leading to the creation of separate "languages." The vast majority of societies in the world are multilingual rather than monolingual. It is estimated that the 140 nation-states of the world share in the region of four or five thousand languages. Even in Britain, which is traditionally considered a monolingual society, it was calculated that in 1987 there were over 170 languages spoken by children in London alone.

One major reason for multilingualism throughout many parts of the world today is imperialism (other reasons include migration and federation). Throughout the Caribbean, South America, Africa, and Asia, European languages (including English, French, Spanish, and Portuguese) became established through the colonial governing classes in the eighteenth and nineteenth centuries. As the British Empire retreated after 1945, the spread of English was sustained by the increasing economic and technological power of the United States of America. Traditional colonial imperialism may now have waned significantly, but a *linguistic imperialism* of sorts still continues. English is currently spoken by 300 million native-speakers in the United States and Britain, but it also has a wide currency among another billion or so speakers of English as a second language from West Africa to India, Singapore, Hong Kong, and the Philippines. English is now the international language of science and technology, business and finance, world communications, and international academic studies.

One of the foremost problems in language planning worldwide has thus been the choice of official or national languages for newly emergent independent states in the developing world. For a variety of reasons this choice has often involved a compromise between an international language such as English and indigenous languages, as can be seen in many postcolonial nations in Africa, India, Singapore, and Malaysia. As a result of colonialism and related factors there are now large numbers of people of African and Asian origin who speak what were originally European languages. In many cases, many such second-language varieties have become at least partly nativized so that it is now possible to speak of Nigerian English, Indian English, Singaporean English, etc.

While it is misleading to assume that speakers of the same language are necessarily members of the same "race," or that speakers of what appear to be related languages are necessarily racially related to one another, language can play a crucial role in symbolizing or signifying membership of a particular ethnic group. Central to the relationship between language and ethnicity is the insight that language behavior by the individual is closely related to the individual's perception of himself and his own identity. This insight has been most coherently and powerfully expressed in the work of the British sociolinguist Robert Le Page, who has put forward a theory of language use in terms of "acts of identity." According to this theory, the individual creates his or her own language behavior so that it resembles that of the group or groups with which he wishes to be identified, to the extent that: he can identify the groups; observe and analyze such groups; is motivated to adapt his behavior; and is still able to adapt his behavior. By so doing the individual is thus able to locate himself in the "multi-dimensional" space defined by such groups in terms of factors such as sex, age, social class, occupation, and other parameters for social group membership, including ethnicity.

Language issues related to ethnicity may be seen in the conflicts experienced by minority language groups in multilingual societies, as with the case of the Francophone population in Canada. The importance of ethnicity may also be seen, however, in the way in which the distinct identity of ethnic groups is expressed not only by different languages but also by different varieties of the same language.

The case of "Black English" both in the United States and Britain provides a good example of the latter point. The study of the Black English Vernacular (or "BEV") was pioneered by the American sociolinguist William Labov. His and subsequent studies have emphasized the distinctive patterns of BEV in terms of both its pronunciation and its grammar. A good deal of controversy has surrounded the origins of BEV, with some linguists arguing that BEV is descended from a creole variety of English, while others have emphasized the similarity of BEV to other nonstandard varieties of American English. Whatever the arguments, however, a historic trial, the so-called Black English Trial took place in Ann Arbor, Michigan in 1979, during which the judge found that the failure of the school authorities to recognize Black English as a separate language had handicapped the educational progress of black children in the area.

Within Britain, recent studies have set out to describe "British Black English." This term is typically used to refer to a type of modified Jamaican creole spoken by second-generation Britishers of Caribbean descent. Whether the creole-based Black English is a fully developed language "variety" is a matter of interpretation (most British speakers of Black English will invariably have a command of other varieties of the language as well). However, one thing is clear: the adoption of creole speech forms by youths of Caribbean parentage in Britain is linked to the assertion of an ethnic identity closely related to black interests and activities (such as rastafarianism and reggae music). In addition, the use of creole or "patois" is also linked to values of solidarity and ethnic pride, expressing at least a symbolic resistance to what many young blacks perceive as a repressive and racist society.

At the same time, throughout the world, the issues of race and ethnicity have recently been linked to the question of "language rights" or "linguistic human rights." A majority of the world's 5,000 languages face "language death" in the next 30 years. Local varieties of speech are being displaced by national and international languages, as a result of economic developments, and the effects of mass education and the mass media. Those working on the issue of language rights are concerned not only by the projected demise of many language varieties, but also by the unequal treatment currently accorded to speakers of minority languages, particularly in education, by governments and state institutions.

The recognition of "linguistic human rights" typically involves the recognition by the majority of both the ethnicity and the language of the minority. Internationally, the claims of minority groups have received formal recognition in agreements such as the UN Declaration of Indigenous Rights and The European charter for Regional and Minority Languages, and minorities such as the Basques, Catalans, and the Welsh have recorded some success in maintaining and reviving their languages. In coming decades, the issue of linguistic human rights is likely to grow in importance, but not just as a linguistic issue – what happens to linguistic minorities in all aspects of their lives in nation-states across the globe.

Reading

London Jamaican: Language Systems in Interaction by Mark Sebba (Longman, 1993) is a study of the forms of Jamaican creole spoken by black youth in Britain.

Linguistic Human Rights: Overcoming Linguistic Discrimination edited by Tove Skutnabb-Kangas and Robert Phillipson (Walter de Gruyter, 1994) provides an overview of the growing debate on linguistic human rights, with discussions of language rights in many societies throughout the world, including the United States, New Zealand, Latin America, and postcolonial Africa.

Acts of Identity by Robert Le Page and Andrée Tabouret-Keller (Cambridge University Press, 1985) is a masterly description of Caribbean creole languages, but also much more, including a theory of language use in multilingual societies and detailed sections on language and race, language, and ethnicity and London Jamaican creole.

Language and Ethnic Relations edited by Howard Giles and Bernard Saint-Jacques (Pergamon Press, 1980) is a collection of articles dealing with language and ethnicity at the level of both theory and case study.

See also: ARYAN; CREOLE; COLONIALISM; ETHNICITY

Kingsley Bolton

Latinos

The designation of Latinos or Hispanics (the terms are used interchangeably) refers to persons of Spanish origin who come from Spanish-speaking Latin America, as well as from the Iberian peninsula. The term also includes individuals whose ancestors come from those regions of the world. Journalists and leaders from the Latino communities began to refer to the 1980s as the decade of the Hispanics. Much of the attention was focused upon the significant growth rate among persons of Spanish origin and the potential for impacting the social, cultural, and political fabric of the United States. The population growth was accounted for by a young population with a high fertility rate, and the significant influx of immigrants from Latin America. There are over 25 million Latinos in the United States (10.2 percent of the total population). Demographic projections suggest that in 2020 they will be the largest ethnic minority, with 49 million. Much of the immigration has come from Mexico, since its revolution at the turn of the century, with more dramatic increases since the 1960s. The other major contributing source countries have been Cuba (since the Castro regime) and Puerto Ricans (since the mid-1950s). Most recently, Central American refugees have migrated from their countries to flee political instability and physical violence.

Thus, the more recent resurgence of Latino politics is tied with the growing presence of persons of Spanish origin. At the same time, the Latino group "umbrella" represents a configuration of many national origin persons (i.e. Mexicans, Guatemalans, Argentines, Cubans, etc.). As a result, previous political efforts have been directed by each of the Latino subcommunities, on their own behalf. The aggregation of Latinos represents a more recent phenomenon that has the net effect of enlarging the group's population and geographical bases to play a role in the national political arena. Another important background consideration in the understanding of Latino politics is the significant numbers of both native and foreign-born persons. As a result, each subgroup is different in socioeconomic status (i.e. foreign-born Latinos are less-educated, more Spanish-language dominant, and occupy lower status and paying occupations), as well as in its contact with institutions and agents of the political system. Puerto Ricans born in the Commonwealth of Puerto Rico enjoy U.S. citizenship status; while other Latino "immigrants" are classified as refugees (more the case for Cubans), permanent resident aliens or undocumented workers.

Thus, these prefatory comments help to establish Latinos in the United States as a fast-growing combination of Spanish-origin groups that forms the second largest minority group in the United States (soon to be the largest minority, according to a 1996 Census Bureau report that predicted the Latino population would grow to 24.5 per cent by 2050). They consist of long-standing "indigenous" members (not so the case for Mexican-origin persons) and recent international migrants. There are both the preservations of native cultural traditions as well as acculturation of American mores and values. For our purposes, Latinos in the United States have achieved some level of recognition and presence in U.S. society and its political institutions.

The Latino "umbrella"

The Latino umbrella comprises distinct national origin groups, of which Mexican-origin people are the largest segment (approximately two-third of all Latinos). They are found predominantly in the southwestern region of the United States. More recent migration patterns have found Mexican Americans in the midwest region, and to some extent, the Washington, D.C., area. The political development of this community had its more recent origins during the socially and politically active decade of the 1960s. The Chicano movement developed an ideology that incorporated determination and community control, and cultural revitalization. It is of note that working-class segments of the Chicano community served as both the leadership and organizational base for this political movement. This period of heightened politicization among the Mexican-origin community served as one of the antecedents of contemporary Latino politics.

To some degree, similar developments occurred among Puerto Rican communities in the northeastern United States, particularly in the New York metropolitan region. Again, issues of community control, a positive self-image culturally, and attacking discrimination and unequal access to economic and political opportunities were the primary foci within many Puerto Rican communities. The political development of Cubans occurred with the significant exodus of Cubanos following the fall of the Batista regime. Since 1969, waves of Cubans have migrated, primarily to southern Florida. Recognized political refugee status, with accompanying governmental aid, and middle-class migration from Cuba helped to facilitate the economic adaptation of the Cuban community. Given their refugee status, the issues of continued support for Cuban refugees, trade embargoes against Cuba, supporting U.S. efforts against Communist regimes, and economic development fostered Cubans' political activities. This brief outline of "pre-Latino" politics serves to characterize distinct national origin communities that were trying to develop their own political bases and resources to address inequalities and policy concerns for their respective communities.

Policy issues
A consensual and well-established Latino policy agenda is still in the process of more refinement and detail. Nevertheless, there are some common areas of interest and concern. One of the primary areas has to do with educational attainment, access, and quality. Besides the needs of limited English-speaking students through bilingual programs, school financing, and equal resources for Latinos, especially those attending segregated schools, and representation of Latinos in all segments of the educational system are major issues for Latinos. Latinos view gains in educational attainment as pivotal for improved social mobility and economic stability. Latinos, over the decade of the 1980s, have experienced higher unemployment rates than nonminority workers. Thus education represents an important vehicle to expand human capital investment. Concomitantly, issues related to the economy, jobs, job training, discrimination, and economic development and small business assistance are among the more important policy areas for Latinos.

With a significant proportion of the population foreign-born, and with continuous migration from Latin America to the United States, the area of immigration reform has placed the Latino community in difficult positions politically. That is, much of the immigration "controversy" has centered on illegal immigration, job competition, and depressed wages due to "cheap" foreign labor. For the most part, Latino immigrants are seen as the major source of both illegal and legal immigration. Thus, discussions of immigration place Latinos on the defensive and opposed to initiatives to curb immigration and tighten labor market controls. The passage of the Immigration

Reform Control Act (1986) represented efforts by Latino leaders to modify this legislative initiative to incorporate Latino policy concerns. They centered on civil rights protection for all Latinos, especially native-born, from employer discrimination. In addition, the "amnesty" provision to legalize the status of residing undocumented persons was largely the result of efforts of Latino leaders. Any effort to alter immigration policy, particularly in a restrictive manner, results in Latino political involvement.

One related issue to the significant percentage of foreign-born Latinos is that of naturalization. Latinos, especially Mexican-born, have among the lowest rates of naturalization among all immigrants. The high percentage of noncitizens serves to decrease the large population base and potential voting bloc. Recent efforts by organizations such as NALEO have targeted the noncitizen Latino segment in order to understand the factors which inhibit naturalization, as well as promotional tasks of encouraging more Latinos to become citizens.

The pattern of political participation among Latinos ranges from lower rates electorally from the nonminority population to greater degrees of involvement in the educational policy arena. Latino rates of voter registration and voter turnout tend to be 5–15 percent lower, although the differential is less for Cubans. Noncitizenship, lower levels of knowledge and interest about politics, alienation, and cynicism are some of the factors for such a pattern. Yet the disparity is lessening as Latinos tend to be more recent participants in American politics.

Organizationally, a lower percentage of Latinos belong to formal groups and contribute money than the general population. At the same time, there is awareness among Latinos of Latino organizations and their activities. Latino representation at all levels of the U.S. federal system has increased over the last twenty years. Much of that increase has been assisted by the decennial requirement to reapportion all legislative bodies based on the "one man, one vote" principle. The Latinos' fast growth and their location in the more populous states, has resulted in new legislative districts or new district boundaries that are competitive for Latino candidates. For example, in 1970, there were five Latinos (all Mexican Americans) serving in the U.S. House of Representatives. That number increased to ten in 1980; and now with the recent 1992 Congressional election, the Latino congressional delegation has been boosted to seventeen members. More dramatic gains have been made at the municipal and school district levels. Again, a recurring theme for

Latino politics is the process of penetrating the U.S. political system and making gains in representation and impacting the policymaking process.

Reading

Latino Voices: Mexican, Puerto Rican and Cuban Perspectives on American Politics by Rodolfo de la Garza, Louis Desipio, F. Chris Garcia, John A. Garcia and Angelo Falcon (Westview Press, 1992) presents the first set of findings of the Latino National Political Survey. This survey was the first national probability face-to-face interviews of persons of Mexican, Puerto Rican and Cuban origin.

Latinos and the Political System edited by Chris Garcia (University of Notre Dame Press, 1988) is a collection of articles and one of the few works on Latinos that specifically focuses on the range of politically relevant topics for this population.

Latinos and the U.S. Political System by Rodney Hero (Temple University Press, 1992) represents an attempt to place the area of Latino politics under a conceptual scheme, two-tier pluralism, in which to explain Latino political participation and impact; specific discussion is directed toward the various forms of political participation for the three major Latino groups.

See also: AZTLÁN; CHÁVEZ; MIGRATION; LAW: IMMIGRATION U.S.A.

John A. Garcia

Law: civil rights U.S.A.

Apart from the brief period immediately after the Civil War, American legislation up to 1938 had the effect of maintaining discrimination against blacks and other minority groups. Reconstruction was an exception to the general pattern, which denied blacks civil rights such as voting, access to education, and so on. The 1866 Civil Rights Act signaled the end of *de jure* discrimination (that is legal racialism), but various federal actions had worked to diminish racialism in various sectors before that time.

In 1938, for example, the Supreme Court ruled that the University of Missouri should admit a black applicant to law school because the state had no comparable institution open to blacks (*Missouri ex. rel. v. Canada*). Four years later, governmental agencies were instructed to end discrimination in employment; and, in 1946, segregated interstate travel was made illegal. Segregated transport was generally more widespread in southern states than in the north, though *de facto* segregation was rife throughout America, with public facilities having all-white and all-black areas.

In housing, blacks were prevented from buying certain properties by restrictive housing covenants (a provision attached to a deed in which the buyer must agree not to sell or rent to a member of a particular group, such as blacks, Jews, or Latinos). In 1948, the Supreme Court, in the *Shelly v. Kraemer* case, ruled that the restrictive covenants were not enforceable by the states any longer. This did not eliminate the covenants, however: it simply meant that they were no longer enforceable. The 1968 Act eventually banned them.

Perhaps the single most important piece of legislation in regard to race relations came in 1954 with the famous case of *Brown v. Board of Education*. The Supreme Court overturned the "separate but equal" principle established in 1896 by the *Plessy v. Ferguson* case in which it was established that different facilities should be made available to blacks. In the area of education, black institutions were truly separate but rarely equal to their white equivalents. The 1954 decision ended this and made segregation in schools illegal. The decision's importance was magnified by the fact that many believed that the whole issue of equality hinged on integrated schooling. The National Association for the Advancement of Colored People (NAACP) precipitated the 1954 ruling by arguing the case of Oliver Brown, whose daughter had been forced to travel by bus to an all-black school even though she lived close to an all-white institution. The NAACP insisted that school segregation was unconstitutional and the Supreme Court agreed, the presiding Chief Justice Warren concluding: "In the field of public education, the doctrine of 'separate but equal' has no place."

Between 1957 and 1960, Civil Rights legislation introduced enforcement powers through a Civil Rights Division of the U.S. Department of Justice. But the critical period in antidiscrimination legislation came over the following four years. Pressure from Martin Luther King's movement resulted in the strengthening of voting rights for blacks (1960) and the banning of discrimination (including sex discrimination) in employment and trade union membership as well as in access to privately owned accommodations, such as hotels, restaurants, and theaters. Enforcement of provisions against discrimination in education was also given more weight.

Constitutionally, the Civil Rights Act of 1964 was something of a watershed in U.S. race relations, extending federal powers to eliminate discrimination in places of public accommodation and the desegregation of all public facilities maintained by public organizations. In addition, public education was desegregated and the Civil Rights Commission granted new powers. Discrimination in employment on the grounds of "race, color, sex, or national origin" was illegalized. The Equal Employment Opportunity Commission was established to investigate and monitor complaints pertaining to this.

The most widespread requirement limiting minority voting was the literacy test that existed in various forms in numerous states in the South, West, and Northeast. This tended to reduce voting opportunities for black, Hispanic, and native American groups, because these groups suffered extensive educational discrimination and, therefore, did not always match up to the literacy test requirements (in some cases, this was compounded by the fact that more stringent demands were made of minorities than of whites). The Voting Rights Act of 1965 largely ended the tests. Discrimination of sorts continued with some states operating policies that governed voter registration that made voting easier for whites; but the 1965 Act made discrimination in access to the ballot box considerably more difficult.

Five key court decisions in 1989 paved the way for new legislation. The most important was *Wards Cove v. Antonio*, which involved the concept of "disparate impact," meaning a practice which is not intentionally discriminatory, but results in a statistically disproportionate effect on minority group members, or women. It was decided that the plaintiff had to prove that a minority was underrepresented in a particular type of job and demonstrate that there were qualified applicants in the labor market. *Price Waterhouse v. Hopkins* deliberated whether a "mixed motive" could lie behind discrimination: for an employee to win a case against an employer, he or she would need "clear and convincing proof" that the motives behind an action were completely discriminatory and not just that discrimination was present.

The 1991 Civil Rights Acts, signed by President George Bush, was effectively a response to the Supreme Court decisions that had narrowed the scope of existing anti-discrimination legislation. It upheld the *Wards Cove* principle that the plaintiff needed statistical proof. But it overturned *Price Waterhouse*. It became necessary to prove that discrimination was only part of the mixed motive. But the major change brought about in 1991 was the fact that parties taking action against intentional discrimination under the terms of the 1964 Civil Rights Act (specifically Title VII) would be entitled to a hearing by jury, which could decide the extent of compensatory damages, both monetary and emotional.

Reading
Rethinking the American Race Problem by Roy L. Brooks (University of California Press, 1990) is a detailed and theoretically informed analysis on the legal apparatus of the United States regarding discrimination.
Eye on the Prize by Juan Williams (Viking, 1987) is a tie-in with the

celebrated television series documenting the civil rights years, 1954–65, and showing how each piece of legislation was hard won.
Unlikely Heroes by Jack Bass (University of Alabama Press, 1992) is an account of the implementation of the *Brown* decision.

See also: AFFIRMATIVE ACTION; JIM CROW; SEGREGATION

Ellis Cashmore

Law: immigration (Britain)

The seventeenth and eighteenth centuries saw Britain and other Western European powers occupy vast portions of Africa, Asia, and the Caribbean. This colonial expansion laid the economic basis for the development of western capitalism: the colonies provided a source of cheap labor, raw materials, and, in some cases, markets. In the years immediately following the end of World War II, Britain exploited this source of cheap labor to the full. The introduction of the 1948 Nationality Act by the Labour government facilitated access to this source and while some members of what is commonly referred to as "the lunatic fringe" of the House of Commons protested publicly at the unregulated influx of black (and later South Asian) migrants, their demands tended to fall on deaf ears; quite simply, while many of their colleagues on both sides of the House shared this concern with the increased settlement of black migrants in Britain, priority was ultimately given to the country's economic priorities. Britain was experiencing rapid economic growth and the import of cheap labor to fill the subordinate levels of the labor market was essential. Nor did central government intervene in the settlement of the migrants in Britain. They were seen and treated simply as factory fodder and no attempt was made to facilitate settlement by the provision of educational, housing and welfare advice and facilities.

It was not until the economy began to take a turn for the worse in the mid-1950s and the demand for labor in major industries began to recede did the efficacy in Britain's approach to immigration come to be seriously questioned. On the one hand, local authorities which had borne the brunt of migrant settlement complained that their limited resources were stretched to the full. On the other, the outbreak of violence between blacks and whites in Notting Hill and Nottingham in 1958 highlighted the resentment felt by some sectors of the white population toward the black migrants. Against this background of imminent social and economic stress, the racialization of Britain's immigration policies emerged as an important fulcrum on which political debate was balanced. At the risk of oversimplification, two courses of action were available to the government: first, the implementation of policies designed to ameliorate the social problems highlighted by the settlement of colonial migrants in certain parts of Britain. Alternatively, central government could abandon its "open door," or noninterventionist immigration policy and impose controls on entry. On the face of it, this second approach was entirely unnecessary; as the leader of the opposition Labour party explained in the House of Commons in the early 1960s, migration was self-regulating: as the economy had entered a downward phase and the number of job vacancies gradually diminished, the number of migrants from the Caribbean had fallen accordingly. Nor was there much prospect of long-term unemployment. In this light, claims that the migrants would spend long periods drawing security benefits were completely untenable.

In the event, the Conservative government eschewed the more constructive and logical step of attacking social problems through policies to improve the living and working conditions of black and white residents. Instead, it embarked on a policy of surrender. The reasons behind this course of action are both complex and, in part, a matter for speculation. Nonetheless, recent research into cabinet and ministerial debates of this period indicate that controls of black immigration had always been favored. What seems to have inhibited, or at least delayed their introduction was the embarrassment which might have accompanied their initiation, given Britain's status as head of the Commonwealth and Colonies.

The Commonwealth Immigrants Act 1962 formally marked the end of Britain's allegedly (if not committed) *laissez-faire* approach to immigration. It established a precedent for the introduction of progressively more restrictive and, *de facto*, racially discriminatory immigration legislation, and presaged the start of what some parliamentary members and others had identified as the defining characteristic of the race relations debate: numbers.

Briefly, the Act qualified the right of free entry into Britain for migrants from the New Commonwealth; that is, black and brown migrants. Although skin color was not openly declared the criterion for entry, the exclusion of citizens of the Irish Republic from the constraints of the Act signified its racially discriminatory nature.

By 1965, selective immigration control had become bipartisan policy. Despite its relatively strong opposition to the 1962 legislation the Labour party had, by 1965, completed a *volte face* on this issue and, for the sake of political expediency, introduced an extension of the earlier Act. In short, 1965 marked the point of public consensus in Westminster based on an identification of black and brown people as "the problem" and "turning off the tap" as the solution to that problem. "Keeping numbers down is good for race relations" became the organizing principle of this bipartisan policy. As Labour MP, Roy Hattersley, put it in 1965: "Without integration, limitation is inexcusable; without limitation, integration is impossible."

This principle has subsequently been put into practice by both major political parties in 1968, 1971, 1981, and 1988. Although blacks in Britain retain formal citizenship, the effect of these laws has been successively to undermine their welfare and security. In all, these selective controls have institutionalized the notion of differential rights and status between white and nonwhite populations in their relation to Britain. The 1971 Immigration Act, for example, effectively ended all primary immigration (that is, heads of households) from the New Commonwealth and placed colonial migrant workers in Britain on an equal footing with, say, "guest workers," or *Gastarbeiter*, in Germany. The 1981 Nationality Act went even further by curtailing, among other things, the citizenship rights of black and brown people brought up in Britain. The 1988 Immigration Act goes further down the line of restrictive and racist legislation by introducing "means tested" conditions on entry. It is quite clear that inequalities in the global distribution of wealth means that potential migrants from Bangladesh who wish to join their families in Britain will be more likely to be hit by this regulation than many of their white counterparts.

In 1978, Ann Dummett pointed out that although immigration laws formally constitute part of the country's external policies, they cannot be divorced entirely from its general policy on race relations; this is because they express "by means of their definition of wanted and unwanted newcomers, what kind of society each Government is aiming for." The pertinence and veracity of this observation in the case of Britain is clear. The external immigration controls in Britain have become more restrictive, so the government's reliance on internal controls, such as passport checking and police surveillance of "suspected" illegal immigrants has become correspondingly greater. The 1981 Nationality Act and 1988 Immigration Act ensured that this pattern of internal harassment was sustained. The Asylum and Immigration (Appeals) Act received Royal assent in 1993 and, over the next two years, refusals of asylum applications increased from 16 percent to 76 percent. Further restriction on asylum seekers were debated in 1996 when the Asylum and Immigration Bill came under consideration. Included among its provisions were: (1) excluding asylum seekers from a "white list" of countries; (2) removing asylum seekers to a "safe" third country if they passed through such a designated country before arriving in Britain; (3) reducing the right of in-country appeal for many asylum seekers; (4) introducing a legal category of "immigrant" which included many long-term residents of Britain who would not automatically have the same rights as other citizens; (5) increasing the powers of police and immigration officials; (6) making employers criminally liable for the status of their employees.

The reintegration of former British colony Hong Kong into the People's Republic of China in June 1997 introduced the question of whether the 3.3 million Hong Kong-born residents had the right to live and work in Britain. Special British Nation Overseas passports were issued and these entitled holders to visit but not work in Britain. Exceptions to this were those passport holders who were prepared to invest £1 million ($1.6 million) in government treasury bonds.

Reading
A Tolerant Country? by Colin Holmes (Faber and Faber, 1991) is a short and pithy account of the patterns of immigration into Britain and the response these have elicited from the white indigenous communities.
"The 1951–55 Conservative government and the racialization of black immigration policy" features in *Inside Babylon* (Verso, 1993) edited by Winston James and Clive Harris. Written by Bob Carter, Clive Harris and Shirley Joshi, it challenges conventional views about Britain's alleged *laissez-faire* immigration policies between 1948 and 1962.
The Immigration Act 1988 is a Warwick University Policy Paper in Ethnic Relations, published in 1991. In it, Chris Platt interrogates the content, effects and implications of this, the latest in a long line of policies which restrict the entry of blacks into Britain and impact differentially on the citizenship rights of Britain's black communities.

See also: LAW: IMMIGRATION U.S.A.; MIGRATION; SCAPEGOAT

Barry Troyna/Ellis Cashmore

Law: immigration U.S.A.

The history of U.S. immigration policy falls into five distinct periods: 1609–1775 (colonial period); 1776–1881 (open door phase); 1882–1916 (regulation phase); 1917–1964 (restriction phase); 1965-present (liberalization phase).

In the seventeenth century, colonial immigration policy was shaped by the need for labor to work the virgin lands of the New World. Schemes were designed to attract people to the colonies from Europe and the British Isles. Transportation was laid on and subsidies for the purchase of land and tools for new settlers provided. Bounties were paid to those who could secure the services of indentured laborers and take them to America.

The availability of work and property was the major incentive for migrating, though the religious policy of most of the colonies was also a magnet. Apart from New England, all areas tolerated most varieties of Christianity. Some places became religious enclaves, such as Maryland for English Catholics, and Pennsylvania for Quakers. There were three important components established in this phase:

- local government exercised jurisdiction over immigration and settlement;
- local government and private entrepreneurs were responsible for recruiting immigrants from overseas;
- economic developments stimulated an active search for new sources of labor, so that policy was directed toward encouraging the flow of immigrants.

The British government's refusal to recognize general naturalization acts bred conflict as it restricted settlement in the areas where labor was required. In fact, this was one of the grievances that led colonists to take up arms against the British in 1775. The War of Independence brought with it a new concept of national identity and the new Americans began to see themselves as a unique "frontier people." This influenced the Constitution drafted in 1787 and made foreign people ineligible for high political positions until they fulfilled residential qualifications.

Congress passed federal laws in 1790 allowing for the granting of citizenship to any whites who resided and abided by the law for two years. This was a very relaxed policy and laid the basis for the massive growth of population in the nineteenth century. From 1820 to 1860, there was some regulation of migrant traffic at major entry ports, particularly New York, and ships' masters were made to give details of their passengers, making it possible to identify and possibly deport the infirm and destitute who could make no meaningful contribution to the labor force. Criteria for entry were such things as medical health, trade or craft, and religion, so there was little control over immigration. Federal officials kept no records of immigrants until 1820. The emphasis was very much on getting as much labor as possible; so much so that there was some intense competition between states.

By the 1870s, over 280,000 immigrants a year were disembarking at American ports. Overwhelmed by the growing volume, Congress

declared existing state laws regulating immigration unconstitutional
and enacted a series of statutes to bring immigration under federal
control.

In the late nineteenth century, the federal government erected
the bureaucratic structure to operate the new immigration control.
Restrictions gradually got tighter as speculation about the links
between immigrants and social problems mounted. One notable
flashpoint arose over the issue of Chinese workers: labor organizations felt threatened by the nonunionized, unskilled laborers who
were willing to work for low wages. Pressure resulted in new legislation preventing Chinese workers from acquiring citizenship (thus
making them more amenable to control).

The Chinese Exclusion Act of 1882 was a significant move in
identifying a group thought to be unassimilable and threatening.
Again, in the 1890s, a group was perceived as undesirable: these
were "new immigrants" from southern and eastern Europe who
were filing into urban centers. More stringent rules were added in
regard to health and competence; about 15 per cent of migrants
were being rejected by the end of the century.

However, the "alien wedge" continued to be driven in, particularly by the Japanese in California. In 1910, the Dillingham Report
on the harmful effects of immigration argued, albeit implicitly, that
the "new immigrants" were racially inferior to those from northern
and western Europe. So people like Slavs and Sicilians became the
source of panic as they were thought to be incapable of becoming
"Americanized."

The 1917 Immigration Act was the first of a sequence of severely
restrictive statutes based on the report. Restricted zones were
located, literacy tests introduced and a ranked order of eligible
immigrants drawn up. No limits on the Western Hemisphere were
imposed and the lack of restrictions on neighbors ensured a steady,
cheap supply of Central American labor. Southern and eastern
European immigration was sharply curtailed and no labor was
allowed from the so-called Asiatic Barred Zone (including India,
Indo-China, and other smaller Asian countries). This effectively
signaled the beginning of the era of restriction. Quota systems were
later introduced, allowing for annual quotas of immigrants from
specific countries. The thrust of later acts was to select those groups
considered best suited to American society.

There were inadequate methods of classifying national origins
that undermined the quota system and the effort to thwart "unassimilable" groups was not effective. However, by the 1930s, the system

was fully operative and immigration began to drop, especially with the onset of the Great Depression; large portions of the quotas went unfilled. In fact, for the first time in its history, the number of people leaving the United States exceeded the number entering. World War II prompted the U.S. Government to make special provisions for groups suffering hardship as the result of war experiences.

Perhaps the most significant piece of immigration legislation in modern times is the McCarran-Walter Act of 1952: this tightened restrictions on migrants from the colonies of quota-receiving countries, so that black immigrants from the West Indies who had previously entered under the British quota were sharply cut down (this, in turn, stimulated many migrants to turn to Britain as an alternative and so precipitate a massive rise in Caribbean migration to Britain). There were, however, liberalizing elements in the Act, such as the allowance of no less than 85 percent of the total annual quota to northern and Western European countries and the extension of quotas to Asian countries.

The Kennedy administration attacked the national origins quota system as having no "basis in logic or reason" and its reform eventually resulted in the 1965 Hart-Celler Act (the provisions of which took effect in 1968). The quota system was abolished and the ceiling on annual immigration raised to 290,000, at the same time removing any preferential treatment for Western countries (this was later revised in 1976 to give Western immigrants with training, skills or family ties priority).

The reforms since the mid-twentieth century have served to dismantle some of the exclusionary measures installed when the federal government assumed control over immigration without removing the crucial link between immigration flow and labor requirements which has become a feature of all industrial societies. The importance of this link is reinforced by the concern over illegal immigration, particularly from Mexico (over half a million arrests and deportations take place annually and between one and eight million Mexicans are thought to reside illegally in the United States).

The Immigration Reform and Control Act of 1986 was designed specifically to combat such illegal immigration: it established sanctions against employers who hired unauthorized workers who could show they had worked at least ninety days in agriculture in the United States in the year ending 1 May 1986. But inadvertently, the law also gave rise to a market in counterfeit documents that undermined the objectives of the legislation. Unless a document was obviously bogus, it was usually evidence enough to protect an employer from the law's penalties, ranging from a $100 fine to six months' imprisonment. A 1992 report on the law by the Commission on Agricultural workers found that the law had made virtually no difference to the flow of illegal immigration; and it proposed changes to toughen enforcement. The report was due to be submitted to Congress in 1993.

The years 1995–6 witnessed a spate of activity to curb immigration. California's Proposition 187, as it came to be known, triggered a national debate: it was an "initiative that bars undocumented aliens from receiving public education and most government-funded social and health services," and, as such, had an adverse effect on illegal migrants from Mexico and their children. In a similar vein, the Clinton administration and the Republican leadership in Congress, advocated stronger efforts against illegal migrants and sponsored separate bills that would reduce legal immigration by about one third.

While much of the debate centered on whether immigrants would take jobs from Americans, the subtext concerned population growth and ethnic diversity. In 1996, a report by the Census Bureau in Washington, D.C., predicted a significant demographic shift fuelled by immigration and high birth rates among Latino women. The proportion of whites would shrink from 74 percent to 53 percent in 2050, with Latinos increasing from 10.2 to 24.5 percent and Asians from 3.3 to 8.2 percent. The African-American population, the report forecast, would rise just 1.6 percent.

Reading
The Distant Magnet: European Emigration to the USA by Philip Taylor (Eyre & Spottiswood, 1971) analyzes the movements from Europe and the "pull" factors drawing people to America – and may be read with *Immigration as a Factor in American History* by Oscar Handlin (Prentice-Hall, 1959) which is a classic text on early migration.

Immigration in America's Future by David Heer (Westview, 1996) focuses on migration trends in the United States and raises questions about the nature of immigration policy. Covering the dispute over Proposition 187, the influx of Cuban refugees into Florida, and the illegal border crossings into California and Texas, Heer links the reaction to these episodes with basic concerns over standards of living, the preservation of "American culture," ethnic and class conflict, and the nation's role in foreign affairs.

See also: LAW: IMMIGRATION (BRITAIN); MIGRATION

Ellis Cashmore

Law: race relations (Britain)

The development of antidiscrimination laws in Britain has to be considered, first and foremost, against a background of increasingly Draconian measures designed initially to reduce the number of black and brown migrants entering the country, and subsequently to eliminate this process entirely. By invoking the principle, "keeping numbers down is good for race relations," both major political parties consistently have presented antidiscrimination laws as a complementary aspect of their policy initiatives on this issue. The imperative for these laws has been to secure equality of opportunity for all people in Britain, irrespective of ascribed features such as skin color. The reality of the situation, however, suggests that they are seen as little more than a token gesture by the nonwhite populations of Britain whose confidence in the state's commitment to "harmonious race relations" has been irrevocably undermined by the obsession with the numbers question, the development of external and internal immigration controls, the division of family units, and so on. These constitute the thrust of state policy and formally legitimate the second class status of the nonwhite communities in Britain. In short, the avowed intention to create a society in which "every citizen shares an equal right to the same freedoms, the same responsibilities, the same opportunities (and) the same benefits" is no nearer its realization in the 1990s than it was when it was first declared in 1968 by the Labour government's Home Secretary, James Callaghan.

Framework

Moves to ensure equal opportunities for the nonwhite communities in Britain has most often been associated with the Labour party, but it was not until 1965 that the development of an exclusionist immigration policy was accompanied by any action to improve the position of these communities. In that year, the Labour government introduced its White Paper, *Immigration from the Commonwealth*, which tried to sweeten the pill of further immigration restrictions by introducing protective laws to combat racial discrimination. Compared to similar initiatives in Canada and the United States, the 1965 Race Relations Bill was very limited in scope. It outlawed racial discrimination in "places of public resort" such as restaurants, hotels, places of entertainment, and on public transportation, and set up the Race Relations Board which was charged with the responsibility to deal with complaints of discrimination and resolve them through conciliation.

But, quite apart from its practical limitations – it failed to protect nonwhites from discriminatory practices in housing and work spheres, for instance – the 1965 Bill was also logically incoherent. On the one hand, it insisted that the black and brown migrants were not depriving whites of jobs, did not have lower health and sanitation standards, and were not sponging off the welfare state. Having denounced racialism and dissociated itself from racialist practices, however, the Labour government then proceeded to orchestrate and support racist views by implementing immigration policies which deliberately excluded nonwhites.

The limited practical use of the antidiscrimination laws included in the 1965 Bill was highlighted by the findings of the PEP investigation two years later. This revealed the extent of discrimination along color lines in employment and housing. The need for an extension to the 1965 measures was further underlined by the eruption of violence in the Watts district of Los Angeles, and elsewhere in the United States around this time. It was precisely the systematic denial of equal opportunity that had precipitated the volatile reaction of blacks in the United States. Fearful of a similar occurrence in the UK, the Labour government initiated new legislation in 1968, the Race Relations Act. This enlarged the scope of the law to the important spheres of employment and housing and crucially, the powers of the Race Relations Board were not extended. It remained a reactive body, permitted to respond to complaints rather than to initiate investigations into racialist practices. Quite obviously, a law that required proof of deliberate acts of racial discrimination could have only a limited effect on the more widespread patterns of inequality between whites and nonwhites; after all, it could do nothing to cope with the more subtle, less visible and conspicuous expressions of racial discrimination.

The veracity of this argument was demonstrated in the next PEP investigation which reported its findings in the mid-1970s. It showed that the proscription by law of racialism in housing and employment had led to a substantial decrease in its incidence; at the same time, this apparent success of the 1968 Race Relations Act may have been mitigated by the replacement of overt racialist practices by less conspicuous and detectable forms of its operation. What is more, the PEP study showed that discrimination along color lines remained common and that many nonwhites who had been discriminated against had failed to inform the Race Relations Board.

Commission for Racial Equality
Along with the development of innovative and antidiscrimination
laws in the United States and the introduction of Britain's Sex
Discrimination Act (1975), the PEP survey provided the catalyst for
further legislation in this field. In 1976, the Labour government
introduced a new Race Relations Act. This totally restructured
the machinery dealing with antidiscrimination and integrated the
functions of the Race Relations Board and the Community
Relations Commission (which had been established in 1968 to promote "harmonious community relations") into a new body, the
Commission for Racial Equality (CRE). Unlike its predecessor, the
CRE had been empowered to initiate investigations where it suspected discrimination has taken place and, where its investigations
proved positive, to issue non-discrimination notices.

Since its inception, the CRE has been assailed on all sides; in
1981, for instance, a team from the Home Affairs Sub-Committee
on Race Relations and Immigrations was severely critical of the
CRE's lack of direction, its incohesiveness and consequently, its
ineffectual attempts at eliminating racial discrimination.

It is difficult to deny the legitimacy of these and other criticism
of the CRE. Put bluntly, the CRE suffers from the tension created
by its two principal, some might say irresolvable functions: the
promotion of "harmonious community relations" and the investigation of alleged discrimination. Which of these should assume
priority remains a dilemma which continues to tantalize. At the
same time, it needs to be recognized that the CRE functions in a
political climate which is not only indifferent to a coordinated policy
on race relations but is wholly antagonistic to such a policy. Regardless of the internal faults of the CRE, any organization integrated
into the state machinery is unlikely to be effective either in combating racial discrimination or assuaging the anxieties of the nonwhite
communities in Britain. How can the CRE or the range of antidiscrimination measures be effective when they are linked to governments which are resolutely determined to prevent black and brown
settlement in Britain and to sanction the low status of these communities? In this context, policies to combat racial discrimination,
however determined and well organized, can never be sufficient to
ensure equality between white and nonwhite citizens in Britain.

Reading
"Racial inequality and the limits of law" by L. Lustgarten and J. Edwards
appears in *Racism and Antiracism* (Sage Books, 1992) edited by Peter
Braham and colleagues. It explores the ineffectiveness of the 1976 Race

Relations Act in particular, and the weakness of antidiscrimination law, generally.

Race and Racism in Contemporary Britain (Macmillan, 1989) by John Solomos provides a readable account of the origins and impact of anti-racial discrimination legalization in Britain.

See also: LAW: CIVIL RIGHTS; LAW: RACIAL DISCRIMINATION; MIGRATION

Barry Troyna

Law: racial discrimination (international)

The accepted definition of racial discrimination is that to be found in the International Convention on the Elimination of All Forms of Racial Discrimination, article 1 (1): "any distinction, exclusion, restriction or preference based on race, color, descent, or national or ethnic origin which has the purpose or effect of nullifying or impairing the recognition, enjoyment or exercise, on an equal footing, of human rights and fundamental freedoms in the political, economic, social, cultural or any other field of public life." This definition specifies [i] a prohibited ground of action (one "based on race" etc.); [ii] four protected classes of persons (those differentiated by race, etc.); and [iii] a sphere in which the protections must operate (in public life).

The international definition is inspired by a concept of human rights as the rights of all peoples, which are above the state and which the state must respect. The United States definition derives from the concept of citizenship in the constitution of 1789. British law stems from a statute passed by Parliament as the law-giver.

Reading

The Lawful Rights of Mankind by Paul Sieghart (Oxford University Press, 1986) and *Equality and Discrimination under International Law* by Warwick McKean (Clarendon Press, 1983) both take a global perspective on the subject.

International Action Against Racial Discrimination by Michael Banton (Oxford University Press, 1996) covers the main initiatives.

See also: INTERNATIONAL CONVENTION; LAW: CIVIL RIGHTS U.S.A.; LAW: RACE RELATIONS (BRITAIN)

Michael Banton

Lee, Spike (1957–)

Perhaps the most original and, in many ways, iconoclastic black filmmaker of his generation, Lee was born in Atlanta, Georgia, the oldest of five children. His father was Bill Lee, an acclaimed jazz bassist, and his mother Jacquelyne (Shelton) Lee, a teacher. Shelton Jackson Lee moved with his family to Chicago and, in 1959, to

Brooklyn, New York – where his early films were set. He took an interest in film during his studies at Morehouse College and, after graduating, gained an internship at Columbia Pictures in California, before returning to New York, where he obtained a master's degree at the Institute of Film and Television, New York University. His master's thesis film, *Joe's Bed-Study Barbershop: We Cut Heads* received a student Academy Award and was screened internationally at film festivals.

His first two commercial films, *She's Gotta Have It* (1986) and *School Daze* (1988) were both popular successes, but his third eclipsed both, in terms of its commercial success and critical acclaim. *Do the Right Thing* (1989) was dropped by Paramount Pictures after Lee refused to change its ending, a violent conflict in which African Americans torch an Italian-owned pizzeria and a white police officer kills a black youth. The film essayed interethnic tensions in New York's Bedford-Stuyvesant district and showed blacks as flawed and fallible. It was eventually released by Universal Pictures. Subsequent films, like *Mo' Better Blues* (1990) avoided the homeboy/drugs/violence stereotype favored by many of Lee's peers. *Jungle Fever* (1991), in particular, portrayed blacks and other ethnic minorities as complex, multifaceted and prone to the kinds of prejudices conventionally reserved for whites. The film told of an ethnic *mésalliance* between a black male and an Italian woman.

Lee's career-defining movie was a film biography of *Malcolm X* (1992), the directorship of which was originally awarded to Norman Jewison, a white male. Lee won the job after arguing forcefully and typically that white directors are unable to convey the richness of black culture on film. He had previously singled out Steven Spielberg for his film version of Alice Walker's *The Color Purple* (1986). Lee has contended that "we (blacks) can't just sit back and let other people define our existence, especially when they're putting lies out there on the screen" (*Washington Post*, October 22, 1986).

Reading
"Spike Lee hates your cracker ass" by Barbara G. Harrison in *Esquire* (October 1992) features an interview with Lee on the subject of Malcolm X, whose philosophies, Lee urges, should be mixed with those of Martin Luther King: "the synthesis is not going to include total nonviolence."
Spike Lee by Alex Patterson (Avon Books, 1992) is an unauthorized biography, which revealingly quotes Lee: "Black people have been dogged in the media since Day One [but] we overreact when we think that every image of us has to be 100 percent angelic."

See also: AFROCENTRICITY; MALCOLM X; MEDIA AND RACISM; RAP MUSIC

Ellis Cashmore

Los Angeles riots, 1992

See RIOTS: U.S.A., 1992

M

Malcolm X (1925–65)

A prominent spokesman for black nationalism in the United States in the 1950s and 1960s, Malcolm Little (as he was christened) has become arguably more influential intellectually since his assassination in 1965 at the age of 40. His radical arguments for black separatism and endorsement of violence make him, in many ways, Martin Luther King's alter ego. At a time when King's Southern Christian Leadership Conference was using nonviolent disobedience as its main strategy in securing civil rights reform, with integration its ultimate goal, Malcolm X urged blacks to disavow themselves of Christianity, reject the very concept of integration and abandon any thoughts that the material conditions of blacks would be improved through white patronage.

Malcolm was born on 19 May 1925 in Omaha, Nebraska. His father, Earl Little, used his itinerant Baptist ministry to preach the black nationalist ideas of Marcus Garvey; he was a member of Garvey's Universal Negro Improvement Association. This was a factor in his murder by whites when Malcolm was six years old. The murderers were never found. Malcolm moved to Boston when he was fifteen to live with his half-sister, Ella. A few years later, he moved to Harlem, New York, and earned a living pimping and pushing drugs, activities that brought him into conflict with the law.

Malcolm became attracted to the Nation of Islam (Black Muslims) while serving a jail sentence which began in 1946. He studied the writings of Elijah Muhammad and, on his release in 1952, went to Chicago to meet Elijah. He took the name of Malcolm X (which he later changed to El-Hajj Malik El-Shabazz). Two years later, he left to lead a mosque in Harlem.

His rift with the Nation of Islam came about in 1963 when he was suspended for regarding the death of John F. Kennedy as a case of "the chickens coming home to roost." (He later explained that, as farm boy from Omaha, he regarded the return of chickens to roost as a joyous event.) He parted with the movement, though he privately had misgivings for some time before, as he revealed in his autobiography: "I was convinced that our Nation of Islam could be an even greater force in the American Black Man's overall struggle – if we engaged in more *action*."

In 1964 Malcolm, having left the Nation of Islam, began to espouse his own distinct ideas of a black international struggle. The organization he founded to express these views was the Organization of Afro-American Unity (OAAU). He retained his Islamic beliefs, making a pilgrimage to Mecca. He also traveled to West Africa, where he personally met several national leaders. His reputation was growing at a time when King was pushing steadily and successfully for civil rights legislation, but also when many blacks, dissatisfied with the slow-paced reforms, were looking for alternative, more direct approaches. Although he actually met with King in 1964, the year before he had strongly denounced him and his movement in a speech (reprinted in *The End of White Supremacy* edited by I. B. Karim, Arcade Publishing, 1971). "I think any black man who goes among so-called Negroes today who are being brutalized, spit upon in the worst fashion imaginable and teaches those Negroes to turn the other cheek, to suffer peacefully, or love their enemy is a traitor to the Negro," said Malcolm. "If it is all right for black people to be drafted and sent to Korea or South Vietnam or Laos or Berlin or some place else to fight and die for the white man, then there is nothing wrong with the same black man doing the same thing when he is under the brutality in this country at the hands of the white man."

During his last three months of life, he linked national progress in Africa to the emancipation of women. He dropped his earlier proposal for an independent black state in the United States and relaxed his strictures on ethnically mixed marriages. He also endorsed voter registration and political involvement, though he warned that civil rights legislation did not defuse the "social dynamite" in the ghetto. It was a prescient warning, as 1965 saw the beginning of a two-year period of black uprising. While he was not alive to witness this, he would have endorsed it, as he taught that "a person who is fighting racism is well within his rights to fight against it by any means necessary" – a phrase for which he is remembered.

His assassination at an OAAU rally in Harlem on 21 February 1965, is still surrounded by mystery. Rumors of plots had circulated when he visited Paris shortly before his death. He was known to be under the surveillance of the FBI. Three members of the Nation of Islam were convicted of shooting him, but speculation remains about the guilt of two of the convicted men and about the complicity of the New York City Police, the FBI, and, possibly, the CIA.

Twenty years after his death, Malcolm underwent a cultural resurrection courtesy of rap music, and a canonization on the authority of film director Spike Lee. The title of Dyson's book, *Making Malcolm*, suggests the process by which legacy was commodified and sold to a new generation of blacks. By the early 1990s, "X" had become a logo and political pronouncements ("by any means necessary"; "I don't even call it violence when it's self-defense, I call it intelligence") mere bromides.

Reading

The Autobiography of Malcolm X written with Alex Haley (Hutchinson & Collins, 1966) and *Victims of Democracy* by Victor Wolfenstein (Guildford, 1993) are two of several life histories.

From Civil Rights to Black Liberation: Malcolm X and the Organization of Afro-American Unity by William W. Sales (South End Press, 1994) focuses on Malcolm's influence on black politics in the 1960s, with particular reference to the O.A.A.U.

Making Malcolm: The Myth and Meaning of Malcolm X by Michael E. Dyson (Oxford University Press, 1995) analyzes the emergence of Malcolm as an icon of militant black nationalism.

See also: BLACK POWER; KING; NATION OF ISLAM

Ellis Cashmore

Mandela, Nelson (1918–)

Nelson Mandela was born in the royal family of the Tembu in Transkei in 1918. Groomed to become a chief, he attended Headtown School in the Eastern Cape and later Fort Hare University College, where he was expelled in 1940 for his activities in student politics. Many African leaders, including Robert Mugabe, later President of Zimbabwe, studied at the time at Fort Hare which became the center of early anticolonial sentiments and liberation strategies. After moving to Johannesburg, Mandela studied law and, together with Oliver Tambo, set up the first African attorneys' practice in 1952.

Together with Walter Sisulu, Mandela was active in the African National Congress Youth League, of which he became national president in 1950. He helped to organize the passive resistance campaign to defy Apartheid laws which led to his first arrest and suspended sentence under the Suppression of Communism Act. Banned from political activity, he nevertheless reorganized the ANC branches into small cells for the expected functioning underground. In 1956 Mandela was among the 156 political leaders charged with high treason, followed by the anti-pass campaign and demonstrations against the declaration of the Republic. In 1961, after the ANC and PAC were outlawed, Mandela went underground and traveled to Addis Ababa, Algeria and London where he addressed conferences and conferred with political leaders.

A few weeks after his return to South Africa in July 1962, Mandela was arrested and charged with incitement and leaving the country illegally. Together with his fellow conspirators on the Rivonia farm outside Johannesburg, he was sentenced to life imprisonment on 12 June 1964.

On 11 February 1990, Mandela was finally released unconditionally after he had rejected earlier offers to be freed on condition that he undertook not to engage in violent resistance.

After twenty-six years' imprisonment, Mandela quickly filled a gaping vacuum in the heterogeneous ANC camp. His leadership unified the oldest and most popular liberation movement as he straddled the divide between a militant youth and older traditionalists, revolutionaries and pragmatists, Africanist nationalists and liberal universalists, orthodox socialists and social-democratic capitalists. Without Mandela's mythos, the ANC would not have been able to rally its skeptical constituency behind the new politics of negotiations, suspend the armed struggle, and soften promises of nationalization and redistribution. Likewise, Mandela's remarkable lack of bitterness and his moderation were crucial in convincing the white segment to share political power and agree to universal franchise without being defeated militarily.

At the same time, the gloss of liberation wore off as Mandela entered the fray of political wheeling and dealing. His failure to reconcile the ANC with rival anti-apartheid groupings, particularly Zulu chief Mangosuthu Buthelezi's Inkatha Freedom Party and the Pan African Congress, contributed to escalating political violence. By placing himself solidly in the ANC as his power base, and subjecting himself to an organizational mandate, Mandela has the role of a reconciling statesman above the petty party competition. His tragic loyalty to his maverick wife, Winnie, before their formal separation and divorce, together with Mandela's support for Arafat's PLO, Libya's Gadhaffi, and Cuba's Castro, have raised questions about Mandela's political judgment. Many critics charge that the erstwhile global prisoner was in danger of becoming a mere figurehead and fundraiser, a symbol more powerful behind prison bars than in the harsher real world. Nevertheless he was elected President in April 1994.

Reading
South Africa in Crisis edited by J. Blumenfeld (Croom Helm, 1987) documents the perceptions and policies of all the major interest groups and their roles in the state of ferment.
State Resistance and Change in South Africa edited by P. Frankel, N. Pines, and M. Swilling (Croom Helm, 1987) is a set of chapters organized around the themes of state, resistance and change and examines the ANC in particular.
Long Walk to Freedom (Little, Brown, 1994) is Mandela's autobiography.

See also: APARTHEID; SMUTS; SOUTH AFRICA; VERWOERD

Heribert Adam

Maoris
See NATIVE PEOPLES

Marley, Bob
See REGGAE

Marxism and racism
Marxist discussion of the interrelationship of class relations and forms of social differentiation based on racial and ethnic categories has become intense over the last two decades. The explosion of Marxist debate on this issue certainly contradicts the oft-cited argument that the preferred response of Marxism to nonclass forms of social division is either silence or an attempt to force a complex reality into narrow and determinist models.

A number of key questions have dominated recent debates. First, there is the issue of Marx's and Engels's views on the subject, or rather their supposed failure to analyze it systematically. Second, there is the problem of how Marxist concepts of class can help us understand the dynamics of societies that are structured by racial and ethnic categorization. Third, there is the question of how recent Marxist debates on ideology, hegemony, and over determination can help us understand the development of racism as an important ideological force in contemporary societies. Fourth, there is the question of how the important debates about class position of women and about sexism interlink with the analysis of race. Finally, a lively discussion has taken place on the alleged Eurocentric bias of Marxist theory.

Class and nationalism
The starting point of the majority of recent Marxist studies of the dynamics of race and class is that classical Marxism contains no systematic treatment of this question. It has been pointed out, for

example, that although the words of Marx and Engels contain a number of scattered references to the pertinence of racial and ethnic relations in certain social formations, e.g. the reference to race as an economic factor in the slavery of the United States, they contain little historical or theoretical reflection on the role of such processes in the capitalist model of production as a whole. Perhaps even more damagingly, a number of critics have argued that several statements on race by Marx and Engels reveal traces of the dominant racial stereotypes of their time and an uncritical usage of commonsense racist imagery. Additionally, a number of critics of Marxism have argued that the reliance by Marxists on the concept of class has precluded them from analyzing racial and ethnic phenomena in their own right, short of subsuming them under wider social relations or treating them as a kind of superstructural phenomenon.

In the writings of Marx and Engels, references to racial and ethnic divisions, along with related issues of religious differences, regional identity, and nationality, are organized around two central themes. The first is the question of internal divisions within the working class. A good example of this strand is the question of the Irish workers who migrated to England and Scotland in search of employment. Both Marx and Engels commented at various points in their work on the impact of this division on the consciousness of the English working class and the manner in which it was perpetrated.

The second theme to be found in the works of Marx and Engels is the issue of the nation and the national question. They frequently drew attention to the significance of national identities and their interrelationship with class relations. For example, they initially highlighted the effect that the development of Irish nationalism had on the consciousness of the English proletariat. Later, they came to perceive the development of a nationalist movement in Ireland as essential to the emergence of a strong labor movement in England. Their historical works are suffused with references to the emergence, development, or demise of nationalities. The analysis provided is by no means as detailed as it could have been, but (a) it does allow us to question the notion that Marx and Engels were silent on forms of extra class differentiation, and (b) provides a basis for later attempts by Marxists to analyze the impact of nationalism and racism within the working class.

Early Marxist work on racial and ethnic divisions concentrated particularly on race and class as modes of exploitation. Oliver Cox's *Caste, Class and Race* (Monthly Review Press, 1948) is an early example of this focus. Cox was primarily interested in the economic interests that produce racist exploitation and ideologies historically, and explained racial inequality as an outcome of the interests of the capitalist class in super-exploiting sections of the working class. Since he saw class divisions as the fundamental source of exploitation in society, the main thrust of his work was to conceptualize racial exploitation as a special form of class exploitation. This model was subsequently to exercise a deep influence on the work of Marxist writers on race in the United States and to a more limited extent in European and other societies.

Reductionism
New life was breathed into this question during the 1960s, particularly as a result of the regeneration of Marxist debates on class and historical materialism which sought to transcend economic reductionism and partly through increasing political awareness that contemporary racial inequalities were being reproduced in a complex manner which could not be reduced to economistic notions of class. This rethinking of class theory and the historical context of race/class relations is evident in new research on slavery in the United States, studies of racisms and labor market segmentation, the analysis of state racism in South Africa and the large body of work on the economics of migrant labor. Out of this large body of research and historical writing since the 1960s a number of main themes have emerged. These have centered on:

- the question of the autonomy (relative or otherwise) of racism from class relations;
- the role of the state and political institutions in relation to racial and ethnic issues;
- the impact of racism on the structure of the working class and dynamics of class struggle and political organization; and
- the processes through which racist ideologies are produced and reproduced.

The question of autonomy in relation to race and class introduced into this field theoretical problems which had been posed through the analysis of class formation and the capitalist stage. This influence is particularly clear in the work of Stuart Hall and other Marxist writers in Britain, the writings of a number of American scholars and the work of several writers on European migration. The starting point of Hall's work is the assertion that it is incorrect to counterpose race to class in a simple manner, since it is the articulation between the two in historically specific situations that is the core issue. For example, in a study of Jamaica, he stresses the manner in which class is overdetermined by race, color, and culture. Thus while one cannot reduce racism to class or other social relations, he also maintains that it cannot be adequately understood in abstraction from wider economic, political, and ideological forces.

Studies by Omi and Winant (*Racial Formation in the United States*, Routledge & Kegan Paul, 1986) and by the CCCS Race and Politics Group (*The Empire Strikes Back*, Hutchinson, 1982) have focused more specifically on the role of the state as a site for the reproduction of racially structured situations. Drawing partly on recent Marxist debates on the nature of the capitalist state, a number of studies have analyzed the interplay between politics and racism in specific historical settings. Studies in the role of state institutions in maintaining racialized structures in a number of societies, particularly the United States and South Africa, have highlighted the importance of the political context of racism. This has raised important questions and problems: what is the precise role of the state in the reproduction of racially structured social relations? How far can the state be transformed into an instrument of antiracist political action? These, and other questions, are currently being explored and debated.

As mentioned earlier, the claim that racism is a source of division within the working class was central to the work of early Marxist writers such as Cox. This theme has once again become central to contemporary debates about racism and class formation, partly as a result of the growth of working-class support for racist political groups and the emergence of black politics. In their study of *Immigrant Workers in the Class Structure in Western Europe* (Oxford University Press, 1973, 2nd edition), Castles and Kosack deal with the way in which the state has intervened to create two distinct strata within the working class through the system of contract labor, which denies political rights to the essentially foreign lower stratum. This lower stratum is said to perform the function of a reserve army of labor. In Britain, the work of Robert Miles and Annie Phizacklea on working-class racism represents another strand of the debate. Their writings reflect a deep concern with overcoming the potentially divisive impact of racism on class organization and radical political action. In the United States similar questions have been raised and, given the political climate in many advanced capitalist societies, this is bound to be a source of concern for some time to come.

Ideology

The final theme to emerge from Marxist debates on race and class is that of ideology. The development of racist ideologies, and the various forms such ideologies have taken at different stages of capitalist development, has traditionally not been an issue which has received much attention among Marxists. But the renewed interest in the analysis of ideology has helped to overcome this neglect, and questions have begun to be asked about the historical, cultural, literary, and philosophical roots of ideologies of race. Specifically, questions are being asked about the role that ideological relations can play in providing a basis for the articulation of racist ideologies and practices.

An important aspect of recent debates about the pertinence of Marxism to the analysis of race and racism is the question of whether there is an intrinsic Eurocentric bias in the core of Marxist theory. This is a theme that has been taken up in recent years by a number of critics of Marxism and by others who profess to be sympathetic to the Marxist tradition. Perhaps the most important statement of this position is Cedric Robinson's *Black Marxism* (Zed Press, 1983) which argues forcefully that Marxism is inextricably tied to Western European philosophical traditions which cannot easily incorporate the experience of racism and ethnic divisions. This and other studies seem certain to raise questions which will play a part in Marxist discussions for some time to come.

At the present time, however, the broader crisis in Marxist theory has resulted in the development of new perspectives which clearly go beyond Marxism. Above all, recent advances have been made in our understanding of the role of racial ideologies and the racialization of social and political discourses. Originating largely from the United States, such studies have looked at a number of areas, including literature, motion pictures, and other popular cultural forms. They have sought to show that within contemporary societies our understandings of race, and the articulation of racist ideologies, cannot be reduced to economic, political, or class relations. The work of literary and cultural theorists in the United States and Britain has in recent years begun to explore seriously the question of race and racism, and has led to a flowering of studies which use the debates around poststructuralism and postmodernism as a way of approaching the complex forms of racialized identities in colonial and postcolonial societies.

Perhaps as a result of broader transformations in social theory this is an area of research which has rapidly developed in recent years. Apart from studies of contemporary trends there has also been a growth of interest in historical research on the origins of ideas about race and in the dynamics of race, class, and gender during the colonial period. This has been reflected in important and valuable accounts of the changing usage of racial symbols during the past few centuries and in accounts of the experience of colonialism and its impact on our understandings of race and culture.

These recent accounts are clearly a long way from the work of Oliver Cox and of contemporary Marxist writers such as Robert Miles. But they highlight the ways in which many writers who were once influenced by Marxism have begun to question the relevance of the Marxist paradigm to the analysis of race and racism in contemporary societies.

Reading
Racism by Robert Miles (Routledge, 1991) provides a critical analysis of racism from a Marxist perspective, while *There Ain't No Black in the Union Jack* by Paul Gilroy (Hutchinson, 1986) provides a critique of contemporary Marxist accounts of racism.
"Varieties of Marxist conceptions of 'race', class and the state" by John Solomos in *Theories of Race and Ethnic Relations* edited by J. Rex and D. Mason (Cambridge University Press, 1986), is a critical review of the main strands of Marxist writing on racism.
"Race," Writing and Difference edited by H. L. Gates Jr. (University of Chicago Press, 1986) and *Anatomy of Racism* edited by D. T. Godberg (University of Minnesota Press, 1990) are two collections that examine strengths and limitations of models of action, including post-Marxist models.

See also: CAPITALISM; COX; EXPLOITATION; HEGEMONY; IDEOLOGY
John Solomos

Media and racism
In 1827 the first newspaper for black Americans was launched: *Freedom's Journal*. In its first issue it proclaimed, "From the press and the pulpit we have suffered much by being incorrectly represented" and "Too long have the publick been deceived." Similar complaints have been voiced over the years with each new mass medium – motion pictures, radio and television. Centrally, the complaints have been that ethnic minorities are both underrepresented and negatively stereotyped in the media.

The importance of such complaints lies in the cultural significance of the mass media. For example, television predominates as a leisure activity accounting for around 30 hours per week for citizens in Britain and the United States where overwhelmingly people cite television as the most important source of information about what's going on in the world.

Although research evidence continues to support concerns over the media's handling of ethnic minorities and race generally, there seems little doubt that notable improvements have taken place over the years in most of the diverse areas of media fare. For example Zinkhan *et al.* in *Journalism Quarterly* (Autumn 1986) note dramatic changes in popular magazine advertisements where black people are increasingly portrayed especially in higher status roles. From the late 1960s to the early 1980s the proportion of advertisements containing blacks nearly doubled but to only 4 percent – well below the 12 percent proportion in U.S. society.

The two largest focused studies of the representation of ethnic minority groups on British television published by the BBC and the IBA in 1996 both concluded that these are now *over-represented*, principally due to stereotypical portrayals of African Caribbeans as musicians and sports performers. Asians were consistently under-represented.

Although negative stereotyping has declined, the problem of adequate representation remains a more intractable problem for various reasons. First of all, the mass media are financed or justified by mass audiences. Minority groups make up the audience of popular television. Unfortunately, minority programs tend to be watched by the small number of people who rarely switch off. Thus, in economic terms, especially with television without frontiers (i.e. satellite broadcasting), there is a strong pull towards what might be described as "wall-to-wall Dallas" where ethnic minorities do not exist.

Concerns about the related aspect of "cultural imperialism," where First World media dominate the Third World and news of the Third World, stimulated UNESCO to propose a "new information order" to allow more representation of Third World viewpoints (see Karl Nordenstreng, 1984, *The Mass Media Declaration of UNESCO*). Although doubtless other factors were influential, the United States withdrew its considerable funding from UNESCO shortly after the UNESCO proposal.

The information we receive through the media about the world – especially foreign countries – is rarely good news. As an earlier UNESCO report (1973) showed, racial matters often have negative overtones. In a content analysis of British Press headlines, on a third of occasions that race appeared it was associated with words to do with conflict or violence such as "Race clash in Texas," or

"Tenants threat on color." However, as the authors later argued (Hartman and Husband, *Racism and the Mass Media* 1974), "the media do not seem to have any direct influence on attitudes as such. It would appear that the media serve to define for people what the dimensions of the situation are." Certainly, simple notions such as advanced during the British riots in 1981 that the media created a "copy cat" effect (e.g. Scarman, 1981), do not stand up to close examination, as the earlier Kerner Commission report observed.

Attempts to demonstrate that racism in the media has a powerful effect on public attitudes have not been well supported by evidence. Various research on a popular television series *Till Death Do Us Part* (U.K.) and its American development (*All in the Family*) indicate the problem. Both programs intended to make audiences laugh at bigotry by poking fun at intolerance. Unfortunately, while both bigoted and nonbigoted audiences laughed at the program equally, it did not significantly change the attitude of its audience. Many prejudiced people quite sympathized with and admired the bigoted Archie Bunker of the U.S. series.

Other research on the effects of the mass media support the theory that the power of the mass media to change society is very limited. This does not mean that the media are irrelevant. Other research, for example Tan and Tan (1979) in the *Journal of Communication*, suggests a more insidious effect – that black self-esteem may be lowered by TV entertainment programs.

The media may not have a powerful effect on prejudice as conventionally defined in the literature on race relations, but they may well have an important impact on self perceptions. As the research on sexism seems to indicate, it could be that the traditional enemy has his most powerful influence by having his prejudices accepted by women rather than by his own discrimination against women. In the field of race relations, the media may have little power to change things but, operating in a climate where ethnic minorities are deeply embedded in a history and culture of discrimination, their passive role of merely reinforcing this experience may provide considerable grounds for concern.

Reading

Minorities and Media 2nd edition by Clint C Wilson II and Felix Gutierrez (Sage, 1995) is an updated review of the historical relationships between the media and the U.S.A.'s four largest ethnic minorities: African Americans, Latinos, Native Americans, and Asian American. Equivalent British studies are *Portrayals of Minorities on BBC Television* (BBC Publications,

1996) and *Ethnic Minorities on Television* (IBA Publications, 1996) both by Guy Cumberbatch and Samantha Woods.

Gender, Race and Class in Media: A Text-reader is 600+ page collection of previously published pieces edited by Gail Dines and Jean Humez (Sage, 1995). It has several excellent chapters on how our experience is structured by media images of ethnic minorities.

. . . *And There was Television* by Ellis Cashmore (Routledge, 1994) has a chapter "Ethnic images" which examines the ways in which ethnic minorities have been depicted on U.S. and British television and how crude stereotypes have been replaced with more nuanced representations. The changes reflect changes in social conditions. Also concerned with television representations is *Race, Myth and News* by Christopher Campbell (Sage, 1995).

See also: HUMOR AND ETHNICITY; KERNER REPORT; LEE; SCARMAN REPORT; STEREOTYPE

Guy Cumberbatch

Melting Pot, The
See ASSIMILATION

Merit
Merit is a term often used in the debate over affirmative action. The debate is complicated by the fact that both sides lay claim to the concept. Both opponents and supporters of affirmative action insist it is their position that protects merit and rewards individuals for meritorious behavior.

Opponents claim that the beneficiaries of affirmative action programs do not "merit" the advantages they receive because advantages are allocated on the basis of gender and skin color instead of individual talent. Talent, supposedly, relates to more legitimate distinctions among individuals, such as intelligence, aptitude, and ability. Opponents of affirmative action would prefer that these traits be recognized as meritorious and that individuals who possess them should receive rewards like college admission or job placements because they "earn" them. The success of talented people ought not be obstructed by government programs that recognize and reward individuals merely on the basis of group membership. Instead, critics of affirmative action advocate an environment of equal opportunity, wherein legitimately meritorious individuals compete fairly for society's perquisites.

For supporters of affirmative action, however, merit is obstructed in an environment without affirmative action. Supporters of affirmative action complicate the concept of equal opportunity by asking: what if society's reward system is so skewed that it becomes easier for people of one color or gender to develop and exhibit their talents? In such cases, the emergence of talent would have less to do with individual traits like energy and creativity, and more to do with genetic privilege. Thus, it is possible, in a discriminatory society, that merit is associated with sex or skin color even though it is ostensibly assigned on the basis of talent.

In response to this problem, supporters of affirmative action argue that *talent alone* does not necessarily define merit, since recognized talent in some societies can be acquired from privilege rather than industry. Instead, supporters of affirmative action argue that considerations of merit ought to include the role of effort, industriousness, and persistence in the formation of an individual's talent. It may be that an African American inner city child has a harder time preparing for college than does an affluent white child living in the suburbs. Supporters of affirmative action argue that this discrepancy in difficulty should be recognized in calculations of merit. Affirmative action policies, whether in academia or the business community, address this discrepancy and provide greater access to true potential because they acknowledge those individuals with unrecognized or unhoned talents.

The debate over merit, then, comes down to a difference in emphasis. Opponents of affirmative action prefer to consider proficiency alone as worthy of merit; they emphasize personal qualities independently of the origin of those qualities. Affirmative action supporters, on the other hand, recognize the sacrifices and efforts expended in the achievement of proficiency. The measure of merit, then, is the distance traveled by the individual instead of just the final destination. And if it is determined that groups like African Americans and women usually have more distance to travel in the acquisition of recognized talent, then it is quite legitimate for society and government to grant them preferential concessions. In any case, if there is to be a consensus regarding the issue of affirmative action, it is clear that differences in concepts of merit must be recognized and resolved.

Reading

"Deserving jobs," by David Miller (*The Philosophical Quarterly*, vol. 42, no. 167, April 1992) examines the underpinnings of social policies designed to ameliorate inequalities in the job market.

"The end of equality: The ugly truth about America's future," by Mickey Kaus (*The New Republic*, vol. 206, no. 25, June 1992) and "The concept of desert in distributive Justice," by Julian Lamont (*The Philosophical Quarterly*, vol. 44, no. 174, January, 1994) are both useful articles.

When Race Counts: The Morality of Racial Preference in Britain and

America by John Edwards (Routledge, 1994) critically examines the principle of merit and looks at conditions under which it can be overriden without damage to justice.

See also: AFFIRMATIVE ACTION; EQUAL OPPORTUNITY; INSTITUTIONAL RACISM; UNDERACHIEVEMENT

Timothy J. Lukes/Bonnie G. Campodonico

Middleman minority

The term has been used to describe the wide range of minorities concentrated in intermediate economic niches in which they engage in trade and broking but encounter hostility in doing so. The term occurs in analyses of the history of the Jewish diaspora but it has also been widely used in descriptions of many other ethnic groups, principally those from the Indian subcontinent, China, Lebanon, Armenia, and Greece.

While there is full agreement on the widespread occurrence of this phenomenon, attempts to explain the mechanisms whereby ethnic status, economic specialization in trading and host society hostility are associated have taken various and conflicting forms. Key elements in the debate focus on

* why particular minorities feature as middlemen,
* how they come to be concentrated in these economic niches and
* what the origins of the hostility to middlemen minorities are.

On the first point, those groups who are most regularly found as middlemen can be usefully compared in terms of economic background, family system, and cultural attributes. It is also notable that there are no well-documented examples of minorities of African as opposed to Asian origin acting as middlemen. The social processes whereby blacks come to be concentrated in public sector employment rather than in middlemen roles provide a related focus of enquiry.

Second, explanations of how middleman minorities come to enter trading and broking niches vary between those stressing features of the structure of economic opportunities ("status gap") approaches (Zenner 1980)) and those which emphasize the possession of relevant qualifications and cultural values that facilitate trading.

Finally, some explanations of the origins of hostility to middleman minorities lay stress on the interests and actions of the dominant elite who may find such groups useful as sources of economic growth and as scapegoats in times of hardship. Other approaches locate the origins of hostility to middlemen in relations with competitors, clients, or employees. Bonacich (1973) argues that middleman minorities are characteristically "sojourners" and that their primary allegiance to another homeland to which they expect to return reinforces the effects of cultural separateness in encouraging negative attitudes within the host society. While this formulation has not stood up well to critical analysis (Zenner 1980), it has stimulated further testable hypotheses which have done much to illuminate the relationship between ethnicity and economic specialization.

Reading
"A theory of middleman minorities" by Edna Bonacich (*American Sociological Review* 38 (1973), pp. 583–94) is a sophisticated version of a theory of middleman minorities.
"Middleman minority theories: a critical review" by Walter Zenner (in Roy Bryce-Laporte (ed.), *Sourcebook of the New Immigration*, Transaction Books, 1980) summarizes the main contributions in this field. Zenner concludes that while a satisfactory theory of middleman minorities has not yet been put forward, the debate has given rise to many useful and testable hypotheses which can be applied in a wide variety of contexts.
Race and Culture: A World View by Thomas Sowell (Basic Books, 1994) has a provocative argument viz: "Middleman minorities have . . . tended to exhibit similarities in certain social traits, despite their great differences from each other in specific cultural features such as religion, food, dress, and language."

See also: BLACK BOURGEOISIE: BRITAIN, U.S.A.; DIASPORA

Robin Ward

Migration

Population shifts are present at the dawn of human history – the phenomena of hunting and gathering, transhumance (seeking seasonal pasture) and nomadism being as old as human social organization itself. The flight from natural disasters, adverse climatic changes, famine and territorial aggression by other communities or other species are also common occurrences. The biblical story of the epic flight of the Jews from ancient Egypt is also well known, but other great empires – notably the Aztec, Inca, Mesopotamian, Indus, and Zhou – also constructed immense monuments using subordinated peoples dragooned to work, often from long distances.

The mercantile period
The "modern world system" was marked by the flourishing of long-distance trade and the opening up of global lines of communication. Along these arterial links flowed not only commodities like spices, precious metals, and ivory but seamen, settlers, merchants, and

slaves. European mercantilism also initiated the hitherto largest process of forced migration – the shipment of ten million slaves from Western Africa to the New World. The Caribbean, Mexico, Brazil, and the southern states of the United States all have large populations descended from these Africans.

At the end of slavery, indentured labor from China, India, and Japan worked the sugar plantations of the European powers in the Caribbean, Indian, and Pacific Ocean areas. Indentured labor was deployed mainly from 1834 to 1920, when the program ceased in British India under the impact of Indian nationalist demands. But the Coolie Ordinance permitting the use of indentured labor in the Dutch East Indies was only finally revoked in 1941.

In addition to compelled and indentured migrants, European global expansion was associated with involuntary and voluntary settlement from Europe itself – particularly to the colonies of settlement and the Americas. Involuntary and state-induced migration from the European mercantile powers included "redemptioners," convicts, demobilized soldiers, and servants. In the English case, a State Paper delivered to King James I by Bacon in 1606 provided the justification of the principle. England would gain, Bacon claimed, "a double commodity in the avoidance of people here and in the making use of them there." The poor rates would be relieved and idlers, vagrants, and criminals would be put to good use in the colonies. Political dissenters like the Levelers, troublesome Irish peasants, and dispossessed Scottish crofters were shipped out in considerable numbers. Even children were not immune from this ruthless logic. Under the various child migration schemes, commencing in 1618 and concluding only in 1967, a total of 150,000 orphaned and indigent children were sent to the British colonies. (Descendants of these children make up 11 percent of the current Canadian population.)

As largely voluntary migrants, British settlers went to the Dominion societies of Canada, New Zealand, and Australia where they monopolized the political and economic life of these countries at the expense of the local inhabitants. British settlers also migrated to the United States, Rhodesia, and South Africa, where their exclusive political hegemony was slowly eroded by other settlers or by the autochtonous peoples themselves. The Portuguese settled in Angola, Brazil, Mozambique, and a few smaller places. Large parts of North Africa and Indochina were populated by the French. Such was the level of identification with their new homes that the Dutch in South Africa called themselves Afrikaners (Africans) while many

French settlers in Algeria called themselves *pied noirs* (black feet), to signify their attachment to the African soil. But, despite the localization of the Afrikaners and the Dominion-British, European settlements did not always endure. The French and Portuguese, in particular, had to absorb large repatriate populations at the end of their colonial empires.

The colonial and industrial era

Mercantilism propelled the commercialization of agriculture, the export of manufactured goods and the growth of the European empire. This was to lead both to massive internal population shifts to staff the colonial enterprises and to the internationalization of the labor market.

The colonial powers needed large gangs of laborers to service the mines, cut the timber, establish the rubber plantations, and to build the docks, railways, roads and canals needed to cement their commercial supremacy and promote their imperial visions. Often the colonial powers adapted local systems of unfree labor recruitment to their own purposes. The Spanish commandeered *repartimiento* workers to dig the silver mines at Potosi in Bolivia and used the *mita* system in Peru. The gold mines in South Africa recruited, through a system of circulating migration, millions of African quasi-free workers from the surrounding countries. Free labor migrants were recruited for work on the various Panama canal schemes, but the death toll was so enormous it threatened the completion of the project.

The free labor market was internationalized notably by growth of the new mass industries in the United States. The collapse of feudalism and the second serfdom in Europe was followed by the Great Atlantic Migration when, over the period 1870–1914, thirty-five million Europeans were transshipped to the United States. Similar international movements of Poles to Germany and the Irish to Britain accompanied industrial development, although the French, Italian, and Japanese were able to staff their factories largely by internal supplies from their floundering rural areas.

Rural–urban migration

Few small countries and only the most remote parts of large countries have been able to resist the seemingly inexorable drift from agriculture to industry, from rural to urban life. This process is often depicted as a natural, if regrettable, fact of life flowing from "population pressures." In trying to develop a more satisfactory explanation of rural-urban migration, it is however, worth recalling Marx's remark that "population does not press on capital, capital presses on population."

This aphorism is a useful reminder that a wide range of phenomena – such as land enclosures, the occupation of land by settlers, fights between ranchers and farmers, the move to cash-cropping, the growth of prairie farming and agribusiness, and the introduction of high-yield seeds needing irrigation, fertilizers and large tracts of land – are all examples of commercial pressures on agricultural areas. They all result too in the migration of landless or small peasants, farmers, and rural craftsmen, who find it more and more difficult to subsist in the countryside.

Projections of the demographic consequences of this process have yielded the following figures: globally, the percentage of population expected to be living in the urban areas in the year 2025 is 65.2 percent. This will comprise 86.7 percent in the most developed regions and as many as 60.9 percent in the least developed regions. The destabilizing effects of such large-scale movements on the capacity to provide housing, food, stable government, and a sustainable livelihood for the majority of the population is self-evident.

Current migratory flows
Four forms of migration predominated in the post-1945 period. First, state formation arising from nationalist pressures resulted in mass displacement. Examples include the swap of Muslims from India with Hindus from Pakistan and the expulsion of Palestinians from Israel. This phenomenon is also currently seen in the former state socialist bloc, notably in ex-Yugoslavia. Mass displacements have also arisen from the two World Wars, localized interstate wars, civil wars, famine, economic crisis and political instability. By the mid-1990s some seventeen million "refugees" (the word being used in a general, not a legal sense) had been compelled to leave their homes.

Second, the unskilled labor migration characteristic of the postwar period has continued despite the immigration restrictions imposed by European countries and North America in the 1970s. Sometimes the flows have gone to new destinations, like the oil-rich countries of the Gulf or Venezuela. In other cases, illegal, undocumented, and contracted laborers have continued to migrate to rich countries in an often desperate search for work.

Third, skilled migrants have used the globalization of the economy to secure their comparative advantage in employment. International

242 *Minorities*

civil servants, independent entrepreneurs, scientists, doctors and dentists, business executives, skilled engineers, and architects are examples of highly mobile skilled workers who cross international frontiers with little difficulty.

Fourth, asylum-seekers, i.e., those hoping for *legal* recognition as refugees under the international Conventions have arrived in Europe and North America in significant numbers. Constitutional provisions in Germany and France and the perception that the United States is willing to accept the world's "huddled masses" act as permissive factors, but the growth in the numbers of asylum-seekers has triggered a xenophobic, hostile, and often violent reaction to the newcomers. Increasingly restrictive measures to slow the flow of asylum-seekers have been imposed or announced in all destination-countries.

Reading
The Cambridge Survey of World Migration edited by Robin Cohen (Cambridge University Press, 1995) provides the most wide-ranging coverage of migration in a single volume. In ninety-five contributions from scholars in twenty-seven countries, the authors cover regional migration patterns, labor migration, the flights of refugees, and illegal migration. The book contains both historical and contemporary contributions
The New Untouchables: Immigration and the New World Worker by Nigel Harris (I. B. Taurus, 1995) describes the conflict between the increasing state restriction on the one hand and the increasing mobility of workers on the other. Harris suggests that the pressures of globalization will ultimately challenge the capacities of the nation-state to control its borders.
The State of the World's Refugees 1995: In Search of Solutions is a report written by the United Nations High Commission for Refugees (UNHCR) and published by Oxford University Press,1995. While arguing that the right of asylum should be scrupulously respected, the authors of the report argue that greater efforts need to be made to tackle the problem of refugees and displaced people at source. The report is trenchantly written and beautifully produced with excellent graphics.

See also: COLONIALISM; DIASPORA; LAW: IMMIGRATION

Robin Cohen

Minorities
In the field of race and ethnic relations, the term "minority" has been confusing because of the double component of its meaning, the numerical and the political. In the United States, where the term has become entrenched in official terminology, a minority group is defined primarily in terms of disadvantage, underprivilege, or some such euphemism for a combination of political oppression, economic exploitation and social discrimination. In recent American

usage, the noun "minority" can refer both to a racial or ethnic group, or to an individual member thereof. Since the groups that are so defined (principally Afro-Americans, Amerindians, Hispanics, and groups of Asian origin) are all numerical minorities of the total U.S. population, this usage is relatively unproblematic in North America, although it may reflect class interests. (The only possible confusion is with the political usage of minority to refer to party representation in government, as "the minority leader of Senate.")

As a term to be used in the comparative study of race and ethnic relations, minority is a liability, since many numerical minorities have been politically dominant and economically privileged. Nearly all tropical colonies of European powers, for example, have been ruled by minorities, often very small ones of under 10 percent, or even 1 percent of the total population. Obviously, to speak of the indigenous populations of India, Algeria, Nigeria, or South Africa as minorities in relation to their colonial masters does not make much sense.

Even in a political context such as that of the United States, where the ethnically and racially disadvantaged are numerical minorities, the term minority is an analytical liability. Its popularity, however, may well be due to the fact that it serves political interests precisely *because* it obfuscates reality.

First, in a representative system, where small numbers are disadvantageous in themselves, it is not clear where the status of minority begins and ends. In the United States, for example, many voices have argued for the inclusion of groups such as Jews and Japanese Americans on grounds of past discrimination as well as small numbers, while others have sought to exclude them on the basis of above-average success on educational or economic indices. If minority status confers preferential access to resources (as under affirmative action policies in the United States), then, of course, the terminological confusion of minority can be manipulated for political and economic gain.

Second, the definition of minority in racial and ethnic terms, and the association of that term with political and economic exclusion from the majority mainstream represents an obfuscation of class realities. Specifically, it ascribes the status of dominant group (WASP, White Anglo Saxon Protestants, in fashionable U.S. parlance) to a group much larger and much more diffuse than the actual ruling class of American society. It also, of course, divides the working class along ethnic and racial lines, and militates against class-based organization by rewarding ethnic and racial affiliation.

Perhaps most insidiously, it disguises the fact that the United States is, like all societies, ruled by a small elite, not by a large amorphous group such as WASPs; that is, the term minority salvages the majoritarian myth of bourgeois democracy.

Reading
Protection of Ethnic Minorities, edited by Robert G. Wirsing (Pergamon Press, 1981) is a good summary of the treatment of ethnic minorities in capitalist, socialist, and Third World countries.

See also: AFFIRMATIVE ACTION; DISADVANTAGE; ETHNIC MONITORING
Pierre L. van den Berghe

Muhammad, Elijah
See NATION OF ISLAM

Multiculturalism
Multiculturalism has the idea, or ideal of the harmonious coexisence of differing cultural or ethnic groups in a pluralist society at its core. However, the principal uses of the term multiculturalism have covered a range of meanings which have included multiculturalism as an ideology, a discourse, and as a cluster of policies and practices.

At the ideological level, multiculturalism has included loosely related themes incorporating acceptance of different ethnic groups, religions, cultural practices, and linguistic diversity within a pluralistic society. When applied to policies, multiculturalism has covered a range of formal state policies with two main purposes: maintaining harmony between diverse ethnic groups and structuring the relationships between the state and ethnic minorities.

At the level of state policy, Canada is identified as the country that has most promoted policies of multiculturalism as manifestations of a political ideal for maintaining relationships between ethnic groups in a manner which implies coexistence, mutual tolerance, and equality. The image of the Canadian "mosaic," with the component groups having distinctive forms but together making a unified whole, is commonly contrasted with the image of the "melting pot," which has been used as a theme to typify the goals of assimilation of ethnic minorities within the United States.

Some critics of multiculturalism have argued that it is socially divisive and tends to threaten the unity of the state. Others have argued that it leads to the creation of cultural or social ghettos, which restrict opportunities for ethnic minorities. Another criticism has pointed to conflicts or tensions between the promotion of multiculturalism and the achievement of gender equality.

Debates about multiculturalism within the context of specific social institutions and state agencies (such as schools, social services, and police services) have clearly shown how multiculturalism stands in relation to other approaches. In education, for example, multiculturalism directs schools toward a curriculum which incorporates material from differing cultures and provides for the celebration of religious and other festivals as a means of fostering awareness of difference cultures and promoting positive relations between students.

In educational contexts multiculturalism has developed through a critique of assimilationist models of education which attempt to impose monocultural education in culturally diverse societies. In turn, critics of multiculturalism in education have argued against multiculturalism from assimilationist and antiracist perspectives. Some have challenged the relativism that underlies the treatment of different cultures as equally worthy of respect.

Meanwhile, others have criticized the celebratory form of multiculturalism that has given emphasis to the arts, culture, and religious festivals. An antiracist critique of multiculturalism argues that such an emphasis dwells on peripheral aspects of schooling while failing to recognize the significance of racism and racialism, which operate through discriminatory practices within schools and in the wider society. Whereas some have argued that multiculturalism and antiracism constitute irreconcilable discourses or lead to incompatible policies, others have sought to develop a synthesis of multiculturalism and antiracism.

Analysis of the growth of debates about multiculturalism reveals underlying changes in power relations, outcomes of such factors as migration, demographic changes, economic changes, or systematic resistance to racism. In this context debates about the principles and practices of multiculturalism are likely to emerge and take different forms in a number of local, national and international contexts.

Reading

Multiculturalism in Canada by A. Fleras and J. L. Elliott (Nelson Canada, 1992) examines the operation of policies to perpetuate the vertical mosaic of Canada.

Education in a Multicultural Society by Roy Todd (Cassell, 1991) highlights problems and policies in plural societies.

A Different Mirror: A History of Multicultural America by Ronald Takaki (Little, Brown, 1993) begins its analysis in the seventeenth century and plots the course of North America's multicultural history.

See also: AMALGAMATION; EDUCATION AND CULTURAL DIVERSITY; INTEGRATION; PLURALISM

Roy Todd

Multiracial/biracial

These terms typically describe persons who have parents of different "racial" heritage. Biracialism refers to those with two heritages, usually one black parent, one white; while multiracialism is a more inclusive term, suggesting a plurality of heritages through several generations.

From the sixteenth to the twentieth century, *mulatto* (the Portuguese term for a young mule) was used in the West Indies and the United States when referring to children of mixed heritage. Other dehumanizing terms included the United States and Britain's use of "half-breed" and "mixed breed." In the present century, "half-caste" has been the predominant term. It was only in countries such as Brazil where persons of mixed heritage became the majority of the population that mixed heritage ceased to be an issue of social reproach.

Traditionally, social attitudes in the United States have been based on the "one drop of black blood" rule (adopted by some states following the abolition of slavery) which classified individuals as black. While most individuals of black and white parentage presumably internalized this rule and identified themselves as black, others "passed" for white. The children from these unions have often experienced rejection from both whites and blacks, and indeed from society.

It was not until 1967 that the remaining antimiscegenist laws were repealed by a United States Supreme Court ruling. *Loving v. Virginia* came as the result of action by Richard and Mildred Loving, a couple who were arrested in their home town in Virginia in 1958 for being married; he was white, she was black. They fled to Washington, D.C., rather than face prosecution, but fought and eventually won their case.

In addition to the repealed antimiscegenist laws, other significant changes during the 1960s in both the United States and Britain may have contributed to the development of more positive identities of multiracial individuals. Such changes include the scientific discrediting of white superiority and the rise of multiculturalism. Ironically, the "one drop of black blood" rule experienced a resurgence as black leaders argued for people of mixed heritage to regard themselves and be perceived by others as black. Although this view was more widely accepted in the United States, the extent of this view's acceptance in Britain remains uncertain.

During the past decade, however, the denial of part of one's heritage has come under question. Individuals identifying themselves as multiracial have argued that it is psychologically damaging to deny the white part of their heritage and to do so would in essence support the discredited theory of distinct biological "races." Multiracial support networks and some demographers estimate there are at least one million multiracial people in North America of all heritages.

Some of the particular problems faced by biracial adolescents were uncovered in a study by Gibbs and Hines (in Root, 1992, below) which found that conflicts regarding ethnic identity could be attributed to the failure to integrate the ethnic and "racial" heritages of both parents into a cohesive identity. While several subjects identified with only the white aspects of their identity, others "overidentified" with the minority parent and rejected whiteness, sometimes taking on stereotyped characteristics. Other experienced pressure to identify with one group or the other and felt ambivalent over the "racial" heritages of both parents. Other biracial adolescents switched between one heritage and the other reflecting "divided loyalties."

Both the United States' and Britain's monoracial census categories are presently being reexamined. Dissatisfied with what they understand to be the inadequacy of existing statuses, advocates of a separate status designated as multiracial rather than "other," believe this category would provide official recognition and a more accurate representation of American and British demographics.

Those who oppose a multiracial category on census forms caution that as more blacks choose this "racial" category and reduce their numbers under the category of black "race," blacks may lose political strength behind governmental policies designed to promote "racial" equality. We might also add that the mere admission of a new "racial" category into an already contested discourse serves to perpetuate divisions that other policies have tried to break down.

Reading
The Multiracial Experience: Racial Borders as the New Frontier edited by Maria P. P. Root (Sage, 1996) is a collection of articles which explore the dynamics of multiculturalism; it is complemented by the same editor's earlier work *Racially Mixed People in America* (Sage, 1992), which looks at multiracial identity and concludes with a section on challenging the U.S. census "racial" categories.

Multiracial Couples: Black and White Voices by Paul Rosenblatt, Terri Karis, and Richard Powell (Sage, 1995) and *Black, White, Other: Biracial Americans Talk About Race And Identity* by Lisa Funderburg (William Morrow, 1994) are both based on qualitative interview studies.

Black, White Or Mixed Race? Race and Racism in the Lives of Young People of Mixed Parentage by Barbara Tizard and Ann Phoenix (Routledge, 1993) examines multiracialism from a historical context and explores the "racial" identities of adolescents of black and white parentage in Britain.

See also: BRAZIL; CREOLE; HYBRIDITY

Amy I. Shepper

Myrdal, Gunnar (1898–1987)

Swedish economist and sociologist, and Nobel laureate (Economics, 1974). Among his prolific works are *Asian Drama, Beyond the Welfare State, Challenge to Affluence*, and *Rich Lands and Poor*. His main contribution to the field of race relations was his monumental study on black Americans, commissioned by the Carnegie Corporation of New York, in 1937, conducted through a large staff of collaborators between 1937 and 1942, and published in 1944 as a 1,300-page, two-volume, forty-five-chapter book, *An American Dilemma*. This massive research effort puts it imprint on at least a quarter-century of scholarship on Afro-Americans, and the list of Myrdal's collaborators was virtually a *Who's Who* in the field: Charles S. Johnson, Guy B. Johnson, Melville Herskovits, Otto Klineberg, E. Franklin Frazier, St Clair Drake, Arnold Rose, Allison Davis, to name but a few.

An influential feature of *An American Dilemma* was its Appendix 2, A Methodological Note on Facts and Valuations in Social Science. This classic statement of the role of the social scientist's values in his research was widely acclaimed and emulated.

The central thesis of the book is that the United States has long lived with a painful dilemma caused by the discrepancy between its democratic and libertarian ideals of freedom and equality for all, and its shabby treatment of Afro-Americans first as disfranchised chattel slaves, then as segregated outcastes. Myrdal predicted that this dilemma would, however slowly and painstakingly, be resolved by bringing the treatment of blacks in line with the lofty ideals of the American Republic.

An American Dilemma was also influential in its analysis of white-black relations in terms of caste and class. The first statement in print of the caste and class school was authored by the American sociologist and anthropologist Lloyd Warner in his introduction to a 1941 book by some of Myrdal's collaborators, but the concept was widely adopted thereafter. Warner, Myrdal, and others saw whites and blacks as representing two almost impermeable castes, characterized by ascriptive, lifelong membership, hierarchy, and endogamy. Each racial caste was internally divided into permeable classes, but class status was not directly transferable from one caste to another because the castes themselves were in a hierarchy.

Myrdal was not without his critics, however. In 1948, Oliver C. Cox published his massive attack on Myrdal and his associates, *Caste, Class and Race*. From a Marxist perspective, Cox regards American racism as a capitalist device to divide the working class, and to produce false consciousness. He attacks Myrdal's idealist formulation of a dilemma, and analyzes the situation in terms of the class interests of the ruling capitalists. He also rejects the description of Afro-Americans as a caste, stressing the nonconsensual nature of the American system, compared to what he saw as the consensual nature of the classical Hindu caste system.

Reading

An American Dilemma: *The Negro Problem and Modern Democracy* by Gunnar Myrdal (Transaction, 1995; originally Harper & Row, 1944) is the towering study of black Americans in the early 1940s; the edition cited here has an introduction by Sissela Bok, Myrdal's daughter.

Caste, Class and Race by Oliver C. Cox (Doubleday, 1948) is the scathing Marxist critique of Myrdal.

The Negro in America by Arnold Rose (Harper, 1948) is a condensation of *An American Dilemma*.

See also: CASTE; CIVIL RIGHTS MOVEMENT; COX; MARXISM AND RACISM

Pierre L. van den Berghe

N

Nation of Islam (or "Black Muslims")

The largest and most important African American sectarian movement, the Nation of Islam, has 15,000 registered members and countless sympathizers, all convinced that whites have been at the center of a centuries-long conspiracy to deny black people their ancestry and conceal their historical achievements. The movement can be described through the activities of its imamate.

Noble Drew Ali

The first twenty years of this century saw many black sects and cults emerge in Chicago and New York City. One such sect was the Moorish Science Temple of America founded in 1913 by Timothy Drew (1886–1929), who later changed his name to Drew Ali. The sect was based loosely on Islamic principles and adapted a version of the Koran. Drew bade his followers to look for their origins in the ancient Moors and explained that whites had stripped blacks of their religion, their power, their land and their culture. In 1929 Drew was murdered, but his followers believed him to be a prophet ordained by Allah and looked for a reincarnation.

Wallace D. Fard

Fard sold silk products door-to-door in Detroit's ghettos. In the late 1920s, he began to claim he was "Arabian" and a prophet sent to help blacks discover their dual African and Islamic heritages. According to Fard, African Americans were descended from the first humans, the "original race" whose descendants could be found in their purest form among Muslims in the Middle East, Africa, and Asia. Fard taught that the world was once ruled by blacks who established a highly advanced civilization: twenty-four scientists populated the earth with animals, created trees, mountains and oceans, and even the moon. According to Fard, they had communication with life on Mars. After 8,400 years, a scientist named Yacub discovered that within blacks there were two "germs," a strong black germ and a weak brown germ. Yacub separated the two and, through some form of genetic engineering, was able to reproduce the lighter and weaker people, who eventually migrated to the cold wastelands of Europe. But the pale race were adept at robbing, scheming, and cheating and used these skills to gain mastery of the world. Once in power, no evil was beyond them and they enslaved blacks, physically and mentally – by convincing them they were inferior beings and the true prophets were white. Only when blacks realized that would their oppression end.

Elijah Muhammad

In 1934, Fard disappeared in mysterious circumstances and one of his converts, Elijah Muhammad (formerly Elijah Poole) – whom he had first met in 1931 – dedicated himself to promulgating Fard's revelation. Elijah proselytized vigorously and built a coherent organization for the movement, which attracted a variety of well-known figures, including Malcolm X in the 1950s and Muhammad Ali in the 1960s, all of whom converted to the Nation of Islam.

In 1963, Elijah became embroiled in a scandal concerning rumors that he was sleeping with his secretaries in breach of his own moral code. Malcolm X believed that this discredited Elijah and this became a factor in his eventual departure from the movement. In the 4 December 1964 issue of the Nation's magazine *Muhammad Speaks*, one of Elijah's loyal supporters, Louis Farrakhan, wrote: "The die is set and Malcolm shall not escape. . . . Such a man is worthy of death." Two months later, Malcolm was assassinated.

Louis Farrakhan

When Elijah died in 1975, his son Wallace Deen Muhammad, took over the leadership of the movement, which by then had over 50,000 members. Farrakhan, born Louis Walcott, was born in 1933 in the Bronx, New York, but grew up in Boston. A one-time calypso artist under the name of Louis X (he made a record, "White man's heaven is a black man's hell") Farrakhan was a strict follower of Elijah and objected to reforms initiated by Deen to relax the restriction of whites' membership and seek a closer integration with Muslims around the world. The movement divided, Deen changing his organization's name to the World Community of Islam, while Farrakhan retained the original. Farrakhan also revived the militant wing called The Fruit of Islam. His teaching was essentially that of Elijah and Fard, though he did take the unprecedented step of aligning himself with a party political candidate, Jesse Jackson. In 1984, during Jackson's Democratic nomination campaign, Jackson was overheard to have referred to New York City as "Hymietown" when in conversation with Farrakhan. It started a series of remarks over subsequent years that was to alienate Jews. This was to elevate Farrakhan into the most infamous imam in the Nation of Islam's history. In a speech in New Orleans in 1989, he professed to have traced the origin of AIDS to the attempts of the U.S. government to destroy the population of Central Africa. He similarly explained the influx of crack cocaine and other hard drugs into black neighborhoods. He proposed reparations for the centuries of slavery; part of these included freeing blacks from prisons and setting aside a separate territory exclusively for blacks. The concept of having a voluntarily separated territory with self-sufficiency has been central to Nation of Islam philosophy since Elijah.

In 1995, after years of relative obscurity, Farrakhan leapt back to prominence when he organized a march on Washington, D.C., where he gave an address to an estimated 600,000 African Americans. And, while he made no claim to such a status, Farrakhan may have been the single-most influential black leader in a period that had witnessed the fall from grace (and later restoration) of Marion Barry, the dismissal of Benjamin Chavis as executive director of the NAACP, and the political disappearance of one-time presidential nominee Jesse Jackson.

Reading
Black Nationalism by E. V. Essien-Udom (University of Chicago Press, 1962) is based on a two-year study in Chicago and New York City, while *The Black Muslims in America* by C. Eric Lincoln is an in-depth analysis of the movement in its historical context. Both are solid works, but dated.
Elijah Muhammad: Religious Leader by Malu Halasa (Chelsea House, 1990) is a short biography of the influential leader in the "Black Americans of Achievement" series. *Malcolm X* (1989) by Jack Rummel is also in this accessible, but rather superficial series.
"False prophet – the rise of Louis Farrakhan" is a critical two-part article by Adolph Reed in the journal *Nation* (vol. 252, issues 1 and 2, January 21 and 28, 1991); Reed traces Farrakhan's development and argues that Farrakhan appeals to whites because he legitimizes the idea that blacks should help themselves. Another critic of Farrakhan's, Nat Hentoff, laments that there are not more credible or inspiring black leaders than the Nation's imam, in "I am to black people as the Pope is to white people" in *Village Voice* (vol. 36, no. 21, May 21, 1991).

See also: AFROCENTRICITY; ETHIOPIANISM; GARVEY; MALCOLM X; *NÉGRITUDE*

Ellis Cashmore

National Front
A British fringe political party which ran in political races with some measure of success during the 1970s. Its premise was that those

Britons of African-Caribbean and Asian descent threatened the job prospects of indigenous whites. In a context of high unemployment, the message gained some credibility among factions of the British working class. The party was launched in 1967 after an amalgamation of other neo-nazi groups. Its avowed aim was to contest by-elections (i.e. local political elections).

The other main thrust of its political activities was its decision to hold demonstrations and meetings organized either around explicitly racist themes or within areas containing relatively large black, brown, or Jewish communities. Quite rightly, these consistently provoked opposition both from the local communities and from antiracist organizations such as the Anti-Nazi League and often degenerated into volatile occasions. In 1974, for instance, an anti-NF protestor, Kevin Gately, was killed at the NF's demonstration in Red Lion Square. A little less than five years later, in April 1979, a London teacher, Blair Peach, was killed as antifascists tried to prevent the NF's pre-general election meeting in the Southall district of London.

Despite its claim to be Britain's "fastest growing party," its successes were minor and it suffered an embarrassing reverse at the 1979 polls. After this time, its membership dropped and it lost its initiative to the more aggressive and youth-oriented British Movement.

Reading
The National Front in English Politics by Stan Taylor (Macmillan, 1982) looks critically at various aspects of the party including its ideological background, its apparent electoral advances in the 1970s and the effectiveness of anti-NF groups such as the anti-Nazi League.
Fascists: A Social Psychological View of the National Front by Michael Billig (Academic Press, 1978) scrutinizes the consistencies between the NF and earlier fascist organizations and personalities. It also includes interviews with members of an NF branch in the West Midlands.

See also: BRITISH MOVEMENT; KU KLUX KLAN; NATIONALISM; NEO-NAZISM

Barry Troyna

Nationalism
A term that refers to an ideology which was formulated after the French Revolution. It became a major determinant of political action in the course of the nineteenth century throughout Western Europe and, in the twentieth century, throughout the world. Many writers want to draw a firm distinction between this conception of nationalism as an ideology and the notion of national sentiment

which refers to a sense of collective solidarity within identified geographical and cultural boundaries. Thus, this distinction can account for the fact that a particular population may express some notion of national identity in the absence of a coherent and organized political movement to bring into being or reproduce territorial boundaries within which a state formation has political power.

As an ideology, nationalism contains three main ideas. First, it argues that an identified population should be able to formulate institutions and laws with which to determine its own future. Second, it maintains that each such population has a unique set of characteristics, which identify it as a "nation." Third, and consequently, it claims that the world is divided naturally into a number of such distinct "nations." This combination of ideas and claims constitute the basis for political strategies and movements which, since the nineteenth century, have had a major influence on the way in which the world is organized politically. The formation and reproduction of national boundaries is, therefore, not a natural or inevitable process, but one which is the consequence of human action in particular historical circumstances. Indeed, that process need not be directly prompted by the ideology of nationalism, as the example of England, France, Spain, and Holland illustrate.

The origin of the ideology is the object of a continuing debate, although there is considerable agreement with the claim that it is connected with what some writers call industrialization and what others define as capitalist development. What unites these different theoretical traditions is the employment of the notion of uneven development. What is claimed is that from the late eighteenth century, the process of industrialization/capitalist development occurred in particular geographical areas, with the result that certain groups in adjoining areas desired to emulate the advances made elsewhere in order to share in the consequential material and political advantages. The ideology of nationalism was a means of politically mobilizing populations to construct a particular political framework for economic/capitalist development, i.e. to "catch up" with the development of those who had developed first.

This process can be observed to have continued in the twentieth century particularly in connection with the consequences of decolonization. A rather different process occurred in connection with the redrawing of political boundaries after the two "world wars" in Europe, although, again, nationalism was a prominent factor. Such a wide diversity of instances where nationalism has been a political force, particularly in the twentieth century, supports the contention that nationalism can be combined with political movements of the "left" and right," a fact that can cause particular difficulties for Marxist writers. One can illustrate this point by referring to the way in which nationalism has been a component elsewhere in the rise of fascism in Europe and in liberation movements in Africa and Southeast Asia. Moreover, the latter examples constituted political inspiration for black people in the United States in the 1960s, where political resistance to institutionalized racism came to be expressed in terms of nationalism. For Marxists, these examples have posed a problem insofar as they claim that classes constitute the major force for revolutionary change. The relative failure of Marxists to be able to account for the political significance of nationalism in the twentieth century has been paralleled by the increasingly common claims by sociologists and political scientists that nationalism constitutes the major political force of the twentieth century.

The fact that nationalism emerged as a coherent and explicit ideology at the same time that racism was formulated as a "scientific" doctrine is of significance. Both ideologies assert that the world's population is naturally divided into distinct groups, although the nature of the group and the foundation for supposed natural division differs. Nevertheless, the fact that racism asserts some form of deterministic relation between attributed or real biological features and cultural characteristics means that nationalism, although ostensibly focusing on cultural/historical differences, can nevertheless merge into or develop out of the former. This is particularly evident in British politics since the 1960s when expressions of British nationalism have increasingly come to contain a form of racism, although without explicit use of the idea of "race" in the case of the main political parties. However, in the case of the neofascist parties, nationalism is expressed explicitly through a notion of "race," in line with central strands of fascist ideology.

Reading

Nationalism: The Nation-state and Nationalism in the Twentieth Century by Montserrat Guibernau (Polity, 1995) examines the political character of nationalism and stresses its importance as a source of identity; the volume also addresses the question of nations without states.

Nation and Identity in Contemporary Europe edited by Brian Jenkins and Spyros Sofos (Routledge, 1996) asserts that "nation" is an ideological construct and that nationalism, far from being a natural response, is a political program.

The Break-up of Britain by Tom Nairn (Verso, 1981) is an influential Marxist analysis of nationalism which breaks with both previous Marxist analyses and sociological explanations.

See also: DEVELOPMENT; FASCISM; IDEOLOGY; RACISM

Robert Miles

Native Americans
See AMERICAN INDIANS

Native peoples

Prior to the expansion of Europe, many regions of the earth were occupied by peoples who lacked the art of writing, and who pursued technologically simple ways of life. Because Columbus thought he had discovered a new route to the Indies, the Europeans described the peoples of the Americas as Indians. The native people of Australia were called Aborigines. In Africa and Oceania the expression "native" was commonly used. The Europeans described themselves as civilized but, ironically, the weaker the native peoples, the greater was the brutality shown toward them. In the United States and Australia, the native peoples were at times hunted by armed whites who regarded this as a form of sport. In Brazil and Australia diseases were deliberately spread among the native peoples and poisoned food left out for them.

In New Zealand, prior to the European invasions, there were about 200,000 Maoris. Before the end of the nineteenth century they seemed to be dying out, so many of them having succumbed to European diseases or having been shot by other Maoris using imported muskets. Then Maori cultural pride and the Maori birth rate began to revive. A similar three-stage sequence of defeat, despair, and regeneration can be discerned among the Native Americans of the United States, whose lands were appropriated more savagely than in the European colonies to the north and south. In North America, European occupation was legitimated by international treaties, the "Indian tribes" being regarded in law as nations on an equal status to that of the invaders. Different European powers were eager to make such treaties because they were in competition with one another. The political claims of Native Americans today are that the whites should observe the promises they made in these treaties.

No issue is more important than that of "Native Title" to land. Aboriginal (or "native") title to land has been recognized under the common law of Canada as existing alongside the treaty-making process, but ownership of minerals rests with the Crown. In Australia, there were no treaties between the invading and indigenous peoples following British setttlement from 1788. In law, the land was regarded as *terra nullius* (land belonging to no one) until January 1992 when, in an historic judgment in the case of *Mabo v. Queensland*, the High Court held that native title had survived the Crown's annexation, and that, under closely specified conditions, persons of indigenous origin could enjoy rights deriving from it.

In New Zealand, the 1840 Treaty of Waitangi was given new life in 1975 with the establishment of the Waitangi Tribunal; this is authorized to assess Maori land claims. In United States law, the British Crown, by discovery, acquired title to all the land, but this was subject to an indigenous right of occupancy. That occupancy has to be protected by the government against third parties but can be extinguished by Congress.

In Sweden, the indigenous people are called Saami (formerly Lapps); though most persons of Saami origin are now urban-dwellers, Saami culture is identified with reindeer-breeding. The law protects the rights of persons belonging to recognized Saami communities to their traditional use of reindeer pasture, and associated hunting and fishing rights, but it does not accept Saami ownership of land itself.

At the United Nations, representatives of the world's indigenous peoples have been pressing for better recognition of their distinctive rights as the original inhabitants of their countries and owners of the land. Since international law recognizes that "All peoples have the right of self-determination" many governments are reluctant to regard indigenous groups as "peoples" and prefer to speak of "indigenous people."

Reading

White Settlers and Native Peoples by A. Grenfell Price (Melbourne, Cambridge University Press, 1950) is a general review.
The Indigenous World, the Yearbook of the International Workgroup for Indigenous Affairs (Copenhagen, annual publication).

See also: ABORIGINAL AUSTRALIANS; NATIVE AMERICANS; UNITED NATIONS

Michael Banton

Négritude

A movement begun in the 1930s by the Martinique-born poet Aimé Césaire and other French-speaking black artists who wanted to rediscover ancient African values and modes of thought so that blacks could feel pride and dignity in their heritage. In its broadest sense, *négritude* was "the awareness and development of African values," according to Leopold Senghor, who helped develop the original ideas into a coherent political movement.

Though principally an artistic and literary critique of western society and its systematic suppression of blacks' potentiality by dissociating them from what were regarded as their true roots, *négritude* took on a more programmatic dimension with Senghor, who became president of Senegal. The impulse was, according to L. V. Thomas, "the rediscovery of one's past, one's culture, one's ancestors and one's language." Inspired by the African ethnographer and historian Leo Frobenius, Senghor delved into African culture to which he attributed the characteristic of being "Ethiopian," as a way of coming to grips with the different conception of reality he presumed existed in ancient African societies.

Leo Kuper writes: "Initially, *négritude* developed as a reaction to white racism, as dialectical opposition to cultural values imposed by whites." But the Africa oriented to was not, as G. R. Coulthard puts it, "of African civilizations or African cultural values, but of Africa itself as a vague geographical region, and the imaginary and emotional fatherland of all the Negroes in the world."

Négritude never advocated a return to Africa in a physical sense, as did Marcus Garvey. Nor did it spurn the other-worldly elements of black religions, as did W. E. B. Du Bois. It sought to make Africa's presence felt by the millions of "exiled," scattered blacks who had been "brainwashed" into Western ways of thinking. It was an attempt to create an African consciousness for blacks wherever they were; a return to Africa through realizing its presence in the *mind* of blacks. As the Haitian poet Jean Price-Mars put it: "We belong to Africa by our blood."

Like other Ethiopianist movements, *négritude* condemned conventional Christianity as a tool of colonialism designed to keep blacks in a state of subjection and perpetuate their physical and mental enslavement; it was seen, as Coulthard points out, in "hypocritical connivance with colonialism and imperialism." Colonialism had culturally denuded blacks to the bone, but as the *négritude* poet Leon Damas wrote:

We have stripped off our European clothes . . .
Our pride in being Negroes
The glory of being black

This sums up the *négritude* effort: to upgrade black people not so much through overt political means, but through instilling them with a sense of history and culture compounded of the distinctive qualities deriving from Africa; a new pride and dignity in being black and being African.

Reading
Race and Colour in Caribbean Literature by G. R. Coulthard (Oxford University Press, 1962) is an assessment and appreciation of *négritude* set in its historical context.
"Senghor and *négritude*" by L. V. Thomas, in *Présence Africaine* (vol. 26, no. 54, 1965), details the poet-president of Senegal's appreciable contribution to the movement and his attempts to convert it into practical policies.
Voices of Négritude by J. Finn (Quartet, 1988) charts the origins and development of the movement and its relationship with the "Negrista" in Latin America, cults in the Caribbean and the Harlem Renaissance.

See also: AFRICA; AFROCENTRICITY; ETHIOPIANISM; GARVEY; NATION OF ISLAM; RASTAFARI

Ellis Cashmore

Neo-nazism
From the Greek *neos*, meaning new or revived, and the German phonetic spelling of the first two syllables of *Nationalsozialist*, the fascist party that seized political control of Germany in 1933 under Adolph Hitler. The term refers to contemporary groups, parties and organizations that exhibit features associated with the original Nazi party: authoritarian, hierarchical, rightwing government; opposition to democracy, liberalism, pluralism, and an assembly of minority groups, especially Jews and blacks.

The term has been applied to white supremacist groups, including the Ku Klux Klan, the Order, and the Aryan Nation Church affiliates, including the Michigan Militia, which was alleged to be responsible for the Oklahoma City bombings of April 1995. That episode revealed the preparedness of such groups to turn to terrorist activities in the pursuit of their goals.

Studies by, among others Aho (*This Thing of Darkness: A Sociology of the Enemy*, University of Washington Press, 1994), suggest that the worldview of members is often shaped by economic insecurity, deep suspicion of government, and, in many cases, a religious fervor that anticipates an apocalyptic battle between good and evil. Many groups, including the Order, harbor conspiracy theories, particularly about the operations of Jews in government and commerce. Christian patriotism is typically invoked to justify such views: there has been a close connection between neo-nazi groups and church organizations.

Reading

"Home-grown extremism" by Scott Heller (in *Chronicle of Higher Education*, section A10–11, vol. 41, no. 35, May 1995) neatly pulls together various pieces of empirical work on neo-nazi groups in the United States.

Religion and the Racist Right by Michael Barkun (University of North Carolina Press, 1994) explores the Christian Identity movement, which believes that white people are the literal descendants of the tribes of Israel; Jews are the product of a sexual union between Eve and Satan; and these are the last days before a cosmic apocalypse. It may be read in conjunction with *The Politics of Righteousness: Idaho Christian Patriotism* by James A. Aho (University of Washington Press, 1994).

Extremism in America (New York University Press, 1995) is an uncredited collection of racist texts including the infamous Turner Diaries, which are revered by many neo-nazis.

See also: LAW: BRITISH MOVEMENT; FASCISM; KU KLUX KLAN; NATIONAL FRONT; SKINHEADS

Ellis Cashmore

New International Division of Labor (NIDL)

First published in English in 1980, the NIDL thesis, as promulgated by Fröbel *et al.* and Ernst, advances the argument that, since 1970, there has been a shift of capital from industrial centers to peripheral undeveloped nations, where cheap and unorganized labor is available. The movement away from industrial centers was hastened by difficulties in securing and realizing high profits, as industrial conflict, increased production costs, and the unionization of migrants and ethnic minorities prevented high levels of labor exploitation.

In Germany, where the thesis was developed, there were obvious economic advantages attached to importing large numbers of temporary migrant "guest workers." But technical and managerial developments in the labor process later permitted use of peripheral labor power, with little training. Third World governments further facilitated the outward tendency by legislating against labor/trade unions' power.

The thesis is, in part, intended to account for the industrial decline in the traditional industrial metropolis. When the policy of attracting cheap migrant labor began to show signs of weakness, a new policy of exporting capital was pursued, often to the cost of those in the centers' job markets.

The NIDL thesis has been roundly criticized on a number of fronts. Cohen, in particular, notices a lack of originality in the observation that global labor markets have been located abroad; this strategy dates back to the mercantile period. He also objects to the "logic" implied in its sequence of phases, forms of labor changing in an inexorable movement. The conception of a single division of labor Cohen also doubts; there are a number of different forms of labor utilization that have implications for the patterning of migration flows.

Reading

The New International Division of Labour by F. Fröbel, J. Heinrichs and O. Kreye (Cambridge University Press, 1980) and *The New International Division of Labour, Technology and Underdevelopment* edited by D. Ernst (Campus Verlag, 1980) are the two basic expositions.

"Migration and the new international division of labour" by Robin Cohen in *Ethnic Minorities and Industrial Change in Europe and North America* edited by Malcolm Cross (Cambridge University Press, 1992) is one of many critical discussions of the NIDL thesis in this volume.

See also: COLONIALISM; DEVELOPMENT; EXPLOITATION; MIGRATION

Ellis Cashmore

O

Others

The theme of otherness originates in philosophical queries about the nature of identity. Wherein lies the identity of a thing? Is the difference between same and other a matter of essence or existence? With Hegel identity and difference translates into the antinomy of being and nothing, spirit and matter unfolds in history. What he calls the life and death struggle with the other, for instance between master and slave, is a relationship that changes dialectically over time. Schopenhauer speaks of will and representation, Heidegger of *Being and Time*, Sartre of *Being and Nothingness*. These and other queries yield various notions of otherness such as the unthought, the implicit (Husserl), the virtual or unfulfilled possibilities (Marcuse). From psychoanalysis and the unconscious as the ego's other arises the theme of oneself as an other. In *I and Thou*, Martin Buber addresses the other in social relations as a potential partner in dialogue.

Cultural difference is a major part of otherness. From times immemorial, peoples have considered themselves as "the people" and all the rest as "others" – the Greeks and the *barbaroi*, the Jews and the *goyim*, the Japanese and the *gaijin*. In the West, the distinction between Christians and heathens long served as the main boundary between self and others. "Heretics" and believers in other faiths such as Muslims, Jews, and Orthodox Christians occupied in-between niches. In the Renaissance the distinction between "Ancients" and "Moderns" overlaid these differences. The Enlightenment introduced the concern with classification and scientific attempts to classify humans on the basis of "race" and language. In the wake of the French Revolution nationhood became a defining element of identity. The notions of "race," language and nationality mingled (nations were thought of as races and races were viewed as language groups).

Romantic preoccupation with the unknown in its ambivalent character of attraction and repulsion was yet another face of the Enlightenment. The pathos of the unknown (the wild, the remote) was like a secular version of pantheism or else of the "hidden God" (*deus absconditus*). "Others" were embodiments of ideals (the good or noble savage), fears (monsters, cannibals), objects of desire, windows of mystery. Others were targets of hatred – scapegoats, as in antisemitism and pogroms. "Nothing but otherness killed the Jews." Genocide of indigenous peoples – American Indians, Tasmanians, Armenians; dehumanizing treatment of slaves, natives – are part of the history of otherness. In nineteenth-century Orientalism and exoticism all these attitudes are reflected, in a general setting of Western expansion, imperialism, and colonialism.

Decolonization destabilized these relations. Imperial identities were decentered. In this context "the question of the Other" became a critical theme, first in structuralist anthropology and its understanding of culture as a system of systems, on the model of language. Tzvetan Todorov is a classic representative of this approach which uses a binary schema of self and other. In Michel Foucault's work relations of power and domination are analyzed through discourse analysis as knowledge regimes or epistemological orders. How others are represented is a key to understanding the structure of knowledge regimes and their claims to truth. Foucault concentrated on others in French society, on those classified as deviant, criminal, heretic, insane, diseased. In *Orientalism* Edward Said applied discourse analysis to the texts produced by European orientalists about the "Orient," the colonized world.

A broad tradition in cultural and postcolonial studies examines how others are represented. The main axes of difference are the "Big Three" of race, class, and gender. Representations of racial (ethnic, national) others often overlap with those of women and lower class people. Increasingly "the Other" has been left behind as too narrow and static a notion. There are so many kinds of "others" that there is little point in generalizing about them. Besides the "Self" no longer represents a fixed identity, witness notions of multiple identity and the "decentering of the subject." The universalist Enlightenment subject (white, male, middle-aged, rational) is no longer being taken for granted.

Jacques Derrida rephrases the question of otherness in terms of identity and difference, returning it to the wider terrain of philosophical questioning where it originated. In feminism, cultural studies and sociology, *difference* increasingly takes the place of otherness. The terminology of identity/difference is more matter of fact than that of self/other. Difference, of course, also comes in many forms: as diversity, ontological difference, metaphysical difference, the difference of God, gender, and cultural difference.

Over time, then, otherness has referred to questions of being and non-being, immanence, and transcendence, and to cultural differences along lines of language, religion, civilizational or evolutionary status (savages, primitives), "race", ethnicity, nationality, gender, class, development, ideology, age, and so forth. All along it has been basic to the construction of boundaries of community.

Reading

The Conquest of America: the Question of the Other by Tzvetan Todorov (Harper and Row, 1984; original French edition 1982) is a classic source in structuralist anthropology and may be read in conjunction with an early collection edited by Francis Barker *et al.*, *Europe and its Others* (Essex University, 1985).

Relevant among the works of Michel Foucault is *Madness and Civilization: A History of Insanity in the Age of Reason* (Random House, 1965) and of Jacques Derrida, *Writing and Difference* (Chicago University Press, 1978).

Orientalism by Edward Said (Penguin, 1978) is an authoritative and pathbreaking study which discusses the construction of the Orient as fundamentally other, different from the West. Useful in relation to colonialism is Nicholas Thomas's *Colonialism's Culture: Anthropology, Travel and Government* (Polity Press, 1994), *Representing Others: White Views of Indigenous Peoples* edited by Mike Gidley (University of Exeter Press, 1992), and *Barbaric Others* by Zia Sardar, Ashis Nandy, Merryl Wyn Davies (Pluto Press, 1993).

See also: COLONIAL DISCOURSE; HYBRIDITY; LANGUAGE, RACE AND ETHNICITY; POSTCOLONIAL; SUBALTERN

Jan Nederveen Pieterse

P

Paternalism

From *pater*, Latin for father, this refers to what is essentially a legimitation of despotism, or tyranny. A model of familialistic relations, especially of father to child, is applied to relations of economic, social and political inequality. Thus, subjects' freedoms are limited by regulations that are ostensibly "well-meant."

There is, of course, an element of despotism in parent–child relations, but the despotism is both tempered and legitimated by "love." In the colder phrasing of sociobiology, kinship makes for a commonality of genetic interests between relatives. Parents can indeed be expected to exert authority for the benefit of their children, if not all the time, at least much of the time, since their children's interests overlap with their own.

In the absence of such a commonality of genetic interests, unequal relations of power are characterized by a highly asymmetrical distribution of costs and benefits, that is, by exploitation. It is, therefore, in the interest of the dominant party to seek to disguise the coercive and exploitative nature of the relationship by claiming that domination is in the best interests of the oppressed. This is done by asserting that the dominated are in a state analogous to childhood, that is, are dependent, immature, irresponsible, and unable to run their own affairs, and that the rulers "love" their subjects, and act *in loco parentis*, to the best interests of the oppressed.

Paternalism is probably the most widespread legitimating ideology of preindustrial societies, and has been independently reinvented time and again in a wide range of social situations. It characterized, among others, patron–client relationships in many preindustrial societies; godparent–godchild ties in class-stratified Latin American countries; the white man's burden and civilizing mission ideology of European colonialism in Africa; master–slave relations in the chattel slavery regimes of the Western Hemisphere, and teacher–student relationships in universities.

The acceptance of the legitimizing ideology by the subordinates is generally a function of the degree of perceived benevolence in the relationship, and of the age difference between the parties. Thus, the model is more acceptable between teacher and students than between masters and slaves. As a type of race and ethnic relations, paternalism has characterized many societies, although acceptance of that ideology by the oppressed has always been problematic. Perhaps the two situations in which paternalism was most explicitly formulated as a legitimation of despotism are European colonialism, particularly in Africa, and plantation slavery in the Americas.

There has been much debate on the extent to which colonial subjects and slaves accepted their masters' view of them and internalized a sense of their own inferiority (the so-called Sambo mentality). There is much evidence that servility and subservience were only opportunistic survival mechanisms, although one cannot entirely discount that some slaves and colonials did indeed develop a dependency complex. This was probably more the case under slavery than under colonialism, because the slave plantation did, in fact, represent a somewhat closer approximation to a large family (though far from a happy one) than the typical colony.

Indeed, extensive mating (often forced, and nearly always extramarital) between male owners or overseers and female slaves was characteristic of all slave regimes. For the dominant males, mating with slaves was a way of combining business and pleasure, hence the popularity of the practice, both in North and South America. (The Latins tended to be less hypocritical and more open in their acceptance of miscegenation than the Dutch and English, but there is no evidence that the actual incidence of the practice differed between slave regimes.) These liaisons across racial lines did, of course, create numerous ties of sexual intimacy and of kinship between masters and slaves, and did make many plantations big families of sorts, albeit of a perverse type. The undeniable fact, however, is that sexual and kin ties across racial lines necessarily affected the master–slave relationship, and consolidated the paternalistic model of legitimation by giving it *some* factual basis.

Reading
Roll, Jordan, Roll by Eugene Genovese (Pantheon, 1974) is an account by a Marxist historian of the U.S. plantation system from the slaves' point of view.
The Masters and the Slaves by Gilberto Freyre (Knopf, 1964) is the classic account of Brazilian slavery by a psychoanalytically oriented Brazilian sociologist.
Race and Racism by Pierre L. van den Berghe (Wiley, 1978) is an analysis of race relations in Mexico, Brazil, South Africa, and the United States, stressing the contrast between "paternalistic" and "competitive" race relations.

See also: AFRICA; APARTHEID; BRAZIL; COLONIALISM; FREYRE; SLAVERY
Pierre L. van den Berghe

Patriarchy and ethnicity

Patriarchy is a social system that emerged during the age of antiquity and continues in various forms to the present. It has existed in various types of nation-states. Whether feudal, capitalist, or socialist, the essential underpinnings of such a system have not differed. In all patriarchal settings, dominance in power and authority have been male-centered, primarily expressed in female sex-gender control and economic discrimination.

Origins

The origins of patriarchy may be traced to primitive sexual divisions of labor, resulting from the transition from food-gathering and for-aging/scavenging modes of survival to hunting, perhaps three million years ago. Women, unable during pregnancy and periods of early child rearing to engage in the more physically challenging feats of big game hunting and, later (10,000 years ago), subsistence agriculture, were relegated to different chores, that were labeled as lesser in worth. Male economic power was augmented with the domestication of animals and male proprietorship of herds and their associated wealth was interwoven into many patriarchy systems. The emergence of property as private rather than communal was a major factor in the establishment of subordinate female sex-gender relationships. The establishment of property as private altered more egalitarian sex-gender relationships for it changed the ways in which basic functions in the family operated. The labor of women was transformed from services of survival or for the betterment of society to an act that enhanced family wealth. In time, many patriarchal cultures denied to women the right to acquire, hold, and dispose of property.

In many ancient city-kingdoms or states, the first components of patriarchy were evidenced in male control of two of a woman's biological capacities, namely her sexuality and procreativity. Female sexual subordination ultimately was written into codes of law which were not only enforced within the family, one of the first and primary institutions constructed on the basis of patriarchial values, but also by the state. Besides laws, males resorted to the use of force, assignment of class privileges, economic dependency, and confirmation of respectability or non-respectability upon women in order to assert control. Within time, patriarchy entailed also the placement of women in a subjugated class devoid of rights equal to those accorded males. The right of women to own, use, and sell property was denied in most ancient societies, and is still a feature of female subjugation in many nation-states today.

In the ancient world, as well as today, patriarchy was expressed in a number of ways. Within a patriarchal family, a male possessed the right to sustain life or inflict death in females. In other patriarchal settings, female right to life was state controlled. The primary subjugation devices utilized by males in such states were the allocation of awards for obedience or punishments, even physical in nature, for disobedience. In all situations, the male was designated head and power figure in the family.

The city-kingdoms of the Mesopotamian world were some of the earliest agencies of state to employ patriarchal ideology to justify sex-gender-class stratification. A patriarchy was established in the Fertile Valley: the ultimate sanction of patriarchy in Mesopotamia was evidenced in the codification of law, most notably Hammurapi's code, which included statutes that guaranteed, in many areas of life, abrogation of the rights of women. Women in the Mesopotamian system were disowned by their husbands for sterility, infidelity, and other types of nonapproved conduct; rewards and punishments were dictated by males. Married Mesopotamian women could be given to their husband's creditors in order to cancel out a debt. Yet, on the other hand, women of Mesopotamia were permitted to own property and to engage in commercial enterprises free of male control.

A genuine expression of patriarchy did not become a major feature of life in every ancient kingdom that was transformed from an archaiac organization into a centralized and structured nation-state with a flourishing culture. Many early horticultural societies, for example, were structured around women as dominant forces in society. If matriarchy is defined as the exact opposite of patriarchy in terms of power and control, a mirror image of a patriarchial system, history does not provide an example of a matriarchal culture.

The Mesopotamian model, was in many ways duplicated in a large percentage of the societies of antiquity and extended, with some modifications, into the modern world. Greek and Roman civilizations were societies in which patriarchy prevailed. English society in the seventeenth century was patriarchal in nature and the same was true in the United States. Aspects of patriarchy remain features of both societies as the twentieth century draws to a close.

In fact, the expressions of patriarchy that still exist in England and the United States are referred to as *de facto* patriarchy, for in both societies the state does not intervene when certain female rights, within a household or in the workplace, are abrogated by a male figure who assigns rewards for what is deemed accepted behavior and inflicts punishment for "unseemly" acts.

African-American matrifocality

Scholars suggest that the African-American family structure represents an exception to patriarchy, by arguing that African-American family life demonstrates the existence of a matriarchal system marked by matrifocality and consanguine households. This view derives from the belief that African-American females, out of necessity assumed control of power and authority in families. The African-American female, from the period of slavery into the modern era, was forced to assert dominance as a result of the need to preserve the family unit because of the absence or prolonged unemployment of the male head of household. Also, African-American matriarchal culture is reinforced by the ways in which modern government assistance is allocated. Most notably, Aid to Families with Dependent Children (AFDC) stipends are allocated on the basis of the absence of an adult male from a household, what is called the no-male in the household restriction.

Opponents of this argument note that the African-American familial experience is characterized by a system of kinship networks. With the destruction of nuclear and polygamous family units, lineage could no longer be reconstructed under slavery, so networks based on marriage, friendship, and relatedness developed. Such a system still exists today, and is made even more necessary, scholars suggest, by other forces that further erode the nuclear family. The boundaries of the African-American family units are elastic and the inner workings of such groupings produce behaviors that allow for a great degree of adaptiveness to crises, such as unemployment, welfare payments restrictions, and lack of permanent dwelling forcing frequent movement of the family unit.

In the African-American system of kin networking, according to many, adult females play a key role in acquiring resources to meet needs. But they do not hold absolute power and authority within the kinship structure. African-American kin networks are cooperative units: all members, males, females, and children are called upon to assist in order that the kinship survives. All members, to an extent not found in white families, expend effort to acquire critical resources to overcome multiple disadvantages. African-American kinship systems are usually three-generational, co-residency households with boundaries that are flexible and exist within a larger kinship system that is extended and adaptive. The role of the woman within this double-tiered social system is *matrifocal*. Her role is both cultural and structural: adult females, primarily mothers, transmit cultural values and are participant in almost all interkinship decision making, the creation of family and kinship ties, and the acquisition of resources.

In the African-American kinship network, young women are socialized to demonstrate strength and to become active members. Both males and females exemplify qualities of assertiveness, initiative, autonomy, and decisiveness. A significant aspect of the socialization process is the training of females to act independently of males. Also, in such a matrifocal, bilateral arrangement, a close affinity between mother, child, and sibling exist, more so than within conjugal relationships. Human bonding in the African-American kinship system is decidedly mother-child oriented as in many other cultures where matrifocality is present.

Among the Ibo of Nigeria, the Javanese, and two Indonesian ethnic groups, the Minangkabau and the Atjehnese, family systems have been constructed in which degrees of matrifocality also exist. Like the African-American kinship system, the Javanese's is also bilateral. Among the Javanese, as in many matrifocal cultures, bonding is mother–child arranged, rather than husband–wife.

Patriarchal families are sometimes consanguine: organized in terms of blood relationships. Male power is vested in senior male members of the family. Examples of this type of patriarchy are found in many Chinese families. Other examples of consanguine patriarchal family structures are ancient Israel and ancient Rome. Both blood as well extended relationships, such as friendship and culture, are the social blocks that create the contemporary African-American family-kinship system.

Religion
Another force that has given rise to patriarchy and sustained its existence into modern times is religion. Religions, such as Judaism, Christianity, Hinduism, and Islam, led to the development of tenets and practices that enhanced existing patriarchal ideologies. Employing a metaphysical rationale, males were able to legitimate extensively their own superiority and establish for women an inferior, and even precarious position in society.

In the Judeo-Christian tradition, a God-ordained male-dominated hierarchy was constructed. Important was the idea that male creation was a primary act, while that of the female was secondary in nature: the female was created to serve the male and bear children. As the rites of Judeo-Christianity unfolded, women were not ordained as priests, denied the position of sacramental celebrants, and were forced to veil their heads, especially in religious gatherings, to signify male authority.

Other ancient metaphysical convenants negated the role of the woman as priestesses, divine healers, or seers. The dominant male-god that surfaced in Hebrew monotheism in some cases destroyed and in others decreased the presence of influential and powerful goddesses in ancient societies.

Under Hinduism, women are deemed to be more erotic than males. If their eroticism is left unchecked, it is believed that the male's quest for spirituality and a high level of asceticism would be impeded. Hindu women have been cloistered, never seen by males who were not members of the family, and wear veils concealing garments. In traditional Hindu society, all property acquired by a wife was transferred to male ownership.

The same was true in ancient Greece, Rome, Israel, China, and Japan. Also in England and America the right to own property did not exist until the modern period. Currently in Islamic Iran and Saudi Arabia, female property rights are still denied.

Theories of patriarchy

Socialist-Marxist feminists contend that a capitalistic-materialistic organization of society invokes patriarchy. It gives rise to a functional arrangement of the work force that is based on sexual divisions; neither equity in labor assignments, pay, nor worth are accorded to women. Patriarchy is sustained by the manner in which class relations occur. Class relations and the sexual division of labor are mutually supportive of one another, under capitalism. Patriarchy in this perspective is a universal system that will not alter *unless* a radical restructuring of society takes place.

Other feminists turn to psychoanalysis to provide explanations for the emergence of patriarchy. They note that once male and female gender classifications were devised, a double standard evolved and women were accorded a lesser position in society. The authority of male as father was the main structural device that was employed for the inclusion of gender in the social order.

Another group of social theorists differ from the more radical feminists and advance the concept that patriarchy was, and still is, only one of a number of sex-gender systems. Their viewpoint rests on the position that patriarchy can and does function independently of political systems and is autonomous. There is general acceptance that not all societies of the past were universally patriarchal. Any assertion included in prior scholarship that such was the case was due in large measure to patriarchal assumptions introduced by ethnographers and anthropologists. While it is contended that a number of societies of the past were culturally more egalitarian than others, and the role of women was more than that of child bearers and child providers, they were not genuinely matriarchal systems. No society of the past was a matriarchy; women acquired positions of importance but did not gain and utilize a dominance in power and authority.

Reading
Women Culture & Society edited by Michelle Zimbalist Rosaldo and Louise Lamphere (Stanford University Press, 1974) comprises sixteen articles that explore various theories that have been offered to explain the role of women in the development of various societies and cultures. This is complemented by *Women, Politics and the Third World* edited by Haleh Ashfar (Routledge, 1996), which examines strategies of resistance adopted by women.
The Creation of Patriarchy, vol. 1, by Grada Lerner (Oxford University Press, 1986) is a stylistic and informative investigation of the evolution of patriarchy in ancient cultures.
Myths, Dreams and Mysteries: The Encounter Between Contemporary Faiths and Archaic Realities by Mircea Eliade (translated from the French into English by Philip Mairet, Harper Torchbooks, 1967) has as its central theme the delineation of two types of thought: traditional thought, as archaic and Oriental in nature, and modern as Western in type. Each affects the culture's attitudes towards women.

See also: AFRICAN AMERICANS; ETHNICITY; KINSHIP

Loretta Zimmerman

Pentecostalism

A term used to describe a collection of religious sects that have proliferated particularly among blacks in the Caribbean, the United States and Britain. Doctrinally, the assemblies revolve around the Day of the Pentecost spoken of in the Bible's Acts, 2:1–2: "And the day of the Pentecost was now come, they were all together in one place. And suddenly there came from heaven a sound as of the rushing of a mighty wind, and it filled all the house where they were sitting."

Pentecostal members, or "saints," were to await this day of judgment when they would reach their salvation; in the meantime, they were to withdraw as far as possible from the "outside world" and restrict contact with outsiders. They believed themselves to be the "chosen people," the saved who would be rescued on the day of the Pentecost when all others would be damned.

The precise origins of Pentecostalism are obscure, but it seems there were antecedents in both America and the West Indies, where there flourished a movement called native baptism. This was based on Christianity but was fused with elements taken from African belief systems. Slavery played a significant part in shaping native baptism, as Malcolm Calley points out: "Possibly the most important role of slavery in the West Indies was to hinder the diffusion of a detailed knowledge of Christianity to the slaves thus stimulating them to invent their own interpretations and their own sects."

Lay native Baptist preachers were exposed to Christian teaching in America and their mixture of biblical concepts and African ritualism was enthusiastically met by American and, later (in the 1780s), Jamaican slaves. Native baptism survived the attempts of plantation owners to suppress it and sprouted a variety of different forms which later transmuted into Pentecostalism.

The sects maintained a presence in the Caribbean and the United States after emancipation and grew in Britain in the 1950s and 1960s – coinciding with the arrival of tens of thousands of Caribbean migrants. The response of the first wave of immigrants to white racialism was characterized by the writer Dilip Hiro as "evasion": they turned inward, developing postures designed to minimize their visibility. Black clubs, shops, and, of course, churches developed. Calley locates the beginnings of Pentecostalism in Britain in 1954 when services were held in private homes. By 1967, Clifford Hill revealed that a single branch of the movement, the New Testament Church of God, alone commanded a following of 10,861 congregations, employed fifteen full-time ministers and owned its own buildings, including a theological college for the training of its own ministry.

The growth of Pentecostalism is even more surprising when we consider the strictures placed on its members: forbidden were the consumption of tobacco and alcohol, the wearing of jewelry, or cosmetics, the use of bad language, and sexual laxity. Avoidance of contact with the "contaminated" outside world was recommended. Observance of these rules and adherence to Pentecostalist practices ensured the believer a special relationship with God, a relationship that was expressed through ecstatic experience in which the individuals became "filled" with the spirit of God and threw convulsions, twitching and being able to speak in tongues (glossolalia): "And they were all filled with the Holy Spirit, and began to speak with other tongues, as the spirit gave them utterance" (Acts, 2:4).

Pentecostalism indicates how many ethnic groups, particularly blacks in the United States and Britain, rather than articulate any outright protest against their treatment by society, develop alternative lifestyles, creating their own autonomous religions, passively withdrawing and seeking salvation not in this world but in an afterlife.

Reading
"Pentecostalism" by Grant Wacker in *Encyclopedia of American Religious Experience* volume II, edited by C. Lippy and P. Williams (Charles Scribner's Sons, 1988) is an excellent summary of the whole tradition and is complemented by the fuller treatment of John T. Nichol's *Pentecostalism* (Harper & Row, 1966).
God's People by Malcolm Calley (Oxford University Press, 1965) is a detailed study of Pentecostalism's growth in Britain, but with useful chapters on the ancestry of the sects.
The Making of the Black Working Class in Britain by R. Ramdin (Gower, 1987) has a section on "black churches" and the rest of the book supplies detailed contextual information.

See also: AFRICAN-CARIBBEANS IN BRITAIN; RASTAFARI

Ellis Cashmore

Phenotype
The visible or measurable appearance of an organism in respect of trait or traits. The phenotype is what one sees, the appearance or behavior of an organism in contrast to the genotype or underlying genetic constitution. For example, all people with brown eyes have the same phenotype in respect of eye color; equally, the behavior of a particular strain of rats when confronted with a series of puzzles in a maze is a behavioral phenotype. The outward appearance of humans in respect of skin color, hair form, bone structure, etc. is best identified as phenotypical variation; this is a relatively culture-free way of designating differences as opposed to the word race, the meaning of which varies from one historical period and one culture to another.

Reading
Personality and Heredity by Brian W. P. Wells (Longman, 1980) is an introduction to the study of psychogenics.
The Race Concept by Michael Banton and Jonathan Harwood (David & Charles, 1975) discusses the concept.

See also: GENOTYPE; INTELLIGENCE AND RACE; RACISM

Michael Banton

Pluralism

This refers to a pattern of social relations in which groups that are distinct from each other in a great many respects share aspects of a common culture and set of institutions. Each group retains its own ethnic origins by perpetuating specific cultures (or "subcultures") in the form of churches, businesses, clubs and media. It also encloses itself with its own set of primary group relations such as friendship networks, families and intra-group marriages. Yet, all those groups participate collectively in some spheres and, collectively, make up a "plural society."

J. S. Furnivall used societies in Burma and Indonesia as illustrations of plural societies: there people of very different ethnic backgrounds did not meet each other except in the marketplace, where they had to dispose of goods and services to other groups. The marketplace was the glue that held the different groups together like different pieces of stone in a mosaic. The mosaic is a useful metaphor for pluralism: one flat entity made up of many separate and distinct elements.

There are two basic types of pluralism: cultural and structural. Cultural occurs when groups have their own religions, beliefs, customs, attitudes and general lifestyles, but have others in common. Structural pluralism is when groups have their own social structures and institutions, while sharing others. For example, several groups may support a single government, and recognize the same law and use the same money; yet they might go to their own churches, speak a second language among themselves, have their own specialist educations and occupations and marry only within their own group.

Pluralism, as an analytical tool, purports to explain how many different groups with different backgrounds and, perhaps, different interests can live together without their diversity becoming a basis for conflict. This is especially so if power is distributed fairly evenly among the groups. Where one of the groups has control of power, conflict is likely to erupt. Historically, pluralism seems to apply to preindustrial or industrializing countries like East Africa or Caribbean societies where there are more or less equal segments rather than hierarchial classes as in industrial societies.

The plural society is based on cultural and social heterogeneity (i.e. it is composed of diverse elements), but one that does not necessarily create deep divisions and produce serious conflict. Groups maintain their own distinct features and corporate identities, thus adding to the richness of society, without being excluded or relegated to lowly positions.

Pluralism has been used as an ideal in some circumstances, something to aim at; a society in which all groups can express their differences and cultivate their uniqueness without engaging in wholesale or even petty conflicts. The ideal encourages self-awareness and development in some spheres and unification and cooperation in others. This has been particularly popular in North American countries which house a variety of ethnic groups, but can foster only a limited unity despite attempts to balance out interests. But, well intended as the goal maybe, it is constantly interrupted by racism which denies different groups access to certain types of resources (like well-paying jobs and good housing).

The term pluralism is also used in political science in a slightly different sense: it describes a situation in which there are several different interest groups segmentalized horizontally with no single group exerting complete dominance. The similarities with ethnic pluralism are apparent: division on the basis of difference without severe inequality of power; horizontal not vertical differentiation.

Reading

Netherlands India by J. S. Furnivall (Cambridge University Press, 1967, first published in 1947) is a very early account of plural societies and provides the theoretical model for the later work by M. G. Smith, *The Plural Society in the British West Indies* (University of California Press, 1965).

"Pluralism, race and ethnicity in selected African countries" by M. G. Smith in *Theories of Race and Ethnic Relations*, edited by J. Rex and D. Mason (Cambridge University Press, 1986), is a more recent re-evaluation by one of the perspective's original proponents.

"Pluralism: a political perspective" by Michael Walzer in the Harvard *Encyclopedia of American Ethnic Groups* (Harvard University Press, 1980) is an assessment of the pluralist development of the United States.

See also: CULTURE; ETHNICITY; MULTICULTURALISM; NATIVE PEOPLES; POWER

Ellis Cashmore

Police and racism

Given the volume of complaints emanating from North America, Britain, Australia, Germany, and France, it is hard to avoid the conclusion that ethnic minorities are still at the forefront of some of the harshest and most controversial policing practices. There are a number of distinctive but interrelated allegations of racist police practices that can be identified. These can be divided into two categories: the over-policing of minority groups and under-policing in relation to the specific law and order needs of these groups.

Over-policing

The allegations of over-policing relate to the discriminatory use of police powers when dealing with members of minority communities, particularly in relation to powers of stop and search, arrest, custody and the use of (in certain cases deadly) force. British Home Office research (Paper 6, 1983) has shown that "young black males are significantly more likely to be stopped than their white counterparts." And community leaders in the United States continue to protest about the aggressive stop and search policies that are *routinely* utilized in relation to male African Americans and Latinos. As well as individual harassment, minority communities have complained about saturation policing by specialist police squads, incursions on cultural and political events, as well as immigration raids. As a result of what they perceive to be constant harassment and discrimination, significant sections of these communities, particularly the young, have become alienated from the police. In Britain the Scarman inquiry, set up after the inner city riots of 1981, acknowledged that the disturbances "were essentially an outburst of anger and resentment by young black people against the police." In a similar vein, the Kerner Report, compiled in the aftermath of serious disturbances in Watts, Detroit, Newark, and Washington, D.C., stated that in the United States the "police force have come to symbolize white power, white racism, and white repression." In Australia, the National Inquiry Into Racist Violence argued that the reason why police–Aboriginal relations were so bad was because of "the widespread involvement of the police in acts of racist violence, intimidation and harassment" (Australian Government, 1991).

Under-policing

The second facet of racially discriminatory policing relates to the alleged refusal of the police to provide an adequate response to minority community needs. Critics of the police claim that responding to the needs of residents in crime-ridden ghettos and inner cities is a lower police priority than responding to the needs of respectable neighborhoods. Thus, for the sake of maintaining public order the police have virtually abandoned certain neighborhoods. Critics also claim to have identified a consistent pattern in the police attitude to racially motivated attacks, that is, a complete lack of response or interest; reluctance to prosecute; the redefinition of such attacks as nonracist; treating the victim as the criminal and reacting harshly to community self-protection measures. With the upsurge of right-wing extremism in France and Germany and the increasing serious-ness of attacks on guest workers, refugee camps, and immigrant communities, the apparent lack of police protection has become a major bone of contention. This lack of intervention stands in stark contrast to over-policing that minority groups claim they are nor-mally subjected to.

Riot/uprising
The ultimate manifestation of the near complete breakdown of the police–community relationship is the riot, or uprising. The British uprisings of 1981–5 were precipitated by what were perceived to be heavy-handed police actions in ethnic minority neighborhoods. More recently, the United States watched in horror as the most serious riot of the postwar period engulfed central Los Angeles, claiming fifty lives and causing millions of dollars' worth of damage. Triggered by the acquittal of police officers for the brutal beating of Rodney King, the ferocity of the May 1992 riots indicated the depth of anger and frustration that existed among many African Americans. For many community leaders the verdict represented a final loss of faith by African Americans in the fairness of the criminal justice system. It also suggested that white middle-class America was willing to condone systematic police brutalization and mistreat-ment of black people.

Explanations
i. Individual   Various explanations have been forwarded to account for the ongoing conflict between the police and minority groups. The orthodox police position tends to deny the problem of racial harassment and discrimination. Police representatives continue to argue that the real source of the problem is the overrepresentation of certain ethnic groups in the criminal statistics. Thus it is argued that the criminality of certain "pathological" communities results in proactive policing practices and that in the "war against crime" there will be casualties. They also point to the antipolice attitudes that are entrenched in these "underclass" communities. More enlightened senior officers would argue that the problem of racial prejudice lies with the attitudes of individual officers rather than the institution. There is little doubt that prejudice exists within

the predominantly white police forces under discussion. However, research suggests that it is not just the prerogative of a few "rotten apples." The Policy Studies Institute study into police–community relations in London reported that "there can be few other groups in which it is normal, automatic, habitual to refer to black people as 'coons,' 'niggers' and so on." This study also noted that supervisory officers did little to curb racialist comments. In the aftermath of the Los Angeles riots there were numerous news reports indicating that in certain American forces racist attitudes were widespread among officers. Following the King case, it was possible for O. J. Simpson's defense team to argue plausibly that L.A.P.D. officers' actions were motivated by racism.

ii. Structural The alternative explanation argues that the source of this conflictual relationship lies with the police mandate and the structural position of minority groups. From this perspective antagonistic relationships between the police and ethnic minorities are not a recent phenomenon. However, from the late 1960s onwards, the antagonism has been exacerbated because of the changing nature of the societies under discussion. During this period, it is argued, there has been a fundamental shift as authoritarian law and order tendencies emerged both in the United States and Britain. Under the aegis of an ascendent radical right, a concerted effort was made to reshape these societies to facilitate a new economic order untrammeled by welfare expenditure and liberal paraphernalia. Those who have suffered most from this restructuring have been minority communities. They have no longer any core role to play within the new economic order and are suffering in a disproportionate manner from structural unemployment, the effects of cutbacks in welfare and urban disinvestment. They are to all intents and purposes politically and socially powerless and economically impoverished, existing outside the reconstituted edifice of citizenship. Within this scenario, the police have the institutional role of controlling and containing the reaction of the ghetto dwellers most affected by the social and economic changes. It is this institutional role that has brought them into constant conflict with certain minority groups. According to this perspective the radical right has also been able to construct a potent ideological connection between race and crime and in doing so has provided the raison d'être for the heavy policing of these groups. As a result, minority communities have been pathologized and criminalized and white support has been mobilized for "the thin blue line."

From this perspective suggestions for improving police training and race relations courses, recruiting minority officers and making racism a disciplinary offense will not work because the source of the problem is structural not individual. Racism is institutionalized in the police. Only when there are wider political changes which will facilitate properly accountable policing and respect for human rights will it be possible to bring the arbitrary policing of minority groups under control. However, in the aftermath of Los Angeles political commentators were pessimistic about whether there would be any radical and wide-ranging policy shifts either in relation to wider social issues or the operation of the criminal justice system. And in this context it is significant to note that, in a manner reminiscent of the British police after the riots of the 1980s, the immediate response of the Los Angeles police was to introduce intensive riot control training for its officers.

Related to this perspective is the observation that police forces have actually utilized scares about the alleged criminal propensities of ethnic minorities to justify gaining material and political resources that enhance their professional autonomy. By fostering an image of a crisis-ridden society in which blacks feature in an inordinate amount of criminal activity, police forces since the war have been able to demand more control over their own practices to be able to meet the challenges of the purported crisis. Police, on this account, have actually contributed to the sense of crisis. The theory is elaborated in *Out of Order?*

Reading
Out of Order? Policing Black People edited by E. Cashmore and E. McLaughlin (Routledge, 1991) is a comparative analysis of the relationship between the police and black communities in Britain and the United States.
The Racialization of British Policing by Simon Holdaway (Macmillan, 1996) relies on secondary sources to argue that the "race" issue manifests itself in British policing and may be read in conjunction with *Racism and Criminology* edited by Dee Cook and Barbara Hudson (Sage, 1993).
The Los Angeles Riots: Lessons for the Urban Future edited by Mark Baldassare (Westview, 1994) collects the views of several scholars on the persistent tension between police and black people.
Black Police in America by W. M. Dulaney (Indiana University Press, 1996) assesses the impact of black officers on law enforcement and crime control.

See also: ABORIGINAL AUSTRALIANS; KERNER REPORT; RIOTS: BRITAIN AND U.S.A.; SCARMAN REPORT

Eugene McLaughlin

Political correctness

A much-derided set of guiding principles and directives, political correctness (PC) became a virtual orthodoxy at many U.S. universities in the early 1990s. While it was based on sound academic concepts, its enactment was quickly interpreted as a form of censorship. It aimed to redress the balance of North American academies, which were understood to be mired in the same racism and sexism that existed in and was promoted by much American culture. The pervasive character of racism and sexism ensured that the language of instruction and the content of curricula reflected these. Given that knowledge is disseminated through educational institutions, it was thought unlikely that such knowledge would serve emancipatory goals unless it consciously rejected racism and sexism and actively embraced alternatives based on multicultural, antiracist, and antisexist articles.

Inspirations behind PC were diverse. Michel Foucault's analysis of the coterminous power/knowledge was important in pointing out that the production of intellect and imagination represent not so much the capacities of the authors producing them, but the relations of power and the ideologies that define the boundaries of discourse – this being, in very general terms, the context in which the knowledge is produced. There has also been a recognition that concepts are not formed in the human mind independently of the language we use to express them. The world is not experienced as a series of facts, but of signs encoded in language. This makes it possible for us to experience the world as "natural" and "right." But, according to writers, such as Roland Barthes, it is possible to uncover invisible codes and conventions through which the meanings of experience are accepted.

Jacques Derrida's method of deconstruction was a challenge to the language in which rational argument is expressed. Derrida argued that the Western tradition of thought is founded on assumptions about a final source, or guarantee, of meaning in language. Language is an instrument, but it is not a neutral one. PC followers believe language has been used to perpetuate racism and sexism, but in ways which almost defy conventional analysis.

Because of this, PC began its attempt to counter the Western, or Eurocentric, conceptions of knowledge by targeting language and the discourse it inscribes. Terms and text did not carry thought; they perpetuated it, often in an unreflective way. Apart from the more obvious cases where "black" or its corollaries were used in a derogatory way and in terms of implied abuse, PC carefully screened out all manner of words, such as "beauty," "burly," "dear," and "leader." Any word with a vaguely sexist or racist inference, or one that reflected poorly on disabled persons, the aged, or the young was anathema.

PC also scrutinized curricula, often finding Eurocentric biases in traditional subjects of, for example, English Literature and Philosophy, the domains of the DWMs "dead white males" (Shakespeare, Aristotle, *et al.*). It sought to make some courses on multiculturalism required for all students. This was so zealously pursued at U.S. universities that it led to hostility from faculty members who sensed an encroachment of "academic freedom." In one notable case at Duke University, classroom behavior was monitored to root out racism. The process uncovered only "disrespectful facial expressions or body language aimed at black students." This kind of finding hastened the trivialization of PC, and so reduced its impact as an intellectual force.

Reading
Unthinking Eurocentrism by Ellas Shohat and Robert Stam (Routledge, 1994) has a chapter "The politics of multiculturalism in the postmodern age" that offers a challenging view of PC by reversing Spivak's memorable question thus: "Can the non-subaltern speak?"
The Politics and Philosophy of Political Correctness by Jung Min Choi and John W. Murphy (Praeger, 1993) explores the assumptions that underpin the PC debates.
After Political Correctness edited by Christopher Newfield and Ronald Strickland (Westview Press, 1995) centralizes the PC debate as a struggle over the very purposes of higher education.

See also: AFROCENTRICITY; EDUCATION AND CULTURAL DIVERSITY; MULTICULTURALISM; SUBALTERN

Ellis Cashmore

Politics and "race"

The idea of "race" has been taken up and employed as an object of political action in a variety of ways in different countries. Put another way, one can trace different forms in which political processes have become racialized. In the vast majority of these instances, the idea of "race" has been employed in order to justify or legitimate discriminatory action of some sort. At the extreme, as in the instance of Germany in the 1930s and 1940s, the idea of "race" was employed by the Nazi party to justify a solution to identified economic and political problems which involved mass murder of the Jews. In South Africa, from the early nineteenth century to the 1950s, the idea of "race" was employed to justify the physical segregation and extreme exploitation of African labor.

Both these examples represent twentieth-century instances of a relationship that characterizes European colonial domination and expansion in the late eighteenth and nineteenth centuries, and the exploitation of African labor in the United States in the same period. In these instances important sections of the dominant class justified their economic and political activity by labeling those whose labor they exploited in various ways as belonging to an inferior "race." The political application of the "race" label was explicitly accompanied by the employment of racist ideology: Africans, both in Africa and the United States, were defined as belonging to the "Negro race," which was held to be inferior, biologically and culturally, when compared with the "race" to which their exploiters allegedly belonged.

The fact that this racism was used to justify mass murder in the heartland of a European continent which various national ruling classes defined as the epitome of "civilization" and "democracy" was one of the reasons why the manner in which politics were racialized changed in Europe after 1945. Another, equally important, factor was the process of decolonization that was well under way by the 1950s. Although direct political control over colonies was conceded, often after direct armed struggle, European and North American capital wished to retain economic control as far as was possible and this necessitated no longer defining the emerging ruling classes as members of an inferior "race." For this same reason, European and North American policy toward South Africa changed to the extent that political opposition toward the manner and content of its ruling class means of domination was expressed while trade and investment continued relatively unhindered. The necessary desire to maintain the international domination of capital was not the sole determinant of this changing ideological content of ruling-class ideology, but it provided the parameters for such a change. It also had major repercussions within European and, particularly, American societies. The contradiction between political legitimation of the American ruling class in terms of "freedom" and "equality," when combined with changing world political relationships in the 1950s and 1960s, was clearly contradicted by the position and experience of the African-descended population within the United States. The result was the rebellion and revolt of those who were the object of that contradiction and, as a longer-term consequence, a redefinition by the exploited of what "race" meant to them.

This general process was neither uniform nor universal. Moreover, it did not mean that the idea of "race" was removed from political discourse. Rather, although the language of biological racism was removed from bourgeois politics, the language of "race" remained and was accompanied by assertions of cultural inferiority. Only the neofascist right retained the "old" racism: parliamentary politicians articulated the "new" racism. The process is particularly clear within Western Europe (in Britain the process is evident in the extreme form) where, since 1945, the racialization of politics has become an internal issue.

Before the major labor migrations beginning in the 1940s, the racialization of politics occurred primarily in connection with colonial affairs. The political reaction to these migrations was at first out of step with the economic reaction: capitalists required labor power and so welcomed migrant labor as a solution to their problem. But there was a hostile political reaction from the start and this gained in strength through the 1960s. The hostility was expressed by drawing attention to cultural differences and linking them with the idea of "race" (in that the migrants were identified primarily by certain phenotypical features). On the basis of this new form of racialization, a wide range of racist legislation was passed in different European countries to confine the migrants to a marginal legal/ ideological position. In some instances, the legislation preceded and directly structured the entry to the migrants.

As a result of this process, "race" is widely defined as a political problem requiring attention and policy decisions in Europe. This is so irrespective of the fact that not only has the language of the nineteenth-century scientific racism been largely absent from official political discourse but also that elected governments have consistently denied being motivated by, or having institutionalized in law, racism. The official explicitly defined object and problem is "immigrants," but the language and imagery used by all classes to discuss this "problem" draws directly, yet separately, upon that store of late eighteenth and nineteenth century racism.

Reading
Race, Politics and Social Change by John Solomos and Les Back (Routledge, 1995) looks at the role of race in politics and the impact of multiculturalism on the shape of politics.
The Politics of Multiculturalism by Bikhu Parekh (Macmillan 1996)

addresses theoretical questions about such matters as national identity, citizenship, and political discourse.

Black Politics in Conservative America by Marcus Pohlmann (Longman, 1990) looks at the major political approaches to black citizens.

See also: COLONIALISM; EMPOWERMENT; MIGRATION; RACIALIZATION

Robert Miles

Postcolonial

A term used to describe theoretical and empirical work that centralize the issues emerging from colonial relations and their aftermath, colonial here meaning the implanting of settlements by imperial powers on distant territories. The "post" aligns it with other intellectual movements, such as postfeminism, postmodernism and, most significantly, poststructuralism, in that it connoted a transition beyond more obsolete discourses; in this case, an age or historical epoch (colonialism) *and* a type of theorizing (nationalistic anticolonial critique). Its ascent in popularity coincided with the descent of the older "Third World" paradigm.

A product largely of European and U.S. academies, postcolonial discourse concerns itself not only with the former colonies that gained independence following World War II, but with the experiences of people descended from inhabitants of those territories and their experiences in the metropolitan centers of the "first world" colonial powers – the diaspora. It focuses on the institutional forces that shape and set limits on the representation of what have been/ are considered subordinate humans and on the efforts of those subordinated groups to challenge the representations.

Postcolonial literary theory concerns itself with the analysis of texts produced by all societies in some way affected by colonial regimes, colonizer and colonized. Edward Said's "contrapuntal reading" of Joseph Conrad's *Heart of Darkness*, for example, uncovers "a structure of attitude and reference" that animates and articulates the relationship between England and Africa in the nineteenth century.

Postcolonial theory encompasses the work of a wide variety of writers from diverse backgrounds, including Frantz Fanon, Jean-Paul Sartre, and Gayatri Spivak. Its critics include Carole Boyce Davies, who objects to it on a number of counts, including the fact that it is too premature a formulation, it is ahistorical and it "remales and recenters resistant discourses by women." The last point refers to the tendency of postcolonial theory to become a single narrative, what Davies calls "the center announcing its own political agenda without reference to indigenous self-articulations." In becoming integrated into "theory," postcolonial work has become the property of western (male-dominated) academies, even if the writing is done by scholars who have no heritage in the west.

Reading

The Post-Colonial Studies Reader edited by Bill Ashcroft, Gareth Griffiths and Helen Tiffin (Routledge, 1994) pulls together a wide range of writings by, among others, Fanon, Spivak and Said; and may be read in conjunction with a similar text *Colonial Discourse and Post-colonial Theory* edited by Patrick Williams and Laura Chrisman (Harvester Wheatsheaf, 1993).

The Wretched of the Earth (Grove Press, 1964) and *Black Skin, Whites Masks* (Grove Press, 1967) by Frantz Fanon are seminal texts about which postcolonial theorists rhapsodize; Fanon's influences include Hegel, Marx, Freud, and Nietzsche.

Black Women, Writing and Identity by Carole Boyce Davies (Routledge, 1994) contains the critique adumbrated above.

See also: DEVELOPMENT; DIASPORA; HYBRIDITY; OTHERS; SUBALTERN
Ellis Cashmore

Power

This is a crucial concept in race and ethnic relations for it refers to the ability to exact a degree of compliance or obedience of others in accordance with one's own will. Power may be vested in individuals, in groups, whole societies, or even blocs of societies; the distinguishing feature is the capacity to influence others into performing and, maybe, thinking in accordance with one's own requirements.

There has been great debate over the exact nature of power and there are many different forms of power. For example, slavery is an extreme example of what might be called "raw power" – an unmitigated coercion based on physical might. It entails one group exercising its will over another through almost total control of circumstances; conformity is enforced through the application of negative sanctions to undesirable behavior. But, as the French philosopher Jean-Jacques Rousseau noticed: "The strongest man is never strong enough to be always master unless he transforms his power into right and obedience into duty."

Sheer compulsion works effectively under some conditions, particularly where there is a large disparity in material resources, but race relations today usually have more complex power relationships entailing a recognition by the power*less* group of the powerholding group's right to exercise its will. For instance, in many situations, a group will retain its power because other groups accept the *legit-*

imacy of its position and so never challenge the unequal relationship. It could be plausibly argued that blacks in the United States, for many years, did not seriously question the legitimacy of the power relationship of which they were part: they acknowledged the right of whites to rule and so accepted their own subordinate position. So the threat of force that lay behind the whites' power in slave days was not necessary to the maintenance of the power relationship.

Power is sometimes operationalized through a unified framework of rules, such as the laws existing in the United States until the civil rights legislation. These institutionalized whites' power and ensured blacks were kept powerless through legal means. The extreme example of this is the law relating to apartheid: this effectively denies nonwhites access to power. This type of arrangement was characterized by the sociologist Max Weber as "rational-legal," but there are alternatives. There may be a "traditional" mode of legitimation in which authority has been vested with one group for a long period of time. On occasions, there may emerge a "charismatic" leader who is attributed with power because his followers believe him or her to be endowed with some special gifts, perhaps from some supernatural agency. In these situations, the ultimate legitimating power may be the "will of God" and they often engender forces for changes in power relationships rather than those securing existing arrangements. Gandhi's successful campaign against British power over India is an obvious example.

The Gandhi case is an illustration of the loss of plausibility of the legitimacy of one power relationship and the gain in plausibility of an alternative. Once legitimacy is lost, then forms of resistance to it are likely to proliferate. Basically, all ethnic struggles are about power relationships. Where there is a diversity of groups with divergent interests and no absolute attribution of legitimacy to a power relationship, a perpetual resistance is likely to take place.

Reading
Race, Ethnicity and Power by Donald Baker (Routledge & Kegan Paul, 1983) remains a model study of the way in which power has factored into ethnic relations in Australia, North America, and Southern Africa.
Power, Racism and Privilege by William J. Wilson (Free Press, 1973) is an old but enduringly useful analysis of race relations, that uses a power framework and some good comparative material.
Max Weber: The Lawyer as Social Thinker by Stephen Turner and Regis Factor (Routledge, 1994) is an exposition of the influential theorist's thought.

See also: COLONIALISM; GANDHI; HEGEMONY; SLAVERY

Ellis Cashmore

Prejudice

From the Latin *prae*, before, *judicium*, judgment, this may be defined as learned beliefs and values that lead an individual or group of individuals to be biased for or against members of particular groups prior to actual experience of those groups. Technically then, there is a positive and negative prejudice, though, in race and ethnic relations, the term usually refers to the negative aspect when a group inherits or generates hostile views about a distinguishable group based on generalizations. These generalizations are invariably derived from inaccurate or incomplete information about the other group.

For example, we might say a person (or group) is prejudiced against Asians; we mean that they are oriented toward behaving with some hostility toward Asians (that behavior is called discrimination). The person believes that, with the odd exception, all Asians are pretty much the same. But the general characteristics they attribute to Asians are faulty. The generalization is called stereotyping and means assigning properties to any person in a group regardless of the actual variation among members of the group. In a recent piece of research it was found that many white residents of British housing developments were prejudiced against Asians, believing them all to be, among other things, "unhygienic, crafty, and antiwhite." The views were not gleaned from valid experience, but from hearsay or secondhand images.

Such prejudices might not be restricted to ethnic groups, but to virtually any group (including whole nations or continents) to which generalized characteristics can be applied. Thus individual members of those groups are denied the right to be recognized and treated as individuals with individual characteristics.

Examples of this process are rife in history, although the antisemitism of World War II stands out: millions were identified as sharing alleged characteristics because of their Jewish background. Gross generalizations were made about Jews and these were used as the basis of all manner of atrocities.

In the aftermath of the war, a large-scale study of prejudice was made by Theodor Adorno and his colleagues. Published in 1950, *The Authoritarian Personality* concluded that certain people are prejudiced because their prejudices meet certain needs associated with their personality. Further, those who were highly prejudiced were likely to have authoritarian personalities; they tended to be submissive and obedient to authority and to reject "out-groups" in a punitive way. They also saw people in dichotomous terms – "either you're with us or against us."

The upshot of this was that, if prejudice was bound up with a fundamental type of personality, people with this type of personality would be prejudiced not just against one particular "out-group" but against all people and groups who were considered different in some way.

This general and complex form of prejudice the researchers called "ethnocentrism" as contrasted to the more one-dimensional anti-semitism. This ethnocentrism referred to a tendency to regard one's own group as the standard and all other, different groups as strange and, usually, inferior. One's own ways of thinking and behaving were seen as normal, the natural way of doing things. The main finding of the research was that there was a strong relationship between this consistently high degree of prejudice against all "out-groups" and a personality with the following features: possession of "conventional values;" intolerance of weakness; rigidity of beliefs and views; tendency to be punitive and suspicious; respectful of authority to an extreme degree. Hence the "authoritarian personality."

Adorno *et al.* traced the development of this personality complex and prejudice to early childhood experiences in families tending to be harshly disciplinarian. As a child, the possessor of an authoritarian personality was insecure, dependent on, fearful of, and unconsciously hostile toward parents. As an adult he or she has a high amount of pent-up anger which, because of basic insecurity, manifests itself in a displaced aggression against powerless groups. At the same time, the individual remains respectful of and obedient toward those in authority.

Though *The Authoritarian Personality* has become a classic study of the causes of prejudices, modern psychologists and sociologists have tended to take the emphasis off unconscious childhood conflicts and to lay them on the pressures and influences in the social context. In particular, many have pointed to prejudice as a matter of learning: people simply pick up prejudices against groups from others with whom they identify. Those others may be parents or they may be peers. Either way the individual feels a pressure to conform, so adjusts his views accordingly. This helps explain why prejudices seem to pass from one generation to the next. Thomas Pettigrew has argued that although personality features may account for some prejudice, the greater proportion of it stems from a straightforward conformity to prevalent standards. So that if one grows up in an environment in which all those with Spanish-sounding names are regarded as imbeciles fit only for menial work, then one strongly feels a pressure to align one's own negative prejudices to conform with this generalization.

Other explanations also invoke social factors. For example, the phenomenon known as scapegoating implicates minority groups in situations that are not of their own making, yet produces high amounts of prejudice against them. A general social decline might lead to sharp contraction of the job market and a general deterioration in material conditions. The underlying causes of decline may be complex, so people may look for something more immediate and locate it in the form of a minority group. So an immigrant or minority group might be made into a scapegoat and negative prejudices against that group can be created.

Prejudice, then, can be explained as a result of childhood experiences, pressure to conform or scapegoating. There are many other explanations; it can be approached as an individual or a social phenomenon. But, however it is explained, one must consider it as an important factor in race and ethnic relations. For being aware of another group's presence and holding negative values and beliefs about that group bears a crucially strong influence on how behavior toward that group will be organized and, therefore, on the general pattern of race relations.

Reading
The Authoritarian Personality by T. S. Adorno, E. Frenkel-Brunswick, D. J. Levinson and R. N. Sanforo (Harper & Row, 1950) is the most influential study of prejudice since the war.
The Nature of Prejudice by Gordon Allport (Addison-Wesley, 1954) was, in its day, a major statement on the psychology of race relations; still an impressive, scholarly account of the causes of and solutions to prejudice.
How Young Children Perceive Race by Robyn M. Holmes (Sage, 1995) is based on participant-observation and shows how children pick up ideas about their own and others' ethnic identities.

See also: DOLLARD; RACIAL DISCRIMINATION; SCAPEGOAT; STEREOTYPE; XENOPHOBIA

Ellis Cashmore

Pruitt-Igoe
The name of two areas in St. Louis that were designated by city planners the sites of a large-scale housing project. In the early 1950s, big, high-rise apartment blocks situated in grounds intentionally left

open for the use of both the resident and surrounding community, were erected in the two areas.

The project was developed in the spirit of good ethnic relations, the idea being that blacks would live more harmoniously together and away from whites. Originally, the plan was to house whites in one estate and blacks in the other, but the U.S. Supreme Court considered this unconstitutional, and the two areas were eventually occupied by some 10,000 mostly black residents. The first families moved in during 1954; by 1959, the project had become a total scandal, not only because of the unusual architecture but because of the high incidence of crime, vandalism, and prostitution. Its unattractiveness was reflected in its vacancy rate which exceeded that of any housing complex in the United States.

Rainwater studied the area and noted: "The original tenants were drawn very heavily from several land clearance areas in the inner city. . . . Only those Negroes [*sic*] who are desperate for housing are willing to live in Pruitt-Igoe."

The place became a "dumping ground" for poor blacks. Street violence became an everyday occurrence, robbery was commonplace and buildings were allowed to deteriorate. Families left as quickly as possible: a vacancy rate of 65 percent attested to the ultimate failure of the project. Twelve years after its construction, Pruitt-Igoe was quite literally blown up.

The "public housing monstrosity," as Oscar Newman called it, served as a reminder of the negative effects of projects based on *de facto* segregation.

A similar policy almost materialized in Britain in 1978 when the Greater London Council announced its proposal for a "racially segregated" area for Bengalis in the Tower Hamlets borough. Its divisiveness was, however, noted and it came to nothing. Herding is a simple "response" to problems of the inner cities, but is in no sense a solution to them; it submits to people's prejudices and fears and can lead to the artificial creation of vast ghettos – as Pruitt-Igoe demonstrates.

Reading

Behind Ghetto Walls by Lee Rainwater (Penguin, 1973) is a study of life as lived by the residents of Pruitt-Igoe with an assessment of the effects.

Defensible Space by Oscar Newman (Architectural Press, 1972) is an analysis of how people's physical environments can affect their social behavior, with particular attention taken of Pruitt-Igoe.

Race and Racism edited by P. Jackson (Allen & Unwin, 1987) examines the geographical aspects of racism, including the territorial basis of residential segregation.

See also: BUSING; DISPERSAL; GHETTO; SEGREGATION

Ellis Cashmore

Puerto Ricans in the U.S.A.

About a third of the total Puerto Rican population lives in the United States with over half of that migrant group domiciled in New York City. Between 800,000 and 900,000 Puerto Ricans live in New York and that is around twice as many as in San Juan, the capital city of Puerto Rico.

Puerto Rico itself is a Caribbean island about 1,000 miles southeast of Florida. It was conquered by the Spanish and made into a slave colony with the introduction of African labor in the early sixteenth century. The dominant cultural influence remains Spanish. After the Spanish-American War, Puerto Rico was given to the United States under the terms of the Treaty of Paris, 1898, and was granted a measure of local government until 1917 when Puerto Ricans were declared citizens of the United States. This precipitated a migration to the mainland.

Improvements in health and sanitation produced a decline in the deathrate, thus swelling Puerto Rico's population and putting pressure on the economy. This hastened migration in the pursuit of employment; access to the United States was simplified by the availability of citizenship and migration grew rapidly in the 1920s.

Natural disasters in 1928 and 1932 devastated coffee plantations (the major source of income for the island) and stimulated more migration. World War II curtailed the movement, but the development of inexpensive air travel after the war (e.g. to New York in six hours for about $50) resulted in a mass migration. By 1973, almost five million people were traveling to and from the United States, in search of work they could not find in their homeland.

New York became the center of gravity for migrants, particularly the area of East Harlem called *El Barrio* (the neighborhood), which is still the prototype Puerto Rican ghetto. Like most other immigrants, Puerto Ricans faced the problems of family fragmentation, inadequate living conditions, poor health, exploitation at work, the handicaps of language and education, and the underlying obstacles of racialism. These had the effect of binding them together and the perception of sharing common problems produced a vigorous ethnicity.

With little improvement, ethnicity was sustained and had the perhaps unwanted consequence of compounding the deprivation. Oscar Lewis, in his study of Puerto Ricans in New York, describes a "culture of poverty" in which Puerto Ricans grow up in a tightly bonded community and assimilate poverty as a way of life instead of trying to break away from it. Catholicism is all-pervasive and enhances the sense of group identity, and family solidarity has worked as a kind of fetter to social and geographical mobility. Often, educational and occupational advancement necessitates moving away from the community and therefore from the family unit (which is rather large – about four people – compared to the New York average). Adherence to this culture alone vitiates any prospect of betterment and locks the Puerto Rican into a world of fatalism and the kind of street violence portrayed in *West Side Story*.

The indications are that today's Puerto Ricans are trying to advance in both education and occupations, but at the expense of the family solidarity and, ultimately, Puerto Rican ethnicity. Marrying outside the ethnic group will also work to weaken the sense of community and identity Puerto Ricans have displayed since the war.

Reading

La Vida: A Puerto Rican Family in the Culture of Poverty – San Juan and New York by Oscar Lewis (Secker & Warburg, 1967) is a classic study of Puerto Rican life, rich in illustrations and theoretically strung together by the author's "culture of poverty" thesis.

"Puerto Ricans and the political economy of New York" by Clara Rodriquez in *From Different Shores* edited by Ronald Takaki (Oxford University Press, 1987) looks at the uneven integration of Puerto Ricans into the New York economy.

The Semiotics of Exclusion: Puerto Rican Experiences of Language, Race and Class by Bonnie Urciouli (Westview Press, 1996) is a study based on ethnography and interviews and maps the workingclass experiences of Puerto Ricans in the U.S.A.

See also: ETHNICITY; LATINOS; MINORITIES

Ellis Cashmore

R

Race – as classification

A group or category of persons connected by common origin. The word entered the English language at the beginning of the sixteenth century; from then until early in the nineteenth century it was used primarily to refer to common features present because of shared descent. But it was also used more loosely, as when John Bunyan in 1678 wrote "of the Way and Race of Saints," or, a little over 100 years later, Robert Burns addressed the haggis as "the chieftain o' the pudding race." The literary usage to designate the descendants of an ancestral figure, or as a synonym for nation, continues to the present day, although it now appears archaic. Since the beginning of the nineteenth century the word has been used in several other distinct senses. It is important to notice these changes because there is an assumption that there is one scientifically valid way of using the word. Physical differences catch people's attention so readily that they are less quick to appreciate that the validity of race as a concept depends upon its use as an aid in explanation. From this standpoint the main issue is not what "race" is but the way it is used. People draw upon beliefs about race, as they draw upon beliefs about nationality, ethnicity, and class, as resources for cultivating group identities.

The changes in the way the word race has been used reflect changes in the popular understanding of the causes of physical and cultural differences. Up to the eighteenth century at least, the chief paradigm for explaining such differences was provided by the Old Testament. This furnished a series of genealogies by which it seemed possible to trace the peopling of the world and the relations which different groups bore to one another. Differences of outward appearances could then be interpreted in one of three ways: first as part of God's design for the universe; second as caused by environmental differences irrelevant to moral issues; third as arising from different original ancestors. In any event, the dominant meaning attaching to the word race was that of descent. In the early nineteenth century increased knowledge about the differences between the world's peoples suggested to many people that they were part of a more general pattern of natural differences encompassing the animal and vegetable kingdoms. Under the influence of Georges Cuvier, the French comparative anatomist, such differences were seen as expressing distinctive types. "Type" was defined as a primitive or original form independent of climatic or other physical differences. Types were thought to be permanent (for this was a pre-Darwinian view of nature). Race came to be used in the sense of type as designating species of men distinct both in physical constitution and mental capacities. This conception survives to the present and forms the core of the doctrines often designated "scientific racism."

Darwin showed that no forms in nature were permanent. His work led to a new interpretation according to which the physical differences between people stem from their inheriting different genes. Race (or geographical race in Darwin's vocabulary) became a synonym for subspecies, i.e. a subdivision of a species which is distinctive only because its members are isolated from other individuals belonging to the same species. If their isolation did not reduce opportunities for mating between these populations, the distinctiveness of their gene pools would be reduced. The theory of natural selection and the establishment of genetics as a field of experimental research had revolutionary implications for the study of racial differences, but it took some two generations for these implications to be properly appreciated. For half a century after the publication of Darwin's *Origin* in 1859, anthropologists continued to propose racial classifications of *Homo sapiens* in the belief that in this way the nature of the differences could be better understood. Subsequent research suggests, to the contrary, that classifications based upon phenotypical variation are of very limited value and that it is of more use to ascertain the frequency with which various genes occur in different populations.

In 1935, Sir Julian Huxley and A. C. Hadon maintained that the groups in Europe which were commonly called races would be better designated "ethnic groups." They wrote that "it is very desirable that the term race as applied to human groups should be dropped from the vocabulary of science . . . . In what follows the word race will be deliberately avoided and the term *(ethnic) group* or *people* employed."

Too few have followed their advice. In the English-speaking countries "race" is widely used as a social construct. For example, in the United States, a person of, say, one-eighth African ancestry and seven-eighths European ancestry, may account himself or herself black and be so accounted by others. This assignment follows a social rule, not a zoological one. In most other countries such a person would not be accounted black. In France (and in some other non-English-speaking countries), the English-language expression "race relations" is regarded as misconceived if not racist. Yet it would not be difficult to stop the use of race as a social construct and substitute references to ethnicity, because the idiom of race is important to measures for combating racial discrimination. In Britain, as in some other countries, the law prohibits discrimination "on racial grounds" and provides protection to "persons not of the same racial group." The use of the expression "race" in the law, in the census, and in official documents, may appear to give government sanction to a classification which is no longer of explanatory value in zoology, and to keep alive a pre-Darwinian belief that it is important to the understanding of differences which are of a social, cultural, and economic character.

Reading
The Race Concept by Michael Banton and Jonathan Harwood (David & Charles, 1975) is an elementary history combined with a simple scientific exposition of the concept.
The Concept of Race edited by Ashley Montagu (Free Press, 1964) is a useful collection of essays.
We Europeans: A Survey of Racial Problems by Julian S. Huxley and A. C. Haddon (Cape, 1935) is the early text that recognized the inappropriateness of race when applied to human populations.

See also: DARWINISM; GENOTYPE; PHENOTYPE; RACE – AS SYNONYM; "RACE" – AS SIGNIFIER; UNESCO

Michael Banton

Race – as synonym

As applied to groups of living organisms, the term "race" has been used in at least four different senses. The most common use of the term in biology has referred to a subspecies, that is, a variety of a species that has developed distinguishing characteristics through isolation, but has not yet lost the ability to interbreed and to produce fertile hybrids with other subspecies of the same species. Today, biologists prefer the term subspecies or breed (in the case of a domesticated species) to "race," and thus avoid the confusion associated with the latter term.

Physical anthropologists used to speak of human "races" in the sense of subspecies, the most common scheme being the great tripartite division of mankind into Negroid, Mongoloid, and Caucasoid. Over the last forty to fifty years, however, it became increasingly clear that no meaningful taxonomy of human races was possible.

Not only were numerous groups not classifiable as belonging to any of the three main groups, but physical anthropologists could not agree with each other as to where the genetic boundaries between human groups were to be drawn, or even on how many such groups there were. The essential condition for subspeciation is breeding isolation, often maintained by ecological barriers. Humans, on the contrary, have migrated over large distances and interbred extensively for thousands of years. Especially with the maritime expansion of Europe starting five centuries ago, this process of interbreeding has greatly accelerated, thereby blurring "racial" boundaries, and contributing more than ever to the genetic homogenization of our species.

A second usage of "race" is as a synonym for species, as in the phrase "the human race." That usage is often deliberately antithetical to the first one, when the stress is put on the unity of humankind.

A third meaning of "race" is as a synonym for what we usually call a nation or an ethnic group, as, for example, "the French race" or "the German race." This third usage has become obsolete, but it was common in the nineteenth and early twentieth centuries.

Finally, a "race" can mean a group of people who are *socially* defined in a given society as belonging together because of *physical markers* such as skin pigmentation, hair texture, facial features, stature, and the like. To avoid the confusion, some people specify "social race" when they use "race" in this fourth meaning. Nearly all social scientists *only* use "race" in this fourth sense of a *social* group defined by somatic visibility. It is important to stress here that any resemblance with the first usage is little more than coincidental. For example, "blacks" in South Africa and in Australia, although they occupy somewhat similar *social* positions in their respective societies, are no more closely related genetically to each other than each of them is to the "whites." Even where there is some shared ancestry in broad parental stocks (as, for instance, between the Afro-American populations of Brazil and the United States, both of which came predominantly from West Africa and interbred with Europeans), the same social label may cover very different blends of ancestry. In Brazil, a "black" is a person of predominantly African ancestry, while, in the United States, the term often refers to persons of predominantly European stock who would be called "white" in Brazil.

The significance of racial labels is thus purely a function of the specific content attached to racial terms at a particular time and place. Social races are *not* genetically bounded subspecies. In fact, members of different social races are frequently close kin of each other in many multiracial societies, particularly those with a history of slavery.

It is also important to note that not all societies recognize social races. In fact, the great majority of human societies have not used physical phenotypes as the basis of group distinctions. Where social races exist, there is invariably an attribution of social and behavioral importance to physical markers. Societies that recognize social races are invariably *racist* societies, in the sense that people, especially members of the dominant racial group, believe that physical phenotype is linked with intellectual, moral, and behavioral characteristics. Race and racism thus go hand in hand.

Reading
The Idea of Race, by Michael Banton (Tavistock, 1977) is a thorough investigation of the development of Western racism.
Race and Racism by Pierre L. van den Berghe (Wiley, 1978) is a comparison of four societies (Brazil, Mexico, South Africa, and the United States), attributing different degrees of importance to "race."

See also: APARTHEID; EUGENICS; PHENOTYPE; PLURALISM; RACE: PERSPECTIVE ONE; RACE RELATIONS; RACISM; UNESCO
                                          Pierre L. van den Berghe

"Race" – as signifier

In contrast to other approaches to race, discourse analysis treats "race" (the quotation marks are conventional) as a *signifier* – an utterance, sound or image whose meanings are made possible only by the application of rules or codes. So the meanings of race are encoded and may be decoded only within the parameters of the discourse. The indeterminacy of "race" (and, for that matter, all signifiers) provides for its *polysemy*, or openness of interpretation (the term polysemy is preferred to ambiguity, which suggests only a double meaning). "Race" is a shifting signifier that means different things to different parties at different points in history and defies definitive explication outside specific contexts. The manner in which the signifier "race" is decoded and read by subjects is known as *signified* and this again is made possible only through appeal to discursive rules.

The approach moves beyond the critique of "race" as a biological misnomer or even as a synonym for cultural difference: it is interested in the popular usage of the term. "Race" is removed from its status as something with characteristics and stable features and conceived instead as diffuse; how it used in a discourse is of paramount concern. Decentering the concept in this way necessarily changes the way it is analyzed.

"Race," it is contended by Gates, has become "a trope of ultimate, irreducible difference between cultures, linguistic groups, or adherents of specific belief systems . . . it is so very arbitrary in its application." The concept has sutured otherwise vague and possibly incoherent beliefs about white supremacy by synonymizing skin color and other phenotypical features with deviance and inferiority.

The admission of the word into our language and so into the discourse enables and encourages us to *will* the sense of natural difference into our formulations. For Gates: "To do so is to engage in a pernicious act of language, one which exacerbates the complex problem of cultural or ethnic difference rather than to assuage or redress it."

In other words, the mere mention of "race" commissions our understanding of a permanent difference and hence a conception of "otherness." Criticism of the term "race" and disclosures of its redundancy as an analytical construct have destabilized and dismembered the understanding of "race" as a meaningful criterion in biological and social sciences, but as long as contemporary conversations continue to include the word, its potency remains. This is so because "race" purports to describe something, but simultaneously inscribes difference.

The focus then is on language not merely as a conveyor of the word and the assembly of beliefs and metaphors it embodies: but as a sign of difference, cultural as well as biological, and a way of maintaining space between superordinate and subordinate groups. Language is both a medium and an active constituent in the process of "racializing."

Cultures are never impermeable and the signifier "race" appears in various cultures of resistance to colonial and racist orders. W. E. B. Du Bois wrote of this in his *The Souls of Black Folk* (first published in 1903) when he argued that a creative solution to the divisiveness of "race" should be sought. Indiscriminate and wholesale attacks on white or Western culture were not productive. He warned against separatist nationalism which was a reaction rather than an imaginative response and, instead, urged an entry into the discourse of white America to make it acknowledge marginalized and suppressed histories. So, while he rejected "race" as a unit of hierarchy, his effort actually needed it not so much to occlude or eliminate as to question and expose.

In contemporary conceptions, there is no race "out there" in the domain or biology or any other part of the world; only "race" as a way of understanding and interpreting difference through intelligible markers. "Problematizing" the concept in this way creates the possibility of unsettling the intellectual foundations on which it has for so long rested.

Reading
"Race," Writing and Difference edited by Henry L. Gates (University of Chicago Press, 1986) contains several articles previously published in volume 12 of *Critical Inquiry* and addresses aspects of the importance of "race" in literature and its shaping influence as "a persistent yet implicit presence" in the twentieth century.
Imperial Leather: Race, Gender and Sexuality in the Colonial Conquest by Anne McClintock (Routledge, 1995) explores the historical instability of the concept of race, embracing, as it did, not only colonized peoples, but the Irish, Jews, and, at times prostitutes in what the author calls "the imperial narrative."
Racist Culture by David Theo Goldberg (Blackwell, 1995) and "Is there a 'neo-racism'?" by Etienne Balibar (in *Race, Nation, Class* edited by Balibar and Immanuel Wallerstein, Verso, 1991) both deal with the near-universal norm of "race" and may be profitably read in conjunction with *The Meaning of Race: Race, History and Culture in Western Society* by Kenan Malik (Macmillan, 1996), is a textbook that attempts to reconstruct the "evolution of the modern discourse of race."

See also: COLONIAL DISCOURSE; POSTCOLONIAL; RACE – AS CLASSIFICATION; RACE – AS SYNONYM

Ellis Cashmore

Race relations: perspective one
A term used in academic writing and in the everyday world to refer to a particular category of social relations. There is an academic tradition that focuses upon these relations and this has come to be known as the sociology of "race relations," now a distinctive and institutionalized subdiscipline within sociological analysis. However, within and outside that subdiscipline, there is a controversy about what characterizes this apparently distinct category of social relations, a controversy which arises from the recognition that *Homo sapiens* is one species. The biological sciences take account of genetic variation, but this does not correspond to what, in the everyday world, is regarded as a difference of "race," founded as it is on phenotypical variation. Hence, "race relations" cannot be naturally occurring relations between discrete, biological groups but have come to be seen as relations between groups which employ the idea of "race" in structuring their action and reaction to each other.

This latter notion of "race relations" links together the pioneering work of Robert Park, John Dollard, Lloyd Warner, Gunnar Myrdal, and Oliver C. Cox in the United States, all of whom were concerned in one way or another with "race relations." A large proportion of the work in the United States in the 1950s and 1960s refracted the new political definitions that arose out of the renewed struggle against racism and discrimination but agreed that "race relations" were a real and distinct category of social relations. Hence, for them the idea of "race" was employed with a new positive content as a collective characteristic of the Afro-American population, one that set it apart from the majority American population of European origin. But they agreed that the relations between these two defined groups were "race relations."

This American-derived conception influenced political, media and academic reaction to the labor migration from the New Commonwealth to Britain in the 1950s, although this reaction also drew upon that deep reservoir of imperialist thought about the inferior "races" of the empire. The consequence was that "race relations" "appeared" within Britain in the 1950s, displaced as it were from the colonies or, more particularly, from Africa (especially the ill-fated Central African Federation). Most writers and commentators took this definition, and its history, for granted. Some academics went further and attempted explicitly and analytically to classify "race relations," not only as a discrete category of social relations, but also as having a specific place within sociological theory. The project was defined as setting out the defining features of a "race relations" situation and the classifying different types of such a situation.

The sociology of "race relations" that has developed from these analytical concerns has been preoccupied with two main themes, first with assessing the extent and effects of racism and discrimination upon those who have been its object, and second with the political struggle against racism and discrimination. It is thereby a sociology of conflict which reflects everyday conceptions of what "race relations" are, although it offers a quite different explanation for that conflict from that employed in the everyday world.

More recently, a new line of enquiry has developed which is critical of this tradition of work and which moves toward a rejection of "race relations" as a legitimate form of study. This emerging position is firmly grounded in historical analysis of both the idea of "race" and the academic study of relations between groups who utilize the idea of "race" to organize their social relations. It is concluded from this analysis that because "race" is no more than a socially constructed phenomenon, then so are relations between the groups that are constituted through this social construction. Consequently, there is nothing distinctive about the resulting relations between the groups party to such a social construction. Put another way, what are called "race relations" are quantitatively no different from other forms of social relations.

There remains the problem of determining how such historically and socially constructed relations are, therefore, to be analyzed. To this problem, one can currently distinguish two solutions. The first sees "race and ethnic relations" as a subdivision of a sociology of intergroup relations. This is premised on the observation that a tradition of enquiry has been established and that any new development should be contained within the tradition established by earlier contributors. But, more significantly, it is argued that the circumstances under which individuals are ascribed, or ascribe themselves, to membership of a "race" (together with the varied and various consequences of such ascription) warrant explanation in terms of a theory of intergroup relations. The second position, developed using Marxist categories of analysis, claims that this process of social ascription should be analyzed as an ideological and political process and, for that reason, it cannot employ everyday conceptions of "race" and "race relations" as either descriptive or analytical categories. This leads to the conclusion that there can be no theory of race relations because this only serves to reify what is a historically specific political and ideological process.

Reading
Race Relations in Sociological Theory by John Rex (Weidenfeld & Nicolson, 1970) is an analysis which claims a theoretical status for the sociological analysis of race relations.
"Analytical and folk concepts of race and ethnicity" by Michael Banton in *Ethnic and Racial Studies* (1979, vol. 2, no. 2) is a critical reflection on what counts as the subject matter of race relations studies, but which continues to assert the need for a theory of "race (and ethnic) relations."
Racism and Migrant Labour by R. Miles (Routledge & Kegan Paul, 1982) is an elaboration of the latter critique but within a Marxist frame of reference which concludes that the analytical task is not to develop a theory of "race relations" but to explain, historically, why certain forms of social relations are racialized.

See also: COX; DOLLARD; MYRDAL; RACE: PERSPECTIVE TWO; RACIALIZATION

Robert Miles

Race relations: perspective two

An alternative approach argues that the term race relations can and, indeed, must be applied to a specific form of social relationship. This approach fully recognizes and endorses the hollowness of the concept of race itself, but, at the same time, insists that, in many situations, people believe in the existence of race and so organize their relationships with others on the basis of that belief. In other words, people predicate their relationships with others on what they believe about those others. If they believe those others belong to a group that is genetically and permanently different (and possibly inferior in some respect) then we have a situation of race relations. And this is the object of enquiry.

The exact nature of race is not at issue, although, the biological concept has been refuted many times over. The point is, however, that people, rightly or wrongly, accept it as a reality and so act in accordance with their belief. This makes race subjectively real: no matter how offensive we may find race and how unimpressed we are by the (largely spurious) scientific research on it, it remains a powerful motivating force behind people's thoughts and behavior. It is as real as people want it to be and cannot simply be wished away. Recognition of this is the starting point of the study of race relations in this perspective.

This allows for the acceptance of Michael Banton's advice that "the student who wishes to understand the nature of the field of race relations study . . . should approach it from the standpoint of the growth of knowledge." Believing in race is tantamount to holding a form of knowledge (even if that knowledge is built on uncertain foundations). This in no way denies the huge influences on race relations which lie outside people's minds and quite beyond their control. In fact, the approach stresses that the study of race relations should proceed at levels: (1) to discover the reasons why people might believe others are so different, culturally or biologically; (2) to find out how this belief affects their actions towards others – this usually takes the form of maintaining social (and often geographical) distance in the attempt to keep unequal relationships and (3) to analyze the ways the belief and the terminology that complements it are used in such a way as to perpetuate a context in which the concept of race continues to have relevance – a racialized discourse.

This sets the scope of the field very widely because the distinguishing feature of race relations is the consciousness of race and it is possible to identify many situations and complexes of social relations where this consciousness is present. It will inevitably influence the conduct of social relations, but will almost certainly operate in combination with other influences. Processes of inclusion and exclusion can be heavily influenced by being conscious of race – or racism – yet it need not be assumed that this is the only, nor indeed, the strongest influential factor. Often we cannot decide the contribution that racism makes to the maintenance of a social activity except in evaluative terms. The precise contribution is the topic of empirical enquiry.

Race relations as a program of empirical study seeks to analyze the relations between sets of factors, one of which is racism. If, for example, (the phenomenon to be explained) – the *explanandum*, in formal terms – is the educational underachievement of black schoolchildren, we may compare samples of black children with their white peers and find something in the experience of black children that accounts for their poor performance. Suspending judgements about innate (genetic) characteristics, we might trace antecedent factors that either lead to or are associated with under-achievement. Clearly, there may be a range of factors, many of which do not involve racism. Yet it may be possible to identify factors involving the awareness of race that will exert an influence on the child's ability to achieve at school. This would draw attention to the value of an emphasis on racism as an approach to some of the problems confronting ethnic minorities. Many ethnic minorities may have problems that are not unique to themselves, but which they share with whites. We can proceed to analyze the two with quite different explanatory factors – *explanans* – or precisely the same. The former may reveal racism as something that affects the position of ethnic minorities, while the latter should disclose broad similarities in conditions and experience.

The presence of racism is presumed from the outset. The analysis then takes the form of a search for its origins (in general or particular settings), tracing back in an aetiological manner an elaboration of racist thinking, a consideration of its effects, behavioral and cognitive, and an assessment of its functional importance in the wider culture.

A narrow conception of this program of study might locate the answer to these types of questions in the individual, suggesting for example why certain groups are prejudiced and examining how this has impact on their behavior and relationships over a period of time. The classic study in this vein is *The Authoritarian Personality* by Theodor Adorno and his colleagues (see PREJUDICE). The preferred approach would be much wider in scope, seeking to integrate historical analyses of the colonial conditions underlying most contemporary race relations situations with an examination of how culture mediates these situations.

In many instances, race relations situations are highly complementary to the perpetuation of capitalism (through, for example, widening divisions between black and white workers and thus undermining working-class solidarity). But it is proposed that this does not prove that race relations cannot exist independently of capitalism; so there may be a close, but not direct, relationship between the two. The present forms racism takes and the forms it has taken in recent history indicate that it is related to the development of modern capitalism, though not caused by it.

Race relations situations are not a perfectly defined series of events, but rather an evolving complex. A mature race relations study should be able to incorporate the investigation of changing events and interpret these in the context of historical, political and social conditions. In this way, it is possible to acknowledge that race as a concept is analytically redundant, yet still identify race relations situations as the focus of study.

Reading
Introduction to Race Relations, 2nd edition, by E. Cashmore and B. Troyna (Falmer, 1990) is an elaborated version of this approach to the study of race relations which argues strongly for the retention of this distinct area of study.
Race, Culture and Difference edited by James Donald and Ali Rattansi (Sage, 1992) asks how the concept of race is produced and sustained in society; the authors argue for the centrality of culture in understanding how race works.
Racism and Society by John Solomos and Les Back (Macmillan, 1996) pulls together copious material on the subject area.

See also: COLONIALISM; PREJUDICE; RACE — AS A SIGNIFIER; RACISM; SLAVERY

Barry Troyna/Ellis Cashmore

Racial discrimination

Also known as *racialism* this is the active or behavioral expression of racism and is aimed at denying members of certain groups equal access to scarce and valued resources. It goes beyond thinking unfavorably about groups or holding negative beliefs about them: it involves putting them into action. Often, racialism and racism are mutually reinforcing in a self-fulfilling way because, by denying designated groups access to resources and services, one creates conditions under which those groups can often do no more than confirm the very stereotypes that inspired the original racist belief.

Racial discrimination, as distinct from many other forms of discrimination, operates on a group basis: it works on the perceived attributes and deficiencies of groups, not individualized characteristics. Members of groups are denied opportunities or rewards for reasons unrelated to their capabilities, industry, and general merit: they are judged solely on their membership of an identifiable group, which is erroneously thought to have a racial basis.

The racial discrimination may range from the use of derogatory labels, such as "kike" or "nigger," to the denial of access to such institutional spheres as housing, education, justice, political participation, and so on. The actions may be intentional, or unintentional. The use of the terms racialist and racial discrimination has diminished in recent years as racism and institutional racism have come into popular use as expressions of both thought and action. Institutional racism, in particular, is now used widely to describe the discriminatory nature and operations, however unwitting, of large-scale organizations or entire societies. A pedant would insist that the correct term should be institutional racial discrimination, or institutional racialism.

Reading
Race and Ethnic Relations: American and global perspectives, 2nd edition, by Martin Marger (Wadsworth, 1991), has an interesting chapter on "Techniques of domination," in which forms of discrimination are analyzed conceptually.
We and They, 4th edition, by Peter Rose (McGraw-Hill, 1990) contains a chapter on "Discrimination," which examines its operation in the contemporary United States.
Clear and Convincing Evidence edited by Michael Fix and Raymond Struyk (University Press of America, 1992) explores the "auditing" method of assessing discrimination in such areas as housing, hiring, mortgage lending, and credit extension: two individuals are matched on all relevant criteria except the one presumed to lead to discrimination: each member applies for the same job, housing, or service and the differential treatment they receive provides a measure of discrimination.

See also: HARASSMENT; INSTITUTIONAL RACISM; LAW: RACIAL DISCRIMINATION (INTERNATIONAL)

Ellis Cashmore

Racialization

A term that emerged in analysis in the 1970s to refer to a political and ideological process by which particular populations are identified by direct or indirect reference to their real or imagined phenotypical characteristics in such a way as to suggest that the population can only be understood as a supposedly biological unity. This process usually involved the direct utilization of the idea of "race" to describe or refer to the population in question.

The use and meaning of the term emerges from historical analysis. This work demonstrates that the idea of "race" is not a universal idea, but, rather, emerges at a particular point in Western European history, and, over time, comes to be used to refer to supposedly fixed and discrete biological categories of the world's population. This shows that "race" is not a biological fact but a social construction. The first use of the notion of racialization arose in the course of establishing these claims and was used to refer specifically to the development of the idea of "race," first in historical writing and, later, in European "scientific" writing of the late eighteenth and nineteenth centuries.

The term's usage has been developed and widened in time with the fact that the process of identifying particular populations as "races" is not confined to the level of "intellectual" activity. By a process not yet adequately understood and analyzed, this social construction of "race" was passed down to the level of everyday categorization and action. In recognition of this, the notion of racialization has been used in a broader sense to refer to any process or situation wherein the idea of "race" is introduced to define and give meaning to some particular population, its characteristics and actions. Hence, the fact that the public and political reaction to the Irish migration and presence in Britain in the nineteenth century employed the idea of "race" to refer to the Irish can be understood, analytically, as an instance of racialization. Similarly, when the political and ideological consequences of New Commonwealth migration to Britain in the 1950s began to be defined by politicians by reference to the idea of "race," one can refer to this process as the racialization of British politics.

In the narrower usage, the ideological content of the process of racialization will warrant description as racism, or more specifically, scientific racism. In the wider usage, referring in addition to the attribution of social significance and meaning to phenotypical/genetic variation in all dimensions of social life, the ideological content of the identified process is not necessarily racist. Before that can be determined, it is necessary to analyze the content of the attributed significance and the populations party to the attribution (both object and subject). In this way we can take account of the fact that those who have historically been the "victims" of racialization may employ the idea of "race" in turn to refer to those who so label them without necessarily concluding that their response is racist in content. This, therefore, requires that the concepts of racism and racialization be kept analytically distinct.

Reading
The Idea of Race by Michael Banton (Tavistock 1967) contains one of the first uses of the term to refer to historical and scientific writing in the eighteenth and nineteenth centuries.
Racism and Migrant Labour by Robert Miles (Routledge & Kegan Paul, 1982) is an example of the utilization of the term in a wider sense.

See also: IDEOLOGY; RACE; RACE RELATIONS; RACISM

Robert Miles

Racism

A word used in several senses. Up to the late 1960s most dictionaries and textbooks defined it as a doctrine, dogma, ideology, or set of beliefs. The core element in this doctrine was that "race" determined culture, and from this were derived claims to racial superiority. In the 1960s the word was used in an expanded sense to incorporate practices and attitudes as well as beliefs and in this sense racism denotes the whole complex of factors which produce racial discrimination, and sometimes, more loosely, designates also those which produce racial disadvantage. Early in 1983, the Greater London Council announced plans "to tackle the problems of racism and racial disadvantage in the capital" including the declaration of London as "an Anti-Racist Zone."

A third usage is to be found in some academic writing. It is said that the expansion of capitalism in the New World required the exploitative use of African labor. This could be achieved more effectively if black labor could be treated simply as a commodity, so a whole complex was created to facilitate this. Beliefs about black inferiority can be adequately understood only as part of a new historical creation which in subsequent centuries has been modified as the economic structure has changed. Racism is the name for this historical complex.

There is no reason why the word racism should not be used in different senses for different purposes. Within sociology, however, it is certain that there will continue to be at least two kinds of definition corresponding to two contrasting theories of knowledge. Those writers who stand within the Kantian philosophical tradition believe their definitions have to be elaborated by the observer in the attempt to formulate theories that will explain as many observations as possible. Those writers who stand within the Hegelian tradition believe that the observer is part of the world that he studies. The observer has to understand the principles underlying the development of the world and first work out definitions which grasp the essence of historical relationships.

The implications of this distinction can be better appreciated if the definition of racism is compared with that of anti-Semitism. Social scientists who use a Kantian epistemology will start from common elements in the prejudice against black people and Jews. Those who use a Hegelian epistemology may, like Oliver C. Cox, assert that racism and anti-Semitism are different phenomena serving different functions in the social system (although it should be noted that not all who write within this epistemology would accept a functionalist analysis). The same opposition of views can be seen in discussions of the attitudes and practices of minority groups. Writers in the first tradition can point to evidence of what they define as racial prejudice expressed by black people just as much as by white, and may call it racism. In Britain, for example, Afro-Caribbeans and Asians can speak as harshly about one another as white people speak about them. For writers in the second tradition, the ideological reaction of those subject to ("white") racism cannot be immediately so defined, not only because of differences in ideological content, but also because explanatory significance is attached to the structural position of the respective groups. From this perspective, hostility between Afro-Caribbeans and Asians will be traced to their historical experience within British imperialism and/ or to conflicts arising out of their structural positions within Britain. It is in the context of such analysis that the ideological content of hostility will be assessed to ascertain whether it can be considered racist.

In recent years, the word has been used in so many ways that there is a danger of its losing any value as a concept. How restricted a definition is to be preferred? Some writers have wished to limit its use to refer to an ideology tied to the development of racial thought in Western Europe. The observation that it was only in the nineteenth century that the idea of "race" came to mean a typological classification of the human species (one that asserted that biological characteristics determined cultural and psychological characteristics) has suggested to them that racism be the name for identifying the doctrine which was first advanced in the mid-nineteenth century and which claimed scientific status. As a concept, therefore, racism would distinguish those claims and arguments

which explicitly assert that people's biological characteristics are
signs of their cultural and psychological characteristics. Since 1945,
such claims have been increasingly less common, from which it has
been concluded that the expression of racism is declining. Some
writers prefer to name this body of arguments scientific racism,
while others call them racial typology.

From another direction, it is maintained that the examination of
the content of the ideological form which is called racism should
be subordinated to consideration of its structure. While biological
arguments are less frequently advanced, new ones have taken their
place which justify by other means the unequal treatment of the
same groups of people. Hence, it is argued that what distinguishes
racism as an ideology is that it asserts a deterministic relationship
between a group and supposed characteristics of that group. Such
a definition of racism broadens its application, but to the point
where its generality renders it analytically meaningless. The ideological process of deterministic attribution of characteristics to particular groups is widespread, with many different types of group
being its object. For example, the exclusion of women from a wide
range of activities is often justified by the deterministic attribution
of such supposed characteristics as physical weakness, emotionalism
and irrationalism. A definition of racism that refers solely to the
structural features of the ideological process must encompass such
claims, thus denying any possibility of distinguishing between racism
and sexism.

The deterministic ascription of real or supposed negative characteristics to a particular group is generally seen as a central characteristic of racism as ideology. This constitutes common ground for the
present authors. However, one of us (MB) believes that what he
sees as racial relations can be analyzed quite adequately without
employing any concept of racism, provided that there is some way of
identifying the nineteenth-century theories that "race" determines
culture. The other (RM) wishes to continue to employ the term,
but with a specific meaning. Thus, it is the attribution of social
significance (meaning) to particular patterns of phenotypical and/or
genetic difference which, along with the characteristic of additional
deterministic ascription of real or supposed other characteristics to
a group constituted by descent, is the defining feature of racism as
an ideology. But, additionally, those characteristics must, in turn,
be negatively evaluated and/or be designated as the reason to justify
unequal treatment of the defined group.

This definition of racism does not presuppose or reify the (real or attributed) biological characteristics which become the identifying feature of the group which is the object of racism. Thus, racism is not an ideology which only has "black" people as its object. This allows us to take account of the observation that, for example, Jewish and Irish people have been the object of racist ideology because they have been identified by reference to real or supposed biological characteristics and, additionally, have been negatively evaluated and treated. It is also a definition that specifically allows for the way that racism takes different empirical forms in different societies at different points in time. It encourages a historical analysis of the emergence of sets of meanings and evaluations about particular populations in conjunction with the expansion of economic and political activity of European merchants (and, later, European capitalists) and of the changes in those meanings and evaluations in relation to changes in the nature and activity of capitalism based in Western Europe and North America. However, the specific relationship between the generation and reproduction of racism and the development of capitalism, dependent as it was upon imperialism, remains the object of a continuing debate.

There is little likelihood that the intellectual gulf between the two philosophical traditions will be bridged in the present generation since they generate different criteria for the definition of racism (and for other concepts too). Each has its attractions and weaknesses. Scholarly progress will be assisted if those who write about these matters appreciate the nature of the gulf and different concepts and empirical emphases that are thereby generated.

Reading

The Logic of Racism by Ellis Cashmore (Allen & Unwin), 1986) is a qualitative exploration of the reasoning underpinning racism among whites and how that reasoning differs according to such factors as class, age, and geography.

Portraits of White Racism by David Wellman (Cambridge University Press, 1977) is an example of a text which proposes a much wider definition of racism, one that refers to structural subordination of particular groups of people. It is a good example of a definition of racism that is so wide that it loses analytical precision.

The Arena of Racism by Michael Wieviorka (Sage, 1995) offers the perspective of a French sociologist who argues that "the spread of racism takes place against a background of the breakdown, absence or inversion of social movements and, more generally, of a crisis of modernity."

Impacts of Racism on White Americans 2nd edition, edited by Benjamin Bowser and Raymond Hunt (Sage, 1996) begins with the central question "What motivates white racism?" and moves on to a number of related issues, especially about the relationship between racism and white identity.

See also: INSTITUTIONAL RACISM; RACE RELATIONS; RACIALIZATION; UNESCO

Michael Banton/Robert Miles

Rap

The term is taken from the slang for talk and refers to the half-spoken, half-sung genre that became musical shorthand for the African American experience in the 1980s and 1990s. It began in the 1970s in the predominantly black neighborhoods of New York and New Jersey. Carried mainly by DJs rather than musicians, it consisted of abstracting, or "sampling," pieces of previously recorded tracks, playing them repeatedly, sometimes backwards, often with another track playing simultaneously, and voicing over them.

DJs would "toast" across the music in the manner of Jamaican DJs: as the music played, the DJs would speak or dub over their own rhymes or doggerel. Many accounts credit a Jamaican-born DJ named Kool Herc with pioneering the approach in the late 1960s. Several U.S. DJs adopted and refined the technique, which, by the 1970s, had become known as rapping. Radio DJs in the New York/New Jersey area, particularly Gary Byrd, had used conversation, or rap, over prerecorded music in his shows, though it was the traveling DJs who originated "scratching," which meant manipulating a stylus on a record to produced new sounds. Used together, the techniques made possible a unique and inexpensive approach to music.

"Rapper's delight," by the Sugar Hill Gang, released in 1979, was the first commercially successful rap record: it logged up two million in sales. This was eclipsed in 1981 by Grandmaster Flash and the Furious Five's "The message" which was a long, spoken rather than sung statement on life in the ghetto as seen through the eyes of a black youth – "Rats in the front room/roaches in the back/Junkies in the alley/with a baseball bat." The lyrics were very different from those of the earlier Sugar Hill hit and showed how music could radicalize the black experience, turning it into an invective against the police and an injunction to challenge its authority; criminal acts could be made political ones. This strain of rap became particularly popular on the west coast.

The first commercially successful record from a Los Angeles rap band was NWA's *Straight Outta Compton*, which, in its credits, thanked "gangstas, dope dealers, killers, hustlers, thugs, hoodlums, winos, bums" and a variety of other bona fide members of the underclass. Two million copies of the album were sold. NWA's infamy, rather than just fame, gave one member, Ice Cube, the exposure he needed to launch a solo career, so that, when he left in 1989, he was already an established writer/producer. He went on to start his own label and management company. On his first album, *AmeriKKKa's Most Wanted*, Cube set out to personify the black criminalized population. He pushed the rap genre by integrating various perspectives from law enforcement officers, judges and so on. The album starts with the character described in the title being led to the electric chair.

Gangsta rap, as it was called, went on to assume virtual hegemony in the 1990s when the genre itself transferred to the mainstream. In 1991, the NWA follow-up album, *Niggaz4Life* entered the *Billboard* pop chart at number two unassisted by a trailer single or a video. The low-budget underground record productions that had been so prized in the 1980s became things of the past as big money began to roll into the ghettos.

Churches, mainstream African American organizations, women's groups, two US Presidents and a battery of other right-minded people and groups condemned Ice-T's "Cop killer," which told of a young man intending to shoot a police officer. "Die, pig, die" he raps as he discharges his "twelve-inch sawed off." In common with other gangsta tracks, it mythologized its eponymous hero. In 1992, Warner Brothers Records recalled copies of the CD after death threats, protests from police associations and denunciations from the White House. Later, Warners dropped Ice-T after a disagreement over the artwork of his album *Home Invasion*. It was the beginning of an extremely vexed relationship between Time Warner and rap. The meda conglomerate sold its interest in Interscope Records, a company that had on its roster Snoop Doggy Dogg, who was arrested on murder charges. His album *Doggy Style* sold four million copies, generating $40 million, despite being banned by, among others, Radio KACE in Los Angeles and New York's WBLS. The artist toured Britain while on a one million dollar bail bond. He was one of many best-selling rap artists who blurred the boundary between life and art.

Rap began as innocent rhapsodies about boys and girls, but changed to angry and often malevolent diatribes often against women. Early evidence of this came in Ice-T's "Six in the morning" – "As we walked over to her, hoe continued to speak/So we beat the bitch down in the goddam street" and Ice Cube's "Gangsta fairytale" "Jack and Jill went up the hill to take a nap/Young bitch gave him the clap."

The "considered" response to rap's abuse of women was to explain how black males were engaged in a search for the causes of their obvious disempowerment. State authority figures, as epitomized by the police, were located, as were black women. Houston Baker suggests that the defense for the crudely sexist 2 Live Crew might rest on the "But, officer, the cars in front of me were speeding too!" plea (1993: 72). Cornel West writes effusively about the rappers' role in "the repoliticizing of the black working poor and underclass" in his book *Keeping Faith* (Routledge, 1993) yet parenthesizes "(despite their virulent sexism)".

Many female rap artists recoiled against this. In her 1994 single "Unity," Queen Latifah asked: "Who *you* callin' a bitch?" Roxanne Shant proclaimed "Brothers ain't shit." Others used names in parody of their male counterparts: Hoes with Attitude was one example. Bytches with Problems was another, though their track "Two minute brother," in deriding a less than spectacular lover, affirmed rap's homeboy patriarchal values, the ones that celebrated the kind of man who could provide for his woman (or, more usually, women) both materially and sexually and ridiculed others as "fruity" or "punks." As Tricia Rose observes: "This sort of homophobia affirms oppressive standards of heterosexual masculinity" (1994: 151).

The popularity of rap with mainstream audiences has ensured the profitability of several once-independent record companies specializing in rap. Over the years, a tier of young entrepreneurs has emerged, the most celebrated being Russell Simmons, of Rush Communications. Others include Andre Harrell, Sean "Puffy" Combs and Antonio "LA" Reid, all of whom have made personal fortunes from what became in the mid-1990s a rap industry.

Reading
Black Noise: Rap Music and Black Culture in Contemporary America by Tricia Rose (Wesleyan University Press, 1994) analyzes rap as an oppositional practice, a vehicle through which the voice from the margins can be heard. Houson S. Baker's *Black Studies, Rap and the Academy* (University of Chicago Press, 1993) takes a similar approach, while *The New Beats* by S. H. Fernando, Jr. (Payback Press, 1995) is in effect an oral history of rap music and the general hip-hop culture of which it is part. All provide generally appreciative interpretations.
"The rap on rap" by David Samuels (*The New Republic*, November 11, 1991, pp. 24–9) and "Jazz, rock'n'roll, rap and politics" by M. Bernard-Donals (*Journal of Popular Culture*, vol. 28, no. 2, Fall, 1994, pp. 127–38) offer a cynical contrast from the above readings and understand the rap genre as a white-driven operation.

See also: AFRICAN AMERICANS; BLUES; LEE; REGGAE

Ellis Cashmore

Rastafari

Arguably the fastest-growing black movement of the 1970s/80s, it first appeared in Jamaica in 1930 just after the decline in fortunes of the leader Marcus Garvey, who organized his Universal Negro Improvement Association around the ambition to return to Africa. "Africa for the Africans" was Garvey's basic philosophy and he worked at mass migration programs, buying steamship lines and negotiating with African governments.

Garvey had some success in the West Indies (he was born in Jamaica), but was more influential after his demise, for he was reputed to have prophesied: "Look to Africa when a black king shall be crowned, for the day of deliverance is near." Around this prediction a whole movement was mobilized. In 1930, Ras Tafari was crowned Emperor of Ethiopia and took his official title of Haile Selassie I. Garvey, at this stage, had slipped from prominence, but at least some black Jamaicans remembered his prophecy and made the connection between "the black king" Haile Selassie and "the day of deliverance" the return to Africa. The connection was reinforced by a new element added by new adherents of Garvey. They made the conclusion that Haile Selassie was not just a king but also their God and Messiah who would miraculously organize a black exodus to Africa (used synonymously with Ethiopia) and simultaneously dissolve the imperial domination of Western powers "Babylon" to the new Garveyites.

It's worth noting that in no way did Garvey endorse this new interpretation of his philosophy. Indeed, he assailed Haile Selassie as "a great coward" and "the leader of a country where blackmen are chained and flogged." Further, Garvey insisted on practical organization and de-emphasized the value of spiritual salvation; his new followers went in the other direction, making no provision for returning to Africa, simply awaiting the intervention of their Messiah, Ras Tafari.

However, what Garvey actually said was less important than what he was reputed to have said and, quickly, the new movement gained followers among the socially deprived black Jamaicans, hopeful of any kind of change in their impoverished lives and willing to cling to the flimsiest of theories of how they might escape their condition. They adopted the Garvey movement's colors of red, black, and green (from the Ethiopian flag) and twisted their hair into long matted coils called dreadlocks as if to exaggerate their primitiveness in contrast to Western appearances. Some made use of ganja, a type of cannabis found in Jamaica, and even endowed this "weed" with religious properties. They used it in ritual worship of *Jah* (the form of "Jehovah" used in bibles before the King James version). Many took to the hilly inner regions of the island and set up their own communes, one celebrated one being led by Leonard Howell, who, with Joseph Hibbert and H. Archibald Dunkley, is popularly attributed as one of the original formulators of the new Garveyism.

Garvey remained a reluctant prophet, although a careful reading of his speeches and published comments reveals his great interest in Ethiopian royalty and his repeated use of biblical, often apocalyptic, imagery to strengthen his beliefs. "We Negroes believe in the God of Ethiopia, the everlasting God," wrote Garvey in volume one of his *Philosophy and Opinions*. His conception of a black god was also significant; he implored his followers to destroy pictures of white Christs and Madonnas and replace them with black versions. "No one knows when the hour of Africa's Redemption cometh," he once warned his followers. "It is in the wind. It is coming. One day, like a storm, it will be here."

Periodically, the Rastas, as they came to be called, gathered at ports to await the ships to take them to Africa and, at one stage, a faction of the movement resorted to guerrilla tactics in a vain effort to assist the destruction of Babylon. More recently, the movement in Jamaica has gained a more respectable status and, nowadays, has become a vital cultural force on the island.

In the middle of the 1970s, the Rastafarian movement manifested itself in such places as the United States, England, Holland, France, New Zealand and Australia. Its growth was stimulated by the rise in popularity of Rasta-inspired reggae music which was given a personal focus by the almost prototype Rasta Bob Marley (1945–1981). It seems that the vision of a united African continent and a black god was a potent one. It was used in sharp counter-position to the imperial dominance of the West. Blacks feeling disaffected with society and searching for alternatives found in the movement a new force which upgraded blackness and instilled in them a sense of identity belonging to a unity.

Despite an infinite variation in interpretation of Garvey's philosophy, two themes remained central to Rastafarian beliefs: the divinity of Haile Selassie (whose death in 1975 did little to dissuade Rastas of his potency in instigating the transformation) and the impulse to return to Africa – if not physically then in consciousness (as the Rasta reggae musician, Peter Tosh, sang; "Don't care where you come from, as long as you're a black man, you're an African").

In 1989, Trevor Dawkins, a Rasta, born in Birmingham, England, won a case of racial discrimination against a British government agency and, in the process, threw the legal status of Rastas into confusion. Under the terms of the 1976 Race Relations Act, Rastas became officially recognized as an ethnic group and, as such, could not be lawfully discriminated against on the basis of their cultural characteristics. They were liable to the same kind of protection afforded to Sikhs (who cannot be refused work for wearing turbans, for example). The decision was subsequently reversed, leading to a legal debate on the subject.

Reading
Rastafari and other Afro-Caribbean Worldviews edited by Barry Chevannes (Macmillan, 1995) is a collection of conference papers, most of which discuss aspects of the movement.
The Rastafarians, 2nd edition, by Ellis Cashmore (Minority Rights Group, 1992) is an update of an earlier report, which documents legal changes in the status of Rastafarians in Britain. It focuses on the Dawkins case.
Rastafari and Reggae by Rebekah Mulvaney (Greenwood Press, 1990) is a dictionary of Rasta terms.

See also: ETHIOPIANISM; GARVEY; NATION OF ISLAM; NÉGRITUDE; REGGAE

Ellis Cashmore

Rational choice theory

Rational choice theory is a family of research efforts grounded in the rational-actor methodology of microeconomics. In this approach, behavioral outcomes are held to be a function of the interaction of given structural constraints and the values or utilities of individuals. The structure determines, to a greater or lesser extent, the constraints under which individuals act. Within these constraints, individuals face various feasible courses of action. The course of action ultimately chosen is selected so as to achieve maximum efficiency. Since rational choice is a deductive and general theory, it offers the prospect of providing the field of ethnic and racial relations with a new research program yielding predictive propositions rather than *post hoc* descriptions.

Applications in this substantive area have begun only recently. For example, Sowell, in his *Race and Economics* (McKay, 1975) uses rational choice principles to explain patterns of racial discrimination in the job market. Consider a society having a low-status racial group whose members command a low price in the labor market. Distancing typically occurs as a result of this kind of racial hierarchy: thus, members of the high-status group prefer to limit their social interaction with low-status individuals. If it is assumed that employers are profit-maximizers, and if they cannot effectively collude against the members of a particular group, then racial discrimination in hiring should be greater in nonprofit and regulated industries than in unregulated and profitmaking enterprises. Even if all employers prefer to exclude low-status workers from their firms, whenever these workers' pay is lower than their productivity there is an economic incentive to hire them. If, however, employers are prevented from maximizing profits by government regulatory agencies, or are legally non profit, then they have no chance to earn more profit by hiring relatively inexpensive (and racially low-status) labor and therefore would tend to discriminate more than unregulated, profitmaking firms which have an incentive to hire low-paid workers.

Landa (in *The Journal of Legal Studies*, vol. 10, 1981) seeks to explain why ethnically homogeneous middlemen are so much more common in Third World societies than in developed ones. Her argument starts from the problematic nature of exchange in rational choice theory. If two parties to a contract are both wealth-maximizers, what keeps either of them from abrogating the contract whenever this becomes profitable? In societies where contract law is both well developed and easily enforced, the judicial system is often sufficient to deter traders from breach of contract. But this remedy is unavailable in countries with poorly developed or nonexistent judicial systems. In such settings, ethnically homogeneous networks provide traders with the best alternative means of insuring against breach of contract. Rational traders will choose to participate in the least costly type of trading network. They are likely to choose ethnically homogeneous trading networks because these economize on coordination and enforcement costs. On the one hand, traditional codes of conduct (such as the Confucian or Talmudic codes) can have many of the same effects as systems of contract law. On the other hand, confining trade to members of one's own ethnic group permits one to take advantage of an informationally efficient screening device. This allows the merchant to predict the contractual behavior of a potential trading partner with a high degree of accuracy. For these reasons, the prevalence of ethnically specialized middlemen should be greatest (*ceteris paribus*) in societies having the least developed judicial systems.

Finally, Hechter, Friedman, and Applebaum (in *International*

Migration Review, vol. 16, 1982) want to predict the conditions under which ethnic collective action will arise. In their view, the likelihood of collective action does not rest on factors such as the degree of interethnic equality, or changing levels of relative deprivation that affect members' desires for structural change in the society at large. Instead, the members of any ethnic group will engage in collective action only when they estimate that by doing so they will receive a net individual benefit. In this regard, ethnic organizations are critical for two reasons. They are the major source of the private rewards and punishments that motivate the individual's decision to participate in collective action. But since the individual's benefit/cost calculation depends in part upon his estimate of the probability of success of any collective action, organizations can play a key role by controlling the information available to their members. When members have few alternative sources of information, organizations can easily convince them that the success of a contemplated collective action is a real possibility, perhaps even a foregone conclusion. On this basis, the likelihood of ethnic collective action varies positively with organizational resources, monitoring capacity, solidarity, control over information, the history of equitable distribution of collective benefits, and the adoption of nonviolent tactics, while it varies negatively with organizational size, and the capacity of antagonists – including the state – to punish prospective participants.

Like most other applications of rational choice theory in this field, these await rigorous empirical testing.

The rational choice research agenda faces two important challenges. The first challenge is to explain the existence of the social institutions that constrain the individual's feasible set of actions – which are usually treated as givens – from rational choice premises; this is discussed in *Social Institutions* edited by M. Hechter, K. Dieter-Opp and R. Wippler (Gruyt, 1994).

The second challenge is to cast light on the problem of value-formation (see Hechter, "The role of values in rational choice theory" in *Rationality and Society*, vol. 6, no. 3, 1994): "Value" is the generic term used in rational choice analysis to designate internal states. Together with institutional and environmental constraints, preferences help determine individual action and social outcomes. Since these internal states are not easily measured, rational choice theorists have constructed their models under stringent assumptions that allow their independent role to be ignored. The task of incorporating more realistic assumptions about preferences into these deductive models lies ahead.

Reading
Racial and Ethnic Competition by Michael Banton (Cambridge University Press, 1983) is an attempt to integrate the theory with comparative analysis.
Foundations of Society Theory by James S. Coleman (Harvard University Press, 1990) is a major statement of sociological rational choice theory.
Principles of Group Solidarity by Michael Hechter (University of California Press, 1987) presents an analysis of the conditions under which groups are more or less solidary.

See also: MINORITIES; PLURALISM; POWER; PREJUDICE; RACIAL DISCRIMINATION

Michael Hechter

Reggae

An amalgam of various musical forms, reggae – probably derived from "raggamuffin," a raggedly dressed person – became a near-universal cultural phenomenon. In the 1970s, it was the music of the rastafari: its messages and motifs were diffused primarily through the music of Bob Marley (1945–81), whose albums continued to sell in the 1990s. Stylistic derivatives of reggae included ragga, moshing and jungle.

Essentially a music of protest, reggae fused several different elements of popular music in Jamaica where it originated. Indeed, Sebastian Clarke has traced its origins way back to the hybrid music that was born out of slave days. But it seems that the significant stage in the development of reggae was in the 1950s when the sound of black American rhythm and blues and soul music filtered across to the Caribbean via radio stations and West Indians who migrated temporarily to the United States to look for work. Early attempts to imitate the American music foundered, but inadvertently gave rise to a unique style that came to be called "blue beat" and, later, "ska." This was popularized in the West Indies, particularly in Jamaica, by peripatetic disc jockeys who operated a "sound system." The DJs stamped their own identity on the music by "dubbing" or toasting over the music, literally speaking into the microphone while the records were playing, in efforts to urge the dancers; this became known as "toasting" and many DJs established more prestigious reputations than the musicians they dubbed over.

In the 1960s, ska was introduced into Britain and was received enthusiastically by sections of white youth without ever growing into a popular music. Occasionally, ska records would become commercial successes, "Long shot kick the bucket" and "The return of Django" being examples.

Late in the 1960s, however, ska underwent mutations and the flavor of its lyrics became altogether more political. Musicians, either adhering to or being sympathetic with Rastafarian ideals, began expressing statements on the condition of black people through their music. The themes of the music included exploitation, poverty, inequality, liberation, and the critical experience of "suffering". They were articulated through Rastafarian imagery, the system of control being Babylon, as contrasted with the liberty of Zion. Predictions of "war in a Babylon" and "Catch a fire, the wheel will turn, slavedriver you gonna get burn" were incorporated into the music.

In his book *The Black Atlantic* (Verso, 1993), Gilroy writes of reggae's contribution to the creation of a "self-consciously synthetic culture"; he writes: "Once its [reggae's] own hybrid origins in rhythm and blues were effectively concealed, it ceased, in Britain, to signify an exclusively ethnic Jamaican style and derived a different kind of cultural legitimacy both from a new global status and from its expression of what might be termed a pan-Caribbean culture." Reggae, in this view, articulates the consciousness of being part of a black diaspora.

Reading

There Ain't No Black in the Union Jack by Paul Gilroy (Hutchinson, 1987) contains a sustained analysis of reggae and may be read as a precursor to the author's later work (above).

Rastafari and Reggae by Rebekah Mulvaney (Greenwood Press, 1990) is a dictionary and sourcebook.

Catch a Fire by Timothy White (Elm Tree Books, 1983) is the best and most comprehensive biography of Bob Marley based on interviews with Marley and members of an "inner circle" of friends in a seven-year period before the artist's death in 1981; chronicles Marley's childhood and early involvement with reggae and shows how he was promoted to the position of "superstar" in the 1970s; also contains full "discography" of Marley, the Wailers, and his backing singers, the I Threes.

Cut 'n' Mix by Dick Hebdige (Comedia, 1987) offers a concise definition of reggae, but also considers other Caribbean music idioms as expressions of the black experience in the New World.

See also: AFROCENTRICITY; BLUES; DIASPORA; ETHIOPIANISM; RAP; RASTAFARI

Ellis Cashmore

322 Reverse racism ("Black racism")

Reverse racism ("Black racism")

In recent years, expressions of hostility, prejudice, discrimination, or even indifference to whites by ethnic minorities have been interpreted by some as reverse racism. In terms of actual content, some of the beliefs and theories held by ethnic minorities, particularly African Americans and African-Caribbeans, resemble a photographic negative of white racism. The beliefs involve an acceptance of the basic categories imposed by whites to justify their historical domination and contemporary privilege, followed by a denial of the validity of the meanings attached to those categories by white doctrines.

Accepted is: that blacks and whites constitute distinct races. Rejected is: that the black race is inferior and degenerate. This is modified to include the view that blacks are superior. We find examples of this in the philosophies of the Nation of Islam. Robert Miles believes that the statements of its leader Louis Farrakhan "warrant description as racism" (in *Racism*, Routledge, 1989). And, while he does not spell out his argument, Miles presumably refers to the sometimes acerbic anti-semitism of Farrakhan, whose theories had a disarming symmetry with the purported Zionist world domination conspiracy of the *Protocols* which has inspired white racist organizations for generations. Jews are depicted as spiders at the center of a vast political web they have spun about the world.

If it were a straightforward question of beliefs, then there would be little argument about the existence of reverse, or black racism. But, content is but one component of racism. Black populations have been affected by the experience of forced migration and enduring oppression. The material element of blacks' relationship with whites has affected both groups' mentalities, or mindsets and approaches to each other. One big difference is that white racism is a legacy of imperialism, whereas the black version is a reaction to the experience of racism. This qualitative difference is disguised by the term "reverse racism," which implies too simple a comparison with its white counterparts.

Blacks' reaction to white racism takes many forms; accepting racial categories and articulating them in a way that mimics those of white racists is but one of them. Analytical purposes would not seem to be served by calling this reverse racism. The term misguidedly suggests that racism today can be studied by examining beliefs and without careful consideration of the vastly different historical experiences of the groups involved.

Reading
Introduction to Race Relations, 2nd edition, by Ellis Cashmore and Barry Troyna (Falmer, 1990) takes the same approach to the term as above and offers an alternative way of handling instances of what superficially appear to be reverse racism.

See also: INTERETHNIC CONFLICT; MALCOLM X; NATION OF ISLAM; RACISM

Ellis Cashmore

Riots: Britain, 1981

The term "race riot" was used in both popular and political discourse to describe and define the wave of violent disturbances which erupted first in Brixton, London, in April 1981 and subsequently in a range of Britain's other major cities during the "long, hot summer" of that year. The typification of these incidents as "race riots" not only helped to shape ensuing political debate on the matter but also helped to determine the nature of subsequent policy interventions.

In fact, careful scrutiny of what took place at Brixton, Southall, Toxteth, Moss Side, and elsewhere in 1981 reveals that "race riot" is a wholly inappropriate mode of classification: not only is it a factually incorrect description, it also denudes the incidents of any political complexion and the participants of any political edge to their protest.

Of the various and often disparate violent episodes of 1981 only the confrontation in the Southall district of London could be labeled legitimately as "racial" insofar as the clashes were primarily between white youth, on the one hand, and the young local Asian residents, on the other. A concert in a local public house by the 4-Skins – a group which constantly made reference to Nazi slogans – had attracted a large following of skinhead youths into the district; a contingent of this group abused an Asian shopkeeper, smashed a few windows, and had set off down the main street of Southall intent on more malicious damage. Local Asian youths reacted strongly and despite (or because of) police intervention the scene outside the concert venue degenerated into a battle. Molotov cocktails were thrown and the public house was eventually gutted.

The violence which had erupted three months earlier in Brixton and which was soon to engulf Toxteth, Moss Side, and other districts was of an entirely different nature. Here, hostilities were directed, first and foremost, at the police and, like the Watts outbreak in Los Angeles in 1965, were precipitated largely by what the residents perceived as racial harassment and intimidation by police officers. What is more, though these disturbances took place in districts containing relatively large black populations, they were not simply black youth versus police confrontations; a substantial number of white youngsters participated. In fact, of the 3,074 people arrested during the disturbances, over 2,400 were white, according to Home Office figures.

Historically, and in its current usage, the term "riot" popularly connotes an image of widespread mindless violence, perpetrated by people who are intent, purely and simply, on creating havoc and inflicting malicious damage on people and property. What came to be called the "burnin' and lootin' " episodes of 1981 were presented via media and political debate largely in these terms. Indeed, the media assumed a major role in this process of "depoliticizing" the incidents; first, by including under the riot heading a whole series of events which on other occasions might never have been reported or which would simply have been recorded as normal crime. The media were also accused of producing a "copycat effect"; by showing graphic and dramatic scenes of the Brixton disturbances, the media were said to have encouraged youths in other parts of the country to imitate their Brixton counterparts. This interpretation of the "burnin' and lootin' " episodes was in part supported by Lord Scarman in his official report. But there is no evidence to sustain this view, nor does it explain why the youths in Toxteth, Moss Side, and elsewhere waited almost three months after the Brixton disturbances before deciding to imitate those scenes. Most importantly, however, the "copycat" interpretation plays a significant ideological role in undermining the notion that the disturbances were inspired by real and substantive political grievances. As one youth in Handsworth, Birmingham, explained: "We're fighting for our rights – against the police – it's not copycat."

If the disturbances were neither "race riots" nor "copycat riots" but forms of protest against specific conditions, one has to establish what these conditions actually were. Clearly, the dramatic rise in unemployment, especially among the young, locally and nationally constituted one of the most significant of the underlying causes. Although as the studies of the "burn, baby, burn" incidents in the United States revealed, unemployment does not directly and inevitably provoke social unrest. What is more, unemployment levels in parts of Scotland and the northeast of England exceeded those in Brixton, Toxteth, and Moss Side but were not scenes of disorder.

When they took to the streets, the youths made it clear that their hostility was directed towards the police: in all the major districts affected in 1981, relations between the police and the local community had reached a low ebb; mutual distrust, suspicion, and resentment characterized this relationship. On the one hand, the communities insisted they were maltreated by the police, subjected to racial harassment and to an intensification of police control such as the Swamp 81 exercise in Brixton in which the Metropolitan Police had saturated the district with extra police, including the Special Patrol Group. The police, on the other hand, justified these modes of action by pointing to the disproportionately high crime rates in Brixton and other multiracial areas.

The characterization of the Brixton and July 1981 episodes as "riots" ensured that the thrust of political debate and policy prescriptions would be firmly with a "law and order" framework. The imperative for action, in other words, has been to ensure that there is no repetition. An intensification of policing in the affected areas and more generally, a broadening of police powers have been the most significant of the subsequent initiatives. But, while the incidents of 1981 may have included some wanton acts of destruction and thieving, the participants in general were remarkably selective in their choice of targets. To have responded to these episodes purely and simply in terms of a law and order crisis degrades and disparages the communities' sense of grievance. Worse still, it is myopic because it leaves untouched the underlying causes of these incidents and increases the possibility of further, perhaps even more severe, rebellions.

Reading

Uprising by Martin Kettle and Lucy Hodges (Pan, 1982) is a detailed account of the 1981 disturbances which discusses the various explanations adduced and identifies policing as the main catalyst of what took place.

Race and Class (Special double issue, "Rebellion and Repression" vol. 23, nos. 2/3, 1982) presents an account of the disturbances with due regard to historical and contemporary factors.

Public Disorder by Simon Field and Peter Southgate (Home Office Research Study no. 72, 1981) comprises two reports: the first considers the "burn, baby, burn" episodes in the United States and the relevance of the studies to the 1981 incidents in Britain; the second is a survey of the views and experiences of male residents in Handsworth, Birmingham – scene of one of the 1981 disturbances.

See also: KERNER REPORT; POLICE AND RACISM; RIOTS: U.S.A.; SCARMAN REPORT

Barry Troyna

Riots: Britain, 1985

The disturbances of 1985, like those of 1981, occurred in major urban centers, involved a great many (but not only) black youths and were precipitated by incidents involving the police. The first three episodes in Birmingham, Brixton (London), and Liverpool, suggested that it was possible to assess the events in much the same terms as their precursors. While there were two deaths at Birmingham, these seemed largely accidental, no one apparently aware that two Asians were trapped in a burning post office. But, at Tottenham, in North London, the final outbreak of the sequence took a new turn when a police officer was attacked and killed in the midst of the riot. Rioters, armed with guns, fired at the police; the police deployed (although they did not use) CS gas and baton rounds for the first time ever in Great Britain.

In Birmingham, events had been spurred by a traffic offense on 9 September. Ironically, the day before had been one of celebration, when residents of Handsworth congregated at their local park (about one mile from the incident) for the district's annual festival. A standard operation was handled indelicately, drawing an overreaction and a burst of violence which escalated through the night. Heavy-handed policing, culminating in the shooting of Mrs. Cheryl Groce, a black mother of six, triggered more violence at Brixton. A week later, another black mother, Mrs. Cynthia Jarrett, fatally collapsed during a police raid on her Broadwater Estate home in Tottenham. A day later, violence broke out; during the violence of 6 October, PC Keith Blakelock was killed.

The popular explanations for the riots were familiar: criminality, inner-city deprivation, institutional racism, mass unemployment, innate indiscipline, left-wing political agitation, and, most implausible of all, drug abuse. The prescriptions were unimaginative: order another Scarman-type inquiry, democratize the police force, crack down in the courts, and increase spending in the inner cities.

One of the interesting political figures to emerge in the aftermath of the riots in Tottenham was Bernie Grant, a local council leader who later became an elected Labour Member of Parliament. To many people, Grant was an extremist who talked coldly of the police getting a "good hiding" (223 police were injured and one died during the disturbance; 20 public were injured). Yet his unequivocal opposition to violence in his discussions with black youth, his attempts to persuade them to use the political process and his refusal to condemn the subsequent trial of forty-five people charged with riot and affray ("You can't support the jury system when it suits you, but not when it results in a verdict you don't like") estranged him from many black youths. Despite being pilloried from all sides, Grant became a politician of note, active in the Labour Party's "black section" and strongly opinionated on all aspects of race relations.

Reading

The Roots of Urban Unrest edited by John Benyon and John Solomos (Pergamon Press, 1987) is a textbook comprising contributions from a variety of scholars and practitioners on the question "what has gone wrong in the 1980s?".

"Forms of collective racial violence" by Terry Davis (in *Political Studies*, vol. 34, nos. 40–60, 1986) is a consideration of the types of explanations of urban unrest.

"Metaphysics of paradigms" by Michael Haas (in *Review of Politics*, vol. 48, no. 4, 1986) analyzes theories of urban violence and the assumptions underpinning them.

Interpretations of Violence, by J. Gaffney (Centre for Ethnic Relations Research, Warwick University, 1987) is a discourse analysis of the three reports that followed the Handsworth riot of 1985. The Police Report emphasized a conspiracy, the Black Report social conditions, and the allegedly impartial Silverman Report unemployment. None dealt thoroughly with the operation of racism as a factor in the experience of blacks in the area.

See also: MEDIA AND RACE RELATIONS; POLICE AND RACISM; RIOTS: BRITAIN, 1981

Ellis Cashmore

Riots: U.S.A., 1965–67

South Central Los Angeles contains the largest concentration of blacks in the city. It includes the district called Watts. On 11 August 1965, blacks took to the streets and for six days engaged in what became known as the "Watts riots". Some whites were attacked, but mostly the destruction was aimed at property: cars were over-turned, stores were looted, and buildings set afire. The watchword of the riots summed up the imperative: "Burn, baby, burn." The burning continued for two years, ravaging ghetto areas in such places as Detroit and New York City.

The actual incident that precipitated the Watts riots involved a white police officer's attempted arrest of a black youth (a similar episode started the Brixton riot, see RIOTS: BRITAIN, 1981). More and more people became involved and police reinforcements were brought in. Five arrests were made before the police withdrew under a hail of stones from an angry mob. Instead of dispersing, the crowd grew and began assailing whites. Over the next few hours, there were periodic bursts when rocks and Molotov cocktails were thrown.

Then came a lull: police called in the National Guard and the situation seemed under control. This tactic, however, served to aggravate matters and the rioting escalated: buildings were burnt and looting was rife. "One of the most ravaging outbursts of Blacks in the history of this nation," is how Douglas Glasgow described the event. "Their rage was directed at white society's structure, its repressive institutions, and their symbols of exploitation in the ghetto: the chain stores, the oligopolies that control the distribution of goods; the lenders, those who hold the indebtedness of the ghetto bound; the absentee landlords; and the agents who control the underclass while safeguarding the rights of those who exploit it."

One estimate placed the total number of participants as over 30,000, or 15 percent of the adult black population of the area. Of the 3,927 people arrested, most were black, but only 556 were under eighteen, while 2,111 were over twenty-five; 602 were over forty. It was not a youth riot as such.

All manner of explanation was invoked to determine the causes of the Watts riots; they ranged from the excessively warm weather (the "long, hot summer theory") to the influence of outside agitators. Glasgow is probably the most plausible when he cites the conditions: "Poverty, racial discrimination, long-term isolation from the broader society." Added to this was the sense of frustration elicited by the failure of the civil rights movement to instigate any immediate, tangible changes after years of campaigning for social reform.

Clearly, there was a frustration that was not just confined to blacks in Los Angeles, but which existed throughout the United States; for over the next two years, similar outbursts occurred at other American cities. They reached a virtual climax in July 1967 when a Detroit vice squad conducted raids on gambling clubs frequented by blacks. There were several arrests (there is an uncanny parallel here with the incident in Bristol, England, in 1980 when police raided a café used by blacks; this sparked a mass disturbance with police eventually withdrawing to leave a virtual "no go area"). By the following morning, some 200 blacks had gathered on the streets; a bottle hurled from the crowd smashed through the window of a leaving police car. The crowd grew to about 3,000 by 8.00 A.M. and the police mobilized for action. As in Watts, rocks were thrown and buildings were burnt, prompting a police withdrawal. Reports of gunfire filtered back to the police, who, in midweek, when the initial outburst had died down, started a series of raids on residents' homes. Once more, the services of the National Guard were invoked. The efforts to restore order and re-establish control only exacerbated the situation and violence erupted again, so that by the end of the week, 7,200 people had been arrested. Forty-three people were killed, thirty or more by the police. Property damage exceeded $22 million.

The mid-1960s were a period of severe black discontent. Rioting may not have been an effective method for overthrowing the social order, but it certainly enlisted the attention of the American population and forced the problems unique to blacks into public visibility. In this sense, the riots were spectacularly successful. As one observer put it: "Reporters and cameramen rushed into the ghettoes; elected and appointed officials followed behind; sociologists and other scholars arrived shortly after. The President established a riot commission; so did the governors." That commission was to conclude that the cause of the riots lay in racism and the resulting poverty suffered by blacks, leading to their being undernourished, underpaid, badly clothed, and poorly housed. The civil rights movement had complained about precisely these features of blacks' lives, but it is arguable that the violent pressure of rioting in two years achieved more than ten years of peaceful protest.

Reading
Fire This Time: The Watts Uprising and the 1960s by Gerald Horne (University Press of Virginia, 1995) documents the impact of race on postwar Los Angeles.
The Black Underclass by Douglas Glasgow (Jossey-Bass, 1980) is a reflective summary of the reasons behind and the aftermath of Watts and an appraisal of blacks in modern America.
Ghetto Revolts by J. R. Feagin and H. Hahn (Macmillan, 1973) examines the reasons for and the effects of the riots in a book that embraces many perspectives. This may profitably, read in conjunction with *The Politics of Violence* by D. O. Sears and J. B. McConahay (Houghton Mifflin, 1973) which has as its central theme "new urban blacks and the Watts riot."

See also: BLACK POWER; CIVIL RIGHTS MOVEMENT; GHETTO; KERNER REPORT; MEDIA AND RACISM; RIOTS: BRITAIN, 1981

Ellis Cashmore

Riots: U.S.A. (Miami) 1980
The disorder that centered on the district of Liberty City signaled a slight variation on the pattern established by the urban disturbances of the 1960s. The earlier riots tended to be precipitated by blacks in response to what they perceived to be police provocation.

Also, the violence was more frequently directed at property rather than persons. The grievances of blacks were about poverty and racialism, particularly that practiced by the police.

Liberty City was slightly different. The first incident started in court. Four police officers who had been accused of beating to death a black Miami businessman were acquitted. Many suspected a miscarriage of justice with underlying racist themes. In addition to this, there was a feeling among blacks that the needs of migrant Cubans in the area were being given priority over their own.

Like the 1960s riots, conflict with the police proved to be a catalyst for violence, but, unlike the 1960s version, the violence was concentrated on white people. As one eye-witness, quoted by Leonard Broom, described it: "the anger is so intense, the feelings are so rampant now, that the attacks have been aimed at white people with intent to do great bodily harm to people."

Whites were attacked as they walked the streets, they were dragged out of cars and chased through the city. Property was vandalized too, but the Liberty City riots were distinguished by the gross violence done to people. Eighteen people were killed and the cost of the destruction was put in hundreds of millions of dollars.

Reading
The Miami Riot of 1980 by B. D. Porter and M. Dunn (Lexington Books, 1984) is a comprehensive account of the riots with due emphasis given to the interethnic conflict between blacks and Cubans that exacerbated the riots.
Race, Reform and Rebellion by M. Marable (Macmillan, 1984), *The Underside of Black American History* by T. R. Frazier (Harcourt, Brace & Jovanovich, 1982), *Race, Ethnicity and Socioeconomic Status* by C. Willie (Prentice Hall, 1983), and *The Black Community* by J. E. Blackwell (Harper & Row, 1985), all cover similar ground and include sections on urban disorders.

See also: GHETTO; INTERETHNIC CONFLICT; KERNER REPORT; RIOTS: U.S.A., 1965–67; SCARMAN REPORT

Ellis Cashmore

Riots: U.S.A., 1992

Disturbances in South Central Los Angeles and other U.S. cities for three days beginning 30 April were touched off by an incident over a year before. Rodney King, an African American male, was apprehended by four white Los Angeles Police Department (LAPD) officers and beaten with batons. An amateur video enthusiast taped the episode, which seemed to reveal excessive violence.

The four officers were brought to trial and acquitted by a jury comprising six males and six females, one of whom was Hispanic, another Filipino, the rest white. The acquittal prompted protests outside the L.A.P.D. headquarters and this later spiraled out of control, leading to 44 deaths, 2,000 injuries, and 1,100 arrests.

Anticipating the reaction to such a verdict, the L.A.P.D. had allocated $1 million in overtime wages. Yet the police response to the initial outbreaks was sluggish and the L.A.P.D. hesitated to restore order. Police Chief Daryl Gates – who was forced to resign because of the King incident, but still held office at the time of the uprising – answered critics by saying he feared a police presence would worsen matters.

The L.A.P.D. deployed only two officers per 1,000 residents, the lowest ratio in the United States (New York City deploys 3.7) and 15 per square mile (compared with 89 for New York). Neighborhood involvement was sought through community policing, but, with so few officers, the approach was largely ineffectual. When the L.A.P.D. failed to quell the initial violence, 1,000 federal law enforcement officers and 4,000 Army and Marine troops were sent to Los Angeles, ready to move in at the express command of the President. 1,400 Californian National Guard members were placed on stand-by. A state of emergency was declared by California Governor Pete Wilson.

In the ten years leading to the violence, Los Angeles county had experienced demographic changes in its ethnic minority population. While the African-American population had dropped from 13 to 11 percent, both the Latino and Asian populations had grown. Collectively, the unemployment level among the three groups was nearly 50 percent. As whites moved out of the area to places like Simi Valley (where the trial was held) and Ventura County, interethnic conflict surfaced – in much the same way as it had done in Miami twelve years before. The predominantly Asian district known as Koreatown was particularly badly damaged.

Reading

The Los Angeles Riots: Lessons for the Urban Future edited by Mark Baldassare (Westview Press, 1994) address three questions: what were the causes of the riots, what actually took place and what were the consequences?

"How the rioters won" by Midge Decter is part of a series of articles in a special issue of *Commentary* (vol. 94, no. 1, July 1992) on the LA disturbances.

"Causes, root causes, and cures" by Charles Murray is in a special collection of papers in an issue of *National Review* (vol. 44, no. 11, June, 1992) devoted to analyses of the uprisings.

See also: DISADVANTAGE; INTERETHNIC CONFLICT; RIOTS: U.S.A. AND
BRITAIN; UNDERCLASS

Ellis Cashmore

Roma

Popularly though misleadingly known as Gypsies, Roma (singular:
Rom) are diasporic people of Indian origin who arrived in Europe
at the end of the thirteenth century before moving to other continents. They now number between ten and twelve million worldwide,
with 6–7 million in Eastern Europe, 2 million in Western Europe,
one million in North America and one million in South America.

The widely held view is that Roma were from Egypt (hence
"Gypcian" or "Gypsy") though others suggest that they came from
10,000 musicians who were gifted from the King of India to the
Shah of Iran in the fifth century. It is now accepted that the source
population was of composite non-Aryan origins (principally Dravid-
ian and Pratihara, though with some African input from the Siddis,
or East Africans conscripted to fight for both the Muslim and Hindu
armies). They were persons marshalled into batallions to resist the
incursion of the Islamic Ghazi (fighter against non-Muslims) into
India in the eleventh century. They began to appear in Europe from
1300.

The Romani word for a non-Rom is *gadzo* (from the Sanskrit
gajjha for civilian). Romani language, in many ways, reflects
migratory patterns: it has elements of Hindi (from northern India),
traces of Iranic (from northern Africa) and Armenian, Georgian,
and Ossetic words (from the Caucasian area of eastern Europe).
The presence of Greek suggests a long stay in the Byzantine empire
in western Asia and southern Europe.

The move into Europe, like the move away from India, was the
result of Islamic expansion. In the Balkans, Roma provided a much-
need artisan population and were employed in the Wallachian and
Moldavian principalities in southeastern Europe. The need for
Romani labor precipitated a movement to other parts of Europe
where their weapon-making skills made Roma sought-after workers
– so sought-after, that legislation permitting the enslavement of
Roma was written into many constitutions. Emancipation came
about in the second half of the nineteenth century.

By 1500, Romani groups had reached every country in northern
and western Europe. The exodus that followed the abolition of
slavery began in the 1860s and took hundreds of thousands of *Vlax*
(Romanian and Bulgarian) Roma to Russia, Serbia, the Americas
and elsewhere. Today, the Vlax Roma are the most numerous and

widely-dispersed Romani group and their dialect of Romani the most popular. Other political events, such as the fall of the Austro-Hungarian empire and two world wars, stimulated migrations. After the collapse of Communism in 1989, a major migration out of eastern Europe took more Roma to western Europe and North America.

Anti-Gypsy sentiment has been a feature of the Roma experience. As nonwhite, non-Christian, nonterritorial people entering in Europe near the height of Ottoman imperialism, they were first identified with Muslims and seen not only as a threat to the Christian church, but to the European economy, which was supported by trade to the East. The dark skin was associated, using biblical rhetoric, with evil; racism was Hitler's rationale for wanting to eradicate Roma. As a diasporic people, Roma were trespassers everywhere. Romani culture itself forbade – and still forbids – overly intimate contact with non-Roma, thereby reinforcing their marginal status to and nonparticipation in various host societies. Laws have been variously enacted to keep Roma at a distance. When western European countries entered the period of colonial expansion, their overseas territories became dumping grounds for unwanted Romani populations: Roma were shipped as slaves from Britain, France and Portugal to their colonies in the Caribbean and elsewhere in the 1660s.

The Balkanization of Europe into several ethnically distinct republics after 1989 led to another wave of enforced Romani migration and harassment. In Bosnia-Herzegovina, Poland, Slovakia, Bulgaria, and the Czech Republic, anti-Romani activity was especially severe. In 1995, 24 houses were set on fire in Bacu, Romania and five Roma were injured in a letter bomb attack in Bucharest, giving rise to the suspicion that, in certain parts, there was a genocidal intent in some of the attacks. In 1994, there was a Congressional Hearing on this very issue: the human rights abuses of Roma. The rise of skinheads in the United States brought fresh problems for Roma, who were regularly victimized by neo-nazi youth.

Reading

A History of the Gypsies of Eastern Europe and the U.S.S.R. by David Crowe (St. Martin's Press, 1995) is a country-by-country account of the history and sociopolitical situation of Roma.

The Gypsies by Angus Fraser (Blackwell, 1991) is a historical treatment of origins and migrations and may profitably be read in conjunction with a collection edited by David Crowe and John Kolsti, *The Gypsies of Eastern Europe* (Sharpe, 1986).

The Pariah Syndrome: An Account of Gypsy Slavery and Persecution by Ian Hancock (Karoma, 1987) deals mainly with the five centuries of Romani slavery, with chapters on anti-Romany laws in Europe and the U.S.A.

See also: ARYAN; DIASPORA; EUROPEAN RACISM; SKINHEADS; SLAVERY

Ian Hancock

S

Scapegoat

The term originated in the Hebrew ritual described in the Book of Leviticus: "Aaron shall lay both hands upon the head of the live goat, and confess over him all the iniquities of the children of Israel, and all their transgressions, even all their sins; and he shall put them on the head of the goat" (16:20–22). In other words, the sins of the people were symbolically transferred to the goat which was then let go into the wilderness taking with it the guilt of the people.

At a different level, a schoolgirl may be humiliated by a teacher at school; she can't hit back at the teacher, so she gets frustrated. When she gets home, she might take it out on her younger brother or sister, who is a more accessible target.

In race and ethnic relations, similar processes often take place: people shift the responsibilities for their misfortunes and frustrations onto other groups and those groups are usually visibly identifiable minorities, such as blacks, Asians or Mexicans, who have little power. These groups can be singled out and attributed with blame for all manner of evil, whether unemployment, housing scarcity, or literally anything else.

Jews and blacks have been recent popular scapegoats; they have had to shoulder the blame for almost everything from the economic decline of whole societies to the escalation of crime rates. Political groups, such as communists, and religious denominations, such as Roman Catholics, have historically been used as convenient scapegoats. It is, of course, no accident that the scapegoated groups are invariably powerless; they can be blamed and picked on without the possibility that they might hit back and resist the attribution. Lynchings and pogroms were carried out against blacks and Jews, when it was reasonably certain that those groups didn't have the power to fight back with any effectiveness.

One important feature of the scapegoating process is the failure of the group doing the blaming to analyze fully the circumstances producing the apparent misfortunes. Economic decline, for example, may be caused by a complex of factors, some rather obscure and difficult to comprehend. Yet scapegoating removes the need to analyze: it provides readymade explanations: "the blacks caused it" is simple and comprehensive – but wrong.

For the scapegoating to work best, there must be an available stereotype, so that the blame can be transferred with a minimum of ambiguity. If people have a fairly well-defined stereotyped conception of Asians as people who work too hard, make too much money, and engage in less-than-orthodox business dealings, then they have a convenient group to scapegoat. If there is widespread recognition that a great many Asians work in bad conditions for poor wages and are overcrowded in rundown homes, then this complicates the stereotype and makes the scapegoating more difficult – depending, of course, on what problems Asians are meant to be blamed for. The abiding rule seems to be not to analyze in any depth the group to be scapegoated.

A final point about the scapegoat should be borne in mind: the image of the group identified and blamed may be created anew for the purpose of scapegoating, but, more frequently, it exists as a stereotype in the popular imagination; the scapegoating adds new dimensions to the image.

Reading

American Minority Relations, 4th edition, by James Van der Zanden (Knopf, 1983) has a chapter on "Personality bulwarks of racism," which considers scapegoating as a "theory of prejudice."

The Nature of Prejudice by Gordon Allport (Addison-Wesley, 1954) is an important, comprehensive textbook on the social psychological aspects of race relations, with a whole chapter on "The choice of scapegoats."

"The ultimate attribution error" by Thomas F. Pettigrew in *Readings About the Social Animal* (Freeman, 1981) is designed to test some of Allport's theories about prejudice.

See also: PREJUDICE; RACIAL DISCRIMINATION; RACISM; STEREOTYPE

Ellis Cashmore

Scarman Report

The findings of a commission headed by Britain's Right Honourable Lord Scarman to investigate the causes of urban disorders in Brixton, London, in 1981 and make recommendations in the wake of them. During the course of the inquiry, violence erupted in the streets of Birmingham, Liverpool, and Manchester (in July 1981) and in his subsequent report to parliament, Scarman made passing reference to these disorders, focusing particularly on the ways they shared with or differed from prevailing social and economic conditions in Brixton. Scarman also considered the claim that there had been an imitative, or "copycat" element, to the July outbreaks, stimulated by media portrayals of the Brixton disorders.

The Scarman inquiry differed in at least two significant ways from its U.S. counterpart, the Kerner Commission's report on the "burn, baby, burn" disorders in the 1960s. First, the gathering of evidence by the U.S. Commission was completed by a team of researchers; in Britain, this role was undertaken solely by Lord Scarman. The result: Scarman collected a less detailed and comprehensive account of the extent of racial disadvantage and the grievances of the black communities than his U.S. counterparts. Second, Scarman presided over a quasi-judicial inquiry, established under section 32 of the 1964 Police Act. The nature of the inquiry, then, enhanced already existing skepticism about its function and relevance and deterred a number of members of the black communities from submitting either oral or written evidence. This further underlined the contention that the report, published in November 1981, presented only a partial view of what actually happened.

Scarman's appraisal of the Brixton district highlighted the social and economic privations experienced by the local black and, though to a lesser extent, white communities. Poor-quality housing, the paucity of recreational and leisure facilities, and the almost obscene levels of unemployment especially among black youngsters constituted some of the most important of the underlying causes of the disorders, wrote Scarman. But the evidence received indicated unequivocally that oppressive – some might say repressive – policing procedures in the locality provided the spark which ignited the flames in April 1981. Scarman was extremely critical of the decision taken by the local police chief, Commander Fairbairn, to inaugurate Swamp 81 on 6 April. The essence of the operation was to "swamp" certain areas of the district with police officers who were empowered to stop and search suspected criminals. Despite the notoriously poor police–community relations in Brixton – especially in the Railton Road/Mayall Road area, the "Front Line" as it is often called – the decision was taken independently of discussions with local community leaders. As Scarman pointed out: "I am. . . . certain that 'Swamp 81' was a factor which contributed to the great increase in tension . . . in the days immediately preceding the disorders" (para 4.43).

Among the various criticisms of the police received by the inquiry – harassment, unimaginative/inflexible policing, overreactions, etc. – Scarman was informed that certain police officers were racists. With some circumspection, Scarman conceded that this might have been a legitimate appraisal of a small caucus of police officers in Brixton and elsewhere. He was insistent, however, in his denunciation of accusations that the police force, and Britain in general, were characterized by institutional racism (see paras 2.21 and 9.1). His remarks on this issue have subsequently attracted considerable and widespread dissent and, as David Mason has argued, are based on an inchoate understanding of this concept.

Scarman's tendency to divide policing into "hard" and "soft" methods and to advocate the latter – in the form of community policing, and putting "bobbys back on the beat" – also attracted criticisms, largely from within the police force. The argument here, then, is that "soft" policing is not a cure-all for crime and is simply not appropriate for all circumstances. Others, outside of the police force, are also critical of community policing, though for distinctly different reasons: they argue that it is a more subtle, though no less invidious, form of ensuring repressive control over the communities.

The notion of "police accountability" figures prominently in the report: "Accountability" wrote Scarman, "is, I have no doubt, the key to successful consultation and socially responsive policing" (para. 5.57). His recommendation that accountability be statutory has met with little enthusiasm from most police forces, however, who maintain that it would undermine the operational independence of their forces. A contrasting view is that policing can only take place, effectively, with the consent of the public; therefore, legislative action was necessary to provide the statutory framework for consultation at the local level.

Scarman's emphasis on the role of the police, both in the context of the disorders and in general, was not surprising in view of the fact that the enquiry was set up under a section of the 1964 Police Act. He did, however, engage in wider questions of social policy both in the substantive sections of the report and in his subsequent recommendations. As he pointed out, issues such as housing, education, local community relations councils and the media, and their specific relation to the needs of ethnic minority communities, "must be kept constantly in view if the social context in which the police operate is not to continue to breed the conditions of future disorder" (para. 6.42).

The Scarman inquiry was designed to function within a liberal-reformist framework; the aim was to identify those factors which precipitated the disorders in Brixton in April 1981 and elsewhere in Britain, three months later, and to recommend those policies and practices necessary to restabilize the foundations and structures of the society. Consequently, those who perceived the disorders as exercises in mindless violence, as a further indication of the erosion of traditional values and mores, criticized the report for its liberal orientation. On the other hand, those who viewed the disorders in terms of an uprising or rebellion against repressive state institutions and who advocate the eradication of those institutions, rejected the report as conservative, myopic and largely irrelevant. Either way, Scarman was bound to disappoint and antagonize – and he did!

Reading
The Brixton Disorders, 10–12 April 1981 by Lord Scarman (HMSO, Cmnd. 8427, 1981. Also published by Penguin, 1982).
Scarman and After edited by John Benyon (Pergamon, 1984) is a set of readings reflecting on the disturbances, the report, and their aftermath.
Out of Order? Policing Black People edited by Ellis Cashmore and Eugene McLaughlin (Routledge, 1991) looks comparatively at the policing of black people in Britain and the U.S.A.

See also: INSTITUTIONAL RACISM; KERNER REPORT; POLICE AND RACISM; POLITICS AND "RACE"; RIOTS: BRITAIN, 1981

Barry Troyna

Segregation

There are two modes of segregation: *de jure* and *de facto*. *De jure* represents the situation where groups defined in terms of putative "racial" or ethnic difference are formally separated by law. In the latter (*de facto*) situation, such group separation exists in the absence of a formal legal framework.

Although there have been countless examples of legal separation historically, the most obvious would be the "Jim Crow" laws of the post-bellum era in the southern states of the USA and apartheid in South Africa. In the former case, levels of residential segregation between the Black and White communities were effectively increased following the abolition of the slave regime. Most commentators saw this as the result of a fear of equal status contact between freed slaves and their former masters: it was certainly a way of maintaining a system of subordination rooted in the notion of an ethnic "racial" hierarchy. In South Africa, from 1948 until the 1990s, apartheid extended and formalized the process of strict residential segregation; this being enshrined in the Group Areas Act and the "Bantustan" policy.

In both countries, legally enforced segregation went much further than the question of residential settlement. "Nonwhites" were prevented from sharing a whole range of facilities with Whites; ranging from education, employment and health to places of public resort such as restaurants, cafes, cinemas, clubs, public transportation and swimming pools/beaches. Apartheid even went as far as providing for separate entrances to public buildings, separate park benches, drinking fountains, and so on.

De facto segregation sometimes follows the formal abolition of its *de jure* equivalent. Thus, in the United States residential segregation in the South remained high for a number of reasons. Poverty, high unemployment levels and institutionalized discriminatory practices within the housing market meant that the mobility of African Americans was severely constrained, and the threat of racially motivated violence deterred those for whom such a move was feasible. Beyond the arena of structural constraints, they would also have been isolated from those who shared their cultural heritage. African Americans who migrated from the rural South to the northern cities in search of work had little choice but to replicate their previous patterns; becoming concentrated in poor urban ghettos.

It is important to recognize, therefore, that *de facto* segregation cannot normally be interpreted as voluntary segregation. There are also certain "gray areas" in the policy sphere in that, even in the absence of a legal framework, "custom and practice" may conspire to produce localized segregation. Thus, in response to complaints of racial harassment from Bangladeshis in Tower Hamlets in London in the 1970s, the local authority elected to place complainants in (for them, totally unsuitable) flatted accommodation (apartments) in a small number of hard-to-let high rise blocks. Enforced segregation therefore resulted from the Greater London Council's unwillingness to tackle the root problem: it was easier to move an already marginalized community than to deal with the perpetrators of the harassment who were for the most part established white residents.

Even more significant in the context of involuntary segregation without a formal legal framework is the process which has become known euphemistically as "ethnic cleansing." Based often on systematic ethnic genocide, as in Bosnia and other parts of the former Yugoslavia in the early 1990s, this is a consciously policy-driven process. In the Bosnian case, the Dayton Peace Accord, signed by all warring parties in December 1995, drew clear "ethnic boundaries" in spatial terms, thus "segregation as a policy" became formal *de jure* segregation.

Except in certain extreme cases, a few of which have been noted here, segregation is not a phenomenon that is either present or absent: it tends to be a matter of degree. The question for researchers then becomes one of measuring the level of segregation.

A number of measurement problems, mainly associated with the arbitrary nature of bureaucratically defined spatial units, complicate comparative analyses (see Massey and Denton article, below). It is important to tackle these problems, however, as the detailed analysis of changing spatial patterns, particularly when looked at in conjunction with issues such as social class, can provide crucial insights into the dynamics of social change.

Reading
Ethnic Segregation in Cities edited by Ceri Peach, Vaughan Robinson, and Susan Smith (Croom Helm, 1981) contains theoretical and substantive contributions from some of the key researchers in the field.
"Trends in the residential segregation of Blacks, Hispanics, and Asians: 1970–1980" by D. S. Massey and N. A. Denton, published in *American Sociological Review* (vol. 52, 1987) discusses the problem of measuring levels of spatial segregation.
Social Geography and Ethnicity in Britain: Geographical Spread, Spatial Concentration and Internal Migration edited by Peter Ratcliffe (Ethnicity in the 1991 Census, vol. 3 OPCS, 1966) contains a detailed appraisal of current and past residential patterns in Britain and assesses the likely direction and significance of future changes.

See also: APARTHEID; GHETTO; PRUITT-IGOE; WHITE FLIGHT
Peter Ratcliffe

Self-fulfilling prophecy
This term, first used to effect by the sociologist Robert Merton in 1948 (*Antioch Review*, vol. 13), refers to the processes by which false beliefs are converted to practical realities. Merton's seminal argument begins with W. I. Thomas' proposition, "If men define situations as real, they are real in their consequences." Merton offered an example of northern American whites who had genuinely held beliefs about the typical migrating black from the nonindustrial south: "Undisciplined in traditions of trade unionism and the art of collective bargaining . . . a traitor to the working class." The whites saw these not as prejudices, but as "cold, hard facts"; that is, they defined the reality. Then they acted on the "facts," excluding blacks from unions so that the only way in which blacks could find work was as scab labor; this served to confirm the whites' original beliefs. (The John Sayles movie *Matewan* brings this point to life.)

"The self-fulfilling prophecy is, in the beginning, a *false* definition of the situation evoking a new behavior which makes the originally false conception come true," wrote Merton. In the 1960s, a study by Rosenthal and Jacobson illustrated this: the researchers selected 20 percent of children on San Francisco school rolls completely at random and informed the relevant authorities, including teaching staff, that these children were intellectually promising, in their terms, "bloomers." Returning to the schools later, the researchers found that the children in the 20 percent were excelling, not, they concluded, because of their own capacities or efforts, but because of the schools' heightened expectations of them and the extra attention they were accorded. Teachers accepted the researchers' completely erroneous observations and adjusted their behavior toward the "bloomers" in such a way as to create conditions under which they could achieve good results. One might easily imagine the experiment in reverse, with specific groups of pupils falsely defined, perhaps through racist assumptions, as "slow learners" and a reality being created to fit the beliefs, or fulfil the prophecy.

Merton showed how this had consequences beyond the school when he wrote, "If it appears to the white in-group that Negroes are *not* educated in the same measure as themselves, that they have an 'unduly' high proportion of unskilled workers and an 'unduly' low proportion of successful businesses and professional men, that they are thriftless and so on through the catalogue of middle class virtue and sin, it is not difficult to understand the charge that the Negro is 'inferior' to the white." One especially damaging effect of this is what Merton called "self-hypnosis" in which the group labeled inferior come to believe this of itself.

"Ethnic and racial out-groups," as Merton called them, have no simple task in breaking out of the self-fulfilling cycle, for, even when they display characteristics that are valued by whites, their behavior can be evaluated differently. Merton described the "moral alchemy" by which key American values, such as industry, resolution, and perseverance, when shown by Jews or Japanese, can bear witness to "their sweatshop mentality, their ruthless undercutting of American standards, their unfair competitive practices." Whites transmute their own virtues into others' vices, so that ethnic "out-groups" are, in Merton's phrase, "damned-if-you-do and damned-if-you-don't." Whether they achieve or not, they are condemned.

Merton's old but absolutely crucial article points out some of the logical paths in the "intricate maze of self-contradictions" of white mentalities, showing how racism, far from being a matter of blind prejudices, is sustained and nourished by actions which at one level seem to defy racist beliefs, but, at another, can be interpreted as support for them.

Reading
"The self-fulfilling prophecy" by R. K. Merton is reprinted in the author's book, *Social Theory and Social Structure* (Macmillan, 1968) and in several texts, including *Social Problems*, 2nd edn, edited by E. McDonagh and J. Simpson (Holt, Rhinehart & Winston, 1969).
Pygmalion in the Classroom by R. Rosenthal and L. Jacobson (Holt, Rhinehart & Winston, 1968), includes details of the school study, while Jacobson's edited collection with P. Insel, *What Do You Expect?* (Cummings, 1975) is a set of studies exploring the general principle.

See also: DISADVANTAGE; STEREOTYPE; UNDERACHIEVEMENT; XENOPHOBIA

Ellis Cashmore

Skinheads

While many other white supremacist movements have declined in recent years, skinheads have continued to attract adherents from all over Europe and the United States. They have followed the examples of British counterparts in the 1970s, who formed alliances with neofascist organizations such as the National Front (NF) and the British Movement (BM) and linked up with established political movements. Although they have no formal organizational structure themselves, skinheads have been welcome supplements to such groups as the Ku Klux Klan, the Liberty Lobby, White Aryan Resistance, and Germany's radical right-wing Nationalist Front and Deutsche Alternativ parties.

Originating in England in the late 1960s, skinheads defined a hostile working-class reaction to the cultural changes sought by youth of the day. Drawing support from young people in Britain's inner cities, skinheads preyed on groups perceived to be "outsiders," most particularly South Asian migrants – in their terms, "Pakis." Their uniform was shorn hair, braces (suspenders), denim jeans, and industrial boots. After a period of decline, skinheads reappeared in 1978 as part of a racist revival.

As skinheads faded slightly in Britain in the 1980s, U.S. equivalents came to light. Many cases of brutality and vandalism involving skinhead attacks on ethnic minorities emerged in the 1980s and 1990s, the best-known involving Tom Metzger, a former Klan Grand Dragon and leader of the White Aryan Resistance (WAR), which had a large skinhead membership. In 1990, Metzger and his son were found guilty by a court in Portland, Oregon, of inspiring a group of skinheads to beat to death Mulvgeta Seraw, an Ethiopian migrant. Metzger was ordered to pay $12.5 million to Seraw's survivors and his assets were liquidated. Metzger was in court again in

1993, when charged with a felony count of conspiracy to violate the municipal fire rules of San Fernando Valley, California, by ritually burning a cross Klan-style. His lawyer invoked the First Amendment, free speech, arguing that Metzger was being persecuted for "his beliefs."

In 1992 the German government banned the sale, manufacture and distribution of the skinhead music known as "Oi!," whose lyrics advocated racism and genocide. According to George Marshall (in *Spirit of '69: A Skinhead Bible*, ST Publishing, 1991), "Oi!" was started in 1980 by the English band The Cockney Rejects. The German bands affected by the ban included Störkraft (Disruptive Force), Endstufe (Final Stage), and Kahlkopf (Bald Head). At the same time, skinheads were appearing in the Eastern European states of Poland, Hungary, Slovakia, and the Czech Republic. Their targets were, variously, gypsies, Jews, and asylum-seekers.

Reading
Blood in the Face by James Ridgeway (Thunder's Mouth Press, 1990) plots the rise of what the author calls a "new white culture," which includes skinheads and other white supremacist movements.
"Long days journey into white" by Kathy Dobie in *Village Voice* (vol. 37, no. 17, April, 1992) discusses female skinheads and their involvement with neo-Nazi organizations.
No Future by Ellis Cashmore (Heinemann, 1984) looks at the origins of the skinheads and assesses their legacy, "the skinhead mentality."

See also: EUROPEAN RACISM; KU KLUX KLAN; NEO-NAZISM; SCAPEGOAT; STEREOTYPE

Ellis Cashmore

Slavery
"Slavery is the status or condition of a person over whom any or all of the powers attaching to the right of ownership are exercised," according to the United States Slavery Convention (I (1), Geneva, 1926). The condition invariably involves the forced, unremunerated labor of the person held as property and his or her exclusion from any kind of participation in politics or civil rights.

The process by which this condition comes about is the "slave trade" defined by the United Nations as: "all acts involved in the capture, acquisition of a slave with a view to selling or exchanging him; all acts of disposal by sale or exchange of a slave acquired with a view to being sold or exchanged and, in general, every act of trade or transport in slaves" (I (2), Geneva, 1926).

Pierre van den Berghe adds the further important point that: "Slavery is a form of unfreedom and disability that is largely restricted to ethnic strangers – to people who are defined as outside the solidarity group." Types of unfreedom have been institutionalized in imperial Rome, in China, and in some quarters of West Africa, though the particular type of interest here is that operated by European powers when expanding and maintaining their colonies between the sixteenth and nineteenth centuries. The especially virulent form of racism that lies at the root of race relations issues was, in large part, born out of the desire and need to justify this slavery.

The conditions for this slavery were quite basic: the conquest of a territory, followed by the capture of its people and their sale to traders, then their transportation to a distant country where they were forced to work. Most of the Europeans' attentions were concentrated on Africa, so the native peoples underwent what Stanley Elkins calls a series of "shocks" in the process of enslavement: "We may suppose that every African who became a slave underwent an experience whose crude psychic impact must have been staggering and whose consequences superseded anything that had ever happened to him." Before the trade in slaves ended in the mid-nineteenth century, between twelve and fifteen million Africans were transported to North, Central, and South American countries to work as slaves (about 60 percent of them were taken in the eighteenth century when the slave trade peaked). Most came from a narrow strip of the West African coast with a significant majority coming from Central Africa. The areas now known as Angola and southern Nigeria were fertile grounds for slave traders. The native peoples' robustness and acclimatization to tropical conditions were thought to make them suitable for cotton or sugar plantation work in such places as Brazil, the Caribbean, and the southern states of America. The physical environments were harsh and demanding, but the first slaves had come from lands rife with diseases and subject to droughts and famines.

Slaves were made to labor on plantations, in mines (especially in Brazil), or in houses (as domestic servants or artisans). The motivation for keeping them working in this way and depriving them of any sort of freedom was in most cases (but not all) profit-maximization. Productivity was paramount and slave owners and traders were unaffected by moral considerations. Racist ideologists served useful purposes in several contexts, for clearly it was morally wrong and unchristian to subject a fellow human being to all manner of atrocity in the pursuit of wealth. If all men were equal before God, then it was simply not right to hold another in bondage and deprive them of all basic human rights.

Racism provided a legitimation of sorts, however, for it proposed a theory of human types in which some races were superior to others. In this instance, whites were thought to be obviously superior: their military and technological advancement demonstrated that. Blacks were considered a race apart, inferior, and even subhuman. So, if they were not equal, there was no reason to treat them equally.

The problem with racist ideologies is that, unlike chalk marks on a board, they cannot be rubbed away when no longer needed. After the abolition of slavery, racism did not disappear. Rather, it endured in the popular imagination and continued to affect relationships between whites and the descendants of slaves most substantially. Racism permanently stigmatized the succeeding generations of those who had previously been enslaved.

In 1772, 10,000 slaves were freed in Britain and, in 1807, the legal slave trade ended after a period of antislavery pressure, mostly from religious groups. The following fifty years saw some small improvements in slaves' conditions, such as housing, clothing, and diet, though the average life expectancy of slaves was at least 12 percent below that of whites by 1850. In 1833, some 800,000 slaves in British territories were freed and ten years later slavery was abolished in British colonial India; one year later it was abolished in Ceylon (now Sri Lanka). Full emancipation came in 1865, though a system of indentured labor in some areas ensured that ex-slaves in the Americas remained tied to plantations.

Technically, emancipation meant that slaves were released from their bondage and relieved of their status as chattel (that is, someone's possession). Yet, various pieces of legislation and other developments made sure that, for the next hundred years, their progress towards some form of equality would be painfully slow.

The particular combination of slavery and racism was a potent one and one which was to have far-reaching effects. There are, however, instances of slavery without racism and it seems that some system of unfreedom can be imposed wherever conditions facilitate slavery; the prime condition being where human labor can be profitably exploited. This is attested to by the endurance of various forms of chattel slavery. The ownership of one human by another persists in the contemporary world, particularly in India where a system of debt bondage ensures that an estimated 6.5 million people are held in a slavelike state. The absence of bankruptcy laws in India means that a creditor can claim back money or goods owed by acquiring his debtor as his property. Another type of slavery in

Asia is the kidnapping of women from Bangladeshi villages, followed by their transportation and sale as servants in the Gulf states.

In South America, there are various types of labor that come very near to slavery, such as in Peru where certain tribes are classed as "savages" and denied citizenship, or Brazil where the "yoke" keeps unpaid laborers working the plantations while in bondage.

There is evidence to suggest that slavery exists in such unlikely places as the People's Republic of China, the ex-Soviet Union, and even the United States. As recently as 1982 arrests were made involving the sale of illegal Indonesian immigrants to wealthy Los Angeles homes as domestic servants. The number of illegally held Haitians, Mexicans, and Salvadorans in the United States is speculated to be in the tens of thousands.

In 1992, the London-based Anti-Slavery International submitted to a United Nations working group reports on slavery in Brazil. 5,000 men, women and children were found in slave conditions, mostly on Amazon cattle ranches or sugarcane distilleries in Mato Grosso. The usual practice was to recruit unemployed people in one state, transport them hundreds of miles to another, promising good pay and conditions. On arrival they would find their fares, and the food and tools they were obliged to buy at inflated prices, were deducted from their wages, leaving them in debt to the rancher or distiller. Escapees were hunted, tortured, or even murdered. The debt-bonded system, as it is called, was not confined to remote regions. Paraibuna, 80 miles from São Paulo, harbored seventy slaves, some of whom were forced to live with livestock.

The most visible state of slavery in recent times is that practiced in the Islamic republic of Mauritania in West Africa. Although technically outlawed, a system of chattel slavery is an integral part of the economy and continues to thrive with about 100,000 held in bondage. Having reviewed the relevant research, Russ Vallance, the Development Secretary of the Anti-Slavery Society (to whom I am grateful for the information on modern slavery), concludes that there are "probably more slaves in the world today than were freed by the great reformers of the 19th century" (personal communication, 13 April 1983). Such a view reinforces the idea that slavery surfaces in virtually any social situation where human labor can be forced and exploited.

Reading

Slavery and Social Death by Orlando Patterson (Harvard University Press, 1983) is an original treatment of slavery, tracing its many historical forms and theorizing why this form of domination and exploitation occurs even when it is economically useless; slavery is seen as a form of "social death" and slaves' membership of society is totally negated; the author's earlier work was *The Sociology of Slavery* (MacGibbon & Kee, 1961).

Roll, Jordan, Roll by Eugene D. Genovese (Pantheon, 1974) is something of a classic text on slavery, complemented by *Race and Slavery in the Western Hemisphere* edited by Genovese with Stanley L. Engerman (Princeton University Press, 1975); *Slavery* by Stanley Elkins (University of Chicago Press, 1968) provides the contrast to these.

The White Man's Burden by Winthrop Jordan (Oxford University Press, 1974) is a historical analysis which argues that English explorers in the eighteenth and nineteenth centuries conceived of Africans as heathen savage beasts which were in need of severe discipline; in this way, the adventurers were able to be consistent with the moral tone of the Protestant reformation. Also on the British experience: *Slavery and British Society, 1777–1846* by J. Walvin (Macmillan, 1982).

See also: AFRICA; BRAZIL; COLONIALISM; IDEOLOGY; NATIVE PEOPLES

Ellis Cashmore

Social Darwinism

Widely, but misguidedly, regarded as a distinctive school of thought which flourished at the end of the nineteenth and beginning of the twentieth centuries. Authors commonly said to be members of this school include Herbert Spencer, Walter Bagehot, Ludwig Gumplowicz, William Graham Sumner, Gustav Ratzenhofer, Franklin H. Giddings, and Benjamin Kidd. Some textbooks identify a separate and contemporaneous, school of "anthroposociology" led by Otto Ammon and Georges Vacher de Lapouge, writers who showed similarities of approach with some of the authors in the first list.

The Origin of Species was published in 1859. Within twenty years Bagehot and Gumplowicz were consciously attempting to apply in the study of society principles they believed to have been established by Darwin, but the expression "social Darwinism" did not make an appearance for almost another thirty years when it was employed by critics to designate a political philosophy that they considered pernicious. Social Darwinism came to be seen as a doctrine defending free-market economics and opposing state intervention. This was far removed from a literal interpretation of the name, which could with greater justification have been applied to the argument that social evolution results from the natural and sexual selection of favorable inherited variations.

Within the early twentieth-century debate about social evolution, several contending schools can be distinguished. As described by R. J. Halliday, the Oxford idealists explained it in terms of the dominance of rational mind over instinct. The Spencerian individualists represented human evolution as primarily a genetic or hereditarian process with a stress upon man's biological make-up rather than his rational mind. A third group, the civics movement, presented evolution as an adaptive process resulting from the interaction between man and his environment. Man was unique because of his ability to plan and to influence his own evolution. A fourth group, identified with the Eugenics Society, was closer to Darwin's conception of natural selection as resting upon a theory of population. Spencer disagreed with almost all the components of the eugenic doctrine and retained in his biology a strong environmental emphasis, insisting in particular upon the inheritance of acquired characteristics. The Eugenists can be seen as the true Darwinians in that they interpreted the social problem of reproduction in terms of the biological problem of competition for resources. On such a view, the conventional definition of social Darwinism as a laissez-faire economic ideology is misleading: the economic theory presupposed an ability rationally to allocate scarce means to competing ends, whereas those who started from biological principles saw human rationality as relatively unimportant. It is also misleading to label particular authors as social Darwinists without allowing for changes in their positions. Gumplowicz and Sumner each at one stage of their careers advanced Darwinist arguments but then moved on to write in quite other ways. Spencer's arguments were so special to himself that nothing is gained by classing him as a social Darwinist.

Arguments appealing to Darwinist principles had a significant influence upon racial relations in the early twentieth century. They introduced an element of ruthlessness and immorality into the justification of European expansion into overseas territories. They gave additional force to the anti-immigration campaign in the United States that resulted in the exclusion act of 1924 establishing quotas for different national groups. They produced a theory which represented racial prejudice as a positive element in human evolution (most elegantly expressed by Sir Arthur Keith). This theory reappeared in the 1970s in connection with the approach known as sociobiology and it has been applied to racial and ethnic relations by Pierre van den Berghe. Whether sociobiology is properly described as a new version of social Darwinism is disputable. It has been maintained that for the study of racial relations the best resolution is to isolate what is called the selectionist theory. This holds that: (1) evolution may be assisted if interbreeding populations are kept separate so that they can develop their special capacities (as in animal breeding); (2) racial prejudice serves this function and in so doing reinforces racial categories in social life; (3) therefore racial categories are determined by evolutionary processes of inheritance and selection. Where the pre-Darwinian racial typologists inferred that pure races must have existed in the past, the selectionists see racial purity as something constantly advanced as humans adapt to new circumstances and cause their groups to evolve. Sociobiologists often advance some version of the selectionist theory; this enables their arguments to be classified without entering upon the dispute as to whether or not they are social Darwinists.

Reading
"Social Darwinism: a definition" by R. J. Halliday (*Victorian Studies*, vol. 4, 1971) is a review of the definitional problem.
Social Darwinism in American Thought by Richard Hofstadter (Beacon Press, 1975) is a more conventional history.
Racial and Ethnic Competition by Michael Banton (Cambridge University Press, 1983, pp. 47–50) examines the selectionist theory.

See also: DARWINISM; ENVIRONMENTALISM; EUGENICS; HEREDI-TARIANISM; SOCIOBIOLOGY

Michael Banton

Sociobiology

Since the popularization of the term by Edward O. Wilson in 1975, sociobiology has referred to the study of animal behavior from the perspective of Darwinian evolutionary theory. The approach goes back to the work of William D. Hamilton and John Maynard Smith in the mid-1960s, however. An older label is ethology, and others prefer behavioral biology or population ecology. Applied to other animals, the subject is relatively uncontroversial, but human sociobiology has been energetically attacked as racist, sexist, hereditarian, social Darwinist, and so on. The core proposition of sociobiology, namely that behavior, like anatomy, has evolved by natural selection, and therefore has a genetic basis, should hardly be controversial.

The sociobiological model is *not* hereditarian; on the contrary, it is premised on the theorem that any phenotype is the product of the interaction of a genotype and an environment. Furthermore, it takes no *a priori* position on the relative importance of each, which is highly variable from species to species, and behavior to behavior within a species. Nor does sociobiology deny or minimize the importance of symbolic language and culture in humans. Human sociobiologists merely insist that human language and culture themselves evolved biologically, and hence are under some genetic influence, however remote, indirect, and flexible that influence might be. They only reject the extreme environmentalism, holding that humans are equally likely to learn anything with equal facility, and that cultural evolution is entirely unrelated to biological evolution.

A central tenet of sociobiology (as distinguished from the earlier ethology) is the emphasis on individual-level selection as against group selection. Organisms act to maximize their individual fitness (measured in terms of reproductive success), not to benefit the group or species, except insofar as group fitness coincides with individual fitness. Ultimately, the unit of natural selection is the gene rather than the organism, which is, evolutionarily speaking, a gene's way of making copies of itself, an idea popularized by Richard Dawkins.

What seems like altruistic behavior is explained in sociobiology as ultimate genetic selfishness. Beneficent behavior can increase an individual's fitness in two principal ways: through *nepotism* or kin selection, and through *reciprocity*. By helping kin reproduce (nepotism), an organism can maximize its own inclusive fitness, because kin share a certain percentage of their genes by common descent with ego (one-half between siblings and offspring; one-fourth between grandparents and grandchildren, uncles, and nephews; one-eighth between first cousins, etc.). Helping kin reproduce is thus an indirect way of reproducing one's own genes. Between kin, nepotism can be fitness-maximizing even if the behavior is not reciprocated, and indeed many forms of nepotism are highly asymmetrical (for example, between parents and offspring). Nepotism has been found to be a powerful explanatory principle of animal sociality, and is obviously also universal in human societies.

Between unrelated individuals, beneficent behavior can only increase fitness if it is reciprocated, though systems of reciprocity are always vulnerable to cheaters and freeloaders (who seek to avoid reciprocation). In nature, sexual reproduction is a widespread form of reciprocity between males and females; each sex benefits by being "nice" to the other, but nature will not select for unrequited love! Many of the most successful applications of sociobiology have been in the field of male and female strategies of reproduction and "parental investment," and in the resulting mating systems of different species. In humans, systems of reciprocity can be extremely complex and sophisticated, because human intelligence allows for extensive deceit, and hence the need to develop complex counter-strategies of foiling cheaters. The conditions for the evolution of reciprocal altruism in humans and other animals have been specified by Robert Trivers.

A neglected aspect of human sociality in sociobiology has been the role of coercion to promote intraspecific and intrasocietal parasitism. Clearly, with the rise of states in the last seven to eight thousand years of human evolution, many relationships are asymmetrical, in that some individuals use coercive means for appropriating resources to maximize their own fitness at the expense of others. Indeed, human societies have become increasingly coercive as they have grown in size and complexity.

Sociobiology should not be seen as a threat to the humanities and social sciences, but as an invitation to incorporate the study of human behavior in the theoretical mainstream of the neo-Darwinism synthesis, the dominant theory of biology for over a century. Its insights complement, specify, and enrich what we have long known about ourselves: that we are a product of both heredity and environment, and that nature and nurture are but the two sides of the same evolving coin.

Reading

Sociobiology and Behaviour by David Barash (Elsevier, 1981) is a lucid, nontechnical summary of the ideas of the main theoreticians of sociobiology.

Sociobiology, Sense and Nonsense by Michael Ruse (Reidel, 1979) is a thorough review of the scientific, ethical, and ideological arguments pro and con sociobiology, and of their human implications.

On Human Nature by Edward O. Wilson (Harvard, 1978) is a statement written for a lay audience, about the relationship between genes and culture, by the man who gave sociobiology its name. The book is scrutinized in *Human Nature and Biocultural Evolution* by J. Lopreato (Allen and Unwin, 1984).

See also: DARWINISM; ENVIRONMENTALISM; GENOTYPE; HEREDITARIANISM; PHENOTYPE; SOCIAL DARWINISM

Pierre L. van den Berghe

South Africa

During the 1970s and 1980s, South Africa's apartheid policy had become one of the great global moral issues, comparable to the debate about slavery or fascism. Apartheid, the Afrikaans word for separateness, denotes a system of imposed racial classification, residential segregation, and denationalization of the majority black population who are excluded from equal rights as citizens.

Among a population of thirty-six million, whites, 12 percent, occupy the top of the racial hierarchy; they are followed by 9 percent so-called Coloureds, as people of mixed origin but Afrikaner cultural background are called; 3 percent Indians, who were mostly imported as indentured laborers in Natal's sugar plantations in 1860; and, at the bottom, the 76 percent blacks, who were classified into nine different language groups with tribal homelands. The whites are divided between 60 percent Afrikaners, who control political power in the form of the state bureaucracy, and 40 percent English-speakers, who historically dominate a First World economy of sophisticated mining and manufacturing in a Third World country of racial poverty and exploitation.

The grossly unequal life chances based on a system of ethnic patronage under minority domination engendered an early tradition of resistance and dreams of liberation from colonial conquest, beginning with the formation of the African National Congress (ANC) in 1911. The opposition, however, has always been split and weakened by strategic differences about the use of violence, boycotts, and sanctions. Since the 1970s, emerging militant trade unions politicized labor relations in the absence of legal working class parties that preceded unionization in Europe and North America.

Faced with stronger adversaries and business imperatives, the Afrikaner government has attempted to modernize traditional apartheid and buy off dissent through selected cooption in a tricameral parliament. However, the rising costs of minority rule, the inside and outside pressure together with the end of the Cold War competition in Africa, finally provided the breakthrough for abolishing formal Apartheid and legalizing the banned liberation movements in 1990. Since then, on-and-off negotiations about political power sharing have, on the whole, replaced confrontation and racial polarization. Nonetheless, the post-Apartheid struggle for power among the contending groups has increased political violence and economic decline. Many doubt that the promised democracy can be realized without an expanding economy. In 1993 less than 10 percent of the new entrants to the market find employment in the formal economy. Rising crime among an alienated youth and disillusionment with the established political parties on all sides has underlined the urgent need for a political settlement as a precondition for economic recovery.

In the early 1990s, the nonracial social-democratic ANC and the tainted but powerful National Party moved toward a system of power sharing. Both major antagonists were too strong to be defeated by the opponent and too weak to rule alone. Both were heading towards an unwilling alliance.

However, all adversaries are part of an interdependent economy which holds a potentially buoyant future, given its developed infrastructure, human capital, and remarkable goodwill among the people of all South African segments. Unlike other plural societies with endemic communal conflicts, most South Africans share a common religion and consumer culture in which skin color was merely an artificial marker for exclusion. With the differential privileges gone in a common society with a federal constitution, proportional voting and a bill of rights but, above all, with imaginative efforts to deal with the legacy of apartheid, South Africa could develop into the exception in an increasingly bleak and marginalized continent.

Reading

The Opening of the Apartheid Mind: Options for the New South Africa by Heribert Adam and Kogila Moodley (University of California Press, 1993) discusses the reasons for the policy change in 1990 and the future of South Africa.

Power and Profit: Politics, Labour and Business in South Africa edited by Duncan Innes *et al.* (Oxford University Press, 1992) provides an overview of new issues in industrial and race relations, educational challenges and economic policies.

Segregation and Apartheid in Twentieth Century South Africa edited by William Beinhart and Saul Dubow (Routledge, 1995) is as comprehensive as its title suggests.

See also: APARTHEID; CONQUEST; EXPLOITATION; MANDELA

Kogila Moodley

Stereotype

Derived from the printers' term for a plate cast from a mould (originally from the Greek *stereos* for solid), a stereotype refers to a fixed mental impression. It is defined by Gordon Allport as: "an exaggerated belief associated with a category. Its function is to justify (rationalize) our conduct in relation to that category." This definition implies a discrepancy between an objectively ascertainable reality and a subjective perception of that reality.

In the field of race and ethnic relations, a stereotype is often defined as an overgeneralization about the behavior or other characteristics of members of particular groups. Ethnic and racial stereotypes can be positive or negative, although they are more frequently negative. Even ostensibly positive stereotypes can often imply a negative evaluation. Thus, to say that blacks are musical and have a good sense of rhythm comes close to the more openly negative stereotype that they are childish, and happy-go-lucky. Similarly, there is not much difference between saying that Jews show group solidarity and accusing them of being clannish.

It is, of course, a difficult empirical question to determine where a generalization about a group ceases to be an objective description of reality and becomes a stereotype. At the limit, almost any statement of group differences can be termed stereotypic, unless it is precisely stated in statistical terms and leaves the issue of causality open. Let us take the example of differential rates of violent crimes between racial groups. African Americans in the United States have conviction rates for crimes of violence that are five to ten times those of whites; they are greatly overrepresented in the prison population; and they also fall disproportionately victim to crimes of violence, frequently committed by other blacks. An unqualified statement such as "blacks are criminals" or "blacks are prone to violence" would generally be labeled a stereotype. "Blacks are more violent than whites," although somewhat qualified, could still be called stereotypic, as the statement implies an intrinsic racial difference in proneness to violence.

The more careful formulations above would probably escape the label of stereotype, because, even though they state the existence of statistical differences between racial groups, they leave open the question of causality. For example, the higher conviction rate of blacks could be due to hidden class differences rather than to racial differences, or to racial bias in the predominantly white police and courts in arresting and convicting blacks. Indeed, probably all of these factors are at work in producing the statistical outcome.

The relationship between stereotypes and prejudice is also of interest to social scientists. Racial or ethnic stereotypes are generally expressions of prejudice against the groups in question, but insofar as they often have a grain of truth, they may also have a measure of statistical validity, and, therefore, be moderately useful guides for predicting behavior. Since we benefit by trying to predict the behavior of others, and since we all have to rely, for simplicity's sake, on rough and ready categories such as age, sex, class, ethnic group, religion, and the like, implicit stereotypes form the basis of much social life. Such stereotypes do not necessarily reflect deeply ingrained prejudices.

Thus, for example, we know that crimes of violence in the United States are statistically correlated not only with race, but also with age, class, sex, time of day, and urban residence. The old lady who walks past a group of young, black, working-class men, late at night, in a street in Harlem is not necessarily a racial bigot if she feels a twitch of apprehension. She merely applies pragmatic formulas for survival. She probably *is* more at risk in such a situation than say, at a church picnic. That she is aware of the difference is a testimony to her common sense, not to her racism, though she *may* be a racist.

Because of the difficulty of ascertaining the gap between the objective reality and the subjective perception thereof, the concept of stereotype is not a useful scientific tool in the analysis of behavior, nor has it been used much in the last twenty years.

Reading
Stereotype Accuracy edited by Yueh-Ting Lee (American Psychological Association, 1995) has an opening chapter which traces the history of stereotypes and includes definitions.
Black Looks by Bell Hooks (South End Press, 1992) exposes the ways in which crude racist representations in advertising, film, popular music, and television reinforce white supremacist thought in the United States.
The Nature of Prejudice by Gordon W. Allport (Addison-Wesley, 1954) is a standard text on problems of prejudice, discrimination, and stereotypes by an American social psychologist.

See also: PREJUDICE; RACIAL DISCRIMINATION; SCAPEGOAT; XENOPHOBIA

Pierre L. van den Berghe

Subaltern

Originally a sixteenth-century military term meaning of junior rank (from the Latin *sub*, below and *alternus*, alternate), this has gained currency principally through the work of Gayatri Spivak and revolves around the questions of whether the experience of oppression confers special jurisdiction over the right to speak about oppression and whether a representation of this is ever possible in a discourse in which subaltern groups are already "spoken for." Her "Can the subaltern speak?" questioned the credibility of the subaltern woman as a subject already represented as mute or ignored; her speech is, by definition, non-speech. Speech, in this conception, is not so much about the abilities of subaltern groups to articulate as the reception they are afforded.

A journal *Subaltern Studies* (published by Oxford University Press) has been devoted to trying "to understand the consciousness that informed and still informs political actions taken by subaltern classes on their own, independently of any elite initiatives," as Dipesh Chakrabarty puts it in the discussion to volume four (1985) of the journal. "Subalternaity" refers to the "composite culture of resistance to and acceptance of domination and hierarchy."

Part of this overall project, according to Spivak, is to disclose whiteness as a culturally constructed ethnic identity – constructed, that is, in contradistinction to subaltern minorities who have been subjugated, or silenced. The privileged position of the White Male in relation to subaltern groups has been "naturalized" to the point of invisibility. Yet the position of centrality is made possible by the denial of a voice to Others.

Reading
"Can the subaltern speak?" by Gayatri C. Spivak in *Marxism and the Interpretation of Culture* edited by Cary Nelson and Lawrence Grossberg (University of Illinois Press, 1987) is the influential argument cited above.
"Gayatri Spivak on the politics of the subaltern" features Spivak in an interview with Howard Winant (*Socialist Review*, vol. 20, no. 3, July–September, 1990).
The Postcolonial Critic: Interviews, Strategies, Dialogues by Gayatri Spivak (Routledge, 1990) edited by Sarah Harasyan is a guide to Spivak's thoughts.

See also: COLONIAL DISCOURSE; DIASPORA; HYBRIDITY; OTHERS; POSTCOLONIAL

Ellis Cashmore

Swann report

An official British government report published in 1985 as "Education for All," this advocated the development of a universalistic conception of multicultural education; an educational ideology, that is, which implicated all schools, irrespective of their geographical location, age-range or the ethnicity of their staff or pupils. Alongside this conviction, the Swann report, as it was commonly known, provided more up-to-date data on the relationship between ethnicity and educational performance (while retaining the limited research paradigm found in its precursor, the Rampton report 1981). It differed from this in the more circumspect view it provided of racism as a variable in the educational experiences of black children in British schools.

It shared with the Rampton report a failure to attract significant support for its recommendations from central government. Its publication was followed by the distribution of a limited amount of funding into in-service education and, through the provision of Educational Support Grants (ESG), some incentive for schools serving predominantly white populations to engage in some version of multicultural education.

In retrospect, and despite the wholly justified criticism of the Swann report, the years 1985–88 now appear almost as the halcyon days of multicultural (even antiracist) education in Britain. The report provided a context for debate, seminars, conferences, and publications on this educational orthodoxy. Although these often generated more heat than light, they helped to ensure that strategies to expedite educational changes linked to social justice concerns suffused initial and in-service teacher education, administrative decision-making and routine practice on the chalk-face.

The passing of the Education Reform Act (ERA) 1988 sounded the death knell for many of these initiatives, however. With the introduction of the National (some say Nationalistic) Curriculum, school-based financial management, Grant-Maintained schools, City Technology colleges, and the correlative weakening of Local Education Authorities, the clarion-call of "Education for All" now sounds more like a faint whisper in the wilderness. The effect of the ERA and associated legislation has been to resuscitate assimilationist conceptions education in contemporary Britain. Universalistic notions of multicultural education, which had a tenuous foothold in the mid-1980s, were dislodged.

Reading
Education, Racism and Reform by Barry Troyna and Bruce Carrington (Routledge, 1990) provides an overview of the ideological and policy developments on "race" and education in Britain. It includes a detailed analysis of both Rampton and Swann reports.
Education for All edited by Gajendra Verma (Falmer, 1989) includes a series of essays which appraise the significance of the Swann report in giving legitimacy to cultural pluralist versions of education.
Racism and Education: Research Perspectives by Barry Troyna (Open University Press, 1993) looks at the role of education in the legitimation and reproduction of racial inequality. It includes chapters assessing the contribution of the Swann report and the 1988 ERA to the development of multicultural and antiracist education.
Racism and Antiracism in Real Schools (Open University Press, 1995) is by David Gillborn. It provides an insight into how schools responded to race-related matters despite the onslaught of the British Conservative government in the 1990s.

See also: AFRICAN-CARIBBEANS IN BRITAIN; ASIANS IN BRITAIN; EDUCATION AND CULTURAL DIVERSITY; UNDERACHIEVEMENT

Barry Troyna

T

Third World

The origin of this term is generally attributed to Alfred Sauvy who, writing in *L'Observateur* in 1952, used the phrase *le tiers monde* to describe nations ridding themselves of colonialism in a manner similar to the struggle of commoners (the Third Estate) to overcome the domination of the nobility and clergy during the French Revolution. Most Third World countries have a past history of colonial domination and have sought a collective identity which disassociates them politically from either of the two power blocs, Soviet and Western-capitalist. The term also has an economic ambience, implying collectively those countries which through the colonial legacy are exploitatively located in the international economy and which generally lag behind in industrial development. Although the definitional criteria are somewhat different, other terms such as "the South" (as opposed to "the North") and "the developing world" are frequently used with the same connotations and often used interchangeably with "the Third World" in the same texts.

As postcolonial states, most Third World countries have economies historically rooted in a system that tapped their natural wealth and expropriated it for the benefits of colonial powers, their function being to provide raw materials, cheap labor, and markets for developing industrialization elsewhere. Political independence in the aftermath of World War II has done little to change the fundamental characteristics of this system, in which the mechanisms of multinational trade and investment have maintained a neocolonial economic dependency within a framework of ostensible political independence. In spite of certain successes by Third World countries in producing dynamic economies (largely in East Asia) or in controlling primary production (e.g. Opec), Third World countries have generally found themselves in a descending spiral of disadvantaged location in the international economic system, thus creating an "international debt crisis" which currently concerns not only themselves but the entire international monetary system. This situation provides regrettable confirmation of President Nyerere's acerbic definition of the Third World as the "Trade Union of the Poor."

The analysis of the Third World's location in a global system of economic exploitation has been largely informed by the works of political economy theorists working within "dependency" and "world systems" paradigms, and by neoclassical economics. While these approaches have undoubtedly been seminal and productive, they have also had the tendency to marginalize the importance of Third World state structures by implying that they have little room for autonomous action. This implication is now being challenged by a Third World scholarship which sees the creation of endogenously derived integrative socioeconomic structures as being a necessary component in economic development. From this perspective the ethnic factor frequently becomes an important variable since many Third World states are ethnically heterogeneous, based as they are on the arbitrary partitions of colonialism. For these polyethnic states the goal of making the state a nation with structures which encourage integrated political and economic participation is a critically central issue. The locus for the resolution of this issue lies largely within Third World state structures themselves and the degree to which this objective is achieved will determine in large part their ability to overcome the dependency dimensions of their current international status.

Reading
The Third World, 2nd edition, by Peter Worsley (Weidenfeld and Nicolson, 1977) is an influential examination of the issues in a sociological perspective.
Third World Cities in Global Perspective by David A. Smith (Westview, 1995) focuses on global inequality and dependency as a way of exploring city growth in the Third World.
Third Worlds: The Politics of the Middle East and Africa edited by Heather Deegan (Routledge, 1996) argues that grouping the Middle East and Africa as the "Third World" has concealed contrasts – though there are historical and cultural similarities.

See also: DEVELOPMENT; COLONIALISM; CONQUEST; POWER
Marshall Murphree

Thomas, Clarence (1948–   )

On 1 November 1991, the commission of Clarence Thomas to sit as an associate justice of the United States Supreme Court was received. With that appointment, Clarence Thomas became only the second racial minority member to sit on the highest court in the United States. And with that appointment, one of the most controversial, if not the most controversial, nominations to the Supreme Court came to an end.

An African American born in poverty and raised in the segregated

South, Thomas was a judge of the United States Court of Appeals for the District of Columbia, having taken the seat held by the equally controversial Judge Robert Bork only eighteen months earlier, at the time of his nomination. The nomination was made by a Republican President, who did not support the 1964 Civil Rights Act and who, in vetoing the 1990 Civil Rights Act, became at that time the only president in the history of the United States to veto a civil rights bill. The nominee, a conservative Republican who built his professional reputation on a steady, often acerbic barrage of criticisms of civil rights leaders and civil rights programs (such as affirmative action), was presented to the nation as "the most qualified" person to replace the legendary civil rights lawyer and liberal justice, Thurgood Marshall. Also ironic and controversial was the fact that Justice Thomas personally benefited from affirmative action programs throughout his scholastic and professional life.

Unprecedentedly, Justice Thomas appeared before the Senate Judiciary Committee twice. The first appearance centered on routine questions of judicial temperament and constitutional interpretation, including the nominee's position on the legality of abortion and the doctrine of "nature rights." During these hearings, the nominee made the famous statement that he never discussed with anyone his personal opinion on the famous abortion case *Roe v. Wade*.

About a week after these hearings ended but before the Committee voted on the nomination, the Committee was called back into session to consider formally a charge of sexual harassment levied against Thomas by a well-respected African-American woman law professor, Anita Hill. In his most effective performance during the confirmation hearings, Justice Thomas numbed the Democratic senators, all of whom were white and liberal, by accusing them of participating in a "high-tech lynching."

Here, the racial ironies were unmistakable. An African American who has strongly criticized civil rights leaders for crying racism ignores his own advice when under fire – he plays the race card and it comes up aces. Also, the most ardent supporters of civil rights in the Senate, in front of millions of African Americans watching the proceedings on television, were made to look like hooded night riders from a bygone era. Finally, the sexual harassment charge brought against Justice Thomas was made by a member of his own race who not only had a strong character but also shared much of his political philosophy, including displeasure over the failed Supreme Court nomination of Judge Robert Bork. For some thirty-three hours, Americans were riveted to their television sets watching the hearings, which in addition to the testimony of Justice Thomas and Professor Hill, included the testimony of twenty character witnesses for both sides. In the end, both the Judiciary Committee and the Senate voted to confirm Justice Thomas by the slimmest margin ever.

Reading

"The legacy of doubt: treatment of sex and race in the Hill-Thomas hearings," by Adrienne D. Davis and Stephanie M. Wildman, *Southern California Law Review*, 65 (1992) 1367–91, is a good overview of the Thomas confirmation.

"gender, race, and the politics of supreme court appointments: the import of the Anita Hill/Clarence Thomas hearings," *Southern California Law Review*, 65 (1992): 1279–1582, is the most comprehensive collection of analyses of the nomination and confirmation hearings, including writings by Anita Hill and dozens of other scholars, many of whom were directly involved in the hearings.

Advice and Consent: Clarence Thomas, Robert Bork, and the Intriguing History of the Supreme Court's Nomination Battles (National Press, 1992) by Paul Simon is a historical perspective of recent controversial Supreme Court nominations by a senior member of the Senate Judiciary Committee.

African American Women Speak Out on Anita Hill–Clarence Thomas edited by Geneva Smitherman (Wayne State University Press, 1995) collects the perspectives of black women scholars and writers.

See also: BLACK BOURGEOISIE; CONSERVATISM; EMPOWERMENT

Roy L. Brooks

Tokenism

As unofficial racial policy or practice in many arenas, tokenism, has been described and analyzed by the media and the academic community. Scholarly works that have described various facets of tokenism as a political resource of powerful white interests, both in the public and private arena in the United States include Ira Katznelson, Benhamin Quarles and Peter Bachrach, and Morton Baratz. The historical work that gave rise to the popular term "Uncle Tom," is, of course, Harriet Beecher Stowe's *Uncle Tom's Cabin*.

Tokenism is usually considered a pejorative term similar to "Uncle Tom," used by many in the black community, but also others to describe a social situation where blacks, or other people of color, are utilized only for "display" purposes. Both Martin Luther King, Jr. and Malcolm X used both terms, tokenism and Uncle Tom, to describe a major obstacle to racial progress in the United States. In one of his speeches in 1964, "Ballots or Bullets," for instance, Malcolm X stated that:

Just as the slavemaster of that day used Tom, the house Negro, to keep the field Negroes in check, the same old slavemaster today has Negroes who are nothing but modern Uncle Toms, twentieth century Uncle Toms, to keep you and me in check, to keep us under control, keep us passive and peaceful and non-violent.

In a featured *New York Times Magazine* article in June 1967 titled, "MLK Defines Black Power," a similar statement was made by Martin Luther King, Jr., about a sector of negro leadership that had allowed itself to become the representative of white power structures, rather than the masses of negroes.

What tokenism suggests is that the presence of individual blacks who may be prominent, or in prominent positions, in white institutional settings does not necessarily indicate that: a) such individuals perform significant or influential roles beneficial to the advancement of blacks as a group; or b) that the presence of such individuals reflects social parity between blacks as a group, and whites in U.S. society.

The function of tokenism as a social phenomenon is to suggest to observers that the rhetoric of racial equality is being adhered to by powerful interests; but this kind of arrangement is not inconsistent with the existence of racial hierarchy where the agendas of powerful white interests, rather than racial or social parity, continue to be the dominant ones. As racial policy or practice, tokenism is a way of neutralizing efforts to integrate fully and institutionalize the presence of blacks and other people of color into social and cultural settings where whites continue to have all the power to make and carry out important decisions.

Reading
Black Men, White Cities, by Ira Katznelson (Oxford University Press, 1973) analyzes the usefulness of tokenism to white society.
Power and Poverty: Theory and Practice by Peter Bachrach and Morton Baratz (Oxford University Press, 1970) notes the relevance of tokenism to the status quo.
The Negro in Making of America by Benjamin Quarles (Collier, 1987) complements the above two in observing the social functions of tokenism.

See also: BLACK BOURGEOISIE; MYRDAL; PATERNALISM; THOMAS

James Jennings

U

Uncle Tom
See TOKENISM

Underachievement
This refers to a persistent pattern in which one group does less well than might be reasonably expected scholastically. It is premised on the ideological notion of schooling as a good thing and tenacious and highly serviceable in modern-day society. It derives from the liberal-democratic assumption that education is the main instrument of occupational and social mobility. Underpinning this is the conviction that the possession of formal educational credentials plays a determining role in the distribution of future life chances. Without these credentials, it is commonly assumed that a person completing secondary education is unlikely to find the sort of job to which she or he aspires, or indeed any job.

Britain's 1944 Education Act was aimed at ensuring that working-class girls and boys had as equal an opportunity of obtaining secondary education as their middle-class counterparts. Nonetheless, research soon revealed that despite obtaining equality of access working-class boys continued to perform less well than their middle-class peers. This concern prompted a new policy in the mid-1960s with the dissolution of the tripartite system of secondary education and the establishment of comprehensive secondary schools. The imperative for this action was clear: to repair the meritocratic credibility of schools by ensuring that all pupils, irrespective of background, be given an equal opportunity to develop their intellectual potential to the full through unimpaired access to educational institutions and the credentials they offer. In Britain, as in other Western capitalist societies, equality of opportunity is the organizing principle of state education.

Despite the introduction of comprehensive schooling and related initiatives, there remained a significant difference in the academic achievement levels of pupils from working-class and middle-class backgrounds. Now, insofar as this pattern is rarely explained in terms of innate intellectual differences between these two social groups, working-class pupils are considered to be formally "underachieving," that is to say, unlike their middle-class peers they are not realizing their full intellectual potential. A group cannot underachieve if its intellectual and attainment levels have been genetically determined to be lower than the group to which it is being compared. On this view, then, the causes of this relatively lower academic performance lay elsewhere. One of the most popular explanations for this trend is that working-class pupils come from culturally deprived backgrounds and that schools must provide a compensating environment in order to increase their academic performance: hence, compensatory education initiatives. Marxists reject this pathological interpretation, preferring instead to locate the causes of underachievement in the institutional structures of society and their relationship to the education system. Different again is the view that microprocesses of school play the most significant part in this scenario. Here it is argued that teachers perpetuate differential patterns of achievement through their expectations and treatment of working-class pupils. These pupils are stereotyped as low achievers and are offered educational opportunities in accordance with these assessments.

A similar range of explanations has been adduced to account for the underachievement of pupils of African-Caribbean origin in British schools. Ever since the early 1960s, research has reported a strong trend toward the lower academic performance of these pupils compared to their white and South Asian pupils. The early and optimistic prognosis that this was a transient phenomenon which derived largely from the pupils' newness in the British educational system and would therefore diminish with the passage of time, was no longer tenable in the late 1970s and the early 1980s. In a range of research investigations, including those conducted under the auspices of the Rampton and Swann committees, pupils of African-Caribbean origin along with children from Bangladeshi backgrounds were identified as "underachievers." That is, performing less well in public examinations than pupils from other ethnic groups.

Of course, certain educationalists and psychologists, such as Arthur Jensen and Hans Eysenck, argue for the lower innate intellect of black pupils. But for reasons already spelt out, those who adhere to this "scientific racism" argument cannot legitimately typify these pupils as "underachievers." What is more, these arguments have been thoroughly devalued and discredited by evidence which shows that the difference in IQ (in itself a highly dubious measurement) within populations is greater than the difference in average between populations.

What the specific causes of this trend are is a question that has tantalized educationalists for many years, and the answer remains elusive. At the same time, many researchers have been so over-whelmingly concerned with establishing differences, or otherwise, along ethnic lines that they have tended to overlook the significant influence of social class background and gender on performance levels. Black pupils in Britain come largely from working-class famil-ies and it has been clearly established that family background has a profoundly moderating effect on school performance levels. Could it be that "West Indian underachievement" is a misnomer and that if the research data were standardized to take into account class and gender backgrounds the results would show few significant dif-ferences between black pupils and their white, working-class counterparts?

Perhaps this obsession with achievement in public examinations is misplaced, anyway. While, traditionally, researchers and policy-makers have concentrated their attention on "who gets what," they have ignored the equally important matter: "who goes where – and why?" Put simply, the debate about "underachievement," especially in relation to ethnicity, has only focused on the tip of the iceberg; namely, observable outcomes from schooling. Those researchers who have taken the trouble to dive beneath the surface and attempt to tease out those decisions and processes that influence the selec-tion and allocation of pupils into examination and nonexamination classes have revealed a range of insidious patterns which, at the very least, need to be taken seriously in this debate. Is there a tendency for teachers to distract pupils of African-Caribbean origin away from academic subjects in favor of developing what they per-ceive as innate sporting prowess? Are pupils whose main home language is not English regarded as less intellectually capable than their peers whose main language at home and school is English? Are African-Caribbean pupils discouraged from competing in high-status examinations because their teachers reckon they have diffi-culty in concentration and perseverance, an "attitude problem," in other words?

Research, based largely on ethnographic methods, has belatedly looked at these and related matters suggesting that "underrated" may be a more appropriate nomenclature than "underachiever."

Reading
The Bell Curve: Intelligence and Class Structure in American Life (Free Press 1994) is the controversial text in which Richard J. Herrnstein and Charles Murray unabashedly assert that scientific evidence demonstrates

the existence of genetically based differences in intelligence among social classes and ethnic groups.

The Science and Politics of Racial Research (University of Illinois Press 1994) is William H. Tucker's exposé of the political and ideological motivations and intentions of those who consider that the "innate inferiority of a race" is still a "proper scientific question."

"Underachievement: a case of conceptual confusion" by Ian Plewis in the *British Educational Research Journal* (vol. 17, no. 4, 1991) lays bare some of the vagueness and disarray associated with the use of the concept in research and may be read with *"Race," Ethnicity and Education* by David Gillborn (Unwin Hyman, 1990) which provides an original and illuminating insight into the complex relationship between ethnicity, education, and achievement.

British Educational Research Journal (vol. 19, no. 2, 1993) includes a debate between Barry Troyna and Roger Gomm about how best to interpret in-school processes governing the selection and allocation of ethnic minority pupils to examination groups.

See also: EDUCATION AND CULTURAL DIVERSITY; INTELLIGENCE AND RACE; MARXISM AND RACISM; SWANN REPORT

Barry Troyna

Underclass

The concept of underclass has been used by sociologists to describe the bottom stratum of complex societies, especially in the urban context. Underclass refers to a heterogeneous group, below the stably employed working class, which is regarded as beyond the pale of "respectable" society. It includes such social categories as the chronically unemployed, vagrants or transients, the criminal "underground," some occupational groups considered defiling or immoral (e.g. prostitutes), and sometimes, some despised outcaste groups which may be either ethnically or racially defined (e.g. gypsies in Europe, untouchables in India, the Burakumin of Japan, or "ghetto blacks" in the United States).

Near synonyms for underclass are *Lumpenproletariat*, subproletariat, pariahs, and outcaste groups. Each of these terms has special connotations, and tends to be used by social scientists of different ideological persuasions. Thus, *Lumpenproletariat* is generally used by Marxists, and refers more to the economic dimensions of status, while pariahs refers more to the moral devaluation of the status group and is used more by liberal scholars. Underclass is probably the most neutral term.

A key feature of the underclass in modern postindustrial societies is its marginality to the system of production, and its relative redundancy to it. In previous periods of industrialization the bulk of the urban working class consisted of lowly trained and, therefore, interchangeable factory operatives, and the unemployed were a reserve army of the proletariat used to break strikes, keep wages low, and perpetuate the exploitation of the working class as a whole. With the emergence of the postindustrial, social democratic welfare states of Western Europe, Australia, and North America, an increasingly sharp line has been drawn between a stable, secure, working class protected by trade unionism and increasingly employed in skilled service occupations, and an unstable, under-employed underclass subsisting on a mixture of welfare payments and an extralegal underground economy (drug traffic, gambling, prostitution, illegal sweat-shop labor, and so on).

The low skill level of the modern underclass in relation to the increasingly high demands for skilled labor in the mainstream econ-omy combines with the dependency syndrome created by the welfare system to perpetuate the marginality and the superfluity of the underclass. In societies like Britain and the United States, where a substantial sector of the underclass is also racially stigmatized and discriminated against, the self-perpetuation of the urban underclass is further aggravated by racism.

Illegal immigration, as among Hispanics and Asians in the United States, complicates the problem yet more, by favouring the super-exploitation of workers whose illegality excludes them from normal legal protection in wages, employment, and social benefits. An additional factor is the rising number of urban children raised by single parents (overwhelmingly mothers) who, in addition to handi-caps of racism and lack of skills, are further marginalized in the system of production by sexual discrimination and their parental responsibilities. For example, an estimated 50 percent of black children in the United States are raised in single-parent families. Many of them inherit underclass status, and are condemned to forming the hardcore of the unemployed ghetto youth. Currently some 40 percent of young urban blacks are chronically unemployed, four times the national average, and subsist largely on welfare and on illegal or fringe activities. The economic dependency of the single mother is often in part the *creation* of the welfare system. The absence of a resident adult male is often a necessary test of qualifi-cation for welfare; this, in turn, encourages male desertion and perpetuates the welfare mother syndrome in the underclass.

Reading
The Truly Disadvantaged by William J. Wilson (University of Chicago
   Press, 1987) is an early work on the analysis of underclass formation.
Social Inequality, edited by André Béteille (Penguin, 1969) is a collection

of classic articles, both theoretical and empirical, covering many parts of the world.

The Other America by Michael Harrington (Macmillan, 1962) remains the most influential book in the "discovery" of the American underclass.

See also: CASTE; DISADVANTAGE; EMPOWERMENT; EXPLOITATION

Pierre L. van den Berghe

UNESCO

The United Nations Educational, Scientific, and Cultural Organization (UNESCO) is a specialized agency of the United Nations which was established in 1946 and has its headquarters in Paris. The preamble to its constitution declares that "the great and terrible war which has now ended was a war made possible by the denial of the democratic principles of the dignity, equality and mutual respect of men, and by the propagation, in their place, through ignorance and prejudice, of the doctrine of the inequality of men and races." In this spirit, the Organization's General Conference (consisting of the representatives of some fifty states members) in 1950 instructed the Director-General "to study and collect scientific materials concerning questions of race; to give wide diffusion to the scientific information collected; to prepare an educational campaign based on this information."

Accordingly, UNESCO convened a meeting of specialists from a variety of disciplines who drew up a "Statement on Race," which was published in 1950. Some of its contentions, and some of the terms used, were much criticized, especially by physical anthropologists and geneticists. Many maintained that the statement confused race as a biological fact with race as a social phenomenon. So UNESCO convened a second meeting which drew up the "Statement of the Nature of Race and Race Differences" of 1951. As it was thought important to avoid any suggestion that this was an authoritative manifesto embodying the last word on the race question, this statement was submitted for comment to a large number of anthropologists and geneticists. The resulting opinions were assembled and presented in the booklet *The Race Concept: Results of an Inquiry*, of 1953. In 1964, a further meeting of specialists was arranged to bring up to date and complete the 1951 declaration. This produced the *Proposals on the Biological Aspects of Race* (1964). A fourth *Statement on Race and Racial Prejudice* was prepared by a committee of experts in 1967. It included several propositions on the nature of racism, a concept that had not previously featured in UNESCO statements. There is some variation in the endorsement of the forstatements by the participants. Only the 1964 statement was described as a text representing the unanimous agreement of those taking part.

In implementation of its mandate, UNESCO commissioned and published (from 1951) a set of short studies in the series *The Race Question in Modern Science* followed by other series, *The Race Question in Modern Thought* (stating the positions of the major religions), and *Race and Society*. It also commissioned pioneering research on racial distinctions in Latin American societies. In more recent times it has been collaborating with the United Nations Human Rights Center in the preparation of teaching materials which discuss racial discrimination in a human rights context. This is part of its continuing Major Program XII concerned with the elimination of prejudice, intolerance, and racism.

A particularly important development was the unanimous adoption in 1960 by the General Conference of the *Convention Against Discrimination in Education*. This defines discrimination and binds states parties to undertake various measures to eliminate and prevent it. The convention was followed in 1978 by the equally important *Declaration on Race and Racial Prejudice* adopted and proclaimed by the General Conference in 1978. After recalling the four statements mentioned above, it begins in Article 1:

> All human beings belong to a single species and are descended from a common stock. They are born equal in dignity and rights and all form an integral part of humanity.

> All individuals and groups have the right to be different, to consider themselves as different and to be regarded as such. However, the diversity of lifestyles and the right to be different may not, in any circumstances, serve as a pretext for racial prejudice.

In the event of a state's being involved in a case before the International Court of Justice, or any other international tribunal, its adoption of the UNESCO Convention of Declaration could be cited as a test of its policies, but UNESCO's measures for enforcing compliance with such instruments are weaker than those of the United Nations International Convention on the Elimination of All Forms of Racial Discrimination.

Reading
Four Statements on the Race Question (Paris: UNESCO, 1969) are the four documents cited above.

The Retreat of Scientific Racism by Elazar Barkan (Cambridge University Press, 1992) has an especially relevant epilogue, pages 341–46.

See also: ENVIRONMENTALISM; HEREDITARIANISM; RACE; UNITED NATIONS

Michael Banton

United Nations

The main source and authority for international action against racial discrimination is the United Nations (UN) Charter which declares in article 55 that the UN shall promote "universal respect for, and observance of, human rights and fundamental freedoms for all without discrimination as to race, sex, language, or religion." The UN includes a variety of bodies with separate but sometimes overlapping functions with respect to human rights: the General Assembly, the Security Council, the Economic and Social Council (with its subsidiary, the Commission on Human Rights), the Trusteeship Council, the treaty-monitoring bodies and the specialized agencies, including the International Labor Organization (an autonomous institution founded in 1919), and UNESCO.

The Commission on Human Rights has its own subsidiary, the Subcommission on Prevention of Discrimination and Protection of Minorities. Responding to anti-semitic incidents in Europe in 1959, and to concerns about racist regimes in southern Africa, the Subcommission took steps that resulted in 1963 in the General Assembly's adoption of the UN Declaration on the Elimination of All Forms of Racial Discrimination and the similarly titled Convention two years later. In 1965 also it proclaimed that 21 March (the anniversary of the Sharpeville massacre in South Africa) should be observed as the International Day for the Elimination of Racial Discrimination. Later it designated 1971 as "International Year for Action to Combat Racism and Racial Discrimination," a step followed by making 1973–83 a "Decade for Action to Combat Racism and Racial Discrimination." It was in this connection that in 1975 the General Assembly adopted, by 72 votes to 35, resolution 3379 which "determines that Zionism is a form of racism and racial discrimination." On 16 December 1992 draft resolution A/46/L.47 was adopted by 111 votes to 25 according to which the General Assembly revoked the previous resolution.

The General Assembly has proclaimed a Third Decade to Combat Racism and Racial Discrimination starting in 1993, but relatively little has been done to implement this plan of activities because money has been short. As a separate measure, the UN Commission on Human Rights in 1993 decided to appoint a special rapporteur "on contemporary forms of racism, racial discrimination and xenophobia and related intolerance." The appointment went to a judge of the constitutional court in Benin. The Commission's resolution emphasized "manifestations occurring particularly in developed countries."

In the following year, it requested him to examine "contemporary forms of racism, racial discrimination, and forms of discrimination against Blacks, Arabs, and Muslims, xenophobia, negrophobia, anti-semitism, and related intolerance, as well as governmental measures to overcome them." The list of victim groups is an indication of the political forces behind decisions of this kind. This was also the first occasion on which such a resolution mentioned anti-semitism.

Working groups of the Subcommission have prepared a draft Universal Declaration on Indigenous Rights and another on the Rights of Persons belonging to National, Ethnic, Religious and Linguistic Minorities. The latter was adopted by the General Assembly proclaimed the International Decade of the World's Indigenous Peoples, starting December 1994, while the proposal to create a permanent forum for indigenous people in the UN continues to make progress. It should also be noted that a Convention on the Rights of All Migrant Workers and Members of their Families was adopted in 1991.

Reading
International Action Against Racial Discrimination by Michael Banton (Oxford University Press, 1996) has details of the initiative enacted.
United Nations Action in the Field of Human Rights (New York, United Nations Sales No. E.88.XIV.2).

See also: INTERNATIONAL CONVENTION; NATIVE PEOPLES; UNESCO; XENOPHOBIA; ZIONISM

Michael Banton

V

Volk

The word corresponding to "people," which in German and related languages is applied to cultural groups and would-be nations. In German, it implies much more than "people" does in English. Since the growth of the Romantic movement from the late eighteenth century, it has signified the union of a group of people with a transcendent "essence." The essence was given different names, like "nature," "cosmos," "mythos," but in each instance it represented the source of the individual's creativity and his unity with other members of the Volk. From it there stemmed a strain in German thought which diverged from traditional Western nationalism and religion. The Volk mediated between the isolated individual, alienated by the forces of modern society, and the universe. In *Mein Kampf*, Adolf Hitler criticized the naiveté of the Volkists but made use of their ideas to describe his vision of a racially powerful and united Germany.

A derived word, Herrenvolk, means a "master-people" and has been used by Pierre van den Berghe to characterize "herrenvolk egalitarianism" and "herrenvolk democracy." In white supremacist societies such as those of southern Africa after European conquest, a white minority have been the masters of a larger black population. To preserve their privileged position the whites needed to maintain a front of solidarity, and this required the cultivation of trust and sentiments of equality within their own group. These attitudes contrasted with the assumption of inequality in their dealings with blacks.

Reading

The Scientific Origins of National Socialism by Daniel Gasman (Macdonald, London and Elsevier, New York, 1971).

South Africa: A Study in Conflict by Pierre van den Berghe (Wesleyan University Press, 1965).

Introduction to Race Relations, 2nd edition, by Ellis Cashmore and B. Troyna (Falmer Press, 1990) looks at the interpenetration of concepts such as *Volk* and *Germanen* in the development of national socialist philosophy.

See also: ARYAN; CHAMBERLAIN; GOBINEAU; HAECKEL; LANGUAGE, RACE
AND ETHNICITY; RACE

Michael Banton

W

White flight

This term implies disillusionment with, even resentment of, social change. It refers to the movement of whites from neighborhoods and schools that have experienced recent changes in their ethnic composition. The nature of this change is sometimes voluntaristic – the pursuit of employment, perhaps, or cheap housing. It might also be contrived, however, stemming from a general commitment to what is known as the contact hypothesis. This is the belief that direct contact between whites and blacks will lessen the formers' fears about the latters' cultures and lifestyles, attenuate racial prejudice, and enhance the likelihood of integration, racial harmony, and social stability.

Social change along these lines derives from various sources. These include the policies of national governments. For instance, changes in the ethnic population of national states and particular regions within them might derive from alterations in the state's immigration policies. They might also stem from more localized initiatives. The determination, perhaps, of local government to ensure that residential areas and their schools comprise a more heterogeneous ethnic character. Another starting point might be the judiciary. In the United States the desegregation of schools gained momentum after 1954 when, in the *Brown v. Board of Education, Topeka, Kansas* case, the Supreme Court ruled that segregated education was unconstitutional.

White flight, then, is a sudden or gradual response to both *de jure* and *de facto* desegregation. Above all, it exemplifies what some white citizens might perceive as their own political inefficacy. Their inability, in other words, to stem the flow of black settlement in their neighborhoods or distract the state from its objective of achieving racial integration. Seen from this perspective, the state's determination to attain the goal of integration is pursued at the expense of the safety of their neighborhoods and schools, the retention of their particular (and traditional) identities, and the sanctity of their cultures and values. In both the United States and Britain, populist alarm at these state-orchestrated maneuvers to contrive a semblance of "racial balance" in neighborhoods and schools has often found a sympathetic ear in respective legislatures. In 1966, Ronald Reagan came to power in California partly on the strength of his committed opposition to the "rioters" in the Watts district of Los Angeles. In Britain, "white flight" was given implicit endorsement and legitimacy by Baroness Hooper, then the Conservative government's spokesperson for education in the House of Lords. In her support of parental choice of schools for their children, a key ideological and policy theme in the 1988 Education Reform Act, Baroness Hooper insisted that the Conservatives did "did not wish to circumscribe that choice in any way." Baroness Hooper's pronouncement on the preeminence of parental choice prefigured what some have seen as the state's official benediction for white flight in the education system.

In 1987, Ms. Jenny Carney wrote to the Local Education Authority (LEA) of the British County of Cleveland requesting that it arrange for her daughter, Katrice, to be transferred from her multiracial, infants school in Middlesbrough to one "where there will be the majority of white children." Ms. Carney's dissatisfaction with her daughter's school centered on its commitment to a multiracial and multifaith education. "I don't think it's right when she comes homes singing in Pakistani," she informed the LEA; "I know they only learn three Pakistani songs, but I just don't want her to learn this language."

While acceding to Ms. Carney's request, the LEA recognized that it was caught between two pieces of legislation which offered contradictory guidance on this matter. On the one hand, section 18 of the 1976 Race Relations Act states that "it is unlawful for an LEA, in carrying out its functions under the Education Acts, to do any acts which constitute discrimination." By recognizing that Ms. Carney's request was influenced by the perceived racial characteristics of the school's pupil population, Cleveland was concerned that it had violated this section of the Act and broken the law. On the other hand, section 6 of the 1980 Education Act places upon LEAs a duty to comply with parental preferences as to choice of school, subject to certain exceptions, which were inapplicable here. According to the Commission for Racial Equality, Cleveland had breached the law; but it had not according to the then Secretary for State for Education, John MacGregor who viewed the 1980 Education Act as sacrosanct on the matter of parental choice. Against this background, the CRE sought a judicial review against Cleveland and the Secretary of State.

In October 1991, Mr. Justice Macpherson resolved in favor of

Cleveland. He insisted that section 6 of the 1980 Education Act placed a singular mandatory duty upon LEAs which was not affected by the nature of the parents' requests. Nor did the judge accept the CRE's contention that "segregate" means to *keep* apart. In his view, Katrice's transfer to a school where 98 percent of the children were white suggested that while she was *moving* apart from ethnic minority children (her previous school included 40 percent of pupils of South Asian origin) she was not segregated (that is, kept apart) from them.

The CRE appealed against the decision. But in July 1992 the Court of Appeal upheld the original decision. Whether or not this gives the green light to white flight from multiracial schools remains to be seen. It does demonstrate, however, the effete nature of the 1976 Race Relations Act and its inability, in particular, to prevent parents withdrawing their children from schools on explicitly racial grounds.

Reading
The Struggle for Black Equality 1954–1980 by Harvard Sitkoff, (Hill and Wang, 1981) provides an historical account of campaigners for desegregation in the United States and the white backlash that these have engendered.
The Logic of Racism by Ellis Cashmore (Allen and Unwin, 1987) provides a testimony to the view that white citizens, especially those in run-down neighborhoods, often invoke cultural differences as a metaphor for their own political impotence and perceived disenfranchisement. The interviews indicate how resentment is evoked once the rights of white individuals are seen to be violated in favor of the rights of groups.
Black and White in School (Teachers College Press, 1989) is by Janet Ward Schofield. It looks at the consequences of desegregation in Wexler Middle School, in a city in the Northeast United States.
"Tolerating intolerance" by Carol Vincent in the *Journal of Education Policy* (vol. 7, no. 1, 1992) examines the background to debates within and likely consequences of the Macpherson ruling on the Cleveland LEA case.

See also: BUSING; EDUCATION AND CULTURAL DIVERSITY; MULTICULTURALISM; SEGREGATION

Barry Troyna

Whiteness
Whiteness as an inclusive category that comprises a segment of a population is no more natural than blackness. It has its origins in the second half of the seventeenth century and was the result of a social transformation of English, Irish, Scottish, and other European colonizers of America. The transformation entailed homogenizing

the statuses of tenants, merchants, planters and so on into a new status – members of a white race. As Bennett writes: "The first white colonists had no concept of themselves as *white* man . . . The word *white*, with all its burden of guilt and arrogance, did not come into common usage until the latter part of the century."

It developed in contradistinction to blackness, which has a longer genealogy, stretching back to the Christian period when the color acquired negative connotations and became associated with sin and darkness. Jan Pieterse (in *White on Black*, Yale University Press, 1992) shows how Islam adopted black to symbolize demons and how blackness appeared in European iconography from the twelfth and fifteenth centuries, blackness was evaluated positively. It seems that only after the seventeenth century and the rise of European colonialism, did blackness become denigrated and yoked with savagery and inferiority; though some scholars argue that blackness was linked with inferiority via traditional Christian associations, stemming from the biblical Curse of Ham.

Jordan contends that, for the colonial English, white was the color of purity and perfection. So the very blackness of Africans' skin was traumatic enough to ensure Europeans' bias against them. The view gains support from Degler's proposal that the negative values deriving from the color black served to set Africans apart from other subservient groups.

The application of scientific reasoning to the understanding of race and the rise of racial typologies occurred after 1790 when the abolitionist movement gathered momentum. It became a "rational" defence against the dissolution of slavery and served to enhance the image of black peoples as naturally suited to servitude and labor. Blumenbach's classification, published in 1795, included Caucasians, who constituted the light-skinned division of the world's population and were supposed to originate from Caucasus, the mountain range in Eastern Europe. They were, he argued the most handsome; in contrast to Mongolians and Ethiopians (his other racial categories). Subsequent racial theories strayed only marginally from this conclusion, Aryans (Müller) and the Germanic race (Gobineau) being synonyms for whites. The gloss of scientific credibility was lent to the belief in the innate superiority of whites and the European domination of most parts of the world reinforced this.

Concurrent with this process was the detachment of blackness from slavery. As the abolitionist movement advanced a humanistic image of blacks, so the supporters of slavery rationalized the treatment of slaves as chattel by projecting a racist argument. Blacks were slaves, it was contended, because the were naturally, geno-typically and so permanently inferior. As the need for a sharper, clearly defined barrier of delineation became more pressing, so the criterion of color became more useful.

In this context, white skin was imbued with new significance – as a means of control. In late seventeenth century North America, poor Europeans, some indentured, were endowed with unprecedented civil and social privileges compared to those of Africans. This privilege was an acknowledgment of their loyalty to the colonial land – and property-owning class and established what might be recognized as race privileges. Primary emphasis on race was not, at first, widespread: it occurred only in areas where plantation owners could not form a social control apparatus without the additional support of propertyless groups of European extraction. Virginia and Massachusetts had plenty of white *de facto* slaves and these states promoted the new status.

For poor whites, this was a welcome adjustment to a well-established system. Bennett points out that white servitude was a precursor to the exploitation of blacks: "Before the invention of the Negro or the white man or the words and concepts to describe them, the colonial population consisted largely of a great mass of white and black bondsmen, who occupied roughly the same economic category and were treated with equal contempt by the lords of the plantations and legislatures." Aligning with the plantocracy as "white" meant unburdening themselves of the harshest aspects of bondage.

Allen favors similar terminology in his *The Invention of the White Race*, which pays particular attention to the experiences of migrant Irish, once victimized and disparaged as degenerate and not amenable to civilizing influences, yet later transformed into defenders of an exploitative order. The Irish were certainly regarded by English colonizers as an inferior racial group (colonization of Ireland took place through the sixteenth century), but were physically indistinct from the English. There were other groups that would today be recognized as white that were readily associated with savagery. But, it became expedient to co-opt them.

There was a comparable expediency about Latin colonial world's invention of whiteness. Faced with a confusing range of phenotypical variation in the eighteenth century (Latin colonies did not legislate against the intermarriage of Africans, Indians and Europeans), the Spanish created *los peninsulares* a category that signified social status and natural advantage. Based on *pureza de sangre* (pure blood) it was a way of separating those born in Spain, including, *los criollos*, from all others.

By the time of publication of John Van Eurie's widely read *White Supremacy and Negro Subordination* in 1861, the concept of whiteness was well integrated into what Smedley calls a "racial worldview" in which social differentiation was understood in terms of natural inequalities. Van Eurie advanced a conception of whiteness that included, among others, Attila the Hun, Genghis Khan, and Confucius – all leaders of one kind or another, but none of whom would be recognized as white today. This kind of racial worldview could not be sustained without a property that at once excluded inferior races and included (and so integrated) the superior ones; whiteness was that property.

Because whiteness signified superiority and privilege, it worked to devalue any skin color that did not qualify and render possessors of that skin Others. In the early twentieth century, many African American leaders, including Marcus Garvey, argued that "Negroes" were caught between self-loathing and the loathing of others. Restoring pride and value in the "New Negro" was a prerequisite for resistance and challenge, according to Garvey. It was not the least function of whiteness that it served to devalue blackness for blacks themselves. Hair-straightening and skin-bleaching treatments attest in some measure to the success of this function. The famous Dolls Test conducted in 1939–40 by psychologist Kenneth Clark (and published in the *Journal of Experimental Education*, Spring, 1940) confirmed this. In the 1950s, Frantz Fanon wrote of an "inferiority complex" that beset Negroes.

The transition from "negro" to "black" in the 1960s involved recoding blackness as beautiful and worth making visible. Afro hairstyles and kente cloth were evidence of this. Stokely Carmichael and Charles Hamilton's *Black Power* (Vintage, 1967) was a signature text of the time. Whiteness, as a sign of all that is good, was forcefully challenged.

In contemporary times, whiteness signifies not so much superiority or purity, but privilege and power: it confers advantages and prestige. It also sets normative standards: up till recently, the term "nonwhite" inscribed deviance and stigmata. Whiteness remains meaningful only in particular kinds of discourses or contexts: specifically, those in which superficial, observable features are supposed to be indices of deeper, perhaps immutable differences. Recognizing color in this way both validates these putative differences and maintains barriers.

Reading
The Invention of the White Race: Racial Oppression and Social Control by
Theodore Allen (Verso, 1994) is a powerful treatise on the construction
of the white race as a discrete entity to meet the demands of changing
social and ideological conditions; it is complemented by *The Shaping of
Black America: The Struggles and Triumphs of African-Americans, 1619
to the 1990s* by Lerone Bennett (Penguin, 1993) which advances the view
that:"Black bondsmen inherited their chains from white bondsmen, who
were, in a manner of speaking, America's first slaves."
"Slavery and the genesis of American race prejudice" by Carl N. Degler
(*Comparative Studies in Society and History*, vol. 2, no. 1, 1959) and *White
Over Black* by Winthrop Jordan (Penguin, 1968) are both historical works
that examine the changing attitudes of whites toward blacks.
Race in North America: Origin and Evolution of a Worldview by Audrey
Smedley (Westview Press, 1993) is a study of the establishment of racial
conceptions and, as such, shows how the meanings of color terms "insinu-
ated their way, perhaps subliminally" into European – especially English –
thought.

See also: CREOLE; GARVEY; RACE – AS CLASSIFICATION; "RACE" – AS
SIGNIFIER

Ellis Cashmore

Xenophobia

A term that means literally fear of strangers (from the Greek *xenos* for strange and "phobia," a fear or aversion). Once regarded as a psychological condition – to describe persons who feared or abhored groups regarded as "outsiders" – its more recent application has been in the context of attacks on immigrants and asylum seekers in western Europe.

The European Parliament's Committee of Inquiry into the Rise of Racism and Fascism in Europe (1985) identified xenophobia as a new type of specter haunting Europe. The committee's report led to the 1986 declaration against racism and xenophobia signed on behalf of the European Union's main institutions and the European Union has continued subsequently to use the two expressions as a pair without differentiating between them. The Heads of State and Government of the Council of Europe in their Vienna declaration of 1993 adopted a plan of action against manifestations of racism, xenophobia, antisemitism, and intolerance" which led to the establishment of the European Commission against Racism and Intolerance. In 1993, the United Nations appointed a Special Rapporteur on Racism and Xenophobia.

In Germany, the word *Rassismus* is uncomfortably associated with the Nazi era. German institutions are more ready to refer to *Fremdenfeindlichkeit* and to translate this into English as xenophobia. This is one factor underlying the increased reference to xenophobia in internationally-agreed documents.

In France, sociologists write of a principle of inferiorization and exploitation which allows the victim group a place in society so long as it is at the bottom; and of a principle of differentiation which represents the other-group as so different that it must be segregated, expelled, or destroyed. Opposition to continued immigration, in France as in other European countries, has in the last thirty years lead to more stress upon cultural than supposed biological differences.

If racism and xenophobia are to be distinguished racism can be seen as relying on ideas of inferiority, where xenophobia relies on ideas of fundamental differences between cultures.

Reading

"Hostility and fear in social life" by John Dollard (*in Social Forces*, vol. 17, 1938) is an early theoretical statement on fears and prejudices.

The Nature of Prejudice by Gordon Allport (Addison-Wesley, 1954) is a classic social psychological text exploring the roots of prejudice.

The Arena of Racism by Michael Wieviorka (Sage, 1995) is a more contemporary treatment of the concept.

See also: EUROPEAN RACISM; OTHERS; DOLLARD; PREJUDICE; SCAPEGOAT

Michael Banton

Z

Zimbabwe

Formerly the self-governing Crown colony of Southern Rhodesia, Zimbabwe's colonial history had its roots in the occupation of the territory between the Limpopo and Zambesi Rivers by white soldier-settlers recruited by Cecil John Rhodes in 1890. This invasion was resisted by the indigenous inhabitants of the area, culminating in the Shona and Ndebele "rebellions" of 1896–97, which were put down through the superior technological weaponry possessed by the whites at the time. The agricultural and mineral potential of the country subsequently attracted a large influx of white settlers. Most of these were of British or South African origin, although numbers of Central European Jewish and Greek minorities were also present.

In 1923 the territory was granted self-governing status within the Commonwealth under conditions which gave the white population virtual autonomy in all internal affairs. The whites, who had established their control through the use of coercive techniques monopolized on racial criteria, consolidated their control on racial lines, ensuring that political and economic power remained in white hands. Land distribution, control of occupational and educational structures, and the manipulation of the franchise were the chief instruments of this process. An edifice of white dominance was evolved which, except at a few critical points, was not explicitly racial in construction. Much of it was apartheid by bylaw, executive device and administrative practice, but its effects in creating a racially discriminatory system of opportunities were as pervasive as those of the racial system in South Africa.

In 1953 Southern Rhodesia joined the Federation of Rhodesia and Nyasaland as the dominant partner. A short-lived experiment in assimilationist policies, the Federation broke up in 1963, the territory's two partners subsequently becoming independent as Zambia and Malawi. The dissolution of the Federation sounded the death knell for assimilationist, "multiracial" policies in Rhodesia, black politics taking a revolutionary confrontationist stance and white politics hardening along more overtly racial lines. In 1965 Ian Smith's Rhodesia Front government unilaterally declared its independence from Britain (UDI), a move unrecognized by the international community. An escalated guerilla war of liberation conducted by blacks, coupled with international isolation, led to the collapse of the white power structure and a negotiated settlement at the Lancaster House constitutional talks in 1979. Independence was granted to Zimbabwe by the British Government in 1980 under the Lancaster House constitution after an election which brought Robert Mugabe's ZANU-PF government to power.

The Lancaster House constitution placed political power firmly in black hands, 80 of the 100 seats in the House of Assembly being assigned to the black electorate. The 20 seats reserved for white constituencies were phased out in 1987, thus removing the last ostensibly racial structure in Zimbabwean politics. Since its accession to power in 1980 the ZANU-PF government has pursued a policy of racial reconciliation, granting full rights to white citizens. At the same time it has pursued a policy of affirmative action that has made many whites – particularly in the trades and public-service categories occupationally vulnerable. The white population, which peaked at 230,000 in 1976, had dropped to 138,000 by 1985. A net emigration of whites continues, but there are indications that this is tapering off. The remaining whites still hold considerable economic power, particularly in the industrial, commercial, and agricultural sectors.

Race therefore continues to be a significant but declining factor in the structure of Zimbabwean society. The significance of the ethnic factor in Zimbabwean society is a matter of continuing debate, some discounting this factor and others (e.g. Sithole) arguing that in certain contexts it is of political salience. The black population of Zimbabwe has its internal linguistic/cultural divisions, the most prominent being that between the Ndebele (largely in Matabeleland, approximately 18 percent of the population) and the Shona (largely in Mashonaland, 78 percent of the population). The Shona are themselves subdivided into the Karanga, Korekore, Manyika, Ndau, and Zezaru culturo-linguistic categories. Both major political parties have pan-ethnic, nonracial policies, but have to contend with the fact that ZAPU support is largely Ndbele and ZANU-PF support is largely Shona. Ethnicity as a political resource thus continues to have salience, and a degree of "ethnic arithmetic" continues to surface at times in the political process.

Reading
Politics in Rhodesia by L. Bowman (Harvard 1973) provides a broad outline
  of preindependence politics in Zimbabwe.
"Race and power in Rhodesia" by M. Murphree, in *Politics of Race* edited

by D. Baker (Saxon House, 1975), focuses on the racial dimensions of colonial Rhodesian society.

"The salience of ethnicity in African politics" by Masipula Sithole (in *Journal of Asian and African Studies*, 1985) is a focused discussion of the ethnic factor in postcolonial Zimbabwe.

See also: AFRICA; APARTHEID

Marshall Murphree

Zionism

Zionism, in its modern form, developed from a late nineteenth-century belief in the need to establish an autonomous Jewish homeland in Palestine. Theodor Herzl (1860–1904), a Hungarian journalist who lived in Vienna, was eventually persuaded by the events of the Dreyfus case in France and the "pogroms" (i.e. the organized massacre of Jews in Russia) to conclude in his book *Der Judenstaat* that the only way the Jewish people could practice their religion and culture in safety was by having their own nation-state. In 1897, at the First World Zionist Congress in Basle, Chaim Weizmann (1874–1952) insisted that this had to be recreated in Palestine, even though there had been no significant Jewish settlement there after the conquest of Jerusalem in C.E. 70.

Nevertheless, it was argued that Jews had always considered Palestine their spiritual home, citing that Jews throughout the Diaspora prayed for "next year in Jerusalem." It is, however, equally arguable that Orthodox Jews thought of this sentiment in a philosophical way: a means of affirming old beliefs, not of recommending the formation of a Jewish state with Jerusalem as its capital.

Herzl and Weizmann faced opposition to their ideas from both Orthodox Jews and those Jews who felt themselves to belong to the countries where they and their families had settled. Even after the Balfour declaration of 1917, expressing the British government's sympathy with Zionist aspirations, favoring "the establishment in Palestine of a National Home for the Jewish people," there was not a large migration of Jews to Palestine, which, for hundreds of years, had been predominantly Arab.

Up to World War II, Zionist claims that Jews throughout the world were persistently longing and striving to return to a homeland from which they saw themselves exiled, had very little foundation in fact. Not until after the genocidal anti-Semitism of the Nazi party had murdered six million Jews between 1939 and 1945 did the classical Zionist theories of Herzl, Achad, and Ha'am, come to mean anything to the Holocaust survivors and Jews throughout the Diaspora.

Just as the Pogroms had convinced Herzl, so the Holocaust convinced millions. The majority of Jews now believed that they were a separate people who had suffered unending discrimination and persecution. The only way they could be safe to practice the Jewish way of life was in a Jewish state, controlled and run by Jews where they constituted the majority. The major theoretical aspiration of Zionism became reality when the Jewish state of Israel was proclaimed in 1948.

While the fundamental demand for the creation of a Jewish state in Palestine had been met, contemporary Zionism means more than pro-Israel support in the Diaspora and more than Israeli patriotism in Israel. Although it includes both of these ideologically, it claims to represent an all-encompassing approach to the problems of the Jewish people. The essential constituents of a Zionist program are contained to a large extent (although not completely) in the resolutions of the 27th Zionist Congress held in Jerusalem in 1978:

- The unity of the Jewish people and the centrality of Israel in Jewish life.
- The ingathering of the Jewish people into their historic homeland, the land of Israel.
- The strengthening of the state of Israel.
- The presentation of the identity of the Jewish people through the fostering of Jewish and Hebrew education and Jewish spiritual and cultural values.
- The protection of Jewish rights everywhere.

The encouragement of "aliya" (immigration to Israel) is the primary task of the Zionist movement.

The Soviet publication, *Pravda*, in 1971, began an anti-Zionist campaign. Moscow's astonishing charges that Zionist leaders had collaborated with Nazi Germany were taken up by Arab states, then on the crest of an oil boom. Together, the countries were able to cull enough United Nations votes to push through what is now an infamous resolution. In November 1975, the UN's General Assembly passed resolution 3379, linking Zionism with South African apartheid and condemning it as "a form of racism and racial discrimination." This implicitly denied Israel's right to a legitimate existence.

Zionists emphatically refuted the links, claiming that the resolution conflated nationalism with racism. Some critics and victims of Israel replied that, once Israel had gained a territorial nation (in 1948), it has behaved no better – and sometimes worse – than other nationalist states and movements. The Arab minority of Israel was denied civil rights; many members of that minority were expelled from the lands of their birth; Israel engaged in acts of violence that went beyond a legitimate response to violence committed against it. Defenders and supporters of Israel answered critics by defining the opposition anti-Semitic.

Changes in political currents in the early 1990s prompted a reconsideration of the resolution. In particular, the Persian Gulf War split the Arab and Islamic worlds and the demise of communism splintered the Soviet bloc. In December 1991, the UN voted 111 to 25 to revoke the 1975 resolution. It was only the second time in its history that the UN had overturned one of its own resolutions.

Reading
The Idea of the Jewish State by B. Halpern (Harvard University Press, 1969) outlines the political developments.
The Origins of Zionism by P. Vital (Clarendon Press, 1975) is a comprehensive guide to Zionism and its roots.
Lost Jews: The Struggle for Identity Today by Emma Klein (Macmillan, 1995) investigates Jews "on the fringes of Jewish life" and how they have sought alternative affiliations to Jewish identity.

See also: ANTI-SEMITISM; DIASPORA; NATIONALISM; UNITED NATIONS
Carl A. Bagley/Ellis Cashmore

INDEX

Note: Page numbers in **bold** type indicate main coverage of an entry.

centralized administrations 11;
Christianity as a tool of 258;
dehumanization experienced by
subordinated groups 136;
determinant relationship between
capitalism and 66; domination 78, 79,
82, 158, 263; empires 79, 240; English
and 377, 378, 379; European 11,
265–6, 378; expansion 333; internal
177–9; Irish and **180–4**, 377; Scottish
and 377; welfare 3; *see also*
postcolonialism
color lines **83–4**, 218
Colorado xiv
"coloreds" 34
Columbus, Christopher 31, 256
Combat 88 (paramilitary group) 197
Combahee River Collective 51
Combs, Sean "Puffy" 314
Commission on Agricultural Workers
(1992) 216
Commonwealth 34, 384; *see also* New
Commonwealth
Commonwealth Immigrants Act
(Britain, 1962) 210
communism/communists 40, 195; black
189; collapse/demise of 127, 333, 388;
former states 109
Community Relations Commission
(Britain) 219
Cone, James 54
conflicts 33, 42–3, 213, 244; affecting
culture 68; African Americans and
Cubans 177; black and white adults
and their children 155; ethnic 12, 99,
123; interethnic 177, 331;
international 146; minority language
groups in multilingual societies 200;
racial 153; racists and antiracists 169;
social 123
Confucius 380; Confucian code 318
Congress of Racial Equality (U.S.A.)
173
conquest 28, 52, **84–6**, 353
Conrad, Joseph 285
consanguine households 269
consciousness 121, 142, 156, 157;
African 258; American 55; black 53;
diaspora as a form of 100, 321;
difference in xii; epistemic shifts in
135–6; ethnic 91; false 167, 249;
manipulation of 82; political 356;
racial 59, 84, 102
Conservatism **86–9**
conservative egalitarianism 115, 116
Conservative party (Britain) 21, 88, 210
conspiracy theories 259

Convention on the Rights of All Migrant
Workers and Members of their
Families (U.N., 1991) 372
Cook, Capt. James 1, 81
Coolie Ordinance 239
"Cop killer" 313
"copycat" effect 234, 324, 337
Cosby, Bill 15, 163
cosmopolitan diversity 101
coterminous power/knowledge 281
Coulthard, G. R. 258
Council of Europe, Vienna Declaration
(1993) 382
Courtet de l'Isle, Victor 151
Cox, Oliver C. **89–90**, 228–9, 230, 232,
249, 301, 309
crack cocaine 70, 252
Crane, D. 164
CRE (Commission for Racial Equality)
62, 119, 219, 376–7
Creole(s) 28, 29, **90–1**, 200–1
crime 277, 353; alleged 69; black males
in their twenties incarcerated or
involved with justice system 19; black
population personified in music 313;
heinous 71; violent, conviction rates
for 355; "war against" 278
Cronon, E. David 141
CS gas 326
Cuba 82, 109, 202, 226; migrations 204,
330
Cuffee, Paul 117
culture(s) 42, 54, 85, **91–3**, 166, 258, 305;
Afrikaans 35; American xvii, 281;
autonomous 58; Celtic 181; common
134; conflicts affecting 68; differences
in 159, 173, 262, 264, 299, 383;
distinct(ive) 44, 90; diverse xix, 121,
172; European 72; fluid conception of
xviii; fusion of groups 27; identity
100; essentialist notions of 166; hybrid
forms xviii, 101, 165; incompatibility
of 176; institutions 53; integrating 74,
136; Italian 123; Jewish 122;
matriarchal 268; matrifocal 270; pan-
Caribbean 321; reindeer-breeding
257; resistance 356; revitalization xvii;
role played by 79; self-consciously
synthetic 321; skinhead 154;
structuralist anthropology and 263;
traditional Indian 139
Cuvier, Georges 159, 295
Czech Republic 126, 333, 344

Daddy Grace 117
Dakar 81
Damas, Leon 258

457055

412   *Index*

whiteness 356, **377–81**
Wierviorka, Michel xviii
Wik people 4
Wilderness Society 171
Wilder, Douglas 88
"wilding" 69
Wilkins, Roger 15
Wilkinson, Bill 197
Williams, Jenny 170
Williams, Sherley Anne 52
Wilson, A. N. 32
Wilson, Edward O. 350
Wilson, Pete 331
Wilson, William Julius 49
Winant, H. and Omi, M.: *Racial Formation in the United States* 230
Winfrey, Oprah 15
Wippler, R. 319
Wirth, Louis 149
Woltmann, Ludwig 153
women 4, 268, 271; acquisition of recognized talent 236; angry and malevolent diatribes against 313; condemnation of rap 313; "considered" response of rap's abuse of 314; discrimination against 7, 234; emancipation of 224; first black U.S. senator 20; humor 164; Japanese 37, 38; kidnapping of 347; Latino, high birth rate 216; postcolonial theory and 285; practices that openly deprecate xix; raped 69, 71; representations of racial others overlap with those of 263; role of 272;

subaltern 356; *see also* female rights; feminism
work ethic 24
working class 124, 158, 367; black/ African American 48, 49, 69; Chicano 203; hostile 343; internal divisions within 228; Latino 69; political organizations 132, 133; race relations, Brazil 59; South Asian 43; support for racist political groups 230; trade union organizations 132; unemployment 253; white 33
World Community of Islam 251
World Heritage listing 4
Wounded Knee, battle of (1890) 30, 31

Xavier University 91
xenophobia 242, 372, **382–3**

Young, Arthur 180
Young, Crawford 96
Young, Robert xviii
Yugoslavia (former) 241; ethnic cleansing 126, 146–7, 340

Zambia 384
zambos 67
Zanzibar 10
Zenner, W. 238
Zhou 238
Zijderveld, A. 162
Zimbabwe 11, 12, 225, **384–6**
Zinkhan, G. M. 233
Zionism 322, 371, **386–8**
Zoroastrians 43